WATERGATE
IN AMERICAN MEMORY

WATERGATE
IN AMERICAN
MEMORY

HOW WE REMEMBER,
FORGET, AND
RECONSTRUCT THE PAST

Michael Schudson

BasicBooks
A Division of HarperCollinsPublishers

Designed by Ellen Levine

93 94 95 96 CC/RRD 9 8 7 6 5 4 3 2 1

Library of Congress Cataloging-in-Publication Data
Schudson, Michael.
    Watergate in American memory: how we remember,
forget, and reconstruct the past/ by Michael Schudson.
        p.   cm.
    Includes bibliographical references and index.
    ISBN 0-465-09084-2 (cloth)
    ISBN 0-465-09083-4 (paper)
    1. Watergate Affair, 1972–1974—Public opinion.
2. Public opinion—United States.   3. Mass media—
Political aspects—United States.   I. Title.
E860.S38   1992
364.1'32'0973—dc20   91–58598
                                          CIP

For Suzie

CONTENTS

PART III
REMEMBERING, FORGETTING, AND
RECONSTRUCTING THE PAST

ACKNOWLEDGMENTS

I HAVE ACCUMULATED MANY DEBTS, LARGE AND SMALL, IN WRITING THIS BOOK. My friends Peter Clarke and Susan Evans, of the Annenberg School of Communication, University of Southern California, showed such enthusiasm for the study of collective memory when I first presented my ideas to them, and such insistence that it should be a fundamental concern in the study of communication, that they asked me to help plan a conference on the topic. That 1986 conference suggested the dimensions of this subject, introduced me to people working on different aspects of it, and kept my interest aflame. Richard Terdiman, then my colleague at the University of California, San Diego, in the Department of Literature, more recently at the University of California, Santa Cruz, co-taught a course with me on "Culture, Ideology, and Collective Memory," and helped my understanding of the topic grow larger and take new turns. Conversation with UCSD colleagues Andrew Wright and Richard Madsen encouraged me in my interest as did correspondence with David Riesman and Barry Schwartz. During a term as a visiting professor at the Joan Shorenstein Barone Center at the John F. Kennedy School of Government at Harvard in 1988, discussions with the Center's director, Marvin Kalb, helped re-awaken my interest in Watergate. Conversations with Jim Miller stimulated my thinking. Jeffrey Alexander shared his thoughts with me, adding to my already great appreciation of his writings on Watergate. David Thelen was both critical and enthusiastic as I tested my thoughts with him when we met in Chicago in 1991.

Rivka Ribak, America Rodriguez, Jennifer Troutner, and Silvio Waisbord were exceptional research assistants for different phases of my research. Rivka Ribak did especially careful work in reconstructing an account of the Bert Lance affair, and as she checked and double-checked footnotes, she added useful, critical observations on the text itself. Colleagues in the Department of Communication discussed my ideas with me or read and commented on parts of the manuscript, and I mention especially Michael Cole, Robert Horwitz, and Vicente Rafael. David Middleton, a British psychologist who has helped revive the Frederick Bartlett tradition of memory studies and insists on the collective nature of memory, encouraged me and improved my thinking during his stay as a visitor at UCSD.

I am grateful to the people I interviewed or consulted in the course of my research, including Scott Armstrong, Ben Bagdikian, Sidney Blumenthal, Benjamin C. Bradlee, James W. Carey, Barbara Stubbs Cohen, Congressman Thomas Downey, Leonard Downie, Thomas Edsall, Mike Epstein, Suzanne Garment, Steven Hess, Marvin Kalb, Marc Lackritz, William Lanouette, Robert Merry, Roger Molander, Lance Morgan, Pamela Naughton, Robert Reisner, Leo Ribuffo, Barry Sussman, Sanford Ungar, Gerald Warren, Senator Timothy Wirth, and Bob Woodward. Lawrence Lichty, director of the Woodrow Wilson Media Studies Project at the Smithsonian Institution, generously arranged study space for me during my interviewing trips in Washington and helped organize a seminar on the role of journalism in Watergate that was enormously instructive for me. Participants in that seminar included Michael Cornfield, Douglas Gomery, William Lanouette, Steven Klaidman, Joseph Laitin, Michael Robinson, Thomas Rosenstiel, Martin Schram, and Joel Swerdlow.

Long-distance telephone or correspondence brought me valuable assistance from David Abshire, Raoul Berger, Howard Bray, Donald Brotzman, Sam Dash, Joshua Gamson, John Hanrahan, Katy Harriger, John Heimann, William Hudnut, Pamela Kilian, Sanford Levinson, Clarence Lyons, Peter Rodino, Jonathan Rowe, Larry Sabato, William Safire, Philip Taubman, Victor Veysey, and Roger Zion. Other colleagues near and far who have been helpful include Harold Berman, Lee Bollinger, Hugh Carter, Steve Chaffee, Daniel Dayan, Thomas Engelhardt, Jan Zita Grover, Raymond Hopkins, Alan Houston, Ellen Hume, Iwona Irwin-Zarecka, Elihu Katz, Helene Keyssar, Anthony Kronman, Stanley Kutler, Anthony Lewis, Burdett Loomis, Andrei Markovits, Martha Minow, Irv Nathan, and Charles Schudson.

I benefited from the use of a number of libraries and special collections: the Nixon collection at Whittier College (and its curator, Joseph Dmohowski), the National News Council archive at the University of Minnesota (and Mark Hammons), and the Mudd Manuscript Library at Princeton University (and Jean Holliday) where I used the Common Cause papers. I also used Common Cause papers at Common Cause headquarters in Washington, thanks to Paul Rensted, and was able to make use of the video oral history of journalism collection of the Poynter Institute for Media Studies, thanks to David Shedden. Thanks also to Donald Ritchie, Senate historian, and Raymond Smock, House historian, and to Greg Harness who helped me at the United States Senate Library. Eleanor Pattison kindly lent me the unfinished manuscript about the Congressional class of 1974 that her husband, Representative Ned Pattison, was working on at the time of his death.

I am grateful to the people who read parts of the manuscript or listened to me read parts of the manuscript. Thanks to Sari Thomas for inviting my participation on a panel at the International Communication Association, to the San Diego Independent Scholars, and at UCSD to the Middle Management Group, the Department of Communication, and the Chancellor's Associates. Thanks to Chandra Mukerji for organizing a conference to honor Bennett Berger's retirement at UCSD, and thanks to Bennett Berger whose ever insightful skepticism provided inspiration for the language of "pious" and "profane" I have employed here. I am enormously grateful to Nancy Bekavac, Todd Gitlin, and Barry Schwartz, not to mention my editor at Basic Books, Martin Kessler, all of whom bravely waded through the whole manuscript at an embarrassingly unfinished stage. Jim Miller, Sam Popkin, and David Thelen offered valuable criticism of several chapters. Along with Robert Manoff, whose editorial suggestions throughout were as deft and demanding as ever, they pushed me to declare my argument more simply and forthrightly. I am appreciative of the excellent editorial assistance I received at Basic Books from Carol Offen and Susan Zurn.

My two older children, Daniel Isaac and Jenna Lorraine, have wondered when this book would ever be done; my youngest child, Zachary Carl, has yet to know a father who is not marking up drafts of chapters in every room of the house. I hope they will all one day know they were in my heart and my mind as I crafted this study of the transmission of culture across generations.

As I have stolen time away from my family to work on this book, there have been costs, some of which have been borne by my wife, Suzie. My comfort is that she has believed in this book from the beginning and has continued to believe in its best intentions even when my doubts threatened to overtake me. She would often hear me out, even at moments far from opportune, sleep-starved as we have been this past year. I hope she will take pride in this book; it is also hers.

This book could not have been completed without four quarters of research leave, thanks to the cooperation of UCSD and the generosity of the Gannett Center for Media Studies (now the Freedom Forum), the Guggenheim Foundation, the Spencer Foundation (which thought it was supporting a different project—that project is underway, too!), and the John D. and Catherine T. MacArthur Foundation. As in my family, friends, colleagues, and students, I have been more fortunate in research support than I could ever have imagined.

PREFACE TO THE PAPERBACK EDITION

W HEN *WATERGATE IN AMERICAN MEMORY* WAS PUBLISHED ON 17 JUNE 1992, timed to coincide with the twentieth anniversary of the Watergate break-in, I was widely interviewed and quoted as the news media ran Watergate anniversary stories. I learned something from this experience that helped to clarify the stand I take in the book. Journalists wanted to know what I took the lessons of Watergate to be. I told them that different people see different lessons in Watergate. Watergate is a piece of our past that we "think with" more than a settled doctrine or an easily encapsulated lesson. But, the reporters continued, isn't it true that people don't remember very much about Watergate at all? In a way, yes, I admitted, but only if you take as "memory" the answers adults give to public opinion polls or teenagers to general-information exam questions. But if, as I argue here, a nation "remembers" institutionally as well as individually, its organs of government altered, its political language rewoven, its repertoire for speaking or doing politics redesigned by past events, then twenty years later America remembers Watergate very well.

That point is one of two central theoretical arguments of my book: remembrance is collective—institutional and cultural, located in language and legislation and in the public face that individual lives take on in careers and reputations; it is not just the sum of private, individual recollections, located in individual brains. (The other theoretical claim, argued most fully in the final chapter, is that we do not remember the past just as we choose. In some respects, multiple interpretations and postmodernism notwithstanding, the past imposes itself on us.)

Some journalists pushed further, asking what I thought Americans *should* learn from Watergate. This is not the question that guided my study. My question is: What can we learn *about learning and about memory* from the way society has learned or failed to learn from Watergate? Still, the journalists' question forced me back from this theoretical issue to the common plane of politics where the interpretation of Watergate is a living controversy. The journalists asked me to abandon my armchair role of surveying and analyzing the various cultural conduits through which the past seeps into the present. They urged me, by virtue of this book a certified "expert," to be an agency of cultural memory myself. What, they inquired, was my own view of Watergate?

Here I found myself professing emphatically what is stated *sotto voce* in the book: advocacy of the "liberal" constitutionalist view of Watergate. I argued that Watergate was a case of presidential abuse of power in violation of the Constitution, that Richard Nixon dishonored the office he held and was rightly forced from it, and that the lesson of Watergate is the simple and hoary one that eternal vigilance is the price of liberty.

This oversimplifies my own position. In the book, I suggest that the radical, liberal, conservative, and ultraconservative views of Watergate all have something valuable to teach us. While I began my research with some sort of liberal view in mind, I learned in my studies to recognize the validity of other positions, to both the left and the right of my own, that pictured Watergate as a piece of political theater, with some of Richard Nixon's accusers delighted to make political hay of the president's distress and eager to present themselves as emblems of all that is right and moral in contrast to the sinning president. Still, their protestations, while theatrical and often pious in the extreme, were not without substance. Nixon did spit on the Constitution and the legal process, both publicly and privately. I felt in 1992, and still do today, that that is the more crucial aspect of Watergate to remember. Editing myself to sound-bite length and speaking to audiences that would never read my book nor entertain my more scholarly questions, I said I believed the Constitution provides an admirable framework for our political system and that protecting "a government of laws, not of men," oversimple a formula as that is, required in the case of Watergate undertaking the extraordinary procedure of presidential impeachment.

There is something to learn from several contradictory versions of Watergate. Even so, I believe that the version that stresses the value of the American Constitutional order and the need to protect it from arbitrary executive power is, today, when the structures of political power are not very different from what they were in 1972, the most important lesson to learn. If we can imagine an American political system twenty or fifty years from now, when the executive is confined and constrained so mightily by Congress, the media, and the public, a Gulliver tied down by Lilliputians, then it could be that other Watergate lessons will arise as more salient, such as the dangers to political order from irresponsible congressional investigation, the unaccountability of the news media, and the overreaching of the judiciary. That is imaginable, although not, to my mind, very likely.

The task of seeking out lessons of history rather than discussing, meta-historically, the interpretations and agents of interpretation in American society was presaged in the last stages of writing the book. In the early chapters, originally, I tried to describe the different leading versions of Watergate without providing a general overview of the events of Watergate myself. I eventually decided this was impossible because a general overview is necessary for almost all readers. Those coming of political age after Watergate ended, nearly half the nation by now, know very little about Watergate; those who remember Watergate in general and can easily recall their own emotional response at the time normally recall few of the details and might well be stumped if asked to specify what constitutional issues were at stake. So I provide a thumbnail sketch of the main narrative of Watergate events (pages 16 to 20), recognizing that the choices I made here, most of all the choice of where to begin the account, prejudges what version of or interpretation of Watergate will seem most plausible. By starting with the Watergate break-in rather than with Richard Nixon's career or the origins of the Cold War or the buildup of the military-industrial complex, I effectively marginalize the radical interpretation of Watergate. But even the radical interpretation of Watergate recognizes that the conventional starting point for the Watergate puzzle is 17 June 1972, and radicals feel obliged to make a case for any alternative point of origin they propose. The narrative hegemony of that moment of surprise and accident is overpowering, and no fancy theoretical footwork refutes the "natural" feel of this once-upon-a-time opening.

Even so, I try in the book to walk a fine line between conventional thought, believing in facts, and modernist or postmodern thought, seeing multiple legitimate versions of the facts; between claiming that there is a settled history that holds us in thrall and noting that the past is subject to radically different versions, even to radically different *plausible* versions. I don't think the theoretical and epistemological issues about where to find facts or foundations in a world that legitimately finds facts to be social constructions and foundations ever shifting are about to resolve themselves. I think we need a lot of hard work along the borders between conventional and postconventional ways of understanding the world. The journalists' questions usefully reminded me that I can refuse to simplify and still choose to take a stand, that I can subscribe to complexity without submitting to relativism in my understanding of where Watergate fits and where it should fit in American political culture.

In the months since this work was published, references to Watergate have abounded in political life both in the United States and around the world. There has been "Collorgate" in Brazil, "Bibigate" in Israel, "Camillagate" in England, and "Nannygate" in the United States. In the 1992 presidential campaign, Ross Perot accused the Bush campaign of "dirty tricks," with unmistakable overtones of Watergate, William Safire pursued President Bush as doggedly over "Iraqgate" as he had Jimmy Carter over "Lancegate." On the twentieth anniversary of the Watergate break-in, CBS, in cooperation with the *Washington Post*, produced a two-hour documentary recounting the Watergate story (managing to dem-onstrate—surprise, surprise!—that the media were the chief heroes, nota-bly the *Washington Post* and CBS News). The same day independent counsel Lawrence Walsh's office hosted its own unintentional commemo-ration by indicting former Secretary of Defense Caspar Weinberger on charges related to Iran-contra. He never had to face those charges in court. Six months later, in one of his last acts in office, President Bush pardoned Weinberger and other key Reagan administration officials for their Iran-contra involvement. This evoked no small outrage at the time, but no lasting outrage either, despite comparisons to President Ford's pardon of Richard Nixon. In March, Charles Colson won the prestigious Templeton Prize for Progress in Religion in recognition of the prison ministry he established after his Watergate prison term was served, while Richard Nixon met with President Bill Clinton to discuss the importance of providing aid to the former Soviet Union. The Nixon meeting was reported with astonishment. Richard Nixon's foreign policy message was reported as part of a calculated effort to advance his own reputation. Again, most public comment assumed, contrary to the evidence (see chap-ter 10), that people must view Nixon either as devil or sage, not, as the polls suggest, both. Liberals are inclined to smirk or roll their eyes at each Nixon reappearance, with mournful comment about his public rehabilita-tion. (They tend to ignore or find anomalous a genuine rehabilitation like Charles Colson's, evidence perhaps that their humanism is not only secu-lar but provincially so.)

Watergate, it seems, is still with us, whether or not teenagers can recognize photographs of John Dean or John Mitchell. That people do not remember Watergate, individually, marks the passing of time, not the passing of literacy or civic-mindedness or historical consciousness. The rhetoric of decline and the rhetoric of nostalgia are strong in contemporary social criticism, but I think them as much in need of deconstruction as the rhetoric of "progress" or "modernization" or "science" that academic thinkers are more apt to take to task. Part of the rhetoric surrounding Watergate, beginning within a year of Nixon's resignation, has been a rhetoric about memory, with exhortations about the dangers of forgetfulness and the necessity of making mental and legal monuments to this national trauma. Events in the former Yugoslavia tragically remind us that collective memory may be too long and too closely held as well as too short and too lightly considered. Memory is always memory *of* some things and not others, and it is always memory *for* some purposes, and these may be uncivil as well as civil. I return to the hope that this study of Watergate's memory may lead people to question conventional wisdom about the virtues and vices of remembering and may help further understanding of how social memory operates in contemporary societies, for better and for worse.

Introduction

I HAVE BEEN MAKING MY WAY TOWARD THIS BOOK AT LEAST SINCE I BEGAN COL-
lecting notes in 1977 or 1978 for a paper (that I never wrote) on what
I called the social significance of statistically insignificant events. I was
interested in the enduring effects of unique events—a traumatic experience in childhood that establishes lifelong patterns of neurotic or fearful
behavior; a revolution in one country with reverberating "demonstration"
effects around the world; a "horror story," true or false, in a school,
workplace, family, or community that initiates and sustains new patterns
of behavior that bear no apparent functional relationship to the environment at hand.

It seemed to me, as I began my professional career as a sociologist, that
the social sciences had unwisely turned their collective back on history. In
seeking generalizable laws of human action and systematic methods for
the study of human behavior, the social sciences had studiously avoided
attention to both the large explosions and the small but fateful accidents
of human experience. I was not prepared to say that there is nothing but
history, and I was certainly not prepared to say that history is just one
damn thing after another. But I was moving toward the view that history
is the record of one damn thing *precluding* another, the record of events
moving people and institutions irretrievably in this direction and not
that one.

Sometimes, I felt convinced, the direction of human affairs has little to
do with the usual stuff of explanation in social science, classes or markets
or political alignments, but derives instead from the simple fact that *some-*

thing happened. Something happened, some untoward event—a leader cut down by illness or an assassin's bullet, a crime committed or revealed, a powerful speech delivered, a stunning idea developed, a community organized to fight on some trivial issue and by that happenstance well prepared to deal with some more troubling conflict later—something happened first, and by happening, precluded something else from happening or enabled something else to happen next, even if the array of classes or political powers or market forces might have led one to predict otherwise.

The past affects the present, I thought, in two ways. First, each human event is a step in a sequence, a node in a branching tree of events that permits only so many next steps and thereby precludes untold numbers of others. Think, for instance, about how critical it is for understanding industrialization that England industrialized first and that therefore the environment in which any next nation sought to industrialize was one with England as an industrial competitor, a radically different environment than the one England itself had faced. Or to take another favorite topic of historical and social scientific study, think about how important to the failed development of a strong labor or socialist political organization in the United States was the fact that universal white manhood suffrage was already achieved in this country, and without struggle. In much of Europe it was precisely the energy directed toward gaining suffrage that helped establish effective labor parties. The sequence of events is sometimes the best explanation for things. In the terms of historical sociologist Charles Tilly, "social processes are path-dependent. That is why history matters."[1]

This "path-dependence" is as critical to understanding natural history as it is to explaining human history, or so Stephen Jay Gould has argued in championing a historicist approach to the study of paleontology and evolution.[2] But in human affairs, the past affects the present in a second way: human beings treat the past as a real, contemporary force. A person defends the "honor" of an ancestor, or a nation fights for a piece of land that has only "historical" value; soldiers who do not believe in any overarching reason for fighting are impelled into battle to pay tribute to the memory of comrades already fallen; a person jilted in love by an aggressive careerist goes "on the rebound" to someone with no ambition at all; and the trauma of World War II leads Western leaders to see the next fifty years of international relations through the prism of Munich—a past experience provides the "frame" or "metaphor" through which the world is viewed.

The remembrance of the past in ways that shape the present is not exclusively dependent on personal trauma or generational crisis, as my examples may suggest, but also on the institutionalization of memory in

cultural forms and social practices, such as "promise" and its institutionalization in "contract" or property and the continuity it endows through
inheritance.[3] Think also of legal terms like "restitution" or "punishment,"
which assume that the past has a legitimate claim on the present, or
political terms like "reform" or "restoration," not to mention sociological
terms such as "reputation" and "career," or educational terms like
"learning" and "role model," all of which likewise recognize in human
action conscious efforts to shape the present according to some understanding of the past, and with some regard to the integrity of the past.

If the first way in which human affairs are shaped by history can be
termed the power of contingency, this second way can be called the power
of continuity. The second way can also be called collective memory or
social memory, referring to the ways in which group, institutional, and
cultural recollections of the past shape people's actions in the present. This
is what I wanted to study.

When I began to talk about my research on how collective memory
works in contemporary life, I found people interested. When I began to
discuss focusing on a case study of Watergate to illustrate general issues
about collective memory, I was promptly warned off the subject. One
friend counseled that the subject was too volatile and too important to use
simply to illustrate something else. Watergate was too important and the
legacy of Richard Nixon too dangerous—the evidence of Iran-contra was
cited—to diminish the political significance of the subject by using it for
academic purposes. I shared my friend's view that Watergate was a serious, living issue. Without having given it studied consideration, I shared
the mainstream position that Watergate represented a threat to constitutional government and that constitutional government is precious, so I
was sympathetic to the view that Watergate should not be trivialized or
aestheticized. But I came to see the constitutionalist position I held as one
perspective among several and that the place of Watergate in our memory
lies not with one interpretation or another exclusively but with the play of
leading interpretations against one another. The contest among differing
perspectives is important, and my subject lies in examining the construction, revision, cultural transmission, and enduring influence of these different perspectives. I believe it possible to pay attention to all of this
without trivializing Watergate's continuing political significance; indeed, I
hope this work helps to give Watergate's meaning new clarity.

But is this not the perfect academicizing of Watergate: to write not
about what Watergate was but about how we have come to talk about
Watergate since? Not to find out new facts about what happened but to
review and relate the existing interpretations and reinterpretations? Well,

yes, if you imagine that the talk about Watergate is not part of the event of Watergate "itself." I do not make that assumption.

Surely there is a difference between obstructing justice—what Richard Nixon and his associates did, among other things—and talking about how or how deeply they obstructed justice or in what context this matters. Talk in the Oval Office is of a different character from talk about the Oval Office. And the talk in 1972 and 1973 in Washington is different from the talk in 1980 or 1990 in New York or San Diego.

But the impact of Watergate on the public mind and political institutions today and the impact it will have a decade or a generation hence, is a function of both kinds of talk. Oddly enough, it may be more directly a function of talk *about* rather than the now long past talk *within* the Oval Office. I am not interested in the "discourse" for its own sake, as if there were nothing but discourse, but for the sake of its role in social action, present and future. In that sense my work is a part of the ongoing accommodation of our culture to the events known as Watergate. But my aim is precisely academic in what I believe to be the best sense: I want to use this study to advance general understanding of human action—in this case, to better comprehend the relations of past and present.

Colleagues have raised the question of how I can know what people remember of Watergate. While I have some useful evidence (from surveys, anecdotes, and interviews) of what individual Americans remember of Watergate, I do not know, in general, what Americans, person by person, know of Watergate. Even if I did, I would not have the evidence I seek: not what people remember but whether and under what circumstances their memories of Watergate affect their views and actions on contemporary issues.

That is what matters, I think, and evidence of it is more retrievable than it may appear at first. Because there is such a thing as social or collective memory—the preservation of the past for current use in a variety of cultural forms and formulae—it is possible to learn in great detail about the reservoir of Watergate versions and the set of Watergate reminders society makes widely available. I use the news media as indices of publicly available knowledge of Watergate: the *New York Times*, *Time*, *Newsweek*, the *Washington Post*, the *Los Angeles Times*, CBS and NBC news (because their transcripts are easily available), other popular television programs, film, books, school textbooks, and so forth. This is the stuff of our collective memory rather than individual and idiosyncratic recollection. Individuals may have personal versions of Watergate, but these will vary from the culturally standard versions most of all in people who participated directly in the affairs of Watergate, and these private versions will grow more rare, and less influential, with passing years. The cultural reservoir of Watergate stories, then, will eventually more adequately map the outlines and suggest the salience of personal understandings of Watergate.

But "reservoir" is the wrong metaphor. Versions of Watergate are not drawn from a common pool but are handed down through particular cultural forms and transmitted in particular cultural vehicles. The forms and vehicles through which Watergate is remembered provide the organizational framework for this book. I examine various forms, including career, myth, reform, celebrity, anniversary, reputation, language, metaphor, expectations, and pedagogical lessons, each of which contributes to collective memory in its own way. The vehicles for these forms may be any parts of the human world with the property of duration. This includes individual human beings themselves; social institutions, designed to transcend the temporal limitations of human lifetimes; and culture, symbols or objects people transmit across generations. The forms of collective memory, attached to human or humanly constructed vehicles, are an aspect of human culture through which time travels. What happens in daily social life is the reverse of H. G. Wells or *Back to the Future:* we do not travel in a machine to the past; the past travels (through a variety of cultural machines) to us.

I received other vigorous warnings about this project. One was from a friend who said that as a Jew I should not write about collective memory without writing about Jewish collective memory. I have ignored this counsel in devoting this work primarily to Watergate and American civic memory, but I have not forgotten it. It is plain to me that my interest in the question of collective memory, which goes far beyond my interest in Watergate, is rooted in my experience as a Jew and particularly in a key ritual act of remembrance in Judaism, the Passover seder. But I will not be probing here just what significance this has for me.

In most discussions of collective memory, it is taken for granted that forgetting is "bad" and remembering is "good." Studies of the Holocaust are the main instance, and there one could scarcely deny that it is good to remember the Holocaust. But this does not suggest that all remembering is laudatory. In other cases, forgetting may be as praiseworthy as remembering. It may be liberating, freeing, forgiving of oneself or others; forgetting may signify not being trapped by the past. That is an important issue Watergate raises in ways the Holocaust does not.[4]

The last warning I received was simply that the subject of Watergate was exhausted. While few scholars have written about Watergate, even before President Nixon resigned there was a sense that the subject had been treated ad nauseum and that any academic study of Watergate could not possibly gain (and would not deserve) an audience. James Nuechterlein wrote in 1979 that historians err to think events judged significant at the time will necessarily have significant meanings. Watergate's circumstances, he wrote, were "essentially banal" and Watergate left "little in the way of usable lessons or enduring implications." It would just "not bear the weight of the portentous meanings that have been attached to it."[5] So perhaps I should not have been surprised at the reaction of the late Howard Simons, one of Bob Woodward and Carl Bernstein's editors at the *Washington Post* on the Watergate stories, when I broached the subject in 1988. Simons's instant response was, "Not another Watergate book!"

I hope, in tribute to Mr. Simons, that this is not another Watergate book.

PART I

VERSIONS OF WATERGATE

CHAPTER 1

Thinking with Watergate:

Constitutional Crisis or Scandal?

Article I.

In his conduct of the office of President of the United States, Richard M. Nixon, in violation of his constitutional oath faithfully to execute the office of President of the United States and, to the best of his ability, preserve, protect, and defend the Constitution of the United States, and in violation of his constitutional duty to take care that the laws be faithfully executed, has prevented, obstructed, and impeded the administration of justice. . . .

In all of this, Richard M. Nixon has acted in a manner contrary to his trust as President and subversive of constitutional government, to the great prejudice of the cause of law and justice, and to the manifest injury of the people of the United States.

Wherefore Richard M. Nixon, by such conduct, warrants impeachment and trial, and removal from office.

Article II.

Using the powers of the office of President of the United States, Richard M. Nixon, in violation of his constitutional oath faithfully to execute the office of President of the United States and, to the best of his ability, preserve, protect, and defend the Constitution of the United States, and in disregard of his constitutional duty to take care that the laws be faithfully executed, has repeatedly engaged in conduct violating the constitutional rights of citizens, impairing the due and proper administration of justice and the conduct of lawful inquiries, or contravening the laws governing agencies of the executive branch and the purposes of these agencies. . . .

In all of this, Richard M. Nixon has acted in a manner contrary to his trust as President and subversive of constitutional government, to the great prejudice of the cause of law and justice, and to the manifest injury of the people of the United States.

Wherefore Richard M. Nixon, by such conduct, warrants impeachment and trial, and removal from office.

Article III.

In his conduct of the office of President of the United States, Richard M. Nixon, contrary to his oath faithfully to execute the office of President of the United States and, to the best of his ability, preserve, protect, and defend the Constitution of the United States, and in disregard of his constitutional duty to take care that the laws be faithfully executed, has failed without lawful cause or excuse to produce papers and things as directed by duly authorized subpoenas issued by the Committee on the Judiciary of the House of Representatives on April 11, 1974, May 15, 1974, May 30, 1974, and June 24, 1974, and willfully disobeyed such subpoenas. . . .

In all of this, Richard M. Nixon has acted in a manner contrary to his trust as President and subversive of constitutional government, to the great prejudice of the cause of law and justice, and to the manifest injury of the people of the United States.

Wherefore Richard M. Nixon, by such conduct, warrants impeachment and trial, and removal from office.[1]

Do Americans remember Watergate? Should we? If we should, which Watergate?

In the years following Watergate, the nation's publicity machine churned out vast quantities of Watergate books and lecture tours and docudramas and jokes and parodies. Watergate figures themselves made their mark in the publishing world, with two books on Watergate by John Dean; two by Woodward and Bernstein; and one each by Haldeman and Ehrlichman and Liddy and Sirica and Jaworski and Ben-Veniste-and-Frampton and Dash and Thompson and Colson and Magruder and Stans and Doyle and Tony Ulasewicz, and others. In 1978 Russell Baker wrote a column that purported to be an excerpt from something called *The Final Watergate Book*, by Sven Eilborg, President Nixon's masseur.[2]

For better or worse, Sven's was not the final Watergate book, and even in 1991 a new interpretation of Watergate stayed on the *New York Times* best-seller list for four months.[3] But whether Watergate is still haunting us is a matter of dispute. How deep did Watergate go and how much does it remain with us? In 1975 conservative legal thinker Robert Bork was passed over for appointment to the Supreme Court because President Gerald Ford believed him too closely associated with Watergate.[4] As solicitor general in the Nixon administration, Bork had carried out President Nixon's order to fire Special Prosecutor Archibald Cox in the "Saturday Night Massacre" of October 1973. He did so after Attorney General Elliot Richardson resigned, refusing to carry out the order, and Deputy Attorney General William Ruckelshaus was dismissed because he, too, refused to fire Cox. But by 1987 President Ronald Reagan felt free to propose Bork for the high court; Bork's role in Watergate, raised by his opponents as an issue, was ultimately treated as irrelevant. Sen. Alan Simpson declared that the Saturday Night Massacre was so long ago that no one paid it any mind except the capital's political junkies. "Fourteen years. This is a curious place," Simpson said. "If you go out in the land and say, 'What were you doing on the night of the Saturday Night Massacre?' a guy will say, 'What are you talking about?' But in this town when you say, 'What were you doing on the night of the Saturday Night Massacre?' they say, 'I was just finishing shaving. I was going out to dinner. I will never forget it my whole life. I went limp. My wife and I talked and huddled together and had a drink and just shuddered in shock.' "[5]

What effect did Watergate have on American politics? One year after Richard Nixon left office, CBS political correspondent Bruce Morton told viewers, "The facts are that Watergate didn't change much." There was a new campaign finance law and a new generation of reformist Democrats brought to Congress, he conceded, but "Watergate had nothing to do with some of the basic things about this country—nothing to do with where the money is, and whose; nothing to do with race, or why the cities are the way they are. Some see it as historic but irrelevant . . . the effects of Watergate a year later seem slight. It has not solved the country's problems, or even had much to do with them."[6]

By the tenth anniversary of Nixon's resignation, Morton's position was, if anything, reinforced. The *Los Angeles Times* reported that "most experts find no evidence that the traumatic ousting of a U.S. President has caused any basic change in public attitudes about either the American system of government or the persons who occupy public positions."[7] Public confidence in government declined after Watergate, the news story observed, but it had been steadily declining for nearly a decade. A highly regarded historian, interviewed in *U.S. News* on the same occasion, held that for her undergraduates "Watergate is already a dim and distant curiosity" and that she expected Watergate to "end up as a relatively insignificant event" in American history.[8] In a 1986 national survey of high school students, 35.5 percent did not know that Watergate took place after

1950. More than one in five associated it with the resignation of a president other than Richard Nixon.[9]

For people old enough to remember Watergate, the fading of Watergate from the national memory may seem astonishing. Watergate was for many at the time a consuming experience, and close observers of Watergate events felt the nation teetering at the brink. Recall, for instance, the unprecedented "firestorm" of protest when Special Prosecutor Cox was dismissed in the Saturday Night Massacre. On the following Tuesday and Wednesday forty-four Watergate-related resolutions were introduced in the House of Representatives, including twenty-two calling for impeachment. One of these was introduced by Ohio congressman Lud Ashley who said that his "great-granddaddy" had introduced impeachment proceedings against President Andrew Johnson more than a century before.[10] The president of the American Bar Association accused President Nixon of trying to "abort the established processes of justice." Newspapers all over the country, Republican as well as Democrat, protested. The *New Orleans States-Item* called Nixon a "dictator"; the *Chicago Tribune* thought his action "may be the worst blunder in the history of the Presidency"; the *Charleston* [W. Va.] *Gazette* urged Congress to "prevent Mr. Nixon from seizing the government."[11]

Or recall the days immediately before Nixon resigned. In late July 1974, Secretary of Defense James Schlesinger asked Air Force General George S. Brown not to respond to any White House directive to use military force without informing him. Schlesinger recognized that his precautions might seem alarmist, but he said, "I had seen enough so that I was not going to run risks with the future of the United States. There are a lot of parliamentary governments that have been overthrown with much less at stake." He determined not to leave Washington in those last days of the Nixon administration; he instructed all military commanders to accept no commands from the White House without his countersignature.[12]

Schlesinger feared what the president might do, either in fomenting a foreign war as distraction or in employing the military to enforce his will against the Congress. Alexander Haig, the president's chief of staff, feared what the president might do to himself. He asked the president's physicians to deny him all sleeping pills or tranquilizers.[13] If the president's closest aides wondered about his stability, it is no surprise that people elsewhere grew fearful. Congressman John Conyers, Democrat from Michigan and member of the House Judiciary Committee, said during the committee's impeachment debate, "Millions of citizens are genuinely afraid that they may have in office a person who might entertain the notion of taking over the government of this country, a politician who has more effectively employed the politics of fear and division than any other in our time."[14] The writer Vance Bourjaily, teaching at the University of Iowa, recalled later that there was "a paranoid nervousness" to the glee that he and other Nixon-haters took in Nixon's repeated Watergate blunders. "We could never feel sure that Nixon, Haig, and Kissinger would not engineer America's first military take-over, in preference to its first presidential act of self-destruction. Not until we saw the final helicopter lift off from the White House garden could we really relax and enjoy it all."[15]

How can all this drama, all this sense of impending disaster have been forgotten so quickly? How can what historian Stephen Ambrose judged "the political story of the century" have left so little impression?[16] This is in stark contrast to other historical events whose memory people hold close. No one questions that the Depression or World War II or the Vietnam War have had lasting effects on American society. No one would doubt that the French Revolution affected France, the Russian Revolution Russia. Those events define their societies. They were "events" of long duration, directly involving hundreds of thousands of people as participants, and issuing in large scale social and political change.

But Watergate? A Gallup poll in 1987 asked respondents which major events most affected their political views. The Vietnam War (19.6 percent) was mentioned most often, followed by the Great Depression, the Reagan presidency, the Kennedy presidency, the assassinations of the 1960s, the civil rights movement, World War II, and then (5.9 percent) Watergate. When asked to list two major events, people again mentioned Vietnam most often (34.4 percent), followed by the Reagan presidency (20.2), the assassinations (17.8), and then Watergate (17.4), ahead of the Great Depression (16.8), the civil rights movement (15.9), the Kennedy presidency (15.4), and World War II (13.6).[17]

Does this tell us that the glass of Watergate importance is half empty or half full? I take it to suggest that Watergate is for the general public one of the most important political events of the past half century, although not nearly as important as the Vietnam War and somewhat less important than the transformation and tumult of political culture in the 1960s that is probably evoked by the category of "assassinations." But while Watergate may be a significant factor when people think back on their formative political experiences, it has regularly seemed to commentators all but invisible in daily American life. On Watergate's tenth anniversary, Richard Nixon's former counsel and chief accuser, John Dean, mournfully reflected, "Now, more than ever, it is clear that Watergate has had no lasting effect, has brought no real changes in government, and has had little impact on the people of the country."[18] Journalist Nicholas Horrock judged Watergate to have "faded to the western horizon of the nation's memory."[19] Ben Stein, a former Nixon speechwriter, was also perplexed by the memory, or lack of it, about Watergate. He confided in the *Washington Post* not only that his college-student assistants did not know what Watergate was but that he himself could not explain it to them. He suggested that something is wrong with our system of government if "the nation chased a president out of office for the only time in 200 years and *no one clearly remembers why.*" (Emphasis in original.)[20]

Few people clearly remember why. My own students in 1990 could not say what Nixon had done. But does this reflect something "wrong with our system of government" or something complex about Watergate or something amiss about how we keep memories—or something else altogether?

We expect large public events like Watergate to leave a visible mark on society. They are, at the very least, important testimonies to a society about itself. Anthropologist Don Handelman defines public events as "culturally constituted foci of information-processing." In them lie "crucial junctures of events and the social orders that formulate them."[21] As such, public events become tools, as well as occasions, for a society's thinking out loud about itself, not only at the time but in retrospect. We think with and through these events; we "think with" Watergate. It is a reference point for thinking about American politics, American journalism, American culture. It is a frame within which we analyze subsequent (and reevaluate prior) historical events. It is a cognitive tool that people use to comprehend elements of the world that might otherwise be harder to place or to define.[22]

But is Watergate "good" to think with? Whether something is a "good" tool for thinking is not settled by the fact that it is a tool. If some cultural materials are good to think with, can others be bad? Some people hold that Watergate is good to think with because it was a profoundly and representatively "American" event, which began to develop the proportions of a grand national myth. Historian James MacGregor Burns felt it emerged as "a morality tale, complete with villains and saints, winners and sinners, and a Greek chorus of Washington boosters and critics."[23] For some, it mirrored the strengths and weaknesses of America as a whole. "What kind of a society is it," historian Henry Steele Commager asked about Richard Nixon's associates, "that produces—and cherishes—men of these intellectual and moral standards? If our own conduct was scrupulous, if our own standards were honorable, would we really have permitted the Mitchells and Magruders and Deans and Haldemans and

Kleindiensts to have imposed moral standards upon us?"[24] Historian Henry Graff explains the revulsion people felt at Watergate as a painful self-recognition: "Because the President is the shining mirror reflecting the nation's values, the people, in a moment of remembered virtue, suddenly and clearly saw their new selves in Nixon. In horror—albeit not in contrition—they smashed the mirror."[25]

Watergate is inseparable, of course, from its protagonist. Is Richard Nixon good to think with? Many observers believe he is; he has been declared a profoundly representative American. After all, he was the dominant political figure in American life for forty years (or so it appears in retrospect; one would not have made any claim for his dominance in the 1950s or in 1960 or in 1962). Just after Watergate, political theorist John Schaar wrote that Nixon is "the mottled image of what we ourselves have become but know we cannot respect ourselves for being."[26] A few years later Robert Herhold wrote in *The Christian Century* that Nixon fascinates "not because he is so different from us, but because he is so much like us."[27] A decade after Watergate, Gore Vidal declared, "As individuals, the Presidents are accidental; but as types, they are inevitable and represent, God help us, us. We are Nixon; he is us."[28] Historian Michael Genovese calls Nixon "the quintessential post–World War II American figure."[29] Nixon biographer Roger Morris holds that Nixon "was so much like the rest of us, so clearly and frighteningly the quintessential American politician of our era."[30] Tom Wicker's recent study of Nixon puts this in its title, that he is *One of Us.*[31] Nixon was, writer Garry Wills observed more elliptically, "an eccentric at the center of our national experience" and a kind of national oxymoron, "our aberrant norm."[32] Does Nixon, like apple pie, baseball, Westerns, and Al Capone, represent something deep and enduring in the American character?

This view has met with some resistance. Some people argue that Watergate is very bad to think with, that Richard Nixon is too bizarre a personality and the circumstances of Watergate too unrepresentative of American culture to ever recur or to symbolize anything profound about our society. In this view the only lesson to draw from Watergate is to keep paranoid personalities from becoming president or, drawing the lesson even more narrowly, to keep Richard Nixon from becoming president again. His personality seems so perverse, his insecurities so overwhelming, his awkwardness in the age of televised public relations so appalling, his guile in an era of sincerity so out of phase, that his unique capacity to be out of touch and to have no ear whatsoever for an audience seems to place him beyond the realm of representativeness. When Nixon resigned his office, economist John Kenneth Galbraith predicted that someone would surely say that "there's a little bit of Richard Nixon in all of us." "I say the hell there is!" Galbraith added.[33]

But whether Watergate is or is not good to think with depends on which Watergate we mean. What is the Watergate we remember (whoever "we" are, and I will be more explicit about several "we's")? What do we talk about when we talk about Watergate? There is no agreement on what Watergate is. The interesting question becomes how, not whether, we remember Watergate, which face or facet of Watergate we recall and why.

Not surprisingly, this varies across different groups. But the varieties of Watergate memory are not infinite and may be catalogued fairly easily; most versions center on some of the same key moments or issues even if they read them differently.

The story the attentive American public most often hears or tells itself about Watergate begins with a burglary, the objectives of which are to this day unclear, and which, so far as we know, the president of the United States did not plan or order or know anything about.[34] I hesitate to provide my own capsule summary of "Watergate" when my task in this chapter is to analyze different interpretations of Watergate, each of which emphasizes different parts of the basic narrative to different degrees. Moreover, to tell a story of Watergate from burglary to resignation prejudices the case. It automatically favors interpretations that center on the cover-up that began hours after the burglary rather than on interpretations that emphasize presidential abuses of power that began soon after Nixon took office or, indeed, interpretations that trace Nixon's abuses to precedents in prior administrations. Still, there *is* a conventionally accepted "basic narrative" and it does begin with the burglary. Since it is not well known to people who did not live through Watergate and since it may not be fresh in the minds of those who did, here is my whirlwind tour of conventional "Watergate":

On 17 June 1972 five burglars were arrested at the Watergate hotel and office complex in Washington, D.C., where they had broken into the Democratic National Committee headquarters, apparently to fix a malfunctioning wiretap set up in an earlier break-in. The White House denied that the Nixon administration or Nixon reelection campaign were in any way connected with the incident, and press secretary Ron Ziegler referred to it as nothing more than a "third-rate burglary." But the press soon reported that one of the burglars, James W. McCord, Jr., had been a CIA employee and was presently employed by President Nixon's campaign organization, the Committee to Re-elect the President (officially abbreviated as CRP but more often referred to as CREEP). Charges flew,

16

with the Democratic National Committee and Common Cause initiating separate civil suits against the Nixon campaign, and the *Washington Post* actively pursuing the story and linking CREEP activities to key White House staff members. The White House retaliated with the accusation that Democrats and liberals in the media were blowing the Watergate burglary out of proportion to gain political advantage in the election.

Five months later President Nixon was reelected by a landslide margin over Democratic challenger George McGovern, and Watergate receded from public view. In the first months of 1973 the Watergate burglars and two others who had organized the burglary team—CREEP's chief lawyer, G. Gordon Liddy, and a former White House consultant and CIA agent, E. Howard Hunt, Jr.—were found guilty of wiretapping and conspiracy in federal court. Judge John J. Sirica, who presided at the trial, imposed stiff sentences but termed them "provisional," holding out the possibility that he would reduce them if the convicted burglars cooperated with current investigations. There was public suspicion that the burglars, some of whom had shifted their pleas from "not guilty" to "guilty," were being paid or pressured by higher authorities in the Nixon campaign to keep silent—which, indeed, turned out to be the case. Unknown to the press or public, the White House was paying E. Howard Hunt for his continued silence with President Nixon's knowledge and approval, and it was holding out to him the prospect of clemency.

In February Senate confirmation hearings of L. Patrick Gray to be head of the FBI revealed that President Nixon's counsel, John Dean, had sat in on FBI interviews when the FBI was investigating Watergate and had received copies of FBI investigation reports. This suggested a collusion to protect White House staff that raised new suspicions about the White House role in Watergate. In March the containment of "Watergate" broke wide open when James McCord, hoping for a reduced sentence, wrote to Judge Sirica that political pressure had been applied to Watergate defendants to plead guilty and to remain silent, that defendants had perjured themselves during the trial, and that other people who helped plan the Watergate break-in had not been identified during the trial.

At that point, nine months after the break-in, "Watergate" became a continuing public issue that would not disappear until President Nixon finally resigned his office. In April credible allegations that Nixon's two closest aides, chief of staff H. R. Haldeman and domestic affairs adviser John Ehrlichman, were implicated in the cover-up of the Watergate affair, along with the president's counsel, John Dean, led to the resignation of all three. Attorney General Richard Kleindienst also resigned, and Nixon named Secretary of Defense Elliot Richardson to replace him. In May

Richardson appointed Harvard Law School professor Archibald Cox to be Special Watergate Prosecutor, making good on his pledge to the Senate in his confirmation hearing; he had insisted there would be an independent investigation of Watergate. Soon thereafter the Senate Select Committee on Presidential Campaign Activities, established by a unanimous vote of 77–0 in the Senate in February, began public, televised hearings under the gavel of Sen. Sam J. Ervin of North Carolina.

These hearings provided captivating public drama through most of the summer of 1973, including two astonishing moments. First, John Dean, in a long and amazingly detailed account, directly implicated President Nixon in the Watergate cover-up. Second, a White House aide, Alexander Butterfield, revealed that President Nixon tape-recorded conversations in the Oval Office. Dean's testimony seemed to pit his solitary word against the denials of the president, Haldeman, Ehrlichman, and others, but the tapes meant Dean might be authoritatively corroborated or refuted.

The Senate inquiry made public not only White House involvement in the Watergate cover-up but other abuses of power prior to and unconnected with the Watergate break-in. This included revelations that President Nixon used the Internal Revenue Service to harass political opponents; that the White House kept an "enemies list" of journalists, intellectuals, politicians, labor and business leaders, and others; and that the White House had established a "Plumbers' Unit" to investigate leaks to the press—a group that, among other things, burglarized Daniel Ellsberg's psychiatrist's office. (Ellsberg was a defense-establishment intellectual and Pentagon insider whose growing disillusionment with the Vietnam War led him to leak a classified Pentagon history of the war, "the Pentagon Papers," to the news media. The burglary was an effort to gather information to discredit him.)

During the summer of 1973, both the Senate committee and the special prosecutor sought access to the White House tapes. The White House refused to turn over the tapes, citing "executive privilege" as a justification. The White House also refused the Senate's subpoenas of the tapes, so both the Senate and Special Prosecutor Cox went to the courts to enforce subpoenas. In August President Nixon responded to Watergate charges on nationwide television, but the public was skeptical and even Republican senators were critical of his evasiveness.

Meanwhile Attorney General Richardson informed President Nixon that Vice President Spiro Agnew was under investigation for corrupt practices while he was governor of Maryland. By October these investigations led to a plea-bargaining arrangement in which Agnew pleaded no contest to one charge of income tax evasion and paid a $10,000 fine in return for resigning as vice president of the United States. While Agnew's alleged corruption bore no connection to Watergate, it seemed one more black mark against the Nixon administration, one more sign of pervasive malfeasance. And the plea bargain did relate to Watergate; Attorney General Richardson was concerned about the president's stability, battered as he was by one Watergate revelation after another, and he wanted to be sure Spiro Agnew would not be in a position to succeed Nixon in office.[35] In October President Nixon nominated Michigan Congressman Gerald Ford as the new vice president; Ford was sworn in two months later.

The temperature of the Watergate affair rose sharply in late October in a moment of tense confrontation over the special prosecutor's access to the White House tapes. Failure to work out a compromise agreement over prosecutor Cox's access to the tapes led the president to order Attorney General Richardson to fire Cox. Richardson refused, believing this inconsistent with his pledge to the Senate of an independent investigation. He resigned. His deputy, William Ruckelshaus, also refused, and was fired. Solicitor General Robert Bork, the third in command at the Justice Department, carried out the order. The offices of the attorney general and the deputy attorney general were closed off and the offices of the special prosecution force sealed. The Saturday Night Massacre, as it came to be known, led to the first serious consideration in the Congress of impeaching the president.

Meanwhile, the battle for the tapes was far from over. A new special prosecutor was appointed, Texas lawyer Leon Jaworski, and the administration hoped he might be easier to work with than Cox had been. President Nixon agreed to turn over to Judge Sirica nine tapes that Cox had subpoenaed. But, the president's lawyers revealed, it turned out that two of these tapes did not exist, one with Nixon's first discussion with former attorney general and CREEP chairman John Mitchell after the break-in and another between the president and John Dean on 15 April. Several weeks later a third tape, covering a conversation between the president and chief of staff Haldeman three days after the break-in, turned out to have a mysterious eighteen-minute buzz on it. The credibility of the president was falling fast. Serious questions were raised about Nixon's own personal income tax returns and about his use of government funds to make improvements on his personal residences. The flurry of accusations led Nixon to one of his most famous disclaimers in November, telling the Associated Press Managing Editors Association meeting at Disney World, "People have the right to know whether their President is a crook. Well, I am not a crook."

The pace of events did not slow. Prosecutor Jaworski pushed for White

House compliance with his requests for evidence. In February 1974, the House Judiciary Committee was authorized by a vote of 410 to 4 to begin an impeachment investigation. In March the Watergate grand jury returned indictments charging John Mitchell, along with White House aides H. R. Haldeman, John Ehrlichman, Charles Colson, and others, with a criminal conspiracy to obstruct justice. Both Jaworski and the House Judiciary Committee issued subpoenas to produce additional White House tapes that the White House had refused to provide upon request, setting deadlines for the end of April.

Nixon announced on 29 April that he would not release the tapes but would provide twelve hundred pages of edited transcripts. When these transcripts were released and quickly printed in "fastback" paperbacks and in newspaper supplements, the public was astonished and outraged at the language of the president and his advisers. The president's talk was foul, vengeful, full of ethnic slurs; it was particularly shocking to morally upright Republicans. His fear and hate, scarcely impeachable offenses, constituted nonetheless a moral offense to millions of Americans, and Nixon's public support fell still further.

A final set of rapid-fire blows brought the Nixon administration to an end. In July the House Judiciary Committee voted in support of three articles of impeachment, a third of the Republican members siding with the unanimous Democratic majority. The Supreme Court voted eight to nothing that President Nixon was obligated by law to turn over the tape recordings of all subpoenaed conversations. Days later the president's attorneys revealed a tape recording from 23 June 1972, that they had not previously known about. On this "smoking gun" tape, as it became known, President Nixon is heard directing his aides to demand that the CIA do what it could to shackle the FBI's investigation of Watergate. Nixon still desperately hoped he might survive the release of this tape, but he hoped in vain. All members of the House Judiciary Committee, including Nixon's most fervent Republican backers, declared they now favored impeachment. On 9 August, Richard Nixon resigned. Gerald Ford took the oath of office and declared that "our long national nightmare is over."

That's a bare-bones chronology of "Watergate" from break-in to resignation. It is in this chronological unfolding that most people experienced Watergate and came to an initial understanding of it. This has been a primary factor in ensuring the continued dominance of the conventional chronological account. Moreover, the chronological account also has the appeal of a detective story, clue upon clue finally demonstrating a connection between the White House and the burglary's cover-up. The detective story form of the Watergate chronology was brilliantly exploited in the most famous and widely read of all Watergate accounts, Bob Woodward and Carl Bernstein's *All the President's Men*. "June 17, 1972," the book begins. "Nine o'clock Saturday morning. Early for the telephone. Woodward stumbled for the receiver and snapped awake." The caller is the city editor of the *Washington Post* informing Woodward that five burglars have broken into the Democratic National Committee headquarters. The mystery novel begins.

Although most popular accounts of Watergate begin with the break-in, some self-consciously declare that the burglary is not the heart of Watergate and is therefore a misleading place to start. There are, indeed, other reasonable places to begin, but there is no other consensual starting point. Theodore White begins in 1952, seeking to trace the "grinding pressures" on the presidency, pressures that would eventually "crack" the incumbent of that office "as surely as a hearing in a giant machine cracks under strains for which it was not designed."[36] J. Anthony Lukas opens with the anxious White House response to Republican election losses in 1970.[37] One might begin with the publication of the Pentagon Papers in June 1971 and the establishment of the "plumbers" unit in the White House. Or with Richard Nixon's election in 1968. Or much farther back, either with the rise of a national security state, or the early career of Richard Nixon, or the early history of the Vietnam War.

Whatever choice one makes, authors who do not begin with the Watergate break-in generally feel called upon to make a case for selecting a different starting point. Lukas notes that Gerald Ford's phrase about "our long national nightmare" is construed by some commentators to refer to the period beginning with the Watergate break-in, but "I have taken it to mean the whole story of Richard Nixon's abuse of his presidential powers."[38] British journalist Godfrey Hodgson objects that the use of the word "Watergate" too often suggests that Nixon "was driven to resign because a team of burglars working for the committee to reelect him was found inside the Democratic National Committee's offices. That was, in the end, the least of it."[39] Stanley Kutler's *The Wars of Watergate*, the first comprehensive history of Watergate by a professional historian, makes a similar point, arguing that Watergate was "more than a burglary" and must be understood in the context of both the political upheavals of the 1960s and of Richard Nixon's political career.[40]

Kutler's work of 626 pages, plus notes, is long, labored, and extremely useful. For all its merits, it is also an extremely odd account in one respect: it tells the story of Watergate without telling the story of Woodward and Bernstein and the *Washington Post*. Publisher Katherine Graham, editor Ben Bradlee, Watergate story editors Barry Sussman, Howard Simons, and

Harry Rosenfeld are nowhere mentioned. Bob Woodward does not get a mention until page 287, when he calls on the president's assistant press secretary on 27 March 1973, and he is described simply as "a *Washington Post* reporter." Carl Bernstein makes his unobtrusive entrance on page 324 when Ron Ziegler apologizes for remarks he made to the *Washington Post* and its reporters Mr. Woodward and Mr. Bernstein. Readers do not learn Mr. Bernstein's first name until page 458, where Kutler discusses the excerpts from *All the President's Men* that appeared in *Playboy* magazine in April 1974, informing us that Woodward and Bernstein "had written extensively on Watergate since the June 17, 1972 break-in."

At first, I thought Kutler's neglect of the *Washington Post*'s Watergate role unexceptional. After all, Kutler is a legal historian with several earlier books to his credit on American legal history. Why not pursue his strong suit? If he offers a partial history, well, all history is partial. Kutler is perfectly forthright in declaring that he has a mission in his book: to remind us "of the importance of most of the characters and the seriousness of the events" of Watergate.[41] Since Kutler believes that Watergate was a severe constitutional crisis, a set of events that "raised weighty issues of governance, especially concerning the role of the presidency and its relation to other institutions in the governmental apparatus," it is reasonable that he focuses on the facts the Watergate investigations revealed rather than on the unfolding process of revelation itself.[42] It makes sense for him to center discussion in the courts rather than in the public press and to renarrate the story from a beginning other than 17 June 1972. Then it also follows that the journalists are bit players in the drama, at best. Woodward and Bernstein come on stage not as fearless investigators but as enterprising self-promoters of a best-selling detective story. Woodward and Bernstein play no role in the constitutional Watergate story, and *All the President's Men*, when it is discussed, is presented as bearing to the real drama of Watergate something like the relationship of *Rosenkrantz and Guildenstern Are Dead* to *Hamlet*.

Kutler thus tends to deny that Watergate was a "story" and a scandal as well as a constitutional crisis. He excludes from consideration the moral complications of scandal, that in a scandal the revealers are themselves vulnerable to pollution by the revelations, their own scandal-mongering morally suspect. The "tattler," the squealer, the gossip—these are morally suspect roles in our culture. In some instances people may judge the morals of the scandal-monger to be as dubious as the behavior of the subject of the scandal. This was apparent in public discussions of presidential-aspirant Gary Hart's extramarital relations in 1987; many people seemed more outraged by the media's pursuit of the story than by Hart's behavior. In the confirmation hearings of Clarence Thomas for the Supreme Court in 1991, many people expressed more alarm about the Senate staffer who leaked Anita Hill's confidential statement to investigators alleging that Thomas sexually harassed her than about the possibility that the charges were true. In Watergate, one side's concern with the Nixon reelection campaign's illegal activities and the Nixon administration's abuses of power and violation of civil liberties was met by the other side's outcry about the self-serving motives of the people who raised these issues. Up until the election in November 1972, the Nixon administration was reasonably successful in deflecting criticism about Watergate by throwing it back on the liberal media establishment and the Democratic party and its allies. In a sense, the White House argued that all the attention to Watergate was no more than electoral strategy, a dirty campaign trick itself on the part of the Democrats. For half a year after the election, the administration and its defenders continued to play this line and, even thereafter, sought to undermine the credibility of Senator Sam Ervin, to attack Judge John Sirica's courtroom tactics, and to cast doubt on the fairness and motives of special prosecutor Archibald Cox.

This was a reasonable strategy, particularly in a Washington that retained vivid and painful memories of past political horrors in which those who made accusations of wrongdoing were themselves the most dangerous men. In the late 1940s and early 1950s, what became known as the McCarthy era, the efforts of the House Un-American Activities Committee and later Senator Joseph McCarthy to rout out Communists in the State Department, in Hollywood, in the military, and elsewhere left the congressional inquiry in very bad odor. Even young liberals coming to work for Senator Ervin's Watergate committee had McCarthy in mind and pledged to themselves scrupulous care in their work lest they become involved in anything that could justly be called McCarthyite; even in Iran-contra a decade later, counsel Arthur Liman had the dangerous precedent of McCarthy in mind as he set about shaping what his inquiry should do and not do.[43]

So I see two faces to Watergate. One face addresses the actual wrongdoing in the Nixon administration as the heart of the event; the other face addresses the process of revelation, the construction of the public scandal itself. The one face sees a constitutional crisis signifying something deep and disturbing about our politics, while the other sees a "scandal." In a scandal the scandal-mongers may well have mixed motives as they go about their business. In Watergate, "scandal" theories draw attention to the anti-Nixon "liberal establishment press," the congressional investigators resentful of Nixon's active assertion of presidential power and prerogatives, the Democrats eager to "get" their longtime archenemy. Without attending to this second face of Watergate, it is impossible to understand how Watergate has been discussed and debated in the years since Richard Nixon's resignation.

Kutler tries by sheer weight of will, rhetoric, and research to solidify the triumph of a constitutionalist version of Watergate. In so doing he pays homage to central American values and constitutional structure. In the terms sociologist Robert Bellah introduced twenty-five years ago, Kutler is celebrating America's "civil religion," a set of beliefs, symbols, and rituals with respect to sacred things that Americans share without sharing a formal religion.[44] The Constitution is surely one of the sacred texts of American civil religion.

But if recognizing the sacred character of the Constitution is a religious act, devotion to the religion can be not only appropriately sincere but suspiciously showy; if there is in economic matters something we may call conspicuous consumption there is in religion something we may call conspicuous devotion. In a word, one may be not only devout but pious. Piety enters in when alternatives to orthodoxy do not get a fair hearing or when professed devotion is not itself critically examined as something that may arise from and promote ignoble or self-serving purposes. Constitutionalist versions of Watergate, I believe, often err on the side of piety.

The constitutionalist interpretation is one of several Watergate versions that can be classified along political lines. The left-right continuum is a clumsy way to categorize political differences, and I use it with some reluctance, but I think it is a helpful first approximation. So I would classify the leading interpretations of Watergate as follows. A radical leftist critique of the American national security state argues that Nixon was conveniently scapegoated, diverting attention from fundamental structural faults in the American system. A liberal position, embodying the constitutional faith, sees Watergate as a crisis over presidential abuses of power and often issues a call to post-Watergate legislative reform along with a ringing reaffirmation of the Constitution, perhaps also noting with alarm the dangers of secret government and the national security state. A conservative view, like the liberal, professes absolute faith in the Constitution but holds that "the system worked," that the way Watergate was handled reasserted the virtues of our constitutional order. The radical right sees Watergate as a witch hunt or coup d'état engineered by the Democratic party and the liberal media establishment.

The most elaborate alternative explanations of Watergate posit a secret conspiracy behind the Watergate break-in. These conspiracy theories oddly fail to engage the broader significance of Watergate, either the constitutional issue of the Nixon administration's systematic and pervasive disregard of law or the genesis, use, and abuse of the phenomenon of the political scandal. Instead, they center attention on the crime story: Who broke into the Democratic National Committee headquarters and why. Both Jim Hougan's argument that the DNC break-in was in part a CIA plot against the administration, and Len Colodny and Robert Gettlin's allegation that the break-in was John Dean's plot to hide his wife's association with a prostitution ring centered at the DNC, bizarrely take it for granted that the break-in is the core of Watergate.[45]

There are at least two things wrong with this picture. First, the DNC break-in was one among several, probably one among many, break-ins authorized by the Nixon administration. David Wise has assembled the longest list in *The American Police State* (1976).[46] It was one among a great many 1972 campaign abuses and dirty tricks. It was one among many invasions of the privacy and civil liberties of law-abiding citizens. Even if there were multiple agendas and multiple purposes for the DNC break-in, with burglars duping burglars (and Hougan makes some points about this not easily dismissed), this may tell us more about the CIA than it does about Watergate. When the CIA is involved, and it was involved in the Watergate break-in, there may be stories within stories within stories that may never be unraveled. But this is a sidebar to the Watergate that precipitated a constitutional crisis, brought down a president, and fascinated and appalled a nation.

Second, conspiracy theories try to establish exactly who was looking for what at DNC headquarters, whose phone was tapped, whose phone was meant to be tapped, and why. But what if the targeting of the DNC headquarters was a matter of happenstance rather than carefully calculated? The DNC was only one of several targets that Howard Hunt, Gordon Liddy, John Dean, Jeb Magruder, and John Mitchell discussed. If Colodny and Gettlin are right that Larry O'Brien's telephone was not the object of the DNC break-in, why did the burglars also consider bugging his hotel suite in Miami Beach during the forthcoming Democratic convention? Why did Gordon Liddy tell Howard Hunt that Mitchell, Dean, and Magruder wanted to bug George McGovern's headquarters? Why did Hunt have a "plant" there as a campaign volunteer? Why did McCord surreptitiously enter McGovern headquarters and case it? And why at the end of May 1972, while making plans to bug the DNC, did McCord, Liddy, and Alfred Baldwin make two unsuccessful efforts to break into McGovern headquarters?[47]

The mystery of the Watergate break-in may be that there is no mystery; the venture was simply "undermotivated and overbungled," as Garry

Wills puts it, like so many of the other schemes of Nixon's "intelligence" and "security" aides.[48] Had Frank Wills not been alert on his job, all the interpreters of the DNC break-in would be deconstructing an entirely different event—a burglary at McGovern headquarters or at the Democratic convention. Burglary for vaguely defined intelligence-gathering purposes seemed standard operating procedure for Nixon campaign aides and White House aides. No one in the Nixon camp required a supremely cogent reason to go ahead with campaign war games. No key decision-maker insisted that there was a legal or constitutional presumption against criminal activity in their cause. Whatever may be revealed down the road about the various motives and cover-up stories that went into the planning and execution of the DNC break-in, no one has yet made a plausible case that *any* alternative version should distract attention from the constitutional issues and the reverberations of public scandal as they have been conventionally conceived.

The dominant constructions of Watergate, as I will show, are the liberal and conservative ones. Both hold to different degrees that <u>Watergate was an aberration</u>, that Nixon was a paranoid of a sort unlikely ever to be encountered in the White House again. Liberal constitutionalism is prominently displayed by the efforts of congressional Democrats along with moderate and liberal Republicans to pass reform legislation, and in works like Bill Moyers' television documentary (and book) on "Secret Government." The liberal version of Watergate teaches that we need to learn some lessons, particularly legislative ones, from Watergate, we need to institutionalize new norms of ethical behavior in government, we need to keep Watergate in mind as a warning of how things can go awry, and we need to keep government accountable to Congress and the public.[49] The conservative "The System Worked" constitutionalism, a view promoted by opponents of post-Watergate legislative reform in the Ford administration and widely available in school textbooks, takes off from Gerald Ford's reading of Watergate: "our long national nightmare is over." In this view, no institutional safeguards, like a regularized procedure for appointing a special prosecutor, are necessary to prevent future Watergates, because they are unlikely ever to happen and, even if they did, the procedures already in place worked to put an end to Watergate. Traumatic and hazardous as it was, Watergate showed that our system works.

The liberal view, to make it more clearly a contrast to "The System Worked" conservative constitutionalism, might well be called "The System Almost Didn't Work" position. Conservatives are satisfied that Watergate reaffirmed the central values of the Constitution and the central virtues of the system it endows. Liberals are more impressed that no "system" operated at all, that a dangerously lawless presidency was cut short only by remarkable good fortune. For instance, Walter Mondale, then senator from Minnesota wrote, "Our system worked, but it worked only with the aid of a good deal of luck and a great deal of hard work." He cites as "luck" the initial detection of the burglary, the selection of Judge Sirica to hear the burglary case, the accidental assignment of Woodward and Bernstein to the story, the presence of Sam Ervin in the Senate, the "throwaway question" asked of Alexander Butterfield that revealed the president's taping system. The lesson in all of this: "Good fortune alone will not preserve a democracy in which there is no will to guard against the abuse of power."[50]

Of different views on Watergate, only the position of the radical right (and to a lesser, and less publicly visible extent, the position of the radical left) gives due attention to the fact that Watergate was a scandal as well as a constitutional crisis. Watergate was a social process of discovery and outrage as much as it was a set of behaviors or violations about which people expressed shock or indignation. It was a public event for the nation as a whole, not just a set of acts by Nixon and responses by the House, Senate, and Supreme Court. For those who emphasize the process of revelation, it is possible even to imagine that the drama of revelation was the whole show, that there was no real offense at the heart of the scandal. The British journalist and historian Paul Johnson has emphatically argued that Watergate was "the first media Putsch in history, as ruthless and anti-democratic as any military coup by bemedaled generals with their sashes and sabers."[51] Watergate was a "maelstrom of hysteria," one of America's periodic "spasms of self-righteous political emotion in which all sense of perspective and the national interest is lost." It was a "witch-hunt . . . run by liberals in the media." For these people, "Nixon's real offence was popularity." There was a conscious effort "to use publicity to reverse the electoral verdict of 1972."[52] All this Watergate hysteria led not only to the resignation of a president but to "the destruction of free institutions in the whole of Indo-China."[53]

This is obviously an extreme position. It absolves Nixon and his associates of all blame. "Watergate *was* a mess and nothing more," Johnson writes, adding that the Nixon administration's abuse of power was in no way worse, in a number of ways not as bad, as that of his predecessors.[54] Johnson's emphasis on the "liberals in the media" (Were there no liberals in the Congress or elsewhere? Were no conservatives dismayed at the president's offenses?) attributes excessive importance to the press and ascribes views to the journalists ("Nixon's real offence was popularity") for which there is no empirical warrant offered and none, I think, possible.

Thinkers of the radical Left share with Johnson consternation that Watergate focused on the specific faults of Nixon and his administration. For Johnson, this was media-generated hysteria; for radicals of the Left, this was the media cooperating with the Congress and even, ultimately, the Nixon administration to manage a crisis, limiting public understanding of basic failings and contradictions in the American system. So the "Bay Area *Kapitalistate* Group" argued that the Congress and "even the liberal press, so often credited with bringing the scandal to the full attention of the American public" helped to manage the crisis. For the *Kapitalistate* group, "All of these political actors had a significant stake in limiting the scope of the crisis, defining it in certain narrow ways, and in the end, turning the crisis itself into a reaffirmation of the virtues of the American system."[55] Journalism was not the hero of Watergate but a coconspirator in limiting its significance: "The press did its damnedest to make Nixon into the devil, so that the proper exorcism—his removal from office— could become the means of restoring faith in the system."[56] Another scholar on the Left, historian Barton J. Bernstein, wrote in 1976 on the growth and abuse of executive power from Franklin Roosevelt on, showing that Nixon "inherited" rather than "invented" presidential deceit and dishonesty. He asks, "Why . . . are citizens, the press, and the Congress so much more disturbed about Nixon's policy (with Watergate) than with his own and his predecessors' policies in foreign affairs?"[57] For Noam Chomsky, the exposures of Watergate were "analogous to the discovery that the directors of Murder Inc. were also cheating on their income tax."[58] Writing in social democratic *Dissent*, historian Leo P. Ribuffo found the Watergate investigation hypocritical; he criticized a tendency to take the Ervin investigation at face value rather than "as the biggest morality play in town." Watergate was a surprisingly "inexpensive expiation," an all too convenient, cheering, and pleasurable way not to examine the failures of American politics.[59]

For both Johnson and critics of the Left, Watergate was stagey, a managed theatrical production. Both see it run by liberals but for different ends—for Johnson, to get Nixon; for the leftists, to maintain the power of the state. But in both cases attention is drawn to scandal, not to constitutional crisis. In both cases the affair was trumped up, a political exorcism designed by and for liberals.

Scandals may be serious but they are also delicious, and Johnson rightly sensed the pleasure that Watergate brought to many of Nixon's enemies. Even to some who were not his enemies. Hedley Donovan, a political moderate and editor of *Time* during Watergate, recalls, "I must also admit I enjoyed Watergate. The plot line was intricate, every revelation seemed to lead to another, and in the end, the American system won.''[60] Journalist Jonathan Rowe recalls the excitement and pleasure of being in Washington during Watergate. "It was what I imagine a crack high must be like, this exhilaration, you just lived for the next issue of the *Washington Post*. The *Post* became almost a psychoactive substance.''[61] Journalist Hugh Sidey remembers that "the media was nearly hysterical. We never had such a story." He recalls that it evoked "a certain exhilaration and perversity that always exists in Washington.''[62]

For most Americans Watergate was action at a distance. Even for most Washingtonians, Watergate was experienced through the media, not through daily decision making or personal involvement. It was an entertainment, a story. During the Ervin committee hearings, people watched Watergate as if it were a soap opera. People spoke of needing their "Watergate fix," watching their six hours of hearings a day during the summer of 1973. This was fun: "a heavy dose of confession, anecdote and insiderism. Instant heroes, instant villains, instant rehabilitation," journalist Peter Schrag wrote of the hearings. The Ervin committee senators, he felt, "were all too obviously conscious of the requirements of performance.''[63] Indeed, the entertainment side of Watergate was to some extent scripted. Sam Dash, chief counsel to the Ervin committee, argued that the hearings were, and should have been "an engrossing educational experience in homes throughout the country." He himself tried to organize them "to impress on the millions of Americans watching the hearings that the people and events presented were real, that they were identifiable with themselves and their families, and that even their own freedoms had been threatened." He hoped the hearings would "demonstrate that the people or their elected representatives could fight City Hall and that the public officials implicated by evidence of corruption and abuse of power, no matter how high their positions, could be made accountable to the people for breach of trust.''[64]

Whether the Senate hearings were entirely successful in their educational effort can be doubted. Godfrey Hodgson, for instance, feared that Nixon was forced to resign "by public indignation about his low crimes rather than about his equally real high ones." Headline-grabbing dirty tricks, not constitutional transgressions, Hodgson worried, captured the public imagination, and the opportunity for a "collective lesson in civic culture" may have been overwhelmed by the emotions of a culture of sensation.[65]

Peter Schrag was severe in his evaluation of the hearings. His mind boggled at the senators' hypocrisy—"the attempt to understand how, given their political experience, they managed to rise to such heights of indignation still staggers the imagination."[66] The call to entertain, he felt, repressed the hard questions and no opportunity for moralizing or for levity seemed to be missed. If the staged drama of Watergate worked to assign guilt to Richard Nixon, it also "accomplished innocence" for others.[67] The Senate committee conducted its inquiry outside the actual context of Watergate, the Vietnam War and the highly polarized struggle between the administration and its foreign policy critics during Nixon's first term. Leonard Garment, a leading adviser to Nixon, argues that the source of Watergate abuses was the frustration Nixon felt when he ran into "domestic political opposition during wartime." With the lives of American soldiers at stake, Garment writes, the battle between the administration and its opposition became virulent, and it is no wonder that "Richard Nixon started thinking that wiretaps and other countermeasures were necessary."[68]

This seems to me an overgenerous defense of Nixon, but it does recall a context—that Nixon and his aides believed America's central values under assault by its own citizens—that rarely entered the Senate hearing room. Instead, as sociologist Jeffrey Alexander has observed, "through their questions, statements, references, gestures and metaphors, the senators maintained that every American, high or low, rich or poor, acts virtuously in terms of the pure universalism of the civic republican tradition." The inquiry proceeded in terms of democratic myths; Senator Sam, Bible and Constitution at the ready, led the pageant of senators embodying "transcendent justice divorced from personal or emotional concerns."[69]

The liberal and conservative views of Watergate as a constitutional crisis too readily turn pious, accepting as transparent the cultural performances of Watergate investigators. The ultraconservative view of Watergate as a scandal, in contrast, is frequently profane. It is an effort at blasphemy, a construction of Watergate that asserts Watergate to be only a construction, the senators nothing but thespians, and their professions of innocence and outrage merely bad faith. The ultraconservative version of Watergate turns the dominant interpretations of Watergate action upside down: now whatever plotting Nixon did is implicitly denied and the focus is entirely on liberal plotters in the media or in the Congress. They are seen as the Iagos of the tale, manipulating the key players, moving the story along, transforming a leader into a hapless victim.

The complexity of Watergate, the continuing interest in it, and the difficulty of getting a purchase on it lie, I think, in the plausibility of *both* the liberal and conservative view of Watergate as a constitutional crisis, on the one hand, and the radical Left and ultraconservative views of Watergate as a scandal, on the other. On one side, Watergate was uplifting public education, on the other, prurient, even contemptible, entertainment; on the one side, politics at its noblest, and on the other, a self-serving morality play; on the one side, fateful events, and on the other, merely their staging.

Putting this another way, views of Watergate as a constitutional crisis take a kind of realist position that emphasizes that there was something "really" there, a set of abuses and transgressions of mammoth proportion that jeopardized the constitutional system. Not that a "crisis" itself is not created by human beings, a matter of people coming to see a certain reality and arguing it into existence, tutoring others in a way of seeing, forcing a situation to a point of confrontation. But the root notion remains that the foundation of the crisis is an actual offense to constitutional principles. Watergate as a constitutional crisis is something people *discovered*.

To see Watergate as a scandal, in contrast, is to see it as something that people *constructed*. Constitutional crises happen, scandals are made; constitutional crises are important for *what* is there; scandals are interesting, and vulnerable to deconstructing, for *how* they got there.[70] So long as liberals and conservatives insist that Watergate was "only" a constitutional crisis and not a scandal, they will not be speaking to people's full experience of Watergate; insofar as ultraconservatives or radicals discuss Watergate as exclusively a scandal, and not a constitutional crisis, they will be talking to themselves just as hopelessly.

Is Watergate good to think with? This chapter does more to raise the question than to answer it. Some things, certainly, are not good to think with. In the legal tradition, "hard cases make bad law," that is, extreme or aberrant situations should not become a basis for legal precedent since they are too likely to offer eccentric guidelines that would not be a good foundation for public policy. In the military tradition, generals should not be fighting the last war but confronting realistically the new. As for Watergate, it may be bad to think with because the Congress almost let the game get away by failing to acknowledge its own powers, by treating a political issue—should we impeach?—as a legal one: Was a crime committed? If we think with Watergate, will we draw misleading conclusions about impeachment and search for "smoking guns" when they are not the real issue?

Is Watergate bad to think with because the greatest dangers of an imperial presidency and a national security state lie in foreign policy and not in domestic abuses of power or their cover-up?

Is Watergate bad to think with because it suggests the news media to be boldly investigative (or irresponsibly adventurous) when the media are actually cautious, statist, establishment institutions? Watergate stimulated New Right media critics, but should it have stimulated media criticism from the Left instead?

And, of course, thinking with Watergate requires thinking with Nixon, and how, from such a man, can we draw a portrait of the nation's soul or destiny? Just because a person is paranoid, the saying goes, doesn't mean he doesn't really have enemies. In Nixon's case, this should be turned around: just because he truly had enemies doesn't mean he wasn't paranoid. If Watergate sprang from his complex, idiosyncratic personality as much as from "the system," then Watergate will be bad to think with.

It may be, of course, that looking at any president, or any person, too closely is like looking at oneself too close up in a mirror. At normal distance, this is a normal face; up close it becomes grotesque, as pores become caverns, veins visible to the eye become red lightning across the sky, crow's feet become furrows in an eroding landscape. As one reads the accounts of Watergate, Nixon becomes not strikingly evil but bathetically and clumsily overlarge, obsessed, and deluded, his mind not the acute instrument many thought it to be but alternately a machine for calculating political score cards—and a slave to distrust and suspicion. Are we to think with this?

When historians or social scientists or social critics assure readers that the issue they treat is a matter of system or structure rather than idiosyncrasy or pathology, lawfulness rather than contingency, it is well to be on guard. This is, after all, an occupational conviction, a proclamation of faith. If accident governed human affairs, if the social study of human business were but a collection of narratives and not an unfolding of regularities, the social scientists would have to fold up their tents, the historians would have to acknowledge history as just one damn thing after another, and the social critics would have no big stories with large lessons to tell, just stories. Frequently, finding regularities in human affairs is not difficult. The difficult cases are those that we recognize as irregular and name accordingly: insanity, self-defeating behavior or neurosis, slips of the tongue, revolutions, crises, scandals. These are the exceptional moments in human affairs, on their face defying explanation. They are eruptions, by their very nature outside routine. With such events especially, the scholar's or journalist's plea that "there is meaning here" is overdetermined and particularly suspicious. These are exactly the cases that not only call out for explanation but threaten the identity of people who devote their lives to explaining.

Can't there be such a thing in human affairs as an aberration? Surely

Watergate raises this issue. Yes, there were continuities with "dirty tricks" in Richard Nixon's own career. Yes, there were continuities with the behavior of other presidents and the rise of an imperial presidency— spying on political opponents, laundering of money, dirty tricks, the use of federal agencies for illegal domestic surveillance—none of this was new. Was the size and scope and singlemindedness of it all different in Watergate? Would such a thing ever recur? What would count as a good argument that this was or was not an aberration?

The question of "aberration," raised at the time of Watergate, changed sharply in the year following Nixon's resignation. The question of Watergate in 1974 was whether to impeach a president; the question that emerged with great clarity by 1976 was not whether to impeach a president but whether to impeach a system that gave rise to an impeachable one. The question, as the next chapter will suggest, became not, "What did he know and when did he know it?" but, "Did he do anything different from the presidents before him?" This second question did not arise spontaneously, but neither was it a conspiracy of Nixon defenders that brought it forth. They promoted it, yet their efforts would have gone nowhere but for circumstances that played fatefully into their hands.

CHAPTER 2

Revising Watergate:

Routine or Aberration?

I F INTERPRETATIONS OF WATERGATE DIFFER ACROSS THE POLITICAL SPECTRUM, they also change over time. They are still changing. If and when "Deep Throat" writes memoirs, we may see Watergate in a new light. After Richard Nixon dies, some people may feel free to put on the record things they have not yet made public. There may be surprises in the Nixon tapes and papers in the National Archives that have not yet come out. The basic evidentiary record of Watergate has gaps, some of which will be filled in.

But powerful post-Watergate changes in the understanding of Watergate have already taken place. Within a year of Richard Nixon's resignation, claims of the singularity of his abuse of power could no longer be maintained or could not be maintained as easily as they had been. History was happening backwards, subsequent events forcing interpreters of all political persuasions to reconsider earlier judgments.

In the terms proposed by Leonard Garment, Nixon's law partner and counselor, there are two kinds of perspectives on Watergate: "Nixon theories" and "imperial presidency theories." Nixon theories typically argue that what Nixon did was unique; "imperial presidency" theories generally argue that what he did was part of a long-term pattern of the aggrandizement of constitutional and extraconstitutional authority by the presidency.[1] These latter theories emphasize that American foreign policy since World War I has been conducted on a wartime footing, that "national security" is a rationale to cover a multitude of sins and crimes, and that Watergate's lesson was that a nation's misconduct abroad "can come home to haunt it."[2]

Was Richard Nixon's offense an aberration or, instead, the logical consequence of a system in which he was no more guilty than other presidents? The House Judiciary Committee was very interested to know if Nixon's offenses could be distinguished from those of his predecessors. Counsel John Doar even asked eminent Yale historian C. Vann Woodward in May 1974 to do a historical study of presidential misconduct. Woodward and fourteen other historians dropped everything else to do the work and determine if Nixon's transgressions were unlike those of his predecessors. Their conclusion: Nixon was unique. Typically American presidents were the victims rather than perpetrators of malfeasance, betrayed by friends or associates. Presidential offense "usually lay in negligence or in indecision about correcting the offensive practices or discharging the accused." Nixon, in contrast, was "the chief coordinator of the crime and misdemeanor charged against his own administration" and "the chief personal beneficiary of misconduct in his administration. For all the many variations of misconduct in the White House from 1789 to 1969, Woodward concluded, "they do little to prepare us for the innovations of the ensuing period of five and a half years."[3]

But Woodward's study looked only at publicly acknowledged presidential scandals, not presidential misdeeds that might have come to light after a president's term of office ended. In 1974 and 1975, a mountain of information poured out from the news media, a presidential commission, and two congressional committees to reveal massive abuses of power by presidents back to Franklin Roosevelt. Woodward's hurried study was irrelevant by 1976. By 1977, when the conservative political writer Victor Lasky published what might be viewed as a rebuttal to Woodward, *It Didn't Start with Watergate*, he had a powerful case.[4] Lasky did not refute a "Richard Nixon" theory with an "imperial presidency" theory. His position was simply that politicians, at least Democrats, are sleazy human beings beneath contempt, particularly if their names are John Kennedy or Lyndon Johnson. Crude as Lasky's book is, it is packed with information gleaned largely from public documents and respectable newspapers. By the time it was published, it was believable in a way it could not have been a few years earlier. In 1973 the kinds of arguments Lasky would later make were stock dodges for Nixon defenders. Humorist Art Buchwald made a list of them, which included "Everybody does it," "What about Chappaquiddick?" "What about Harry Truman and the deep freeze scandal?" "Franklin D. Roosevelt did a lot of worse things," and "LBJ used to read FBI reports every night."[5] By 1977 such rationalizations for Nixon's conduct were not so easily dismissed.

The impeachment inquiry promoted "Nixon" theories, but the

meaning of Watergate by 1977 had shifted, "Nixon" theories losing ground to "imperial presidency" theories, and views of Watergate as symptom of systemic faults coming to compete with views of Watergate as aberration. Three factors made this possible. First, the legal and cultural need to attribute blame for criminal activity to specific, morally responsible individuals had been at least partially satisfied. President Nixon left office in disgrace, and many of his aides had served or were still serving prison terms. With the matter of criminal responsibility resolved, there was more room to consider broader interpretations of Watergate without necessarily suggesting Nixon's exoneration. Second, the meaning of Watergate was to some extent fuzzy to begin with, because Watergate was in no small measure a crime against memory itself. The Watergate cover-up was an effort to misdirect attention, to destroy evidence, to make accurate historical reconstruction impossible. Though the cover-up fell apart it was successful enough to leave ambiguity about just what went on. Bolstered by the pardoning of Nixon, it left wiggle room for varying interpretations.

Third, as I have indicated, investigations in the years after Watergate brought out new and damning information about the abuses of power by presidents before Nixon. C. Vann Woodward worked only with public historical records. The question he examined was: What kinds of malfeasance in office or abuse of power have presidents or their chief aides been responsibly charged with through the years? The question that became of greater interest in 1975 was quite different: What abuses of power have presidents been guilty of even if the public never knew about them? How was Watergate routine rather than aberration? While this question was asked during 1972 to 1974, it never became a matter for intense public attention. It slid, or was pushed, to the side. But once asked seriously, it reconfigured the meaning of Watergate. It propelled to new prominence the question, "Did Richard Nixon just have the bad luck to get caught?" It forced people connected with earlier administrations and campaigns who had themselves engaged in dirty tricks painfully to rethink their own deeds.[6] It reestablished what would pass as plausible interpretations of Watergate.

THE COVER-UP

Part of what we mean by Watergate is the protracted effort of the Nixon administration to deceive Congress, the courts, and the public about what illegal or dubious activities the president's campaign committee and the Nixon administration had been involved in. I will not recount all of this in detail. The story of the Watergate cover-up has been well told in the congressional investigations, in the newspapers, and in the accounts of Watergate that followed. But a quick listing of activities designed to prevent an understanding, let alone a memory, of the Watergate break-in, should give a sense of how extensive and powerful the cover-up was:

James McCord, the CREEP security coordinator and Watergate burglar, buried some of the equipment used in the burglary and threw some of it in the Potomac River.

A CIA operative, Lee Pennington, either destroyed or watched James McCord's wife destroy incriminating evidence at the McCord home two days after the Watergate break-in.

E. Howard Hunt, an accomplice of the burglars, hid some of McCord's wire-tapping equipment in his Executive Office Building safe within hours of the arrests at the Watergate.

G. Gordon Liddy, the CREEP's general counsel and a burglary accomplice, went to the CREEP offices the day after the burglary and shredded evidence.

In a statement to the press on 18 June, John Mitchell intentionally understated McCord's role at CREEP. Since the CREEP director's wife, Martha Mitchell, was well aware of McCord's position at CREEP, Mitchell instructed aides to keep her from reading news accounts of McCord's arrest.[7]

Martha Mitchell's bodyguard prevented her from making phone calls for several days. He ripped the telephone out of the wall while Mrs. Mitchell, who had feigned sleep to get to a phone unobserved, was talking to Helen Thomas of UPI. Mrs. Mitchell, who said—not inaccurately—that she was "being held a political prisoner," was forcibly restrained and sedated.

On 19 June, Jeb Magruder burned the "Gemstone" file, including transcripts from the listening device that had been placed at the Democratic National Committee at an earlier break-in, in his fireplace at home.

The next day, John Dean, counsel to the president, and Fred Fielding, associate counsel, examined the contents of Howard Hunt's safe. This included papers on antiwar activist and Pentagon Papers principal Daniel Ellsberg; State Department cables on Vietnam, including two that Hunt had fabricated himself; memos from Hunt to Nixon's special counsel, Charles Colson, about the Plumbers' operations; and a Colt revolver and live ammunition. John Ehrlichman, Nixon's domestic affairs adviser, instructed Dean to shred the documents and "deep six" the briefcase. Instead, Dean turned over sensitive materials to the acting FBI director, L. Patrick Gray. Gray was told, by either Dean or Ehrlichman, that the files bore on national security, not on Watergate. Dean told him they "clearly should not see the light of day." While Gray testified that neither Dean nor Ehrlichman told him explicitly to destroy the files, he took that to be their implication. In December he burned the files at his home in Connecticut.[8]

The CIA kept information from the FBI to cover up its own involvement with the Watergate burglars during the first six weeks after the Watergate break-in.[9]

None of these activities was directed by or even known to President Nixon, so far as is publicly known. But quickly President Nixon entered into the cover-up, too:

On 22 June Nixon was cheered by Haldeman's news that the FBI did not yet know that Howard Hunt had been at the scene of the Watergate break-in and that the FBI was so far unable to trace the hundred-dollar bills the burglars had been carrying—and so could not link the money to CREEP. The president, in short, had knowledge relevant to an FBI criminal investigation that he was not volunteering to the FBI, hoping the criminal investigation would flounder.[10]

On 23 June President Nixon instructed Haldeman and Ehrlichman to direct the CIA to ask the FBI to curtail its investigation of Watergate, under the guise of protecting national security matters that might come to light. The tape recording of those instructions would later be known as the "smoking gun" tape.

On 15 September 1972, President Nixon, in a meeting with Haldeman and Dean, directed Dean to find ways to scuttle the Watergate investigation begun by Rep. Wright Patman's Banking Committee. The president made it clear that Dean should indicate to cooperating congressmen that the desire to keep the investigation from proceeding came "from the top."[11]

On 21 March 1973, John Dean met with the president for two hours and told him that the Watergate burglars had received payments for remaining silent; that these payments were an obstruction of justice; and that Haldeman, Ehrlichman, Mitchell, and Dean were all involved in the payments. At that point, as the House Judiciary Committee report states, "The President did not express either surprise or shock. He did not condemn the payments or the involvement of his closest aides. He did not direct that the activity be stopped. He did not report it to the proper investigative agencies."[12] Instead, the president considered strategies for continuing payments to the burglars and maintaining the cover-up. He authorized continued payments to E. Howard Hunt.

The president personally and through his aides led the Watergate burglars to expect clemency in return for their continued silence or their perjured testimony.[13]

CREEP and White House officials lied under oath. Indeed, H. R. Haldeman was convicted of perjury; John Ehrlichman and President Nixon's appointments secretary, Dwight Chapin, were convicted of lying to a grand jury; Egil Krogh, an aide to Ehrlichman, pleaded guilty on perjury counts; Herbert Porter, an official at CREEP, pleaded guilty to lying to the FBI. President Nixon was informed in March 1973 that several key members of his staff were committing perjury. The president, far from condemning this conduct or reporting it to an appropriate authority, condoned it and even went farther, advising his aides how to instruct witnesses to mislead investigators. On 21 March he told Dean and Haldeman to "just be damned sure you say I don't . . . remember; I can't recall, I can't give any honest, an answer to that that I can recall. But that's it."[14]

The president repeatedly lied to the public in televised speeches and press conferences devoted to Watergate. On 22 June 1972, the president denied that members of CREEP or the White House staff were involved in the Watergate burglary, although he knew by then that they were. On 29 August he declared that John Dean's investigation of Watergate showed that no one then employed in the Nixon administration was involved in the Watergate incident, a statement he knew to be untrue. On 30 April 1974, the president released transcripts of forty-three presidential conversations to the public, declaring that they told "the whole story" of the Watergate matter, a statement he knew to be false. These transcripts omit important words and passages, including Nixon's express approval of clemency for E. Howard Hunt.[15] As Nixon writes in his memoirs, the 30 April speech gave the impression that the president had known nothing of the cover-up until 21 March. "In fact, I had known some of the details of the cover-up before March 21, and when I did become aware of their implications, instead of exerting presidential leadership aimed at uncovering the cover-up, I embarked upon an increasingly desperate search for ways to limit the damage to my friends, to my administration, and to myself."[16]

The president refused to comply with subpoenas of the House Judiciary Committee in April, May, and June 1974.

Eighteen and a half minutes of a tape recording of the president's conversation with Haldeman on 20 June 1972, were erased at a time when the tapes, according to the president, were under his "sole and personal control." Responsibility for the erasure has never been established, but few doubt that the erasure was intentional.

In all these, and other ways, President Nixon and his aides edited the story of Watergate as it unfolded, indeed, tried to keep it from unfolding. As it turned out, this effort to keep from public memory matters embarrassing to the president and his closest staff became the clearest, most palpably criminal basis for impeachment. Of the three articles of impeachment approved by the House Judiciary Committee, the "obstruction of justice" article had the largest majority. And once the "smoking gun" tape was released, even those who voted against this article changed their views. Congressmen Edward Hutchinson, Henry P. Smith, III, Charles W. Sandman, Jr., Charles E. Wiggins, David W. Dennis, Wiley Mayne, Trent Lott, Carlos J. Moorhead, Joseph J. Maraziti, and Delbert L. Latta, all Republicans, the ten "no" votes on Article I, acknowledged that President Nixon's statement of 5 August 1974 amounted to a confession of obstruction of justice and conspiracy to obstruct justice.[17]

While not altering their opposition to Article II or Article III, these stalwart defenders of Richard Nixon took it upon themselves to observe that they could not assent to the proposition that Richard Nixon was "hounded from office" by political adversaries and critics in the media. "We feel constrained to point out . . . that it was Richard Nixon who impeded the FBI's investigation of the Watergate affair by wrongfully attempting to implicate the Central Intelligence Agency; it was Richard Nixon who created and preserved the evidence of that transgression and who, knowing that it had been subpoenaed by this Committee and the Special Prosecutor, concealed its terrible import, even from his own counsel, until he could do so no longer. And it was a unanimous Supreme Court of the United States which, in an opinion authored by the Chief Justice whom he appointed, ordered Richard Nixon to surrender that evidence to the Special Prosecutor, to further the ends of justice."[18]

Differences remained among the congressmen about the appropriate extent of presidential authority and whether the president overstepped it in dealing with the Congress, but there was finally unanimity about Nixon's responsibility for obstruction of the legal process. Nearly everyone, including every single member of the House Judiciary Committee, could agree that Nixon's effort to rewrite the Watergate past was both criminal and impeachable.

The cover-up tends to be ignored in ultraconservative accounts of Nixon's "hounding" from office. *It Didn't Start with Watergate* is devoted to precedents for the abuses of power of Article II of the articles of impeachment, as if that is a refutation of the unique and unprecedented nature of the cover-up activity detailed in Article I. Liberal accounts, in contrast, ordinarily see Nixon's Article I efforts to cover-up as behavior consistent with the kind of contempt for law and due process evident also in the Article II abuses of power.

In the continuing memory of Watergate, the "cover-up" did not end with Richard Nixon's resignation. The most important subsequent event in the cover-up was that, one month after Richard Nixon left office, President Gerald Ford pardoned him for crimes he "committed or may have committed" while president.

This was a shocker. Inside the White House it prompted the embarrassing resignation of press secretary Jerry ter Horst, specifically on the grounds that he had not been kept informed of the pardon decision and had thus unintentionally misled reporters.[19] The pardon very likely cost Ford the 1976 election. It was an act widely condemned at the time. The public hue and cry was enormous. There was, according to the *New York Times*, a "firestorm" of protest "only a little less intense than that Mr. Nixon set off last October when he fired special prosecutor Archibald Cox."[20] President Ford was booed in Pittsburgh the day after the pardon and a flood of phone calls to the White House ran two to one against the pardon. The *New York Times* editorialized against the decision three days running.[21] Historians have tended to evaluate the pardon more generously.[22] Even at the time, there is some question as to whether people's public condemnation of the pardon squared perfectly with their private views. William Hildenbrand, then an administrative assistant to Senate Minority Leader Hugh Scott, recalled later that Nixon's Republican supporters in the Senate thought Ford's act both "proper" and "humanitarian." Other Senate Republicans thought it was "dumb," but they were glad to have Watergate behind them. Senate Democrats, too, did not really want to live through a trial of Richard Nixon.[23]

Wise or unwise, Ford's decision to pardon Nixon cut short the legal process that would have confronted Richard Nixon directly with the charges against him and would have aired and very likely resolved certain factual matters at issue. This was, in fact, a major concern of some of the voices protesting the pardon. Fred M. Hechinger, of the editorial board of the *Times*, suggested the Senate vote approval of the articles of impeachment.[24] *Times* columnist Tom Wicker suggested the impeachment process continue or the Congress formally vote censure.[25] The *Times* editorialized that the House should resume the impeachment process.[26] On the op-ed page Arthur L. Liman, a man who would become known to a wider public only with Iran-contra, argued that Richard Nixon should be brought before the Watergate grand jury or a special commission to be cross-examined about all the allegations against him. He urged adoption of a constitutional amendment to prohibit pardon or immunity for any president or vice president for acts committed in office "at least until after trial and conviction."[27] Anthony Lewis of the *New York Times* argued for a House Judiciary Committee inquiry into the pardon power and suggested Congress authorize Special Prosecutor Jaworski to make a report of what his case against President Nixon would have been if it had gone forward.[28]

The pardon was of far-reaching significance for the construction of a national memory of Watergate. Gerald Ford pardoned Richard Nixon for whatever crimes he "committed or may have committed or taken part in" during his presidency. Nixon, in accepting the pardon, confessed to neither the abuses of power nor the obstruction of justice with which the articles of impeachment charged him. He acknowledged only that his "mistakes and misjudgments" in handling Watergate (a term he seemed to use to refer to a set of offenses perpetrated by his associates and subordinates unbeknownst to himself) might, reasonably but falsely, lead others to conclude that he himself had acted in illegal and self-serving ways.

If the pardon failed to elicit from Nixon a statement of contrition, it succeeded in curtailing further legal proceedings against him. This is made clear in what may be the single most interesting book in the Watergate corpus, *Stonewall*, written by Watergate Special Prosecution Force attorneys Richard Ben-Veniste and George Frampton.[29] On 28 August Ford had publicly declared that he was holding open the possibility of pardoning Nixon but would make no move until after any legal action against Mr. Nixon was undertaken. Within two days he had changed his mind. He asked his attorney, Philip Buchen, to study the pardon power and to seek to learn from special prosecutor Leon Jaworski what indictment might be made against Nixon and how long Jaworski would expect a trial of the former president to last.

There is no clear information on what negotiations transpired between Jaworski and Ford, but it appeared to Ben-Veniste and Frampton that Jaworski must have intimated that he would not oppose a pardon if it was grounded in the view that prejudicial pretrial publicity would make a fair hearing for Mr. Nixon impossible.[30] Buchen told the press in the days following the pardon that Ford's decision was influenced by Jaworski's view that it might require a year's delay before Richard Nixon could get a fair trial. Many Watergate Special Prosecution Force staff members were upset that the special prosecutor had helped push Ford toward a pardon before presenting formal charges against Nixon.[31]

Because of the pardon, formal charges against Nixon were never made a part of any judicial proceeding. The special prosecutor turned over to the House Judiciary Committee a summary indictment of Richard Nixon and entered material into the trial record in *United States v. Mitchell, et al.* in the fall of 1974. The case against Nixon is also outlined in the memoirs of Jaworski, as well as Ben-Veniste and Frampton.[32] But there was no focused, dramatic public hearing of the case against Nixon. Nowhere was a prosecutor pitted against a defendant and his attorney. If the nation drove a president from office and "no one clearly remembers why," one reason is that the pardon granted by President Ford with the acquiescence, perhaps the relief, perhaps the encouragement, of the special prosecutor prevented the courts from impressing on the public mind just what Richard Nixon had done.[33] However unwittingly, the pardon became just what House Judiciary Committee member Jerome Waldie called it, "the ultimate cover-up."[34]

HISTORY BACKWARDS: CIA REVELATIONS AND THE "YEAR OF INTELLIGENCE"

The Ford administration was barely in place when the nation was stunned by a series of revelations about American covert military and intelligence operations. In mid-September, while responses to the pardon were still electrifying the media, Seymour Hersh wrote in the *New York Times* that CIA covert operations had been designed and enacted, with some success, to bring down the government of the democratically elected Marxist leader of Chile, Salvador Allende. On 22 December 1974, Hersh broke an even more explosive story: that the CIA had spied on domestic antiwar protesters and other left-wing organizations during the 1960s. Daniel Schorr, the CBS News correspondent covering the story, recounts that this disclosure "caused a public stir in a way that a covert operation against a distant South American regime had not. It twinged the Watergate-raw 'invasion of liberties' nerve that the Ford administration had been trying to assuage."[35]

"Watergate-raw" is a term that certainly fit the CIA. In May 1973, the public learned that Howard Hunt, a White House "plumber" acting with authorization from John Ehrlichman and using CIA equipment to collect materials for a CIA "psychiatric profile" of Daniel Ellsberg, broke into Ellsberg's psychiatrist's office. The administration was looking for information to discredit Ellsberg in retaliation for his release of the Pentagon Papers. CIA director James Schlesinger was outraged. He directed all CIA employees, past and present, to disclose any improper agency activity they knew of. The Inspector General's office came up with a 693-page report of possible violations of the CIA's legislative charter, known inside the agency as the "family jewels" or, by Deputy Director of Plans William Colby, as "our skeletons in the closet."[36]

So when Ford asked William Colby, Schlesinger's successor as CIA director, to respond to the *New York Times* charges, Colby delivered "the family jewels" to the president. On 4 January 1975, Ford appointed a commission of inquiry headed by Vice President Nelson Rockefeller to examine CIA domestic operations that violated its charter. While this was intended to cool things off, Ford unintentionally provoked another bombshell. In an off-the-record luncheon with *New York Times* editors, he defended the generally conservative cast of the Rockefeller commission by saying he wanted people who would stick to the mission at hand (illegal and unauthorized domestic surveillance) and not get into matters that could blacken the reputation of presidents back to Truman. "Like what?" asked managing editor A. M. Rosenthal. "Like assassinations!" said Ford, adding, "That's off the record!"[37]

The *Times* did not print the remarks or investigate the story, but word began to get around. After Daniel Schorr obtained an unintentional confirmation from Colby that the CIA may have assassinated foreign leaders, he broke the story for CBS News, and assassinations were added to the topics within the Rockefeller commission's mandate.

By then the Rockefeller commission was not operating alone. Senator Frank Church, Democrat from Idaho, was running a Senate investigation of the CIA, too, as chair of the Senate Select Committee to Study Government Operations with Respect to Intelligence Activities, established 27 January.[38] The House set up a comparable committee in February, although internal bickering left it floundering for months. The Rockefeller commission ran out of time, or will, even with a two-month extension, to complete a study of assassination attempts; it turned over its assassination materials to the Senate Intelligence Committee.[39] Even so, the Rockefeller report, made public 10 June, was anything but the whitewash many had expected. It documented the domestic surveillance charges, including "Operation Chaos," in which the Johnson administration and later the Nixon administration had collected files on foreign contacts of left-wing American activists. Although the CIA had no statutory authority in domestic intelligence, it developed files on Americans and infiltrated New Left organizations.[40] The CIA during the Nixon administration helped draw up a plan "at the President's personal request" for a major assault on the peace movement, under the direction of a White House aide, Tom Huston.[41] The infamous Huston plan was squelched by FBI director J. Edgar Hoover's opposition.

As for assassination plots, the Church committee revealed that there had been assassination plots or coup attempts under Presidents Eisenhower, Kennedy, Johnson, and Nixon directed against a number of foreign leaders. Efforts had been made, but failed, to assassinate Patrice Lumumba in 1960 in the Congo (internal opponents assassinated him). Efforts were made to assassinate Rafael Trujillo, the dictator of the Dominican Republic, in 1961. Trujillo was killed by dissidents who apparently had received American arms. The CIA aided a coup against South Vietnamese president Ngo Dinh Diem in 1963 that led to his death. The CIA sought to kidnap General René Schneider, chief of staff of the Chilean army, who had foiled a CIA-backed military coup against President Allende; when he resisted, Schneider was killed by CIA-supported Chileans. A number of imaginative CIA plots had been launched to assassinate Fidel Castro. Poison cigars were delivered to Havana, but it appears no one got them to Castro. Mafia gangsters were retained to help poison Castro's drink. A diving suit with disease-bearing fungus was to be delivered to Castro as a gift for his recreational diving.

No foreign leader, as Daniel Schorr reported for CBS, "was directly killed by the CIA. But it wasn't for want of trying."[42] On 18 July Senator Church suggested that the CIA may have been acting like "a rogue elephant on a rampage," but that was a conclusion Church did not have evidence to support. It was not clear whether the CIA acted on its own or with the knowledge of presidents. The Church committee could not demonstrate either that the CIA acted under presidential directive or that it did not. It is still not clear. Robert McNamara, testifying before the Church committee, avowed that all senior officials in the Kennedy administration opposed assassinations but claimed at the same time that the CIA took no major actions without proper authorization from senior officials. "I understand the contradiction that this carries with respect to the facts."[43] Richard Helms, defending the CIA, felt the Church committee hypocritically conducted an assault on U.S. intelligence. Surely the senators knew that the CIA was the agency of the president precisely to provide a policy option midway between persuasion and military conduct; the point of covert activity is that it be covert. When the committee asked how the CIA could engage in horrible acts like assassination without presidential authorization, Helms felt they surely knew there *was* such authorization but that no president would be so stupid as to put it in writing.[44]

Assassination plots were not the Church committee's only bombshell. The committee revealed that CIA scientists developed and retained deadly poisons, violating President Nixon's directives to comply with international treaties.[45] The public learned also of twenty years of CIA opening of mail, including that of Martin Luther King, Jr., Arthur Burns, Senator Edward Kennedy, and Senator Frank Church. Mail opening stopped only in 1973 because of fears inspired by the Watergate investigations.[46] The FBI, too, had been engaged in unauthorized interception of mail.[47]

The investigations of the abuses of the intelligence agencies led to new patterns of congressional oversight of the CIA and, at least in the short term, major demoralization within the agency. In the long term, it may have led to a more conscientious effort to reconcile the irreconcilable forces of secrecy and democracy than had existed since government secrecy rapidly expanded during and after World War II.

The CIA revelations reshaped the public's image of Watergate. They achieved what President Ford had feared they might: They depressed the reputations of presidents before Nixon, especially Kennedy and Johnson. They lent credence to Nixon's own fumbled defense of himself: that in many of the abuses of power detailed in Article II of the Watergate bill of impeachment, he was pursuing politics as usual. While Article I obstruction of justice charges were untouched by "the year of intelligence" events, Article II abuse of power charges were shown to be ones that might well have been leveled with equal merit at John Kennedy and Lyndon Johnson—and perhaps other presidents, too. Then was there any legitimate basis for distinguishing Richard Nixon's offense? In terms of scope? Perhaps. In terms of central direction? Perhaps. In terms of how Nixon's use of intelligence agencies for political purposes dominated White House activities and provided a central thrust in the administration's outlook? Perhaps. In the Nixon administration's obliviousness to legal and constitutional issues, in its mode of operation less embarrassed and, indeed, less covert than that of earlier presidents? Perhaps. In the warlike footing in which opponents were transformed into enemies and dissension perceived as civil war? Perhaps this, too. All of these are plausible bases for distinguishing the character or scope of Richard Nixon's abuses of power from those of his predecessors. But there is no definitive or consensual judgment among lawyers, judges, or scholars on these matters. The blurring of the line remains between what offenses Richard Nixon alone committed and which offenses were a habitual part of an arrogant, imperial presidency by the time he assumed office.

In the last chapter I discussed one dimension along which interpretations of Watergate divide: whether Watergate is judged a crisis or a scandal. The "year of intelligence" underlined a second dimension: whether the offenses of Watergate should be seen as the responsibility of Richard Nixon or of the system of an imperial presidency; it made the latter view more plausible. Taking the two dimensions together, Watergate interpretations can be roughly arranged into four groups, as follows:

	Crisis Theories	**Scandal Theories**
Nixon Theories	Conservative Article I (obstruction of justice)	Ultraconservative Article II (abuse of power)
System Theories	Liberal Articles I and II (obstruction of justice and abuse of power)	Radical Left Article II (abuse of power)

For radicals of the Left, Watergate was a scandal, not a crisis, managed by establishment forces to preserve the general system of the national security state. As Marcus Raskin put it, "to forestall a politically revolutionary consciousness, it was necessary to develop a theory that Nixon and his activities were distinguishable from the System's usual operations."[48] Watergate posed danger to the system by revealing a fundamental corruption of democracy incompatible with national aspirations and popular expectations. To keep these obvious contradictions from threatening the system as a whole, Congress, the media, and other leading forces helped make Richard Nixon the scapegoat for systemic dysfunctions. A political issue of overriding importance was turned into a criminal matter that the nation would after a time be able to put behind it.

For ultraconservatives, Watergate was likewise a scandal but one in which Richard Nixon (and the political forces he represented) was genuinely the object, not a scapegoat. Powerful institutions were not united to save their power as a whole; instead, power was sharply divided between liberals and conservatives. The liberals used their hegemony in the media and in the Congress to drive conservatives from office. The proof that Article II–type presidential abuses of power were rife among Nixon's immediate predecessors strongly reinforced the legitimacy of conservative and ultraconservative charges that liberal forces had been out to get Nixon and not out to locate truths about the presidency.

For liberals Watergate was a constitutional crisis of a troubled system, one that should force the nation to legislative reform to prevent future Watergates, educational reform to prevent the socialization of the kinds of people who made Watergate possible, and general soul-searching to uproot the failings in all of us that enabled Watergate to happen. But central to the liberal position is that Watergate was a constitutional crisis in which the separate branches of government stared each other down. The executive and the legislature—the president and the Congress—went eyeball to eyeball in Watergate, and the president blinked first, honoring the Supreme Court decision on the tapes and choosing to resign for lack of political support in the legislative branch. For liberals Article I obstruction of justice was a kind of subset of Article II abuses of power; both revealed an overreaching presidency and a dangerously reckless president who believed himself above the law.

The liberal position waffles, moving first to Article I to indict Nixon, then to Article II to reform the system. Take, for instance, Theodore Sorensen's lectures at MIT on presidential accountability in the fall of 1974. Sorensen, chief speech writer for President Kennedy, took issue with *both* those who saw Watergate as "a culmination of past trends" and those who asserted that Nixon was "a total aberration." Nixon, he said, was not the first president to receive and dispense unreported campaign contributions, to engage in political espionage, to sanction dirty tricks, to deal ruthlessly with opponents. But, Sorensen argued, turning exclusively to Article I transgressions, "I know of no other President who was personally and directly involved in the cover-up of crimes, the obstruction of justice, and the defiance of those congressional committees, courts, and prosecutors who then investigated these misdeeds."[49] This is unarguable. But see how Sorensen first recognizes but then dodges the more complicated and fateful issues of Article II transgressions to rest on the more plainly established uniqueness of those detailed in Article I.

It is not illogical to claim both that the growth of executive power made possible someone like Nixon and that Nixon was distinctive, unlikely, unprecedented. It may be a virtue of the liberal position that it alone maintains a focus on *both* Article I and Article II abuses, but it opens liberals to charges of confusion. Liberals emphasize systemic explanation while still insisting on the moral and legal accountability of individuals.

For conservatives, as for liberals, Watergate was a constitutional crisis, but it was caused by the follies of one man and his administration, not by systemic distress and disproportion between the powers of the executive and the legislative branches. What Watergate demonstrated is that the political system was strong enough and flexible enough to handle even so serious a threat to political liberty as Watergate turned out to be. For conservatives, Watergate should be viewed ultimately as an opportunity for national self-congratulation rather than for soul-searching and reform.

The question of whether Watergate abuses were aberrational and Nixonian or common and systemic was raised before the Church committee, the Pike committee, and the Rockefeller commission. The "year of intelligence" simply added powerful corroboration for the "system" theories. No one doubted the validity of the CIA inquiry revelations. No one questioned the veracity of Seymour Hersh's reporting. Now no one denied that the CIA under Kennedy and Johnson had been involved in trying to assassinate foreign leaders. And no one could easily define a bright line separating Richard Nixon's Article II abuses of power in office from the abuses of other presidents.

After the cover-up, the pardon, and the "year of intelligence," the shape of Watergate discourse was set. This is a somewhat arbitrary conclusion, of course; the meaning of Watergate has changed in some measure since 1975 and may one day change again. But I think the framework for debate about Watergate today was well articulated by the end of 1975. Was Watergate a personal aberration or a systemic fault? Were Nixon's abuses of power the same as or different from those of other presidents? Was Watergate a constitutional crisis of mammoth dimensions or a scandal of malfeasance blown out of proportion? Was it a turning point in American history or no more than a systemic spasm at the end of the Vietnam era?

These questions figure in the Watergate story in most of its renditions. While this leaves plenty of room for significant debate, the framework of Watergate discussion also precludes consideration of some topics. What is left out of Watergate memory may be more important than what is contained in it. If the Nixon administration did its own frantic editing of Watergate, the Congress did editorial work, too, but more deliberately. Of real importance, a fourth article of impeachment concerning Nixon's prosecution of a secret war in the territory of neutral Cambodia rarely receives more than passing mention in accounts of Watergate. This article (as well as another one concerning Nixon's tax returns and his use of federal money for personal home improvements) was voted down in the Judiciary Committee 26 to 12. The Judiciary Committee was reluctant to challenge the president's authority in foreign policy, especially when the administration had in fact notified a few members of Congress of the military action in Cambodia.[50] The Congress was thus compromised; what was secret from the American public was not entirely unknown to the Congress. The Cambodia issue was thus removed from the story of Watergate, shearing off the largest source and original center of conflict between President Nixon and the Congress: the Vietnam War. Watergate has come to mean, in some interpretations, the matters of the cover-up detailed in Article I; and, in other interpretations, the abuses of power in the domestic sphere discussed in Article II. But the issue of presidential prerogatives in foreign policy raised by the Cambodia article is left aside, too painful a topic to pursue and too divisive a topic on which to reach consensus. Both liberal and conservative versions of Watergate may have provided a signal to presidents that foreign policy is safe territory for unilateral action.

The questions asked about Watergate, nonetheless, as well as the ones unasked, are powerful and important, living public questions animating our politics and culture. They have been questions both legislative and journalistic, both personal and generational. My aim is less to answer them than to identify them and their continuing influence. My goal is neither to revilify nor to rehabilitate Richard Nixon, and my primary purpose is not to promote my own vision of Watergate. Instead, I seek to map the Watergate flood plain in the geography of American public life, to show how Watergate and our various reconstructions of it have endured—with what purposes and with what effects.

All that said, I do have my own view of Watergate, as should be clear. My research has not weaned me from the constitutional view with which I began; indeed, it has strengthened my conviction that grave constitutional issues were at stake in Watergate. At the same time, I have come to see for the first time that there is validity in the "scandal" version of Watergate, too. I now believe that constitutionalist views frequently oversimplify and often proceed naïvely as if partisanship, showmanship, and the possibility of manipulating public sentiment have nothing to do with our national politics. Scandalist interpretations of Watergate correct for this even though, in the form in which they have normally been stated, they tend to deny altogether that constitutional questions were at issue and that the Constitution required some extraordinary efforts to protect it from executive lawlessness.

My own position, then, is that the way we *should* think about Watergate is to recognize in it elements of both constitutional crisis and scandal, and various dimensions in which it was both an aberration and a routine occurrence. But it is not my point to argue how we should think about Watergate but to demonstrate that, in fact, we do. I want to show how different views of Watergate have warred with one another through the past twenty years and to analyze how different forms and forums have carried these views on in American memory.

CHAPTER 3

Collective Memory
and Watergate

H OW DO SOCIETIES REMEMBER? IN EVERYDAY LANGUAGE, MEMORY IS GENER-
ally understood as a property of individual minds. We make excep-
tions when discussing the information storage capacity of computers or
the ability of fabrics to retain their shape but, generally speaking, locating
memory outside of individual minds is likely to seem suspect to people not
trained as sociologists or anthropologists.[1] Still, as a member of this small
social-scientific tribe, I maintain that *we* have it right in identifying memory as essentially social and that general usage has it wrong in a number
of respects. First, memory is sometimes located in institutions, rather than
in individual human minds, in the form of rules, laws, standardized procedures, and records. These include cultural institutions or practices
through which people in the present recognize a debt to the past (including
"debt" and moral or financial obligation itself, punishment, retribution,
restitution, restoration, reform, inheritance, and promise and its enforcement through contract) or through which they express moral continuity
with the past (for instance, tradition, identity, career, curriculum). These
cultural forms and institutional practices store and transmit information
that individuals can make use of without themselves "memorizing"
it; individual memory piggybacks on the resources social institutions
provide.

Second, memory is sometimes located in collectively created monuments and markers: books, holidays, statues, souvenirs. Third, where
memory can be located in individual minds, it may characterize groups of
individuals—generations or occupational groups. While memory in this

51

respect is indeed an individual property, it is so widely shared as to be accurately termed social. Fourth, where memories are located idiosyncratically in individuals, they remain social and cultural in that *(a)* they generally operate through the supra-individual cultural construction of language, and *(b)* they generally come into play in response to social stimulation, rehearsal, social cues. Fifth, the act of remembering is most often social and interactive, occasioned by social situations, prompted by cultural artifacts and social cues that remind, employed for social purposes, even enacted by cooperative activity. Of course, remembering can be undertaken alone, walking through the woods or sitting in a prison cell, but such instances, paradigmatic as they are in the psychological laboratory, may be exceptional.[2] Sixth, the cultural dimension of memory also suggests a normative dimension: memory of the past may be valued more or less in different societies at different times and so encouraged or discouraged, enabled or blocked.[3]

In the case of Watergate, attitudes toward memory are at center stage. Much discussion about Watergate takes as its subject, in part, the question of memory itself: The recall of Watergate is surrounded with cries about the dangers (or, much more rarely, the virtues) of forgetting. In talking about Watergate, people frequently express an anxiety that in our society, historical memory is currently fighting a losing battle against the siren song of the present.

Why is there a fear of forgetting? Why does oblivion seem so likely and so threatening?

This question goes well beyond Watergate and what I can explore here, but it is worth noting how difficult it seems today to know how to think about the past, not just a particular past whose recollection promises to stir conflict, shame, or embarrassment, but "pastness" in general. People are wary of the past, recognizing that it is often used as an ideological weapon and knowing that any account is vulnerable to challenge and revision. Doubts today among professional historians about the value of their enterprise for the education of citizens may be as grave as they have ever been in this century.[4] Historians have become reflective about their own specialized role in memory-making rather than taking for granted a sovereign role.[5] As historian Peter Burke has observed, "Remembering the past and writing about it no longer seem the innocent activities they were once taken to be. Neither memories nor histories seem objective any longer. In both cases this selection, interpretation and distortion is socially conditioned. It is not the work of individuals alone."[6]

The view that the past is vulnerable to present interests is presented in extreme—and classic—form in George Orwell's *1984* where poor Winston

Smith is daily charged with the task of adjusting written records of the past to accord with the present interests and policies of the State. "Who controls the past controls the present, who controls the present controls the future" is the watchword of Big Brother's Party. Smith, like his co-workers, puts facts inconvenient to the State's present interests down the "memory" hole, where they are irretrievably lost.

As long as our society is not totalitarian, *1984* is not a full picture of how the past is remembered or how history is written. Still, Orwell captures a disturbing part of what happens even in liberal societies. It may seem exotic and pathetic that the Soviet Union cancelled final examinations in history for schoolchildren in 1988 because the Glasnost-inspired authorities could no longer determine what was truth, what was myth, and what was lie in the Soviet curriculum.[7] But it hits closer to home when historians report convincingly that the John F. Kennedy of legend in reality was neither liberal nor idealistic. He proved only a reluctant spokesman for civil rights and social justice, lied to the press about his health and his intellectual achievements (he was not the author of *Profiles in Courage*, for which he shamelessly accepted the Pulitzer Prize), and was a notorious philanderer.[8] During his life Kennedy's image was assiduously cultivated to promote his political fortunes, and, since his death, it has been maintained by family and friends eager to keep his memory sacred and the Kennedy political magic active; popular reluctance to let go of the shining Camelot image has conspired to support the Kennedy fiction.

In the Kennedy case, there has clearly been an effort to control the present by editing the past. There are much more humble examples, too. The labor historians Daniel and Isabelle Bertaux have gathered evidence that bakers who rose from apprentice to master tended to forget the humiliations of apprenticeship, while those who remained workers tended to recall them vividly.[9] Interest guides memory to its own purposes, whether in the organized intentions of a totalitarian state or simply in the information control any powerful political figure may exercise over a public willing or wanting to believe—or even in the self-justifying ways of the ordinary person in everyday life.

Apparently opposed to this "interest theory" of how we use the past is a "cultural" theory. If every society's symbols form a vast cultural system whose job is that of telling stories that represent and reproduce the existing society, then for good or ill, and whether or not it accords with our "interests," culture constrains how we tell the tale. Barry Schwartz, Yael Zerubavel, and Bernice M. Barnett, for instance, examine the Israeli commemoration of Masada first promoted in modern times by Palestinian Jews of the 1920s. They argue that the Palestinian Jews' appropriation of

Masada cannot be understood as instrumental, that is, it cannot be understood to have been selected for its value in legitimating their power or promoting their solidarity. It did not in fact appear to promote solidarity but instead offered a way of thinking about it. "Its function was not instrumental, in the sense of producing practical effects, but semiotic, in that it formulated meaning." Collective memory, they argue, "is drawn not to that which is useful but to that which is appropriate." The recovered memory of Masada did not reduce worries of the present but expressed them; its role was "that of a symbolic structure in which the reality of the community's inner life could be rendered more explicit and more comprehensible than it would have been otherwise."[10]

Historian Carl Degler adds that "appropriateness" means appropriateness to contemporary values as well as circumstances. In "Why Historians Change Their Minds," he observes that historians are obliged to rewrite history as the values of their society change. He argues that "if historians did not change their minds about the past as the great values of the society shifted, their history would cease to be a living part of the culture and therefore incapable of illuminating the present with the light of the past."[11] A contemporary historian of slavery who did not begin with the assumption that slavery is bad, he suggests, would not be a historian but an antiquarian, someone for whom there is no vital connection between present values and telling the story of past events.

"Interest" theories tend to be over-economistic, seeing self-conscious "interests" behind every idea, ideology, and history book. The "cultural" school tends to be over-anthropological, seeing general "values" or "culture" between the lines of every text. "Interest" theory assumes there is a personal (or social or class) intention or motive for every historical interpretation, while the cultural position assumes an underlying symbolic logic, even if the historian is unaware of it.

Both positions assume that historical interpretation works on an independently existing body of facts, documents, and recollections that are the raw materials of "history." This axiom is strenuously resisted by a third group I will call radical social constructionists. An academic joke tells of three baseball umpires at an umpires' convention, speaking at a panel on the theory of umpiring. The first umpire expounds his theory, "I call them as I see them." The second umpire, more positivist in inclination, declares, "I call them as they are." The third philosopher-umpire declares, "They aren't anything until I call them." The third umpire is a radical social constructionist like Richard Handler and Jocelyn Linnekin, for instance, who argue that "tradition" is nothing more than that which people call tradition, a category of thought, not a residue of the past. "We suggest," they write, "that there is no essential, bounded tradition; tradition is a model of the past and is inseparable from the interpretation of tradition in the present."[12] People of the present are the umpires, and the past does not exist until they call it.

All three of these positions usefully map a portion of the phenomenon of historical memory. But they are incomplete and, oddly, inhumane. The ways people make use of the past, and the reasons they seek to, are more devious and complex than any of these general positions allow. "Interest theory," "values theory" or cultural theory, and radical social constructionism all implicitly deny historicity altogether. They portray actors, unconstrained by their own pasts or by their own location in time, as either ensnared by overweening personal aggrandizement or ensconced in inescapable cultural logics or completely free of interpretive constraints.

By any of these models, everything works out. Nothing is left astray. And thereby the starting point of history, story, and narrative, is denied: "Once upon a time." Once upon a time, something happened. Something happened, and on that, not on interests or values or free interpretation, hangs the tale. Tracing the consequences of "something happened" is what an interest in the past is all about. Historical accidents or branching programs or two roads diverging in yellow woods (and, sorry, we cannot travel both) and the choices made at those crossroads and the ways those choices are conceived and remembered: this is the core of human historicity, and it makes us what we are.

People are not solely rational actors who use history to their own ends, nor are they merely cultural puppets pulled by the strings of deep-set values. They are, instead, I believe, creatures who are themselves inescapably historical. In the notion of humanness is a temporal dimension, a necessary orientation both to past and to future, an understanding of self for which a sense of the past is not instrumental but defining. Because humans live for a span of time and then die, and know that this is their fate, in a narrow sense they have no "interests" apart from interests across the span of a lifetime, although "lineages" and "traditions" and even the "self" are cultural fictions giving people a sense of what time period is relevant for achieving their interests. Bodies (culturally interpreted, to be sure, but within compelling biological limits) regularly remind people of their lifetimes. An obvious instance is women's consciousness of their "biological clock," which in our day, at least, sharply affects the career decisions of many women in their thirties and forties.

Much of human behavior is incomprehensible without keeping "the lifetime" in mind as the cultural and moral, as well as biological, framework for action. People may act "for the moment" and not maximize their interests over a lifetime. Or people may take as more important than the lifetime a span of generations or a long tradition. But the lifetime is the most familiar and most widely accepted moral framework for daily life, at least in the West. This obvious point has not had much impact on the social and behavioral sciences, although Anthony Giddens, the contemporary social theorist most self-consciously concerned with how human beings are situated in time and space, takes it as a central point: "Human beings do not just live in time, they have an awareness of the passing of time which is incorporated in the nature of their social institutions."[13]

The lifetime is a central framework for our ethics, our interests, our cognitions. Probably the most important distinction in recollection of the past is between matters within and matters beyond living memory. This is obviously important in understanding the remembrance of Watergate. As I write this, Watergate is well within living memory for many people. This makes it available—and, importantly, "actionable"—in ways events beyond the reach of living memory rarely are. That is, it continues to motivate action. Bismarck is supposed to have remarked that fools learn by experience, wise men by other people's experience. No wonder wisdom is so rare. We learn more from past events the more our own time, energy, and ego are involved in the events themselves (perhaps up to some limit, beyond which ego involvement may very well be an *obstacle* to learning).[14] As we will see, the preservation of a memory of Watergate has in many respects been motivated by people deeply moved or hurt by Watergate who feel a commitment to one or another version of it that they want to see others accept.

Watergate is a distinctive event for the study of collective memory not only because it falls within living memory for many, but because it was, or was quickly treated as, a unique event rather than a process. That may make it easier to remember. It has a beginning, a middle, and an end. It has heroes and villains. It has moments of conflict and high drama. It is the sort of phenomenon that both journalists and historians know instinctively how to handle, unlike, say, the movement of blacks from the southern countryside to northern cities or the emergence of AIDS as an illness of epidemic proportion or other such social processes with no identifiable beginning or ending point, and where the actors are primarily Everyman and Everywoman, not key individuals of celebrity status.

Because events to which we can readily assign beginnings, middles, and ends can be apprehended as dramas, they encourage immediate notice, and immediate notice is certainly better adapted for enduring memory than no notice at all. Still, historians and, even more, social scientists are occupationally inclined to take "events" as superficial and ultimately not worthy of great attention. What is the relationship of the daily events of government policy and government scandal and constitutional crisis to underlying forces of social-demographic structure, alterations in the international balance of economic and political power, or basic developments in technology and the economy? It may be that there is little or no relationship. Or that the events on the "surface" can be understood as "volcanic eruptions that reveal deep shifts in the geological structures."[15] I suspect it could be that the metaphor of deep structure and surface events is misleading and that "surface events" may not only reveal shifts in deep structure but propel them. In any case, the appearance of Watergate as a drama on the surface of history rather than a structure deep in the bowels attracted immediate popular notice but reduced long-term interest by social scientists and historians.

A third distinctive feature of Watergate for the character of its remembrance is that most people experienced it at a distance. When attorney Fred Thompson left Nashville for Washington in February 1973, to be minority counsel for the Senate Watergate Committee, Watergate was already "the biggest action in town" in Washington, but it meant very little to anyone in Nashville.[16] Even a year later, when the House Judiciary Committee was undertaking its impeachment inquiry, a White House aide said of Watergate, "It's an obsession of politicians and editors in Washington, but where else?" U.S. News set out to answer that question, calling on staff in seven bureaus. Their conclusion was that the energy crisis and the price of gasoline, not Watergate, preoccupied people in Atlanta, Chicago, Los Angeles, Houston, Detroit, San Francisco, and New York.[17]

Watergate was, for the vast majority of Americans most of the time, a distant and abstract event in the way an energy crisis was not. Experienced overwhelmingly through television, Watergate could not help but take on the quality of entertainment rather than real life. This is not to say people did not experience Watergate in powerful ways. Millions sat before their television sets for hours watching the Senate hearings in the summer of 1973. Not everyone could be in the Senate hearing room, but nearly everyone could watch the proceedings on television. This is a distinctive mode of publicness, as Daniel Dayan and Elihu Katz argue. A national society, which cannot provide the experience of "being there" for many, institutes televisual ceremonies "to encapsulate the experience of 'not being there.'" Dayan and Katz rightly urge that we try to picture this participation in national affairs through the media not as "an impoverished and deviant experience" but as an "altogether *different* experience, a new style of publicness."[18]

It certainly felt that way to many. The hearings were electrifying; for the first time, a year after the Watergate break-in, "Watergate" became a focused, national public event. It would be so again several more times: at the Saturday Night Massacre in October 1973; when President Nixon made public transcripts of White House tapes in April 1974; at the televised House Judiciary Committee impeachment debate in July 1974; and when Nixon resigned in August. The primary medium of public participation at these times was television, but not only television. With the release of the White House tapes, for instance, the print media responded in spectacular fashion: nineteen metropolitan newspapers printed supplements with the full thirteen hundred pages of transcript, and within a week three publishers put three million paperback copies of the transcripts in print.[19]

Even apart from these major moments of public fascination, an attentive political public across the nation monitored the Watergate story. The writer Mary McCarthy observed that when she traveled across the country in April 1973, she found that "the story was being told, democratically, to the entire population, which was discussing it, democratically, as if at a town meeting. . . . In every city I arrived at, the local papers were full of Watergate; regardless of their politics and of pressure, if any, from their advertisers, they were keeping their readers in touch with the most minor episodes in this fantastic crime serial."[20]

Still, on television or in print, Watergate was a story narrated more than an experience lived. This is not to deny importance to Watergate but to put it in its place. Unlike a war or a depression or an energy crisis, Watergate was directly an affair of the state, only indirectly and through the media an affair of society.[21]

A fourth distinctive feature of Watergate's memory is that it is deeply affected by the power of the presidency as the symbolic center of American public national life. The presidency magnetizes events as nothing else in our civic life can. A scandal over a vice president (who now remembers Spiro Agnew or would argue that we should?) or a Speaker of the House (can you identify Jim Wright or anything about the scandal that drove him from office?) will fade quickly in ways a presidential scandal cannot.

Fifth, Watergate has only one strong memory agent, and he keeps the memory of Watergate alive despite himself. In a later chapter I will examine Richard Nixon's campaign against memory, arguing that it has been more successful at keeping Watergate alive than burying it. Apart from Nixon, Watergate has few continuing sponsors, even though historians, journalists, publishers, and others keep it alive for their own purposes and according to their own codes—but *not* because they have a personal stake in Watergate itself.

To put this another way, Watergate is an uncommemorated event in our history. Contemporary societies often ritualize recognition of the past. Anniversaries—commemorations marked in time—and shrines—commemorations marked in space—invoke and evoke the past, stressing continuity with it.[22] Were my topic the American memory of Vietnam or World War II or the Civil War or George Washington, commemorative practices would be a central part of my discussion. Watergate was ignoble, and few want to celebrate it. There is no shrine for Watergate, even though Washington, D.C., tour guides will point out the Watergate condominium and office complex as the bus drives by. For a time the National Archives listening room for people who wanted to hear the Watergate tapes attracted tourists.[23] The Nixon Presidential Library in Yorba Linda, California, pays tribute to Richard Nixon and his achievements, not to Watergate, though it is inescapable there.

But, clearly, Watergate is not a tourist industry any more than it is a holiday or ritualized anniversary.[24] William Safire has noted that the infamous headquarters of the White House plumbers in room 16 of the Old Executive Office Building cannot be visited, because it has "disappeared." A General Services Administration spokesman said that the room disappeared in the 1970s, but Safire was unable to pinpoint whether this was a Ford administration or Carter administration move or why it was initiated. "Where," Safire archly inquired, "are the preservationists who usually rally to the salvation of historic bars and battlefields? Where is the old Watergate cottage industry now that one of its shrines is not merely imperiled, but metaphysically denied?"[25] But no one noticed or cared, which of course was Safire's point.

Watergate is better served by anniversaries than by shrines or tourist attractions. There is no celebration of 17 June, although on the break-in's tenth anniversary there were private celebrations in Washington.[26] There is no holiday for 9 August, the date of Nixon's resignation. There is rarely even media notice of 20 October, the date of the Saturday Night Massacre, although, on its tenth anniversary in 1983, 120 former staffers for the Watergate special prosecutor's office, including Archibald Cox, gathered at a Washington restaurant.[27] There is media coverage of Watergate on the anniversaries of 17 June 1972 and 9 August 1974, especially in anniversary years divisible by five or ten. Publicity-generating industries cultivate the memory of Watergate, as of so much else.

This is a defining feature of our time, the so-called "post-modern" era that feasts on imagery and luxuriates in spectacles, pseudo-events, and celebrities, emphasizing a form of consciousness shaped most of all by the visual stimulation of television and film. Watergate receives its post-modern, image-conscious, spectacle-fixated due, but not more than its due. The news industry keeps track of important political and cultural anniversaries, and Watergate is one to which it seems attached. On anniversaries of the break-in and of Richard Nixon's resignation, the newspapers, news magazines, and radio and television programs are full of reports, retrospectives, reflections, and updates on key Watergate figures.

People accept the anniversary as a cultural form that legitimately demands their attention to something other than the present. In the absence of any stronger commemorative form, the media-recognized anniversary keeps alive a memory of Watergate. But the media that make use of Watergate anniversaries do not promote a particular Watergate interpretation. A leading topic of these reconsiderations is simply an examination of the Watergate legacy and what people still remember of the event. The general media are not agents for any particular Watergate memory in the sense in which Jews sponsor memory of the Holocaust or Vietnam veterans memory of Vietnam. The media honor liberal and conservative versions of Watergate more than radical or ultraconservative versions. These versions are, after all, the ones that have been sponsored by the president (Ford), the Congress, and other centers of power and opinion leadership. But the media do not seem to have any axe to grind in this, not even the glorification of their role in Watergate, a subject that receives surprisingly modest attention in the press on these anniversaries.

This absence of formal commemorative practices makes memories of Watergate an unusual topic in the study of collective memory. Even the memory of the bombing of Hiroshima and Nagasaki has an agent in peace organizations that annually commemorate the bombings in the first week of August as a time for vigils, demonstrations, meditation, and a renewed commitment to a world without war. The memory of Abraham Lincoln has not only obvious national backing but a specific agent—the state of Illinois, promoting itself through pride in its native son. The state announces itself as the "Land of Lincoln" on automobile license plates and supports the Lincoln-connected historical monuments and tourist sites throughout the state. But the Watergate anniversaries, so marginally institutionalized, will grow more and more faint as the generations that knew Watergate age and die.

A sixth and final distinctive feature of Watergate memory, one deserving of somewhat fuller comment, is that Watergate is an *American* event. Americans are notoriously present-minded and are said to have no regard for the past. Ten years after the Watergate break-in, the *Los Angeles Times* pronounced that "even after the gravest Constitutional crisis since the Civil War, the American people have demonstrated their profound inclination to put bad times behind them, let memories fade and ultimately allow those guilty of wrongdoing to gain a measure of rehabilitation."[28] The reporter and his editors saw no need to document this "profound inclination" beyond the survey data the story provides. Nor did they ask if the data showed an admirable forgivingness rather than a deplorable forgetfulness. That Americans forget the past, and that to do so is bad, goes without saying. So there is an expectation of public alarm when a study reveals that American students study very little history in American high schools compared to Europeans, and that today they study even less (usually one year) than they did twenty-five years ago (usually two years).[29] It is easy then to make a remark like, "We are a people who drop the past, and then forget where it has been put."[30]

Alexis de Tocqueville's *Democracy in America* is the *locus classicus* for this view. In discussing the philosophical attitude of Americans, Tocqueville observed "the relaxation or the breaking of the links between generations. It is easy for a man to lose track of his ancestors' conceptions or not to bother about them."[31] Tocqueville believed this lack of historical consciousness in Americans was a natural outgrowth of the actual absence of a history. "The United States," as Daniel Bell has written, taking up the Tocquevillian theme, "began with no 'history,'— the first such experiment in political sociology—and for much of its existence as a society, its orientation was to the 'future,' to its Manifest Destiny and mission."[32]

The past, insofar as Americans regard it at all, is said to be remarkably unproblematic. The American past is unitary. We share, and share a high regard for, the Constitution and the Founding Fathers. Our tradition is one of what Richard Hofstadter called "comity," a shared sense of the basic humanity even of our opponents. For Hofstadter, the creation in the United States of a two-party system early in the nineteenth century was a unique achievement, because it created a *legitimate* opposition, a set of rivals to be respected in limited conflict rather than overcome in all-out political war.[33] People disagree over the implications of the past for us today, but this "never brings into question which history one should be faithful to," the historian Charles A. Miller has observed.[34] While this is less true today than when Miller wrote a generation ago, the American case can still be distinguished from that of France, where there are distinct royalist and revolutionary traditions; from that of England, where relatively separate Whig and Tory histories survive; and from that of Germany, where political disunity has until recently stymied the emergence of a unitary political tradition.

There is remarkable consensus, at least among academic and journalistic elites, that Americans do not respect or know much about the past, but I think the consensus is wrong.

I do not believe the failure of young Americans to identify key Watergate figures or of Americans young and old to be able to list Richard Nixon's abuses of power is evidence of a shallow sense of history. I do not believe that contemporary America is amnesiac. This is the conceit of the academy, of historians, of culture critics who take their views of what culture is and what history is from European high culture and from the classroom. If one accepts a more anthropological understanding of culture, Americans are awash in historical remembrance. I would point to four features of American life in particular. First, Americans are more concerned than most peoples about preserving the natural world. Today's environmentalist movement and yesterday's conservation movement can be understood as movements dedicated to memory of a peculiarly American sort. Americans carved a nation out of a wilderness; the myth of "man against nature" is readily recalled in a country where "the frontier" closed only a century ago and the imagery of a "new frontier" animated exploration of space just a generation ago. Our past is not cathedrals and forts and Roman walls; it is Yellowstone and Yosemite and the Everglades. In America "natural history" is national history. It is perhaps only now, in an intellectual climate alert to ecological concerns, that this feature of America may be appreciated. What seemed naive, even absurd, now may seem prescient.

Second, Americans are vigorous amateur historians even in the most conventional sense of the term. State and local historical societies, national organizations dedicated to collecting old campaign buttons or old baseball cards or antique furniture or the restoration of old homes or the building of new ones with the equipment of a century ago—these are everywhere. There is a vigorous memory industry, one might even say. People collect old jukeboxes, Elvis memorabilia, vintage comic books, political campaign items, old toys, or circus posters, and many others cater to these collectors' desires.[35] Nostalgia may be a yearning for a past we ourselves remember or for something we never, in fact, experienced. Either way institutions, voluntary organizations, businesses, and enterprising swindlers seem ready to respond to the yearning.[36]

This does not mean that Americans have a profound "sense of history." It may even characterize, or caricature, a peculiarly postmodernist historical sense, shallow, distanced from the self, the past treated at arm's length as an item for consumption. Perhaps. But it is no less a brand of historical knowledge than was the nineteenth-century elite's schooling in Greek and Roman history or the early twentieth-century schooled citizen's memorization of the presidents and state capitals. It is different from these other ways of knowing a past, but I do not see that it is self-evidently any worse. Moreover, this consumerist history is only a part of the contemporary American sense of the past.

A third feature of American memory is that Americans are busy unearthing not only their common history, of a city or region or nation, but their separate histories. There are individuals and institutions dedicated to ethnic histories of dozens of immigrant groups. As this has been increasingly recognized in the past generation, there has been a growing struggle over the common history. American collective memory is now a contested terrain. Debate over the teaching of American history is scarcely new, but it is unusually intense today.[37] Widespread recognition of the partiality of any historical view and of the partisanship of many contributes to the belief in many groups that they should seize the tools of historiography themselves, taking the past into their own hands. Subordinate groups—notably women and ethnic minorities—have become very sensitive to dangers posed when the writing of history is controlled by someone else. "We do not have to believe Santayana when he said that those who fail to remember the past are doomed to repeat it," historian Stephen Vaughn writes. "Still, those who do not remember are in jeopardy of suffering at the hands of those who say they do."[38]

A final feature of American memory is its peculiar focus on a document written two hundred years ago that established the outlines of our form of government. Certainly the battles over the importance in constitutional interpretation of getting at the "original intent" of the writers of our constitution which were recently renewed in Senate confirmation hearings on Supreme Court nominees and in the pronouncements of President Reagan's attorney general Edwin Meese, represent a concentration on the past almost pathologically intense. It is plausible to claim, with the legal historian Leonard Levy, that judicial attention to original intent is so much eyewash, a kind of irrational rhetorical cover for justices who simply adopt the conventionally accepted language of legitimation for the pursuit of policy.[39] But, even in Levy's terms, why this language of legitimation and not some other? Why should historicity be so compelling a rhetorical trump in American culture of all cultures?

The American sense of the past as I have sketched it may be inadequate. Nothing I have asserted here prevents me from also believing that Americans should have a better grasp of our own history and that there is a lot of educating to be done. But the educating can proceed without assuming that we are uniquely deficient in our attention to the past. A consciousness of the past, in anything like the sense in which it is understood today, is a product of the great revolutions of the eighteenth century and of the rapid transformations, since that time, wrought by industrialization and by the rapid transnational movements ever since of people and ideas through trade, travel, printing, and war. Still, the American consciousness of the past is—and must be—different from the Western European sense of history to which it is inevitably, and parochially, compared.

If lack of attention to the past is treated as a fault in the United States, too much attention to the past has been seen as a fault elsewhere. The British affection for their own remembered or invented past has come under critical scrutiny. Critics have attacked Britain's "heritage industry," appalled at the discovery that a new museum opens in Britain about once a week.[40] The historian Martin Wiener has criticized Britain's longing for an idyllic village past, arguing that Britain's industrial decline has been in part brought on by leaders imbued with a love of a (partly mythical) rural tradition.[41] Remembering the past is not automatically virtuous. It depends on how one remembers and to what end, and there may be virtues in not clinging too closely to a world gone by.

The memory of Watergate, twenty years after the original events, is richly and deeply with us. To look for it only in surveys or classroom quizzes takes on an impoverished notion of collective memory and of knowledge in general. Societies may vitally remember without the memory residing in each of its individual members. If the legal profession remembers well the Constitution and the constitutional abuses of Watergate, even if the rest of us are not prepared to recite the Constitution or the Bill of Rights, then the recollection of Watergate may well be substantial without being popularly shared. Moreover, a substantial memory need not be conscious. I believe this is the case with Watergate: memory seeps into the cultural pores even if not in a form readily retrievable by seventeen-year-olds answering a quiz. Schoolroom historical knowledge is not without value, but to assume that it constitutes all there is to historical knowledge short-circuits real analysis of the American sense of the past.

The task in examining how contemporary Americans view and use the past is to understand it, to characterize it, and not to presume in advance that it is uniquely faulty or uniquely noble. This is the task I hope to contribute to here.

"Collective memory," as the political theorist Sheldon Wolin puts it, "has to do with the formation, interpretation, and retention of a public past."[42] The social institutions and processes that do the forming, interpreting, and retaining will not be the same for all cases where the past is preserved. The chapters that follow represent as much an inventory of the institutions of collective memory in the Watergate case as an argument about how they have operated. With a different case, there would be a different inventory. To examine the transmission of memory of World War II, war films and veterans' groups would be of central importance. To look at the transmission of memory of the Bill of Rights, history textbooks, classes for new citizens, the everyday work of defense attorneys, and the education citizens receive whenever they are empaneled on a jury or present in a courtroom would require special attention.

I am not offering, then, a comprehensive list of the agents of social memory. The pattern of the persistence of memory of Watergate is unique, even though the carriers of this memory I examine certainly operate in other cases, too. With different cases of collective memory, there will be different agents and institutions involved, but always one can look for the transmission of memory through the cultural constitution of individual lives, of social institutions, and of public discourse. With Watergate, I examine the cultural constitution of lives through "career" and "reputation," the cultural establishment of institutions through "myth" and "reform," and the cultural construction of public discourse through "language," "expectation," "metaphor," and "celebrity."

There is an argument in the inventory itself: I want to insist that the past endures in the present not only in formal commemorative practices that historians in recent years have done so much to analyze but also in fundamental processes of social life that are not specifically or self-consciously dedicated to memory.[43] The inventory suggests, further, that collective memory does not operate only with a mass audience. The forms of social memory that are most influential in shaping public life and social action are not necessarily the most widely distributed. As I will argue in chapter 7, the Watergate remembered through schoolbooks and through continuing media attention to Watergate celebrities is bowdlerized and depoliticized. These Watergate renditions, well-institutionalized and widely available, drain the Watergate trauma of emotional intensity. The media and the textbooks keep Watergate alive in public consciousness but mask any good reason for doing so. In contrast, the Watergate whose memory is rehearsed in congressional debates and institutionalized in legislation on government ethics (see chapter 5) has had a decisive influence in setting the tone and agenda of national politics, just as the mythic Watergate celebrated inside journalism has colored journalistic practice (see chapter 6).

Some versions of the past persist more successfully than do others and different agencies of memory operate to different effect. In the case of Watergate, there is no great mystery about why liberal and conservative versions dominate the public memory rather than radical Left or ultraconservative interpretations: They have been officially sanctioned by the political establishment. They vie with each other for dominance when the executive branch or the Congress take up questions of governmental ethics or executive wrongdoing. Like the two-party system itself, the field of battle between liberal and conservative versions of Watergate is a terrain of genuine and significant controversy, but its dramatic engagements distract attention from and marginalize other conflicts. Still, less conventional versions of Watergate have had their influence. As we have seen already, the "year of intelligence" reconfigured the meaning of prior incidents and gave greater legitimacy to system theories of Watergate.

Without close, empirical examination, my general framework cannot say which versions of the past will survive best or why any survive well. But there is still a general lesson to be told, and it goes something like this:

Even in the world of television and home computers and cellular phones and twenty-four-hour news from around the globe, people acquire culture primarily from their family, their friends, and their neighbors, and they do so in the homes, schools, streets, and parks where they live their face-to-face lives. But part of the culture people typically acquire is a sense of national identity, a sense of themselves as tied to the national society as a whole. This national identity is present only in small ways in everyday life, as in the daily Pledge of Allegiance in schools. It is routinized in national holidays and quadrennial presidential elections. It is powerfully established through military service or through the experience of war for both soldiers and civilians. It is also instituted through people's shared attention to explosive and traumatic national events judged historically significant. Americans have collectively put everyday life aside to attend to the Army-McCarthy hearings, the television quiz-show scandals, the assassination of President John F. Kennedy, the Watergate committee hearings, the *Challenger* disaster, and other such events. These cultural flashpoints generate collective, widely shared experiences through which people establish, and come to care about a relation to public discourse and public action. That is my subject in the following chapters: the public discourse and public action emerging from Watergate that have kept that event alive in American culture—in weakly or strongly institutionalized ways, in emotionally intense or coolly distant fashion, out of self-serving calculation or out of unintentional circumstance, and sometimes with fateful consequences for public understanding of subsequent events.

PART II

WATERGATE IN AMERICAN MEMORY

CHAPTER 4

Memory Mobilized:
Making Careers Out of Watergate

C ELEBRITIES, AS WE WILL SEE LATER, ARE LIVING MONUMENTS TO WATERGATE, because the institutions of mass culture keep them and their Watergate connections in public view. Another set of people are more subtly and indirectly—and sometimes more consequentially—carriers of Watergate memory because the event propelled their careers or moved their careers in particular directions. This includes people whose careers were destroyed by Watergate and those whose reputations were made by it. It includes individuals for whom Watergate was a crisis of conscience redirecting their efforts and reshaping their sense of themselves, perhaps even precipitating a spiritual crisis and religious conversion, as in the case of Charles Colson. For a few people, Watergate became a career in itself. John Ehrlichman, through fiction, nonfiction, and public appearances, lived off it for years. John Dean, obsessed with Watergate, did the same for a decade. For many others, younger and far from the center of Watergate action, the event was a decisive moment in forming political consciousness.

Others made use of Watergate to establish their political identity and careers. In this chapter, I will examine two contrasting cases. For Democrats elected to Congress in 1974, the so-called "Watergate babies," Watergate was a fortuitous circumstance that helped establish their political careers without necessarily engaging them in its issues or enlisting them as agents of its memory. This is a case of the power of contingency in human affairs; an event moved historical forces in one direction rather than another and gave a set of politicians an opportunity they otherwise might never have had.

In contrast, there is the case of two influential political figures, Jimmy Carter and William Safire, who made use of Watergate in their careers; for one urgent moment in American politics that I will detail, their alternative uses of Watergate put them on a collision course with each other. This is an example of "continuity" where through individual careers the memory of Watergate is self-consciously maintained, serving a career by preserving a particular memory of the past. Though Carter and Safire self-consciously used the memory of Watergate for their own advantage, their use of the past cannot be understood in baldly Orwellian terms or in the simple language of "interest theory." They did not randomly choose Watergate as a theme to embroider. A platform of virtue was certainly appropriate to Carter's personality and Puritan style; and Safire, through his close association with Nixon, surely realized that he could not escape identification with Nixon—and confrontation with Watergate—even if he wanted to. In the eyes of many in his audience and among his colleagues, he would always be "William Safire, former Nixon speech writer," even after twenty years of trying to be "William Safire, *New York Times* columnist." Big Brother could erase the past at will; Jimmy Carter and William Safire used the past precisely because they could not erase it. It was the indelible context for their careers. The only question was: could they make it serve their own purposes?

WILLIAM SAFIRE AND
JIMMY CARTER

In 1959 William Safire, a former journalist, was working as a public relations agent for All-State Properties, a home-builder client that had set up a "typical American house" at an exhibition in Moscow. Vice President Richard Nixon was showing Nikita Khrushchev the exhibits; as they wandered the halls, Safire yelled out, "This way to the American house!" steering them to his exhibit. There, while Safire took what was soon to be a famous photograph, Nixon skillfully debated Khrushchev on the virtues of American consumerism.[1] In 1965 Safire went to work for Nixon and later served as one of his key speech writers in the White House.

Safire left the White House in March 1973 to take a job as a regular columnist with the *New York Times*. He has held that position ever since, in addition to writing fiction and other works. The decision at the *Times* to hire him was important for an institution judged a paragon of responsible liberalism. To place a conservative and Nixon insider in a prominent position on the recently created op-ed page was a kind of compensatory conservatism, an effort to bend over backward and show the *Times* to be fair-minded. This placed on Safire's shoulders a burden familiar to beneficiaries of affirmative action: to demonstrate that he had been selected for his merits as a writer and thinker, not just for his representativeness.

Safire's first column appeared 16 April 1973, not the most auspicious time, as he wryly acknowledged, for an ex-Nixon staffer to begin work as a columnist for the *New York Times*. He quickly wrote a column expressing pleasure that President Nixon had taken control of the Watergate affair and nipped a scandal in the bud. By the end of the year, in a column "On Being Wrong," he acknowledged that this was "not mistaken, not slightly off base, not relatively inaccurate—but grandly, gloriously, egregiously wrong." And he observed, too, that if April 1973 was perhaps "the wrong time to start writing a column" it was "the right time to leave the White House."[2] David Halberstam, a former *Times* reporter, wrote to the *Times* publisher after the first few months of Safire's columns that Safire was not a conservative but "a paid manipulator. He is not a man of ideas or politics but rather a man of tricks, which is the last thing *The Times* needed."[3] But publisher Arthur O. Sulzberger showed no inclination to dismiss his new man.

Safire did not hesitate to write about Watergate in his new position, sometimes raising the "everybody does it" defense. Why, he asked in August 1973, was there no investigation of vote fraud in the 1960 election? Or no outcry about John Kennedy's improper use of the Internal Revenue Service? Or the tapping of Martin Luther King's telephone during the Kennedy administration? Or the dirty tricks in Lyndon Johnson's 1964 campaign?[4] He acknowledged, upon Nixon's resignation, that Nixon was "not unfairly ejected."[5] But he kept on with his theme that Nixon was not alone in his disregard for the law. He attacked Judge Sirica for corrupting the criminal justice system in pursuit of Watergate defendants.[6] On the conviction of Haldeman, Ehrlichman, Mitchell, and Mardian, he urged "a searching look at who else was guilty, what set the pattern for the excesses being paid for today." He noted, among other matters, Johnson's surveillance of newsmen, FBI wiretapping of Martin Luther King, Jr., and CIA spying on the Goldwater campaign.[7]

A month later it was Franklin Roosevelt's surveillance and wiretapping of War Production Board chief Donald Nelson and FBI surveillance of the 1968 Nixon campaign that interested him. Why, he asked, was the Johnson matter not pursued when the Senate Watergate Committee had testimony on the matter? Because, he claimed, "The thrill is gone because Mr. Nixon is gone." As the precedents for Nixon's actions unfold, Safire told readers, "Nixon-haters will assure us that the 'cover-up' was far more serious than any of the abuses of power that so enraged the nation two years ago." True, agreed Safire, but then he wondered how to judge the cover-up of all these earlier abuses that investigators had been sitting on "until well after Mr. Nixon had been struck down."[8]

Safire was quick to draw lessons for Nixon's reputation from the investigations of the "year of intelligence." In December 1975 he took as epigraph for his column an excerpt from the second article of impeachment; he cited leftist intellectual Noam Chomsky, maverick journalist Nicholas von Hoffman, and his liberal *New York Times* colleague Tom Wicker—not his usual pantheon—in support of the proposition that "We are all now permitted to recognize as truth one central point that Richard Nixon's defenders have been making for two years: that the use of the F.B.I. for political purposes in the Nixon Administration was mild compared to the misuse of the agency in the Johnson and Kennedy years."[9] He returned to the Senate Watergate Committee's roads not taken, citing the committee's Republican counsel Fred Thompson to argue that the committee did not pursue the Kennedy and Johnson abuses of the FBI because Sen. Lowell Weicker opposed doing so, holding that it would look like an effort to justify the Nixon administration. Of course, for a committee whose charter was to investigate campaign abuses of the 1972 campaign, this would indeed have looked like, and would have been, just that: an attempt to shore up the Nixon administration.

Safire calls this "the greatest cover-up of all . . . the suppression of the truth about Democratic precedents to Watergate."[10] He did not distinguish between covering up done by a president in office through lying, counseling perjury, approving bribery, and otherwise obstructing justice and "covering up" done by a Senate committee operating legally and in keeping with the committee's charge. Safire's columns on Watergate are a leading instance of profane Watergate commentary, an insistently provocative, even outrageous, effort to defile received wisdom on the subject.

But Safire was rarely willing to own up to his own blasphemy. His is a curiously pious profanity. He pictures himself as eminently fair-minded, seeking not partisan redress but journalistic balance. Denying that to claim that "everybody does it" is an effort to justify Nixon's doing it, Safire nonetheless kept returning to that theme. In discussing the Church committee's findings, he concluded that they "demonstrate conclusively that the seeds of Watergate were planted and nourished in two Democratic administrations."[11] The column complains that John Mitchell's career was in ruin for doing much less to harm civil liberties than did his predecessor attorneys general in the Johnson administration. But, even if this were true, what lesson about politics does Safire ask us to draw from it? Should new legislation better guard the citizenry against their guardians? That is not Safire's subject; his aim is defilement, not analysis or reform; his rhetoric is pitched in a way to get even, not to get on. He is, for better and for worse, a partisan as he decries partisanship.

During his first few years at the *Times*, Safire has written, "nothing angered me more than the double standard of political morality applied to Richard M. Nixon by old admirers of John F. Kennedy."[12] He wrote a Watergate-inspired column on Kennedy's sins in February 1975 ("The Kennedy Transcripts"), detailing Kennedy abuses of power, Kennedy campaign hardball, and other questionable practices for which Kennedy, unlike Nixon, was never punished.[13] In June he thought it useful to re-count some items that Nixon "has not yet been accused of having done."[14] At the top of the list are things Safire says John Kennedy did do: ordering the murder of a foreign leader and wiretapping a civil rights leader. In December Safire called attention to the Church committee's evidence concerning President Kennedy's liaison with the girlfriend of mobster Sam Giancana and refers to the Church committee's efforts to keep this information from leaking to the press a "plumbers'" operation.[15]

But it was not only Kennedy versus Nixon for Safire; it was anyone-getting-an-easy-ride-in-the-press versus Nixon. In September 1974, it was Rockefeller. Safire urged "equal treatment under press" and argued that Nixon's effort to avoid his taxes was "stupid, selfish, arrogant, and technically illegal," and that Rockefeller's 1970 tax return was "stupid, arrogant, probably technically legal, and—for a billionaire in politics—reprehensible."[16] During the Democratic primaries in 1976, it was Carter. In "Richard Redux," he held that "those who still defiantly wear Richard Nixon tie-clasps . . . can find much to admire in the campaign techniques of Jimmy Carter."[17]

In the spring of 1977, Safire promoted Victor Lasky's book, *It Didn't Start with Watergate*, calling it the "first carefully researched blast of criticism at the fusion of hypocrisy and hysteria that gripped this nation in 1973 and 1974." Lasky, Safire wrote approvingly, believes that matters that might embarrass the Democrats are not pursued by the press because of "a partisan double standard, a visceral media hatred of a political man named Nixon, and the blood-lust of a running pack." Lasky, Safire held, "should convince all but diehards that the crimes, lies, and abuses of power of the period from 1961 to 1969 beat anything that happened before or since."[18]

Safire's most important Watergate revisionism was not to raise up ghosts of the past but to affix the Watergate label to contemporary affairs. He did this most conspicuously (even earning a Pulitzer Prize) and consequentially in the case of Bert Lance in the summer of 1977. Journalists, Safire notable among them, used the fresh memory of Watergate to stir questions concerning the dubious banking practices of a key Carter aide into a scandal raising serious doubts about the upright moral posture of President Carter himself. In the Lance affair, a president who rode into office assuring the public he was an honest politician or an honest anti-politician politician, found himself ambushed by his own pretensions. In the Lance affair, the Watergate-invested career of William Safire came face to face with the Watergate-propelled career of Jimmy Carter.

As early as 1972, Carter aide Hamilton Jordan wrote a memo that distrust of government was a strong sentiment in the country and that Richard Nixon would not satisfy the American people's "desire and thirst for strong moral leadership."[19] Gerald Ford's pardon of Richard Nixon in 1974 could only reinforce that conclusion, helping to make morality the central focus of the 1976 campaign, and so helping elect Jimmy Carter president. The pardon tainted Ford in a way that he could not wish nor wash away.[20]

Jimmy "I will never tell a lie to you" Carter took full advantage of the Watergate stain on the Ford record. In the primaries, Carter ran against Washington, making character the chief issue. He cornered the market on trust, as the reporter James Wooten put it. Once Carter had managed this rhetorical feat, Wooten wrote, the outcome of the election "was never really in doubt, so deep was the country's thirst for someone—anyone—it could trust."[21] A few days before his nomination, Carter said he would not use Watergate as an issue, but his whole stance of ethical purity made political sense only with a Watergate backdrop. Watergate became foreground when Peter Rodino, one of its heroes as chairman of the House Judiciary Committee, put Carter's name in nomination. At the Democratic convention, vice-presidential candidate Walter Mondale reminded his party, to an uproarious response, "We have just lived through the worst political scandal in our history and are now led by a President who pardoned the person who did it."[22] Mondale pursued the Watergate theme with special vigor in the final days before the election. He held that "the question is whether Mr. Ford and his running-mate truly saw and understood the Watergate crisis for what it was—the worst political scandal in American history—and whether they responded to it with the leadership which placed respect for the law above politics."[23]

In accepting his nomination, Carter alluded to both Watergate and

Ford's pardon of Nixon: "It is time for our governmental leaders to re-spect the law no less than the humblest citizen, so that we can end the double standard of justice in America. I see no reason why big-shot crooks should go free while the poor ones go to jail."[24] Carter chose to be "above" direct mention of Watergate, but no one had any difficulty filling in the blanks. Pledging not to discuss Watergate, Carter discussed it. In September, overreacting to revelations that the FBI carpentry shop had undertaken $335 worth of work on FBI director Clarence Kelley's apart-ment, Carter objected: "When people throughout the country, particu-larly young people, see Richard Nixon cheating, lying, and leaving the highest office in disgrace, when they see the previous Attorney General violating the law and admitting it, when you see the head of the FBI break a little law and stay there, it gives everybody the sense that crime must be okay. If the big shots in Washington can get away with it, well, so can I."[25]

The use Jimmy Carter made of Watergate in his presidential campaign is obvious. The use Watergate made of Jimmy Carter, however, was just as momentous. If Carter used popular concern with government ethics as a rhetorical device to shoehorn the presidency, he was also stuck to that rhetoric in ways that came back to haunt him. This began in the campaign itself. The press watched Carter more closely than Ford, taking his self-righteous claims to purity as a challenge. His mantle of purity distin-guished him from other candidates, as Jules Witcover observes, but this had a price: scrutiny from "a particularly tenacious press corps that had been lied to by experts for years and that tried its damnedest, day after day, not to get burned."[26]

"Our first movie in the White House," Carter confided to his diary two days after taking office, "was 'All the President's Men.' I felt strange occupying the same living quarters and position of responsibility as Rich-ard Nixon."[27] In office, Carter would soon realize, the memories of Water-gate would be with him still, whether he wanted them or not. The press remained on alert, and not only the press. Though he was a Democratic president coming in with a Democratic-controlled Congress and a presum-ably liberal establishment press, the new assertiveness of Congress, like the new aggressiveness of the media, would prove an obstacle to his administration.

The first serious confrontation between Carter and the press came with the Lance affair, beginning with media revelations in July 1977, and con-tinuing through Lance's resignation two months later. Thomas Bertram "Bert" Lance was a Georgia banker and confidant of Carter whom Carter appointed director of the Office of Management and Budget in December 1976. Early in January the Associated Press and the *New York Times* reported on what seemed to be unusually permissive overdraft policies at Lance's Calhoun Bank, but nothing came of this.[28] On 20 January 1977, the Senate Governmental Affairs Committee approved Lance's appointment on the assurance that Lance would not participate in bank legislation or policy-making on banking matters while he sought to sell his 21 percent stock holdings in the National Bank of Georgia. Lance pledged to sell his stock by 1978.

Although *Time* magazine reported on some suspicious Lance banking practices at the end of May and Sen. William Proxmire objected in June to Lance's involvement in a piece of bank-related legislation, in apparent violation of his pledge, there was no general controversy around Lance until 12 July when President Carter asked the Senate committee to waive the deadline on Lance's stock sale. The announcement that Lance would sell his stock had apparently depressed the stock's value and selling at current prices would have placed on Lance an "undue financial burden." On 15 July Lance met with the Senate committee. The committee intended to come to agreement with him by 22 July on a new plan for the sale of his stock, but news stories about the circumstances of Lance's personal indebtedness led the committee to delay its decision pending further inquiry.

There were two relevant news stories. In a column in the *New York Times* on 21 July, William Safire accused Lance of being a cause, not the victim, of the National Bank of Georgia's financial difficulties, and on 22 July the *Washington Post* raised new questions about Lance's banking behavior. Safire's column repeated the information *Time* had reported in May when it questioned Lance's banking practices and personal debts. Like *Time*, Safire reported that Lance received a $3.4 million personal loan from the First National Bank of Chicago. What Safire added to this was speculation and innuendo—that J. Robert Abboud of the First National Bank of Chicago sought through this loan to buy influence in the Carter administration, to "gain life-and-death financial control over the man closest to the President." No evidence ever appeared that J. Robert Abboud was seeking to curry political favor through his loan to Lance, plausible a supposition as this might be, but Safire, with the freedom of the columnist, could suggest what news stories could only leave to the reader to consider.

What the *Washington Post* added the next day was not that First National of Chicago went out of its way to please Lance but that Lance may have gone out of his way to satisfy Chicago. Lance's National Bank of Georgia had opened a non-interest-bearing "correspondent" account at First National of Chicago six days after Lance applied to First National for a personal loan. (A correspondent account is ordinarily established to serve a bank's customers conducting business in another city, but the National Bank of Georgia already had such a relationship with another Chicago bank.) This fact, not Safire's speculations, raised Senate concern about Lance's possible misapplication of bank funds in violation of banking laws.[29]

Despite Safire's allegations and the *Washington Post* story, the Senate committee found no serious problems with Lance and approved his proposal to put his stocks in a blind trust with the trustees instructed to sell the stock on a flexible schedule as market conditions warranted. Moreover, at the committee hearing on 25 July, Sen. Abraham Ribicoff told Lance, "you have been smeared from one end of the country to the other, in my opinion unjustly."

The smoke, however, prompted a continuing outcry about fire. On 27 July, a *New York Times* editorial criticized Ribicoff and the Senate committee, holding that press questions about the circumstances of a $3.4 million personal loan was not a "smear" but a journalistic "duty." On 31 July reporter Anthony Marro, who had been covering the story for weeks, wrote that "legitimate issues . . . were raised that are likely to linger," and he noted, with apparent disapproval, that the senators had questioned Lance "quite gently." In the meantime, John G. Heimann, Carter's newly appointed comptroller of the currency, began an inquiry. His report, issued on 18 August, raised questions about Lance's banking practices but concluded that prosecution of any individuals did not seem warranted by the evidence. At this point Carter introduced Lance at a news conference: "Bert Lance enjoys my complete confidence and support. I am proud to have him as part of my Administration." Carter turned to Lance, saying, "Bert, I'm proud of you."

Carter thought that was the end. Instead it became, unhappily for him, a defining moment in his presidency. Allegations continued to appear. Despite Lance's strong public appearance before the Senate Governmental Affairs Committee in mid-September, suspicions of his pre-administration conduct continued, and on 21 September he resigned. (Lance was later indicted and tried, but none of the allegations against him ever led to a conviction.) Lancegate, as Safire had dubbed it in a column on 11 August, was a devastating moment for the Carter administration. Its "immense" cost, as Clark Clifford remembers it, included the loss to Carter of his "most savvy political adviser."[30] It was first blood, the definitive end of the presidential honeymoon, and it embittered the administration in its relation to the press in ways that were never overcome. Hedrick Smith wrote in the *New York Times* that it "tarnished the post-Watergate good government image of the Carter Administration and robbed the President of some of the early magic of his moral authority with the public."[31] Smith suggested that, though Lance's business affairs were "no Watergate," the White House handling of the affair "exposed political frailties in the Carter camp that hark back to the Nixon era and before, and that have rubbed the lustre from the clean government image that Mr. Carter so carefully fashioned." Carter was "vulnerable to charges of cronyism, of hasty judgment and overlooking flaws in friends that he might not tolerate in others, of being defensive about his judgments, too quick to commit his prestige in the midst of a controversy and too reluctant to concede that he may have made a mistake."[32] Carter, in a time of "post-Watergate morality" that he himself helped install in Washington, was hoist by his own petard.

Joseph Kraft found that most of the charges against Lance "could be passed over if it were not for the relation of Lance to Carter and the case Carter has been making for the superhonesty of his administration."[33] Indeed, as Safire kept insisting, the issue was Carter, not Lance. On 25 August the *Washington Post* had reported that Carter knew about the overdraft problems before deciding to nominate Lance OMB director.[34] On 20 September the *New York Times* found that an FBI report on Lance was concealed from the Governmental Affairs Committee before it approved the Lance nomination. Safire, back from an August vacation, insistently tied Lance's woes to Carter personally: "The issue is the way the sanctimonious Mr. Carter and his men have covered up wrongdoings and conspired to deceive the public."[35]

When Lance resigned, most observers were content, praising Carter and Lance for the resignation. Not William Safire. He called for a special prosecutor and decried "the abuse of governmental power after the election of 1976 by the President elect and a clique of cronies."[36] He argued that Carter was implicated personally in a cover-up and obstruction of justice.[37] Throughout his writing, Safire made full use of Watergate words: "cover-up" (1, 11, and 16 August; 12, 13, 22, 26, and 30 September), "Lancegate" (11 August, 16 October), "smoking gun" (11 August), "stonewalling" (22 September), "presidential pardon" (15 September), "obstruction of justice" (22 September), and "special prosecutor" (11 August, 12 and 19 September).

The Lance affair lingered on in the careers of Jimmy Carter and William Safire. For Carter it was a devastating loss of Washington innocence. It stimulated the press and got the scandal juices flowing again. For Safire, Lancegate was vindication of his conviction that Nixon the Terrible was not really so different from Carter the Good. Even more, it was a personal vindication of his own skills and instincts as a journalist. Safire was already an influential journalist in Washington by the time Carter came to office. His columns accusing the Church committee of a pro-Democratic bias in investigating CIA abuses had a significant impact on the committee's activities, according to a committee staffer.[38] But the Lance affair gave him new national recognition. Publicist ever, he sang his own praises in a *New York Times Magazine* analysis of the Lance affair 16 October 1977. He employed the same rhetoric he did in his columns—first denying the comparison to Watergate and then insisting upon it. "Lancegate is no Watergate," he wrote, but then found the only notable distinction to be that Nixon's men had a lot longer to establish a pattern of conspiracy. The "quality" if not the quantity of the two affairs, he argued, is similar. Both show that "power tends to confuse, and that there is no tactical way to rectify a strategic error at the center of power."[39]

This is an astonishingly tendentious reading; it's at the same time a *very* generous interpretation of Watergate, in which government power was systematically used to deprive "enemies" of their civil rights in a wide range of cases (Safire himself was illegally wiretapped!), and a very abstract way to summarize the Lance affair—a case of small-time cronyism in which pressure was very likely applied, and shortcuts surely taken, to assist one friend.

Safire then held that his "hard-earned understanding" of how power works enabled him "to break the Lance story originally, to weather the self-righteous storm of indignation and to be sadly certain even now that the most important revelations lie ahead." Safire asserted that the Carter administration was "blindsided" by his 21 July column charging Lance with receiving a "sweetheart loan" of $3.4 million from the First National Bank of Chicago.[40]

While largely true, this misstates what happened in two ways, both of which enhance the importance of Safire's own role. Safire does not mention that *Time*, not Safire, broke the "sweetheart loan" part of the Lance story on 23 May. What Safire demonstrated on 21 July was not investigative skill but good timing, reviving the languishing *Time* story on the eve of Lance's appearance before the Senate committee. Safire reported that his column led an examiner from the comptroller of the currency's office to investigate the First Chicago loan. I do not know that he is wrong about this, but the new comptroller, John G. Heimann, who took office 12 July, ordered his inquiry into Lance's banking practices 14 July on the request of the Senate Government Operations Committee.[41]

Safire recalled his early commentary on the Lance affair as "not too well received," saying he was engaged in a lonely struggle. "I hung in there, annoying some people with a 'single-standard' argument."[42] On 1

August he listed questions the press seemed reluctant to ask the president and predicted that journalists would be asked where they were "during the cover-up of the first scandal of the Carter Administration." He recalled that his editor, Abe Rosenthal, asked him after a few weeks what specific law he thought Lance had broken. Safire told him: misapplication of bank funds. Rosenthal then "walked out into the city room of *The Times* in New York, called an investigative team together, and I no longer felt alone."[43] If that's what happened, Rosenthal must not have been reading his own paper where the question of misapplication of bank funds was explicitly discussed in news stories on 23 and 25 July. By mid-August the investigative team included Nicholas Horrock and Anthony Marro, both of whom had been reporting on the subject in prominently placed articles for a month; and, by late August, Wendell Rawls, Jr., and Judith Miller, both of whom also had been writing on Lance since mid-July.

Still, Safire may have had good cause to feel isolated, a lone Nixon sympathizer in a sea of Nixon-haters in the *New York Times* Washington bureau, accused by a prominent United States senator (Abraham Ribicoff, in a remark he would later regret and apologize for), of "smearing" Bert Lance. And the press was not at first eager to jump on the story. *Time* magazine, which broke the first story in May, seemed "uncomfortable in a vanguard role on a story so close to the White House," according to reporter Philip Taubman, who left *Time* in part over its handling of the Lance story.[44] The *Washington Post* began vigorously pursuing the story in July, but only late in August did Safire's companions on the *New York Times* op-ed page come to his aid.[45] Safire portrays his crusade for single-standard morality as a lonelier venture than the journalistic evidence suggests, but he *was* under attack.

I dwell on this because Lancegate was, for Carter, a turning point and, for Safire, a peak experience in his journalistic career. Propelled by the power of the Watergate analogy that he brought fully to bear, Safire helped turn Lancegate into a major embarrassment for the Carter administration. His role has been exaggerated, not least of all by Safire himself. He cheerfully acknowledges that he benefited from the Lance affair. "Whatever happens," he later wrote of Lance, "I hope he makes a comeback in politics—he's got a lot of gumption, and he's done a lot for me."[46] Safire was awarded a Pulitzer Prize for his Lancegate columns. When Safire crossed swords with Carter, he won. His career as a journalist reached a new height while Carter's presidency and moral stature plummeted.

Lancegate, the most successful of Safire's efforts to Watergatize Carter administration scandals, was by no means the last of his attempts to turn Watergate to rhetorical effect. He contributed to the journalistic overkill on Billy Carter's Libyan influence peddling. Led by the *Washington Star*, but quickly followed by the *Post* and other papers, this was a good case of a journalistic feeding frenzy, which is to news coverage what a police riot is to law enforcement.[47] In a column headed, "Waterquiddick," on the tenth anniversary of Chappaquiddick in 1979, Safire drew attention to the similarities between Chappaquiddick and Watergate. He conceded that Nixon's misdeeds were greater than Kennedy's: "Nobody drowned at Watergate, but nobody challenged the Fourth Amendment at Chappaquiddick." But again, this piety is a glove on the fist of profanity; the point of his column was to impress readers with the parallels, not the distinctions.[48] This evoked outrage from fellow *New York Times* columnist Anthony Lewis, who wrote three days later of a "calculated effort . . . to obscure the meaning of Watergate." The mechanism, he said, is to treat any suspect activity of politicians as "another Watergate." Lancegate, Koreagate, "peanutgate" (concerning charges of criminality in Carter's warehouse business) and now "Waterquiddick" all try to make Watergate "our common political denominator." This, Lewis argued, "is to trivialize a profound event."[49]

I think Lewis is quite right, but Safire was unimpressed; his use of Watergate as a reference point is some kind of itch he cannot stop scratching. On the tenth anniversary of the Watergate break-in, Safire continued his tortured condemnation/exoneration of Nixon. While nothing he knows absolves Nixon of "eavesdropping paranoia nor moral paralysis," he says he is more interested in criticizing the media's "orgy of nervous self-justification" on the anniversary than in criticizing Nixon. Acknowledging that Nixon obstructed justice, he nonetheless pairs this with "the determined effort on the part of prosecutors and investigating legislators to conceal any evidence of precedents in preceding administrations." For him this "selectivity of interest in wrongdoing" is something that "manipulates public outrage." He concludes: "McCarthyism was practiced in the name of anti-McCarthyism."[50]

Watergate is a theme in Safire's work to this day. In 1991 he commented on Clark Clifford's memoirs as further evidence that Lyndon Johnson planted the seeds of Watergate.[51] He used Watergate as a framework for examining the Charles Robb campaign's bugging of Virginia Gov. Douglas Wilder's car phone and other sleaze on both sides of the Wilder/Robb disputes.[52] When Procter & Gamble's chief executive was caught in the act of using his influence to subpoena records of 803,000 home and business phones to uncover who had leaked confidential information to business rivals, Safire urged him to "take it from an old Nixon hand" and learn that full disclosure now would save major embarrassment later on.

"Abuse of power and invasion of privacy are no mere errors of judgment, regrettably inappropriate—but are unethical, bad, improper, wrong."[53] He dubbed the to-do over House of Representative members' bouncing checks "Housegate."[54]

For William Safire, Watergate was a decisive moment in his career; as an influential journalist, he has helped keep Watergate a decisive reference point for American political culture in general.

"WATERGATE BABIES" AND POLITICAL OPPORTUNITY

On the heels of the Nixon pardon, the House of Representatives and a third of the Senate came up for reelection. It was to be a stunning electoral defeat for the Republicans. There was no question in popular accounts at the time that revulsion at Watergate swayed the election, bringing in the largest crop of new Democrats in a generation. In the House, there were seventy-five Democratic freshmen and a net gain for the Democrats of forty-three seats. The "Watergate babies," as the class of '74 became known almost at once, bore a major responsibility for bringing to fruition a series of far-reaching reforms in congressional procedure.[55]

Analysis by political scientists has since raised some questions about the role of Watergate in the election. Some scholars have found a "Watergate effect" on voters, but others have argued that there is little evidence of "retrospective voting" on the part of the electorate. But whether Watergate operated directly through voters' efforts to toss out Nixon supporters in Congress, or through the beliefs of strategic elites more willing than ever before to fund Democratic candidates, or through the disillusionment of Republican voters who simply chose to stay home on Election Day, as several of the politicians I interviewed suggest, it seems clear Watergate was a significant source of the Democratic surge of 1974.[56]

The newcomers to Congress who took office in 1975 were not only new but also different from typical congressmen before them. Younger than most new classes and much less experienced in electoral politics, they embodied a new political style, exemplifying, in Burdett Loomis's phrase, the "new American politician."[57] According to Loomis, the new American politician is individualist and entrepreneurial, rather than deferential and oriented to a seniority system; he or she is "issue-oriented, publicity-conscious" rather than partisan and organizational in style.

This new political style by no means originated with the class of '74. In fact, the new class reinforced established reformers in the Congress who finally, with its votes, made some of the important procedural changes they had sought to establish for years. The Congress the Watergate babies entered was already changing. Some powerful changes, growing directly out of Watergate, were already in place, particularly in the relations between executive and the increasingly assertive legislature. The War Powers Resolution of 1973 and the Budget and Impoundment Act of 1974 both asserted congressional authority in relation to the president. Still, the new Democrats were instrumental in moving reform in the Congress along quickly. They helped shift power from House committee chairmen to subcommittee chairmen. They helped empower the Democratic caucus with the adoption of a new procedure requiring the caucus to approve nominations for committee chairmen, which made the chairmen responsible to the congressional party. The caucus rejected incumbent chairmen W. R. Poage as chair of Agriculture, F. Edward Hébert as chair of Armed Services, and Wright Patman as chair of Banking and Currency in 1975, thereby dramatically announcing the new congressional regime. Committees were required to have standing subcommittees with fixed jurisdictions, and the power of chairmen within committees was in other ways limited, too.

For veteran congressional reformers, the new members of the class of '74 became "cannon fodder," as Sen. Tim Wirth recalls it. "They suddenly had the votes." Wirth raised a little money to get an office and hire staff for the class of '74, and that had, he recalls, "enormous symbolism." The whole class met and someone suggested that they interview committee chairs to learn more about the committee system. The committee chairs declined. Then, Wirth recalls, "we said we'd vote against any chair who didn't come talk to us." They came. "Change was in the air," he said. "Anything went."[58]

When Jimmy Carter came to the White House in 1977, the task of working with the Congress was significantly more difficult, and more complex, than it had been when he first gave thought to running.[59] The House had become "more like the Senate, and consequently less amenable to presidential persuasion." With weakened chairmen and weakened committees, the "influence structure" in the House was flattened.[60] Moreover, in the increasing dominant new-politician style, incumbents were more and more safe in their seats, more and more protected in their positions by the everyday services they provided their constituents—thus more and more independent of presidential campaigns and coattails.

So the Watergate babies had a substantial impact on the mode of operation of the U.S. Congress, moving it in a direction consistent with "post-Watergate morality." This does not mean that Watergate as such was for members of the class a central concern, but the class came into existence in part because of Watergate. In Colorado's second congressional district, Democrat Tim Wirth unseated longtime-incumbent Donald Brotzman. Brotzman recalls that Watergate was the key factor in the race: "I think I would have won without Watergate." University of Colorado students were mobilized by Watergate to oppose Republican candidates, and, Brotzman recalls, "a lot of Republicans didn't go to the polls," disillusioned either because they felt the system had failed Richard Nixon or Richard Nixon had failed the public.[61]

"I am the classic Watergate baby," says Wirth. However, it was not Watergate that brought him into politics but a year in Washington as a White House fellow and active involvement in Robert Kennedy's campaign for president in 1968. "I was never quite sure what Watergate was," he concedes, recalling it more as a culmination of the Vietnam War and the assassinations of John Kennedy, Martin Luther King, and Robert Kennedy than as an event with a distinct meaning in itself. In 1972 Democrat Patricia Schroeder was a surprise winner in the congressional district Wirth had hoped to capture, so he moved to another district, traditionally Republican Jefferson County. In a 1970 redistricting controlled by the Republican legislature, a heavily Hispanic section of west Denver was attached to this district. It seemed clear that the district was so thoroughly Republican that it could absorb the Democratic votes of west Denver and improve chances for Republican candidates in the city of Denver. Certainly it appeared that Donald Brotzman was safe in 1974. Wirth recalls that a Labor Day poll put Brotzman thirty points ahead.[62]

When Wirth sought the nomination, it was his for the asking—no one else wanted it. But Watergate made it a more attractive prize, though this was not immediately apparent. "Brotz never heard the footsteps, never heard a sound, didn't know what had happened, stayed in Washington." He returned to the district only in the last two weeks before the election. Wirth recalls a rally at Bear Creek High School in the most conservative part of the district. Wirth's campaign packed the gymnasium with three hundred young people in Wirth T-shirts who had been ringing doorbells for their candidate. Brotzman was stunned. Brotzman refused to debate Wirth, so Wirth appeared on television debating an empty chair, Wirth talking on so that "the poor guy had Watergate hanging all over him." Wirth's victory was by about seven thousand votes; west Denver was the difference.

Congressman Tom Downey tells a similar story. In 1972 his Suffolk County, Long Island, opponent, incumbent Republican James Grover, won in a traditionally Republican district with more than 66 percent of the vote. President Nixon received a larger plurality in Suffolk County than in Orange County, California. The second district, though very Republican, was newly carved in 1970 redistricting; for more than half of it, James Grover was a new representative. Still, Grover's 1972 victory had been so overwhelming that "he didn't take me very seriously." Downey, who at twenty-five became the youngest member of the class of '74, had twice won election to the county legislature. He had been motivated to enter electoral politics by the war in Vietnam and ran against the war as an issue in his 1971 race for county legislature.

Downey decided to take on Grover in 1973 as he waited unhappily in a long gasoline line, thinking, "I'm going to blame this on the incumbent." He entered the race with no understanding of the power of Watergate for voters, especially the sense of anger and betrayal among Republicans, "There was more champagne sold that August than New Year's Eve, the liquor store operators told me. So there was an enormous sense of betrayal and relief on Long Island. I mean they had voted for this guy in big numbers and now he left in disgrace, so they were very angry and disillusioned, as best as I can determine. I, of course, had no understanding of that at the time." Indeed, he did nothing to exploit Watergate as a campaign issue. When he announced for the House seat at the beginning of 1974, he did not urge impeachment, because polling did not show support for it. He just said that "the legal process should be brought to bear, which was the same thing, I just didn't want to say 'impeached.' " Later, in television debates, Downey sought to paint Grover with a Watergate brush, attacking him for not recognizing it as a serious scandal.

Downey won with 49 percent of the vote to Grover's 44 percent, 6 percent going to New York's Conservative party candidate. Ford's pardon of Nixon, he suspects, was crucial in his victory. "Republicans were so sick of what had happened. The Ford pardon caused them in droves to stay away from the election. That's how I read that. Republicans did not vote for me. They just didn't vote."[63]

Rep. Victor Veysey lost in the 35th California district to Democrat Jim Lloyd. Here reapportionment worked against the Republican, as it led Veysey to run against a popular local mayor in an area far from his political base. He lost by just over a thousand votes, so certainly Watergate was a factor in the race. Lloyd did not openly use Watergate as an issue. "He did not need to do so," Veysey recalls. "Our analysis of election returns revealed that over ten thousand registered Republicans in the District declined to vote, which was a devastating margin. We could not get them to the polls."[64]

Watergate was openly an issue in the hotly contested election in the 11th congressional district of Indiana. Andrew Jacobs was a four-term incumbent who had been challenged and defeated in 1972 by Republican William Hudnut. In 1974 Jacobs came right back and took the seat away from Hudnut. Hudnut recalls that he might have been able to beat anyone else, but that Jacobs "had too much recognition and was just too strong, and the undertow of resentment about Watergate was too strong in a close race." During the race Hudnut forthrightly declared his support of Ford's decision to pardon Nixon. Commenting that it would be scandalous to see the president of the United States in the docks, Jacobs returned that the real scandal was Watergate itself. "So I had to defend the Nixon Administration," Hudnut recalls, "and the election really turned on Watergate and not on any local or international issues."[65]

The scandal of Watergate brought a new generation to the Congress at a propitious time for institutional change and helped create new sets of congressional habits, institutions, folkways, and policies. The Watergate babies did not self-consciously keep it alive, however, as an issue or a metaphor, a tradition, a precedent, a memory. In this their relationship to Watergate is very different from that of Jimmy Carter or William Safire. There is no policy statement by the Watergate babies on Watergate, not even among the Democrats. What "Watergate" meant to the class as a whole was impressed upon them by speaker after speaker in a Democratic Study Group briefing a few weeks after their election. The DSG experts insisted that the newcomers were *accidentally* members of the Congress. More than half of the congressional class of 1964, swept in by the Johnson landslide, they pointed out, failed to win reelection. The class of 1974, beneficiaries of the Watergate windfall, could expect the same fate unless they quickly learned to exploit the advantages of incumbency in their districts.[66] (They did just that, a large majority of them winning reelection in 1976.) Watergate was the occasion for their advance to national political office. It was also, thanks to the DSG and the class of '74's self-consciousness as a group, a warning about what they would have to do to stay in office. It was not a mission to which they felt beholden or an event they have sought to commemorate. They are Watergate's children but not its custodians.

For Jimmy Carter and William Safire, in contrast, Watergate was more than an occasion or an opportunity; it was almost the necessary condition of their careers as politician and political journalist respectively. A career is a socially constructed *location* of an individual in a culture over time. Watergate influenced the careers of Carter and Safire; Carter and Safire sought in turn to shape their careers through Watergate. Their careers thus emerged as agents of collective memory, keeping Watergate in the public mind, keeping it alive as warning, as precedent, as metaphor, as irritation and incitement. Carter used Watergate as a platform for placing ethical behavior at the center of his political identity, thereby helping to establish the moral accountability of public officials as a central issue on the national political agenda. Safire, seeing Watergate more as a scandal than as a constitutional crisis, used the situation as license to do unto others as he believed they had done unto Nixon. Relying on the recency of Watergate, secure that any reference to it, subtle or direct, would resonate with the public, Carter and Safire mobilized the memory of Watergate for their own purposes and kept it a vital force in public life.

CHAPTER 5

Memory Contested:
Reform and the Lessons
of the Past

If men were angels, no government would be necessary. If angels were to govern men, neither external nor internal controls on government would be necessary. In framing a government which is to be administered by men over men, the great difficulty lies in this: you must first enable the government to control the governed, and in the next place oblige it to control itself.[1]

—James Madison, Federalist 51

Of the many consequences of Watergate, one of the worst will be the panaceas it puts into circulation. Generals fight the last war, reformers the last scandal. Reformers therefore run the risk of deforming the constitutional system forever in order to put to rights a contingency of fleeting moment.[2]

—Arthur M. Schlesinger, Jr., *The Imperial Presidency*

In liberal democracies, "reform" is one of the ways the present pays debts to the recent past. Reform is a key instance of collective memory in action.

In the case of Watergate, this is most vividly illustrated in the legislative efforts that became Title VI of the Ethics in Government Act of 1978, a provision for the appointment of a special prosecutor or independent counsel when officials high in a presidential administration are suspected of criminal behavior. This was probably the single most important legislative response to Watergate. But despite the political pressure on the Congress to "do something," despite the good will that went into this act, including strong support from the Carter administration, and despite the noble rhetoric about learning from the mistakes of the past, many people opposed the special prosecutor law at the outset and criticized it still a decade later. John Doar, House Judiciary Committee impeachment proceedings majority counsel, testified that legislative provision for a special prosecutor was unnecessary. Minority counsel Albert Jenner argued that such legislation "demeans the Congress of the United States and the Department of Justice."[3] Former attorney general and Watergate hero Elliot Richardson held that an act designed to enhance public trust in government had "contributed substantially to the enhancement of public cynicism in the United States."[4] Title VI, he believed, drew precisely the wrong lesson from Watergate.

In congressional efforts to prevent future Watergates, conflict over Watergate's meaning became heated. Its invocation was more than a rhetorical flourish; this was the very stuff that motivated debate and deliberation. It tested the conservative and liberal memories of Watergate, pitting The System Worked theory against The System Almost Didn't Work theory. Congress was the primary forum where the important differences between liberal and conservative interpretations of Watergate were played out—and where, by their absence, other interpretations were marginalized.

Title VI originated in the appointment of a Watergate special prosecutor and in the dismissal of Special Prosecutor Archibald Cox in the Saturday Night Massacre. Within a week of Cox's departure, bills were introduced in both House and Senate to provide for a judicially appointed special prosecutor. By the spring of 1974, Sen. Sam Ervin proposed legislation to create an "independent" Justice Department with an attorney general appointed by the president for a six-year term and not subject to removal by the president. Archibald Cox, among others, testified against this proposal. Sen. Alan Cranston proposed a commission to study the need for a permanent special prosecutor. Not long after, the Senate Watergate Committee issued its final report, including a recommendation for the establishment of a permanent Office of Public Attorney entrusting the courts, not the attorney general, with the power to appoint and dismiss.

In 1975 Sen. Abraham Ribicoff's Committee on Government Operations took up some of the Watergate committee's ideas and held hearings on a proposal to establish an independent public attorney to investigate the executive branch. The public attorney would be appointed for a five-year term by a panel of retired court of appeals judges selected for this purpose by the Chief Justice of the Supreme Court.[5]

The first witness before the committee, Sen. Walter Mondale, called Watergate "the worst and most dangerous political scandal in American history." Nevertheless, he said, "The memory of Watergate, I think, is beginning to fade. In a real sense, I suppose, that is good for the country because we can change our focus to other matters that need to be dealt with. But if we let the history of Watergate fade without taking those steps that need to be taken in the legal sense we may well find in later generations a threat which will succeed and destroy American democracy itself."[6] He urged legislative reform, in other words, to institutionalize collective memory. He saw law as a permanent repository of collective lessons that individual minds and memories could not reliably preserve.

Ervin committee majority counsel Sam Dash urged the Congress to "learn the lessons of Watergate." He believed that former special prosecutors Archibald Cox, Leon Jaworski, and Henry Ruth, all of whom were on record opposing a permanent office of special prosecutor, had not learned these lessons and would leave the country as vulnerable as it had been during the Nixon administration.[7]

But others did not see legislative reform as a way to prevent future Watergates. Michael M. Uhlmann, assistant attorney general in the Office of Legislative Affairs in the Justice Department, representing the Ford administration, opposed the bill as unconstitutional and unwise. Uhlmann asked the senators to consider whether the provision for a public attorney was not "an overreaction to the events of the recent past." He argued that Watergate was "if not unique" then at least an "exceedingly rare" sort of transgression. The Justice Department could handle ordinary executive branch wrongdoing perfectly well without an independent prosecutor.[8]

Some legislators shared with Uhlmann a concern about overresponding to Watergate. "In general, Mr. Chairman," Sen. Charles Percy said in his opening remarks as a member of the committee, "I want to prevent future Watergate abuses, as we all do, but I want to be sure that we do not just react to Watergate and create new institutions or procedures that might not serve us well in the long run."[9] But Sen. Lowell Weicker complained of the slowness of the Department of Justice in focusing on the issue of independent investigations of government crimes, more than three years after the Watergate break-in. He urged the Department of Justice to "be leading the charge, along with the Congress." Without executive and congressional leadership, he said, "the American people will forget. It is not a hard political issue any more. The issues will fade away in the distance. We can sit here, and we can remember what has happened, and we will make sure it will not happen again, but what about those children who are unborn, and fifty years from now, have had no relationship whatsoever with these events."[10] Lloyd Cutler, an insider Washington attorney later to be counsel to President Carter, agreed that the Nixon people were not unique: "What happened then will happen again; the memory of the last few years may very well prevent it from happening for a decade or so, but we all know it will happen again, just as it happened fifty years earlier in the Teapot Dome scandal.''[11]

In these remarks, reform is explicitly entertained as a functional alternative to memory: in the short run, personal memory could prevent Watergatelike abuses; but in the long run, there would be no personal memory and the deterrent of law would have to substitute for the protective coating of memory.

Sen. Howard Baker, in his testimony, argued against an independent prosecutor. In retrospect, he said, the system worked rather well in Watergate, and now he feared "there is a danger, that in trying to rectify the problems of Watergate, we may diminish the legitimate authority of the Presidency."[12] He felt that "we can overlegislate as well as underlegislate." He argued that Watergate, though a culmination of practices that grew up over many years, was a unique event, that the hearings provided a cathartic influence on the political system, and that the Watergate experience showed that our governmental system worked. For Baker, the fact that the country dealt directly and effectively with Watergate was more remarkable than that the abuses occurred. "I do not know of another nation on Earth that could have faced the challenge, the embarrassment, and the disarray of Watergate and have emerged on the other side essentially intact, and I believe stronger than we were before."[13]

Sen. John Glenn took issue with this, arguing that the "system of checks and balances" did not save us. It "did not work initially in Watergate. It did not protect us against those abuses. That is fundamental." Only the work of the press, in Glenn's interpretation, brought the abuses to light. What the Congress should be doing, he argued, was to create a system "where we do not depend on the press." Baker, in contrast, called the press a "quasi-official part" of government, saying he was pleased to leave to it the task of bringing to light allegations of misconduct of public officials.[14]

Baker's general position was supported in what may seem unlikely quarters. Former Watergate Special Prosecutor Leon Jaworski testified that "I have the feeling that Watergate has been a lesson that this Nation has learned. It has been a tragic lesson, of course. But I believe it will have a long-lasting effect."[15] Former Watergate Special Prosecutor Henry Ruth, Jaworski's deputy and later his successor in mopping up the Watergate-related inquiries and prosecutions, likewise argued that Watergate was "a unique combination of abuses of power, and future possible abuses will not require the permanent existence of a special prosecution force as a deterrent."[16]

No legislation came out of these hearings immediately, but they laid the groundwork for the Ethics in Government Act. Jimmy Carter came into office on a platform of post-Watergate reform, championing the idea of an independent attorney general along the lines of the Ervin bill. Once in office, Carter asked Attorney General Griffin Bell to provide an opinion on the constitutionality of the proposal. Bell came down against it. "There is a legal maxim," he wrote, "that hard cases make bad law. We believe that implementing the special proposal mentioned above would be permitting a hard case, Watergate and its aftermath, to produce bad law."[17] With that, the Ervin idea died. But with the support of President Carter, the Ethics in Government Act of 1978 passed, including Title VI, a provision for a judicially appointed special prosecutor, despite the strenuous opposition, behind the scenes, of Carter's own attorney general.[18]

There have been several troubles with the special-prosecutor provision in action. First, and constitutionally foremost, the question has been raised whether a prosecutor appointed by a panel of judges, upon the request of the attorney general, and answerable to the judiciary rather than to the Department of Justice or some other agency of the executive branch, violates accepted understandings of the separation of powers. Is not prosecution an executive rather than a judicial branch function? Second, is the procedure for appointing a special prosecutor or independent counsel too easily triggered so that frivolous cases are pursued, wasting taxpayer dollars on pointless investigation and damaging reputations where there is little or no significant evidence for proceeding? Third, are the officers who may be investigated by an independent counsel inclusive of all those who should reasonably be included—and at the same time not overinclusive? A fourth question concerns not just the independent-counsel legislation but the whole pattern of governing-by-prosecuting: does the special-prosecutor law turn into criminal litigation matters that are more appropriately handled by a political process of political pressure, public exposure, or even impeachment? Fifth, does the special-prosecutor law and other post-Watergate legislation create a puritanical rule that discourages good people from seeking public office?

All of these questions participate in a kind of "metalegislative" discussion that perennially plagues reform and reformers: Did we overlearn from the past? Was the lesson of Watergate that the system works, as the conservative version maintains? Or that it did not work, or only worked by dint of accident and luck, as the liberal version insists, and required reform? Even if Watergate implied some sort of legislative remedy, could such legislation distance itself enough from the Watergate case to ensure the legal system's presumption of innocence in people investigated under its provisions?

The Ethics in Government Act, incorporating a five-year sunset clause, came up for reconsideration. The Senate Governmental Affairs Committee held hearings in 1981, and there seemed a measure of agreement that Title VI had flaws that derived from remembering Watergate all too well. Sen. Warren Rudman asked Rudolph Giuliani, associate attorney general in the Reagan administration, "Do you think possibly that one of the problems with this whole statute, if indeed there is a problem, goes to the fact that we have gone from what was designed in a particular case, the whole Watergate incident, and drawn a statute, with that background, to apply to an entirely different class of people? Do you think that is one of the problems with this statute?" Mr. Giuliani agreed that it was. "We used as an example, an historic event that was somewhat aberrational, and that focused on the President of the United States and the people very closest to him. And we have created a statute that has a much broader range than that. And to that extent, it creates—we have overincluded, to a very large extent." Giuliani agreed with Rudman's view that this was an instance of "the old cliché that hard cases make bad law."[19]

At that point, Title VI had been invoked only twice. One case concerned a charge of cocaine use against President Carter's chief of staff, Hamilton Jordan. Attorney General Benjamin Civiletti, although holding that "the matter is so unsubstantiated that prosecution is not warranted," felt nonetheless that the letter of Title VI obliged him to appoint a special prosecutor to investigate. This led the *Washington Star* to refer to the law as "asinine" and to cite the Ethics in Government Act as "a not very discriminating congressional response to the Watergate scandal." A law meant "to slay dragons of official corruption" was instead using "this heaviest of hammers on every gnat of petty rumor."[20]

The second case seemed just as frivolous: a special prosecutor was appointed to investigate alleged cocaine use, several years before, by Carter aide Tim Kraft. The *Washington Post* held that this showed Title VI to have "a trigger so sensitive that a senior official's slightest misstep is likely to bring him face-to-face with the full array of government power." The *Post* called for a change in the law: "Special prosecutors ought to be saved for special cases."[21]

But the law had its defenders. In the four years of the law's operation, Lloyd Cutler testified in 1982, though no special prosecutor had yet filed an indictment, the statute significantly alleviated public concern about government corruption. For Cutler, the events of Watergate "are a tribute to how well our system works," but, he added, repeating the liberal refrain, "it was a very near thing."[22]

The Ethics in Government Act was amended and signed into law by

Ronald Reagan in 1983 for a second five-year run despite Reagan administration urgings that it be repealed. The amendments changed the standard for the attorney general's removing a special prosecutor from "extraordinary impropriety" to "good cause." They also gave the attorney general more discretion in invoking the law, alleviating concern about the law's hair-trigger mechanism. The language of the law changed, too, the "special prosecutor" becoming the "independent counsel," to reduce the perceived presumption of guilt in any investigation under the provisions of Title VI.

The independent counsel, née special prosecutor, law came up for reconsideration again in 1987. The Justice Department now made a stronger case against the law than it had in 1981 and 1982. Michigan senator Carl Levin, chairing the hearings, characterized the Justice Department position as leaving the independent counsel's jurisdiction and hiring and firing entirely up to the attorney general. Lecturing his committee's witness, John R. Bolton, assistant attorney general for legislative affairs, Senator Levin said the Department of Justice's position amounts to the attorney general wanting "to return us to where we were in 1973." He said:

> That is what this is all about. This is not some dry academic legal exercise that we are going through this morning about some dry statute. What we are talking about is the confidence that people have in their government to do justice to high officials who are suspected or accused or where there is evidence of criminal wrongdoing. . . . Now what you want to do is say let's just forget what has happened in the 1970's with that Saturday Night Massacre. Just forget all that. Give us back the appointment power. Give us back the removal power. Give us back the power to set the jurisdiction for the independent counsel. I think you are going to find the Congress resisting that advice.[23]

The independent counsel provision, renewed again, got a Supreme Court hearing on its constitutionality in 1988. In oral argument, the justices were reminded of the connections of the case to its Watergate origins, so much so that Solicitor General Charles Fried, arguing against the constitutionality of the law, felt called on to specifically reinterpret what "Watergate" meant. That episode, he argued, does not teach the necessity of a special prosecutor provision but "teaches the exact opposite lesson." The dismissal of Archibald Cox, he argues, "was regrettable, but it was not a constitutional catastrophe." The prosecutions "proceeded to their denouement without missing a beat." They did so "not because of jury-rigged [sic] constitutional innovations such as we have here, but because of public pressure and the long, deep shadow of Congress's power of impeachment." That, Fried held, is the constitutional system, and it worked. He continued:

> To be sure, it did not work without struggle and strain, but it is a central fallacy of this statute to think that a supremely political object—and I use the word politics in its high sense, of those occasions which concentrate the moral and practical sense of the people—can be accomplished without politics; that, in some sense, it can be turned over to serene persons operating outside of the political process, platonic guardians of sort.[24]

But the Court upheld the constitutionality of the statute by a vote of seven to one. In an opinion written by Chief Justice William Rehnquist, the Court held that the statute did not violate the "appointments clause" of the Constitution and that a committee of the judiciary could constitutionally appoint a prosecutor. The Congress may vest the appointment of "inferior officers," according to the Constitution, "in the President alone, in the Courts of Law, or in the Heads of Departments." Was an independent counsel an inferior officer if in fact so independent of the executive? Yes, the Court argued, observing that the attorney general was empowered to remove the independent counsel and that the independent counsel's role is limited to certain temporary and specific duties.[25]

The controversiality of the independent-counsel provision did not end with a Supreme Court opinion. The Reagan administration continued to oppose the act; that it is constitutional, Attorney General William French Smith observed, does not make it desirable.[26] The law has come up for discussion and criticism repeatedly in the law reviews.[27] Terry Eastland, an official in the Reagan administration Department of Justice, devoted a cogently argued book to the topic, essentially a brief for the law's repeal.[28] Suzanne Garment attacked the law at length in her recent study of post-Watergate Washington politics.[29]

Eastland and Garment have been particularly scathing in denouncing the special-prosecutor statute. For Eastland, it "has had perverse and unintended consequences, not least of which is to wire the Washington political culture in such a way as to make it think another Watergate is around the corner whenever there is some allegation of malfeasance involving the executive branch." Of course, no one thought Hamilton Jordan or Tim Kraft would turn out to be Watergate; few people even know of the Theodore Olson investigation, taken by some observers to be the most egregious misuse of the independent-counsel provision. But Eastland insists that the statute "has helped elevate the pursuit of government malfeasance to such a high priority in Washington that elites in the city seem to believe, perhaps unconsciously, that the whole point of our political system is to root out official wrongdoing."[30]

Garment's rhetoric is not so wild but just as bitter. She sees the independent-counsel provision as part of Washington's "ethics police," an element in a "self-reinforcing scandal machine." For her, post-Watergate ethics laws were passed "to empower Democrats in Congress and put Republican presidents on a short political leash," neglecting to note that much post-Watergate legislation passed under President Carter at a time when few people were talking, as they do now, of a permanent state of "divided government."[31] Congressional Democrats in 1978, benighted fools though they may have been, expected to work with Democratic presidents in their lifetimes. For Garment, the special-prosecutor law, though by statute it empowers a three-judge panel and a prosecutor, actually empowers Congress, giving it "increased power—of a sometimes frightening sort." The law creates fear among senior government officials, which, she holds, "is a major means through which scandal politics and its demands come to pervade the operations of government."[32]

Eastland and Garment, I think, speak not so much analytically about a process but more personally, and painfully, from positions close to potential or actual objects of prosecutorial discretion. Eastland served in the Department of Justice from 1983 to 1988; Garment is married to Leonard Garment, the prominent Washington attorney who has represented several people investigated under the provisions of the special-prosecutor statute. This is not to deny that some of their specific charges hit home but to suggest that they may exaggerate altogether the importance of their topic.

Supporters of the law also exaggerate its importance. The special-prosecutor act has been repeatedly advocated and defended as promoting the appearance of fairness to the American public and thereby restoring faith in government that Watergate so deeply undercut. But, as the political scientist Katy Harriger observes, there is no evidence that the general public places any emphasis on, or for the most part even knows about, the independent counsel.[33] The intensity of sentiment both for and against the statute seems to be a Washington phenomenon. Much more than a local ordinance, the independent-counsel provision is still much less than the linchpin of a new political culture.

When Attorney General Edward Levi testified in 1976 on the special-prosecutor legislation, he expressed some disorientation, sensing a cultural divide between "those who had lived through the Watergate experience in this city, and those who like myself had come lately.'' Still, he thought, the whole country experienced Watergate, not just Washingtonians, and "whatever the perspective we have we all agree we must learn from the past but not cherish—or at least overly cherish—the scars.''[34] The debates since that time indicate that there are scars aplenty and that conservatives now display their post-Watergate wounds with some of the indignation and overheated rhetoric that liberals once demonstrated regarding Watergate's blows to civil liberties and a government of laws. There is a disproportion, however, in victimage and in damage. The Nixon administration, operating covertly and outside the law, violated the rights of private citizens, while post-Watergate reforms, to the extent that they have misfired, have victimized relatively high ranking government officials through procedures legally constituted and publicly accountable. Only if Garment is right that post-Watergate reforms have helped create a "scandal machine'' that does fundamental damage to our whole political system is there warrant for her rhetoric.

Even if we now have a "culture of mistrust'' in American politics that did not exist before (and I am not convinced of this, despite the tendencies toward mistrust that Garment identifies), Garment's emphasis on the folly of overzealous reformers is not the only explanation that deserves consideration. Perhaps the Reagan administration was truly more "sleazy'' than ordinary administrations; many Reagan Republicans, after all, were not public-service tradition, old-school Republicans but cowboy entrepreneurs. Or perhaps the high-flying "go-go'' economy of the 1980s corrupted public servants left and right who might have stayed on a straight and narrow path under more ordinary circumstances. Or perhaps there is just a necessary period of awkward testing and adjustment with a new regime of ethical expectations, that people in both the executive and the Congress genuinely do not know where the boundary lines lie between acceptable and indictable behavior. Or, more fundamentally, as Benjamin Ginsberg and Martin Shefter argue, perhaps scandal politics emerges when parties decline; when the electorate is demobilized; when the media grow more powerful; and when Democratic control of the Congress and Republican control of the presidency make institutional conflict a more comfortable form of combat for politicians than electoral mobilization.[35]

More moderate critics, like political scientist Harriger, nonetheless see much to revise in the independent-counsel statute. Few cases, she suggests, truly require independent investigation, and in most of these an independent counsel would be appointed even without the statute. The statute aggravates distrust of the Justice Department. She urges a specification of categories of cases where a special prosecutor should be used, greater discretion for the attorney general in declining to appoint a special prosecutor, and continued diligence in oversight and reauthorization.[36] Whatever position one takes on Title VI, it is clearly hard to come to a judgment on the law's merits unclouded by a particular vision of Watergate.

Hard cases may indeed make bad law, as the lawyers say, but it is equally true that without hard cases, a complex, pluralistic democracy may get no laws at all. It often takes exceptional circumstances to motivate Congress into actions when, with inaction, nobody in the Congress loses. Making laws often requires making a coalition, and making a coalition of people who have other things on their minds is difficult without being able to focus significant public attention beyond the Congress on the issue at hand. When public attention is so mobilized, there is a rich opportunity for legislative action. That does not mean it is easy to take advantage of the opportunity. It does not mean that the legislation that follows will be wise. It means that laws, however generally they may be written—and however clearly they are intended to govern actions that have not yet happened and behaviors that perhaps have not even been conceived—hold a particular history within them.

The Ethics in Government Act is not by any means the only Watergate-inspired legislation. There were a number of acts passed in the white heat of Watergate in 1973 and 1974, others directly derived from Watergate in the years thereafter, and still others not directly related but passed in the ensuing spirit of reform. Both before and after Watergate, the 1970s saw new laws enacted to increase congressional oversight of or participation in executive policy-making. Watergate, and more generally the arrogation of executive power that grew in the Vietnam years and came to a head in Watergate, was the context for this legislation.[37] This included legislation that limited or specified executive power in foreign policy, most famously the War Powers Resolution, passed over President Nixon's veto in the wake of the Saturday Night Massacre.[38] The Hughes-Ryan Amendment (to the Foreign Assistance Act), signed into law 30 December 1974, required the president to "find" necessary any non-intelligence-gathering activities of the CIA and report that activity to the relevant congressional committees. Superseded by the Intelligence Oversight Act of 1980, this legislation required that findings be reported in a "timely" manner; this provided a key statutory basis for concern about illegal activity in Iran-contra.[39]

Watergate stimulated legislation concerning privacy. Concern about privacy had been growing in the 1960s and early 1970s. Popular books worried about invasions of privacy in the early sixties, and from 1965 on privacy became a recurrent topic in congressional hearings. In February 1974 President Nixon himself gave an address on "The American Right to Privacy" and established a Domestic Council Committee on the Right of Privacy. At the same time, Congress moved toward what would become the Privacy Act of 1974. Senator Ervin introduced a privacy bill in May 1974 and accepted a compromise between his stronger measure and weaker legislation favored by the Ford administration. The compromise passed in part because of "the desire to pass some privacy legislation in the wake of the Watergate affair" and "the desire to honor Senator Ervin in his last term."[40] "The climate of the times" lubricated passage and the Privacy Act of 1974 became law.[41] It requires federal agencies (exempting the CIA and most law-enforcement institutions) to limit personal data they collect, to then limit disclosure of that data, and to annually report on the character of their personal-data record systems. The Tax Reform Act of 1976 restricted governmental use of tax information for other than tax collection purposes. This grew out of the Watergate revelations that the Nixon administration had used the Internal Revenue Service to harass political enemies. The Foreign Intelligence Surveillance Act (1978) legalized the use of electronic surveillance in the United States where foreign espionage was suspected, but required the government to seek a warrant for surveillance before a special panel of judges.

Campaign finance reform also came out of Watergate. The Federal Elections Campaign Amendments of 1974 amended the Federal Election Campaign Act of 1971, an act whose provisions for public disclosure of campaign contributions made the investigation of Watergate and the tracing of campaign contributions to the burglars possible. The 1974 amendments passed a Congress influenced by Watergate. The House Administration Committee, chaired by Wayne Hays, was not favorably inclined toward the bill but went along "because a majority of the House members felt strongly about the matter during the Watergate years."[42] Floor debate in both houses was full of references to Watergate.[43] The wisdom of this response to Watergate has been contested. Congressman Bill Frenzel said at the time, "We couldn't go back to the American people and tell them that we had no answer to the abuses that they had seen. This is our answer, and we have to make it work." Like President Ford, the Congress felt pressure to show results and show them quickly, to prove responsiveness to Watergate, even at the expense of sound policy.[44]

Other ethics and conflict-of-interest legislation, too, grew out of Watergate. In 1977 the Foreign Corrupt Practices Act responded to the Watergate special prosecutor's discovery of corporate slush funds maintained to buy political influence abroad. Watergate influenced the revision and renewal of the Freedom of Information Act. Originally passed in 1966, it was significantly strengthened by amendments passed in 1974. When President Ford vetoed the amendments (Congress overrode the veto), Rep. Bill Alexander referred to Watergate, asking, "Hasn't the White House learned that Government secrecy is the real enemy of democracy?" Sen. Howard Baker said that both the Vietnam War and Watergate "might not have occurred" if the executive branch had not been able to act in secrecy.[45]

Much of this legislation, on privacy and campaign financing and other matters, carries Watergate into the present more contingently than continuously, although a sharp line cannot be drawn. Because all of the legislation I have mentioned grew out of Watergate, these laws may be an unspoken commemoration of the past, their roots in Watergate always capable of being exposed. My claim for the special prosecutor law, however, is much stronger: Title VI and the persistent debate over it exemplifies the process of continuity; Title VI advertises Watergate and implicitly renews discussion of Watergate's meaning every time it is invoked. The visibility in Title VI of its historical origins will be reduced over time but, for now, the law serves as a living reminder of events of two decades past.

The reformist impulse lies close to the heart of the liberal view of Watergate. Archibald Cox declared, in the wake of his dismissal as special prosecutor, that now we would see "whether ours shall continue to be a government of laws and not of men." The "right answer," of course, is "government of laws," and that no one, not even the president, is above the law. The "right answer" renews the deep American distrust of power and distrust of anyone holding power. The rhetorical thrust of Cox's remarks, and of others that have echoed it, is that the freedom of the president should be constrained by law.

The phrase reverberated through the Title VI hearings. Sen. Jacob Javits in 1975: "The extraordinary eruption of Watergate and impeachment has shaken and at the same time vindicated our system as a government of laws—and not of men."[46] Walter Mondale, attacking the Ford administration during the 1976 presidential campaign for opposing Watergate reforms: "If you want to restore trust in government, it must be achieved not just by electing nice people, but by establishing rules and laws and institutions that make it clear that if ever again a person in high office abuses his trust by violating the law, he will certainly have to respond and be accountable to the Constitution and to the laws of the United States."[47] Senate Watergate counsel Sam Dash, testifying in favor of the special-prosecutor law: "We must always remember that ours is a government of law, not of men, and that our laws are fashioned to cover all times, not for any particular times or any particular men."[48]

This liberal invocation of the "laws or men" phrase to command attention for reform legislation is not the only view of the matter; indeed, it may not be the most prominent view. A conservative position has also been well represented. Michael Uhlmann, testifying in the special-prosecutor hearings, shifted the rhetorical weight of the famous phrase from "laws" to "men." He urged the Senate to consider the limits to legislation. He said that passing a law is "a characteristic American solution" to problems and may well be necessary. "But, at the same time, I think we tend to underestimate how much of the law reform, or political reform is a consequence of good men, and I think that we must examine a change in public attitude, perhaps even a shift in measurable public optimism in respect to the law enforcement processes of the Federal Government, by considering the character of the people who are now in charge of it." He held—obviously acting as a one-man cheering section for both President Ford and Attorney General Edward Levi, "I think we sometimes tend to lose sight of what the character and integrity of the particular person holding office can do to restore public confidence."[49] And Elliot Richardson, also arguing against a special-prosecutor law, echoed these sentiments in 1977: "The outcome of Watergate, we keep hearing, proved that our system works, that our government is still one of laws and not of men. That's so. But it was never intended to mean good laws without good men, who will always be needed."[50] Here again the rhetorical emphasis shifts weight, to men, not laws.[51]

Richard Ben-Veniste and George Frampton, both assistant special prosecutors under Archibald Cox and then under Leon Jaworski, accept this position and argue that the lesson of Watergate is not that the system works but that "the system doesn't work by itself." Cox, they argue, is a case in point to prove "that whether we care to admit it or not ours must be a government of laws *and* men." Prosecution, they observe, is not an automatic process but requires a great many judgments along the way by prosecutors. "The abilities, personalities and biases of the prosecutors play an important and sometimes determinative role in the outcome." If Cox had been a different sort of man, if Leon Jaworski had been a different sort of man, they conclude, President Nixon might have served out his term. They give equal credit to Woodward and Bernstein and their editors; to John Doar and Peter Rodino; and to John Sirica. "Without all of these men," they conclude their book, "we might not have had a 'government of laws.' "[52]

The phrase about "laws, not men," like reform itself as an institutionalization of memory, keeps discussion centered on the civic meaning of the abuses that led to Watergate rather than on the cultural creation of the Watergate phenomenon as a scandal. It reaffirms the pious interpretations and gives no quarter for the profane. There is an opening for profane interpretations only if one stands back from the pros and cons of legislation contemplated or enacted to look at the ways that publicly considering or enacting legislation serves the public relations needs of legislators. In the meanwhile, the contest between reverent liberal and conservative readings of Watergate persists and establishes in the Congress not agreement but, through the deliberative process itself, the legitimate plane of conflict. Radicals of left or right may make arguments of great intellectual cogency, illuminating one or another aspect of Watergate in ways that raise profound questions. But these arguments and questions remain on the sidelines of political debate when the headlines of civic discourse are made in the Capitol and when the laws that emerge from this discourse set a new stage for action, a new set of contingencies to which future political activity is hostage.

CHAPTER 6

Memory Mythologized:
Watergate and the Media

There is filth on the floor, and it must be scraped up with the muckrake; and there are times and places where this service is the most needed of all services that can be performed. But the man who never does anything else, who never thinks or speaks or writes save of his feats with the muckrake, speedily becomes, not a help to society, not an incitement to good, but one of the most potent forces of evil.[1]

—Theodore Roosevelt

Perhaps (now mind you, I'm not saying this myself) the press even concocted the whole Watergate saga out of personal spite. It's a good moment to suggest this. Edward Jay Epstein warned at the time . . . that the press was giving itself much too much credit for Watergate. The cops and the grand jury didn't exactly need the Washington Post to start the ball rolling, but that's how it sometimes seemed. And since people don't really like the press to overthrow presidents all by itself, the press has been in medium to bad odor ever since. Folks may be getting fuzzy about the Watergate details, but at least they remember the movie: a couple of nosy journalists and an informer, wasn't it? Next question.[2]

—Wilfrid Sheed

Watergate overwhelms modern American journalism. According to one close observer of the press, Watergate "had the most profound impact of any modern event on the manner and substance of the press's conduct."[3] According to another, the *New York Times* publication of the Pentagon Papers and the *Washington Post* coverage of Watergate "inspired a whole generation of young journalists to dig below the surface of events."[4] No other story in American history features the press in so prominent and heroic a role. Students may learn in their history classes that John Peter Zenger bravely dared attack the royal governor of New York or that the *New York Times* went after Boss Tweed or that "muckrakers" at the turn of the century exposed corrupt politicians, but these tales are scarcely the stuff of enduring legend. If the pen is mightier than the sword in American history, it is more likely the pen of a novelist than the typewriter of a reporter—Harriet Beecher Stowe stimulating antislavery sentiment or Upton Sinclair enlisting citizens in outrage against the food-processing industry. Perhaps the most enduring (if only half-accurate) story of the American press is that yellow journalism pushed the nation into war against Spain in 1898; hardly a heroic endeavor of struggling journalists yearning for truth, this is recalled as a classic case of unscrupulous capitalists going to any length to make a buck.[5]

The story of Bob Woodward and Carl Bernstein in bold pursuit of the perpetrators of the Watergate break-in is resonant and powerful in both the world of journalism and the culture at large. The *Washington Post* received a Pulitzer Prize for its reporting on Watergate. Woodward and Bernstein's account of their own role as investigators, *All the President's Men*, became an extraordinary best-seller, and the film by the same title became a box-office sensation. The film, even more than the book, ennobled investigative reporting and made of journalists modern heroes. A mythology of the press in Watergate developed into a significant national myth, a story that independently carries on a memory of Watergate even as details about what Nixon did or did not do fade away.

At its broadest, the myth of journalism in Watergate asserts that two young *Washington Post* reporters brought down the president of the United States. This is a myth of David and Goliath, of powerless individuals overturning an institution of overwhelming might. It is high noon in Washington, with two white-hatted young reporters at one end of the street and the black-hatted president at the other, protected by his minions. And the good guys win. The press, truth its only weapon, saves the day.

That is the myth in its most general form, but this is only a portion of a larger complex of themes about modern journalism that the Watergate story opens up. The Watergate myth is available for comment and criticism, not just for reverent attention, and the initial romantic construction of the myth has been challenged on at least three points. First, did "the press" as an institution act courageously to keep power in check? Or was it especially one lonely newspaper or even a few lonely individuals within that lonely newspaper who acted in ways *uncharacteristic* of the press in general?

Second, was the press unaided in its battle against the evils of Watergate? Or was it but one institution and one set of individuals among many, with the Congress and the courts standing stalwart at its side while other institutions of investigation, including the FBI, made equally important contributions?

Third, was the press morally pure, which is to say, professionally unbiased, in its pursuit of Watergate, driven only by its sense of responsibility to the public weal? Or was the press partisan, even petty, all too delighted to bring down a man journalists had long abhorred?

On each point, a critical look at the myth of journalism in Watergate forces some telling adjustments. First, "the press" as a whole did not pursue Watergate, at least, not in the beginning—the *Washington Post* did. From the break-in in June 1972 until after the election in November, the *Post* frequently felt itself alone on a story that many leading journalists regarded as a figment of active election-year imaginations, no more than the political shenanigans Nixon claimed it to be. *Washington Post* publisher Katherine Graham remembers saying to editor Ben Bradlee, "If this is such a hell of a story, where is everybody else?"[6]

Where indeed? Of 433 Washington correspondents, at most 15 worked full-time on Watergate in the first five months after the break-in, and some of these only briefly.[7] The *Post* Watergate stories went out on the *Post* news wire, but few papers picked them up.[8] Even at the *Post* there was plenty of skepticism. *Post* White House reporters discouraged Woodward and Bernstein and their editors from following up the story. The national staff was dismissive.[9] The whole thing began so accidentally and grew so unpredictably, it made *Post* executives nervous. The decision in 1971 to publish the Pentagon Papers, Katherine Graham recalls, was self-conscious and carefully considered. But with Watergate, "there really wasn't a decision." When the story began, "it was small and sort of a farce . . . .It just looked sort of lunatic and not very consequential."[10] While a few other leading papers competed with the *Post* on Watergate, contributing new leads and new revelations—notably the *Los Angeles Times*, the *New York Times*, and *Time* magazine—"journalism" or "the press" as a whole did little investigating and showed little courage.

Second, journalists did not uncover Watergate unassisted. In a mini-classic of press criticism, Edward Jay Epstein asked in *Commentary*, "Did the Press Uncover Watergate?" and answered in the negative. *All the President's Men*, Epstein correctly points out, tells very little about how Watergate was in fact uncovered. The contributions of the FBI investigations, the federal prosecutors, the grand jury, and the congressional committees are "systematically ignored or minimized by Bernstein and Woodward." What they report, instead, are "those parts of the prosecutors' case, the grand-jury investigation, and the FBI reports that were leaked to them." This calls attention to two lacunae in the mythic account of Watergate journalism. Agencies besides the press were instrumental in pursuing Watergate. The journalistic contribution was one among many, and there would have been no presidential resignation had it not been for Judge John Sirica, the Ervin committee, the existence and discovery of the White House tapes, and other factors. Even the matter of "keeping the story alive" was not exclusively a reportorial function: candidate George McGovern kept talking Watergate throughout his campaign; the General Accounting Office, Common Cause, and the Democratic National Committee and its lawsuit against the Nixon campaign all forced disclosures that kept the Watergate story in the public eye. Moreover, the journalistic contribution itself was dependent on government officials who risked their jobs or their careers by leaking to the press. Epstein insists that it was less the press that exposed Watergate than "agencies of government itself."[11]

This skeptical view of the Watergate myth has been endorsed by many people in journalism, not least of all *Washington Post* publisher Katherine Graham. Graham has observed that the press did not bring down a president. In the spring of 1974, with Richard Nixon still in the White House, she gave a speech at Colby College, where she insisted that Woodward and Bernstein were successful only because some people, including "many inside government and mostly Republicans," were willing to go out on a limb and talk with them and that Judge Sirica, the Senate Watergate committee, the grand juries, and other agencies of investigation produced "many of the key revelations."[12]

Third, skeptics have argued that it was not journalism's devotion to truth but the *Washington Post*'s or the liberal news media establishment's contempt for Richard Nixon that led it to pursue the Watergate story. The *Post* was a liberal paper and long had been a liberal, if thoroughly establishment, institution. *Post* editor Ben Bradlee had been a Kennedy intimate. "The press," as *Washington Post* reporter Thomas Edsall told me, "is a liberal entity, with a commitment to liberal values and the 'rights revolution.'" This, he said, is "inherent in the press—opening things up."[13] Press scholar Larry Sabato argues that the press is in fact, whether or not in principle, liberal.[14] Conservative media critics, of course, have been complaining about this for years.[15]

In the view of some conservatives, this is enough to explain the *Post*'s chase after the Watergate story, but no one in journalism I spoke to and no student of journalism I know believes this. "Liberal bias" does little to explain why the *Post* followed up every allegation that came to it of Democratic campaign spying against Republicans, why journalists at the

Post resented McGovern supporters who told them what a great job they were doing, or why editors working on the Watergate stories were nervous and self-doubting about them. "I had harbored misgivings, story by story, as had the reporters and the editors above me, writes Woodward and Bernstein's immediate editor, Barry Sussman. "We all wanted to push our coverage to its proper limit, but not any farther, and we didn't want to be tools in anyone's election campaign."[16] As for Ben Bradlee, he backed up his young reporters and their editors because he was after a good story, not after Richard Nixon. The media scholar and former *Washington Post* national editor Ben Bagdikian recalls Bradlee saying, "I want every fucking cocktail party in Georgetown talking about this." Bradlee "got excited by a story that was going to make a difference."[17]

But the *Post* was also an establishment newspaper, generally cautious at its highest levels. The management struggled over the decision to publish the Pentagon Papers in 1971, finally forging ahead against the counsel of company lawyers.[18] The *New York Times* published the Pentagon Papers first. This rankled Bradlee, and there was a delicious sense of revenge in the *Post*'s pursuit of Watergate. If Bradlee was out to get anyone, it was the *New York Times*, not Richard Nixon. He is said to have walked around the *Post*'s newsroom in the midst of Watergate, shouting, "Eat your heart out, Abe!"[19] Bradlee's counterpart at the *New York Times*, Abe Rosenthal, was Bradlee's real rival.

Nixon long had friends as well as adversaries in the press, and his early career was sponsored by the powerful *Los Angeles Times*, but he felt battered and betrayed by the press in 1960 when it was apparent that reporters were not charmed by him as they were by the Kennedy entourage. (Newspaper management was more favorably inclined: 54 percent endorsed Nixon, 15 percent Kennedy, and the others did not endorse.) After his embarrassing loss for the California governorship in 1962, he lashed out at the press, though some historians doubt that he was treated badly.[20] In his presidential bids in 1968 and 1972, some analysts hold that the press treated him well, perhaps even too well, not probing hard enough and, in 1972, not pushing enough to get him out of his Rose Garden retreat.[21] Sixty one percent of American newspapers endorsed Nixon to Humphrey's 14 percent, while 71 percent endorsed Nixon in 1972 compared to McGovern's 5 percent.[22] Newspaper endorsement was significantly related to Watergate coverage. In a study of thirty of the country's leading daily newspapers representing 23 percent of newspaper circulation, Ben Bagdikian found that many papers did not carry important Watergate stories available on the wire services, and, when they did, the stories typically were not given much prominence. Papers endorsing Nixon put Watergate stories on page one at half the rate of the nonendorsers.[23]

So Nixon may not have had as much cause to damn the press as he believed. He was aware that the leading Eastern establishment press—the *Times*, the *Post*, and even *Time* magazine—was critical of his Vietnam policy and deeply suspicious of government pronouncements on Vietnam. Still, as British journalist Godfrey Hodgson observes, leading journalists did not get where they were "by being quixotic or sentimental. Their job was to get on with those who had access to stories, which meant with those who had power. They were good at that." Nixon could have had a sympathetic media, Hodgson believes: "The price would only have been a little tact, a little openness. It was too high a price for Richard Nixon to pay."[24] Perhaps Nixon longed to be treated with the deference accorded Eisenhower, but he did not have Ike's affability, competent staff, or good luck to not preside over an unpopular and divisive war. Moreover, Nixon followed in office a president whose administration repeatedly lied to the public about the progress of the war. Lyndon Johnson was battered by the press on this, and the term "credibility gap" became common political parlance.

Even if the notion of a "liberal press" is only a weak assault on the myth of journalism in Watergate, it is clear that the myth, in its unadulterated form, is overblown. Nonetheless, it remains a powerful force in the news media. When I interviewed Leonard Downie, Ben Bradlee's successor at the *Washington Post*, and at the time of Watergate one of several editors working with Woodward and Bernstein, I distinguished between "what the *Post* did in Watergate and . . . the mythology about it, two lone reporters versus the government." Downie objected:

> I want to correct you a little bit about mythology. The movie was fairly accurate but it did overly focus on just the two reporters. There were obviously other people involved, editors who were helping them figure things out and other reporters who were doing other things. But it was a small group of people against the government. And as someone who edited Carl and Bob directly through the second half of that, the question of whether the President was going to fall or not, we felt small. We did not feel big and powerful. We were not swaggering. Our responsibilities were huge to us. We didn't really believe the president was going to resign. Most of us were dysfunctional the night that he resigned because the role which we had played in that looked overwhelming to us. We were very concerned about being right all the time. We were very concerned about the judgments we made. And we were a small group of people. As Ben [Bradlee] liked to say, we didn't have subpoena power. We didn't have the FBI. It was a small group of people

doing this. . . . That's still what this business is about. That's still what makes a difference. That's a lesson of Watergate I want to remind people about. It was hard. It was not glamorous at the time. Later on it was glamorous with movies and movie premieres at the Kennedy Center and so on but at the time it was dirty. People weren't sleeping, people weren't showering, Bernstein's desk was a mess, he and Woodward were fighting all the time, they were fighting with their editors all the time, we were all under such great pressure, it was difficult to figure out what was going on because everybody was against us, because people were whispering to Katherine Graham that they'll ruin her newspaper, and that's still what it's about, you know, initiative and bravery and enterprise. That's what makes a difference.[25]

Downie's objection is eloquent, I think, but it only underscores the power of Watergate mythology. "Watergate" is indeed a myth in journalism, and I think the impact of Watergate in journalism has more to do with the carrying power of this myth than with any specific social changes in the practice of journalism after Watergate. But the myth among journalists is multifaceted. Downie, knowing that he spoke on the record to an outsider, insisted on advocating the full-scale romantic version of the myth and not a more skeptical revision. Speaking to insiders, Downie was more willing to criticize journalistic practice. Upon being named managing editor, he acknowledged to his colleagues his continuing interest in investigative reporting but added that "there was a period—after Woodward and Bernstein became household names—[in which] a number of journalists lost their perspective. Too many got caught in the thrill of the chase and it was a very, very dangerous period when a lot of people got burned."[26]

A responsible editor might well, as does Downie, emphasize different faces of the Watergate legend, depending on his different purposes and audiences. Indeed, it is fair to say that there are two myths about Watergate and journalism and Downie is drawing on both. If there is a myth of journalism-in-Watergate, there is also one of Watergate-in-journalism. It is a myth spun about a myth, a set of tales and feelings about how journalism has changed in the past generation expressed as a set of propositions about how Watergate changed journalism. The second myth, Watergate-in-journalism, is that Watergate led to a permanently more powerful, more celebrated, and more aggressive press. This is often supported by reference to a set of presumably empirical propositions: (1) Watergate led to an extraordinary increase among young people of interest in journalism as a career; (2) Watergate created unprecedented bitterness between the president and the White House press corps; (3) Watergate turned journalists into celebrities; (4) Watergate stimulated extraordinary (and, it is often added, excessive) media interest in the private affairs of public persons; and (5) Watergate caused an unprecedented and, it is often added, excessive increase in investigative reporting. These propositions about post-Watergate journalism are widely believed, but are they true? If these changes happened, did they last? If they did, are they attributable to Watergate?

The rush to journalism. Watergate did not initiate a wave of interest in journalism among students. The best available data show that the number of majors in programs in journalism and communication began shooting upward in the mid- and late 1960s.[27] Undergraduate degrees awarded in journalism doubled between 1967 and 1972. The trend continued to move upward through the midseventies at the same pace as in the late 1960s. One can always argue that, without Watergate, it might have tailed off more quickly (enrollments plateaued in the late 1970s but picked up again in the 1980s). But Watergate clearly did not start the rush to journalism.

Why, then, does almost everyone think otherwise? Perhaps people remember an *Atlantic* magazine cover story by Ben Bagdikian called "Woodstein U.: Notes on the Mass Production and Questionable Education of Journalists," published in March 1977. It documented the rapid growth in journalism majors at the nation's colleges and universities. But it offered nothing to indicate that Watergate or even *All the President's Men* was a cause. In fact, Bagdikian's article expressed serious concern that the advertising major within journalism schools was growing, accounting for a significant part of the overall rise in journalism and communication enrollments. Bagdikian's essay was never intended to explain increasing journalism enrollments, and the *Atlantic*'s striking cover of, not Woodward and Bernstein, but *All the President's Men* film stars Robert Redford and Dustin Hoffman, is nowhere justified by the article. The *Atlantic*'s editors were already trading on the currency of the myth of Watergate journalism.[28]

I do not say that Watergate did not affect how young journalists thought about journalism. It did.[29] I recognize, too, that charting journalism majors is not a perfect index of the interest of young people in journalism as a career. Students majoring in history or literature or economics may have sought positions in journalism more than they did before Watergate. Even if this is true, surely any turn toward journalism was caused not by Watergate alone but by the whole context of the moralism of the sixties and the general turn to public affairs. To take Watergate as the sum and substance of what brought young people to journalism is mistaken. But it is a mythic mistake; the mythic attraction of Watergate as a key to modern journalism distracts attention from alternate sources of explaining why contemporary journalism is what it is.

It is impossible to distinguish a Watergate effect on the growing interest of young people in journalism from the vital influence of other forces contemporaneously at work: the still-fresh inspiration of John Kennedy's live television press conferences; the growing prominence of news to young people subject to the military draft; the growing opportunities for women in journalism; the increasing salaries of journalists at least in national publications; the increasing profitability of local-broadcast news programming; and most of all the continuing influence of national events of the 1960s—from John Kennedy's assassination to Martin Luther King's and Robert Kennedy's, to the succession of shattering reports from Vietnam, not only about the slow progress of the war but about its moral horrors.

The white house press and the president. Journalists and observers of journalism agree that for a time after Watergate a tone of civility between the White House press corps and White House staff vanished. Before then, the White House press corps had been a passive press corps; after Watergate it became more angry but not less passive.[30] Ron Nessen, President Ford's press secretary, attributes this to a frustration White House reporters felt at being scooped by Woodward and Bernstein, who "broke that story without ever going inside the gates of the White House." The White House correspondents decided to be investigative reporters, too, but "they thought the way to become an investigative reporter was to bang on the press secretary or ask nasty questions . . . of the president."[31] David Broder writes that White House reporters, outgunned by two unknowns, developed a "professional fury" and a style of questioning at White House briefings that became "almost more prosecutorial than inquisitive."[32]

The appearance of civility began to return to the White House press conference in the Reagan administration, perhaps less because the press grew more civil than because the White House grew more astutely managerial. The "Deaver Rule," named after Reagan aide Michael Deaver, was that reporters jumping up and down and shouting at press conferences would not be recognized. Reporters "would sit in their chairs and raise their hands," Deaver insisted, "or there would be no press conferences."[33] But relations were still not the way they had been before. Former NBC News anchorman John Chancellor recalls, "I grew up in an America where you could win debates in school by reaching in your pocket and reading official government figures. During Watergate that went out the window." (More accurately, during Vietnam it went out the window.) "I think Reagan brought it back to some degree. But not much, and the distrust is still there."[34]

How deep does the distrust go? What Watergate may have produced in the White House press conference was a public relations need of journalists to appear adversarial rather than a motivational drive to actually be adversarial. Leonard Downie insists that Watergate did not reduce the civility between press and government, with the solitary exception of the press conference. "It's misleading," he said, "to see the theater of press conferences as being representative of the actual interaction. Press conferences account for very little information gathering by the press. They're mostly stagey events."[35] But Gerald Warren, deputy press secretary to Richard Nixon and now editor of the *San Diego Union*, remembers it differently. He saw a sharp decline of civility not only in White House press conferences but in private press briefings, not only at the White House but at the State Department, where, traditionally, reporters had been more diplomatic than the diplomats.[36]

Ben Bradlee, at the time I spoke with him in 1991, thought the White House press had grown all too civil. "I worry about the lack of *in*civility. The Gridiron Club? That's an embarrassment, the way that the press aspires to the establishment and, in fact, has made it."[37] Civility is not something easy to measure, but it seems clear that Watergate contributed to the uncivil expression of surface tensions between the press and the government, at the White House certainly and most likely beyond, even if the press did not become fundamentally more adversarial.

Celebrification. The proposition that Watergate propelled journalists to fame and fortune is well supported by the experience of Woodward and Bernstein. The book *All the President's Men*, when it appeared in May 1974, was the fastest-selling nonfiction hardback in the history of American publishing. It sold nearly three hundred thousand copies, and paperback rights were auctioned for a record $1,050,000.[38] A few months before the book's publication, actor Robert Redford, who had acquired film rights, asked screenwriter William Goldman if he had heard of Carl Bernstein and Bob Woodward. He had not, but he liked the manuscript Redford showed him, signed on to the project, and kept with it even though his acquaintances assured him that people had heard quite enough about Watergate.[39]

The film *All the President's Men* was released amid much publicity in the spring of 1976, during the presidential primaries. The premiere, at the

Kennedy Center in Washington, was picketed by striking *Washington Post* pressmen but, as CBS News reported, "serious Washington showed up, its men in sincere coats and ties."[40] Like the book before it, the film was critically acclaimed. It was also praised for its realism; as Nat Hentoff wrote, "In some places the gritty familiarity is so compelling that a watching reporter may get hit with the nagging feeling that he's missing a deadline while sitting there."[41] *New York Times* film critic, Vincent Canby, found it the most successful work ever by director Alan Pakula and screenwriter William Goldman and praised it for its ability "to make understandable to non-professionals the appeal and the rewards of American journalism at its best."[42]

As the film begins, before the credits appear, the screen is white. Has the film in fact started? The audience is entitled to a moment's hesitation. Then a typewriter key vigorously and loudly slaps a "J" on what we now recognize as a blank sheet of paper: "u" "n" "e" follow as a date in June 1972 is written out. Then, suddenly, there is a cut to what appears to be old news footage, with the president's helicopter landing outside the White House and President Nixon entering and being announced at the House of Representatives to a thunderous standing ovation. Then the screen goes black. The next thing we see is security guard Frank Wills finding a taped door; the discovery of the Watergate burglary begins. It is almost as if the film announces itself as myth—white and black, the purity of the page with which the journalists work, the dark night within which the burglars operate.

All the President's Men pushed the David versus Goliath myth of Watergate journalism to its height, but in doing so it also evoked a skeptical response. The journalist as celebrity is a paradox. When journalists are doing their jobs, according to journalists' own professed ideals of objectivity, they are on the sidelines, the transcribers, perhaps the watchdogs, but not the central actors, of society's dramas. CBS news executive Barbara Stubbs Cohen, at the time of Watergate an editor of the *Washington Star*, remembers joking with Carl Bernstein that the problem with *All the President's Men* as a film is that "in most movies, when you get to a climax, somebody punches somebody, or something like that happens, and in this case they would go back and pound furiously on the computer. It didn't quite have the same dramatic impact."[43] But Woodward and Bernstein came out of *All the President's Men* (not out of Watergate itself) as national celebrities. For a journalist in 1976, this was unseemly.

It was all the more unseemly because, just as the film was released, Woodward and Bernstein had the bad taste to publish a second stunning book, *The Final Days*, an extraordinarily detailed and intimate account of

Nixon's last weeks in office.[44] Critical comment within the journalistic fraternity came fast and furious. CBS news commentator Eric Sevareid spoke disapprovingly of both book and film the evening after *All the President's Men* premiered. In what seems almost a parody of journalistic "balance," he compared the excesses of Nixon with the excesses of Woodward and Bernstein: "Mr. Nixon and his intimates did not know where to stop in their quest for power; the two reporters did not know where to stop in their quest for fame and money. A pause, at least, was in order. There is something in life called the decent interval." He concluded with the observation that Kennedy and Roosevelt were in the grave before their private peccadillos were exposed. "Not even the cannibals feasted on living flesh."[45]

Reaction to journalism's heroics in Watergate had in some measure already set in. In March 1974, William B. Arthur, executive director of the watchdog National News Council, warned that "the press must be wary of overkill" in Watergate.[46] Speaking before the Magazine Publishers Association, *Washington Post* publisher Katherine Graham worried soon after Watergate about a "new and rather indiscriminate emphasis on disclosure as the index of fitness for public office."[47] But this rivulet of cautionary comment became a torrent of criticism with *The Final Days* and the transformation of Woodward and Bernstein, heroes of the myth of journalism-in-Watergate, into Redford/Woodward and Hoffman/Bernstein, the trickster figures of Watergate-in-journalism. In May 1976, a month after *All the President's Men* opened, Associated Press general manager Wes Gallagher complained to the American Newspaper Publishers Association (ANPA) annual meeting that Watergate had let loose "an investigative reporting binge of monumental proportions." He chided his colleagues: "The First Amendment is not a hunting license, as some today seem to think." ANPA chairman Harold W. Anderson criticized journalists who "almost joyously cast themselves in the role of an adversary of government officials."[48]

The Final Days became very controversial. Several people whom Woodward and Bernstein interviewed, including Henry Kissinger and Nixon sons-in-law Edward Cox and David Eisenhower, disclaimed parts of the work that the book suggested they could confirm. Some fellow journalists were up in arms over a narrative constructed primarily of unattributed statements, including the technique of citing as direct quotations statements from conversations Woodward and Bernstein obviously reconstructed from the fallible, and self-serving, memories of their informants. This was, wrote *New Republic* White House correspondent John Osborne, "the worst job of nationally noted reporting that I've observed during 49 years in the business." There were some glowing reviews, ecstatic reviews, but even these mentioned the widespread reservations about journalistic method.[49]

Watergate certainly contributed to the celebrification of journalists and the notoriety of celebrification. However, other factors contributed decisively, too. The development of the Public Broadcasting System, with a new range of news programs, and cable television's rapidly growing appetite for relatively cheap, easy-to-produce news programs, created a growing *organizational* demand for journalists to appear on TV. By the 1980s, the call for televisable journalists was enormous, from "Nightline" to "The McLaughlin Group," both of which, as James Fallows observed, "magnify journalists' celebrity and blur the distinction between journalists and politicians."[50] Once celebrified on television, journalists became more and more bankable on the lecture circuit, too.[51]

Celebrification is a part of a larger development, the rising status of Washington journalists. In Washington, people are measured by their clout, and after Watergate, rightly or wrongly, the clout of journalists has been judged greater than ever before. Salaries have increased, and educational levels may have risen, too, although the evidence on the latter is more equivocal than popular accounts of journalism generally assume.[52] But there is certainly a widespread perception of rising status. "There're no drunks in this business any more, you know, we really dressed up pretty good," Ben Bradlee remarked.[53]

Ironically, the improving status of journalism as a field may owe more to Richard Nixon than to Woodward and Bernstein. From the beginning of his presidency, Nixon insisted on treating the press as the enemy and on identifying it as a distinct power center in American life rather than as a representative of the public or a medium through which other power centers speak.[54] "In all the world of 'us against them,' " William Safire wrote in his memoir of the Nixon administration before Watergate, "the press was the quintessential 'them,' the fount and the succor of other 'thems.' "

In terms of power, the academic "them" was insignificant; the social-cultural elitist "them" was useful as a foil that would help attract working-men to a Nixon coalition; the liberal, political "them" was in the process of destroying itself by narrowing its base along severe ideological-faddist lines; but the journalistic "them" was formidable and infuriating, a force to be feared in its own right, but even more important, a magnifying glass and public address system that gave strength and attention to all the other "thems."[55]

Nixon came into office with Lyndon Johnson's credibility gap standing between the presidency and the public. At first he proclaimed openness and sought to contrast his administration to Johnson's. His communications director, Herbert Klein, declared, "Truth will be the hallmark of the Nixon Administration. . . . We will be able to eliminate any possibility of a credibility gap in this Administration." But quickly Nixon treated the press as his enemy. By the fall of his first year in office, he regularly instructed his staff to "get" this or that reporter or news institution.[56] In November 1969, he unleashed Vice President Spiro Agnew for a speech in Des Moines, Iowa, that blasted the television news establishment.[57] Agnew's widely discussed speech was written by Nixon's own speech writer, Patrick J. Buchanan. A week later Agnew struck again with a speech adding the *New York Times* and *Washington Post* to the list of dangerous elite media. Harassing the news media became established White House policy.

For all the importance of Agnew's public attacks, perhaps the more important war went on behind the scenes. White House officials were generally uncooperative with the press. Reporters were frozen out of relations with the president or his aides, often on Nixon's explicit instructions.[58] The White House "press conference" was renamed the "news conference" to emphasize that it belonged to the president, not to the press.[59] Moreover, Nixon's concerns about leaks—a perennial presidential concern—led him to illegally wiretap a number of journalists, including syndicated columnist Joseph Kraft, reporters Hedrick Smith and William Beecher *(New York Times)*, Marvin Kalb (CBS), and Henry Brandon *(London Sunday Times)*.[60] The administration prosecuted the Pentagon Papers case, seeking "prior restraint" of the press—suppressing publication rather than prosecuting after publication—for the first time in American national history. The Nixon-appointed FCC chairman, at the request of the White House, sought to intimidate uncooperative newscasters while the White House office of telecommunications policy prodded local affiliates to pressure their networks to report on Nixon more favorably. The *Washington Post*'s Florida broadcast stations were challenged in license renewals by known friends of Nixon on advice from the president.[61] The FBI investigated CBS correspondent Daniel Schorr at the request of the White House. White House pressure on CBS executives led CBS just before the 1972 election to cut short a special report on Watergate.[62]

The administration's aim was not only to make the president look good but to make the press as an institution look bad. H. R. Haldeman wrote Herb Klein a memo in early 1970 urging him to get the story out in the media that Nixon had overcome the "great handicaps under which he came into office," namely, "the hostile press epitomized by the NEW YORK TIMES, WASHINGTON POST, TIME, NEWSWEEK, etc., the hostile network commentators, the generally hostile White House press corps, the hostile Congress, etc."[63] This was a persistent theme in the Nixon White House. H. R. Haldeman's assistant Larry Higby wrote to Klein later the same year that an important public relations point to be made was that "RN is the first President in this century who came into the Presidency with the opposition of all . . . major communication powers."[64]

In the heat of Watergate Nixon personally lashed out at the press. After the Saturday Night Massacre, Nixon gave a televised press conference in which he called television news coverage of him "outrageous, vicious, distorted." Asked by CBS correspondent Robert Pierpoint what in particular about the coverage made him angry, Nixon replied that he was not angry. Pierpoint said he got the impression he was. Nixon explained, "You see, one can only be angry with those he respects."[65]

The outcome of the Nixon administration's calculated attacks on the press was just what *Chicago Daily News* reporter Peter Lisagor suggested at the time—that the Nixon administration successfully promoted for the news media an identity separate from that of the public.[66] The very term, "the media," was promoted by the Nixon White House because it sounded unpleasant, manipulative, a much less favorable term than "the press."[67] The Nixon administration insisted that the media were not, as they often claimed to be, the voice of the people. Nor were they, as many had traditionally understood them, the voice of wealthy publishers, on the one hand, or the organs of political parties, on the other. Instead, they were an independent and dangerously irresponsible source of power. The aggressiveness of the *Washington Post* in Watergate, then, not only enacted and enlarged an old script of muckraking but at the same time played out a scenario drafted by the Nixon White House.

Not surprisingly, like the myth of journalism-in-Watergate, the myth of Watergate-in-journalism serves two masters: both government, which employs it to portray itself as unfairly besieged; and journalism, which uses it to present itself as a brave and independent social force. Both usages veil the fact that, for the most part, there remains a comfortable and cooperative relationship between public officials and the press in Washington.

Rise of prurient reporting.   The private lives of national public figures have been featured more prominently in the news in the two decades since Watergate than in the two decades before. Watergate helped stimulate this, particularly when the White House transcripts produced extraordinary shock and prurient interest in the private language and private attitudes of President Nixon and his top advisers. Later, *The Final Days* renewed this. Still, contemporary journalistic fascination with writing about the private lives of public figures owes more to Edward Kennedy and Chappaquiddick in 1969 than to Richard Nixon and Watergate in 1972–74.[68] It owes much, too, to the way Jimmy Carter, first among equals in this regard, promoted "character" as a chief criterion for presidential candidates in 1976. It owes something to the women's movement and its insistence that private life is political, and that the dividing line between public and private is a politically constituted boundary. No doubt the newly intimate reporting of politics is indebted also to Theodore White and the new brand of behind-the-scenes political reporting he pioneered, as well as to the face-to-face, close-up approach brought to television news by "60 Minutes."[69]

In any event, prurient reporting has brought down on journalism a tidal wave of criticism. Robert Redford, speaking in 1983 to the American Society of Newspaper Editors about celebrity coverage in the press, questioned whether Watergate's lasting impact on the press was a good one. Ten or twelve years earlier, he wishfully and wistfully claimed, there had been a clear line between privacy and what the public needed to know.[70] But this is not so. Watergate was a factor but not the key factor in creating new patterns of intimate inquiry in political reporting.

Rise of investigative reporting. Did Watergate lead to an increase in investigative reporting? This depends on what "investigative reporting" is. Of course, Watergate was not the beginning of an adversarial relationship between the government and the Washington press corps. The key event was Vietnam, not Watergate, and the "credibility gap" that drew the press toward deep distrust of government voices first came to a head in Johnson's administration, not Nixon's. But the real question is not whether investigative reporting increased—all signs indicate it did—but when this increase began and whether it was transient. Only a few news institutions devoted significant new resources to investigation, even in the aftermath of Watergate, and many of these began their investment in investigation before that. *Newsday* established an investigative team in 1967, the Associated Press in 1967, the *Chicago Tribune* in 1968, the *Boston Globe* in 1970. The *New York Times* devoted increasing resources to investigative work through the 1960s. Auxiliary institutions appeared to stimulate more critical and investigative journalism: some two dozen journalism reviews (only a few of which held on into the 1980s) beginning with the *Chicago Journalism Review* in 1968; the Fund for Investigative Journalism (1969) to provide small grants to journalists doing investigative work; and Investigative Reporters and Editors (1975), a membership organization to promote investigative reporting.[71]

But investigative reporting is not today a priority for most institutions nor has it ever been. "A main thing to say about newspaper editors is they're not crusaders," former *Washington Post* editor Barry Sussman told me.[72] Steve Hess argues that investigative work became fashionable "for a relatively short time." Journalists "took great satisfaction in thinking of themselves as great investigators, but that's not what most of the press is most of the time." After editors assigned reporters to hunt for a new "-gate" a few times and they came back not with a "-gate" but with a mouse, Hess suggests, only institutions with enormous resources would take that risk again.[73]

The influence of Watergate on investigative journalism was most evident in the immediate aftermath of Watergate, and most devastating after the brief Ford interlude, for President Jimmy Carter. Carter, as I have suggested, cooperated in opening his administration up to all charges of hypocrisy or corruption because he had so willingly taken up Watergate as his unsung presidential campaign anthem. In the wake of Watergate, it would have been hard for the press not to take that as a challenge. Journalists in Washington were newly aware of government deceit and newly hungry for investigative work. "One by-product of the Watergate adventure," wrote Charles Seib in the *Washington Post* in 1977, "was a journalistic fad: investigative reporting."[74] As Ben Bradlee put it, reporters, especially young reporters, "covered the most routine rural fires as if they were Watergate and would come back and argue that there was gasoline in the hose and the fire chief was an anti-Semite and they really thought that was the way to fame and glory."[75]

Early in his term, Carter was faced with the Bert Lance affair, as we have seen. That it rocked the administration as badly as it did was in many ways a post-Watergate phenomenon. But Lancegate was just the beginning for the Carter administration. The Carter years were a time, Jimmy Carter himself has noted, "when every reporter thought, well, since they found horrible events in the president's life in Watergate, maybe there's something here. If we dig deep enough, we'll find it."[76] Both Gerald Ford's press secretary, Ron Nessen, and Carter's, Jody Powell, complained that the media saw Vietnam and Watergate everywhere. *St. Louis Post-Dispatch* White House correspondent James Deakin agreed: "the imprint of catastrophe is slow to fade. When a full realization of disaster sinks into the fabric of 200 million people, it is hard to dislodge. It was a long time before Americans forgot the Depression of the 1930's. It was the same with Vietnam and Watergate. The public had been badly burned and was wary. The reporters, intensely so."[77] Jody Powell quotes Bob Woodward on the case of Hamilton Jordan's alleged cocaine use at a New York disco: "You have to remember that our experience for the past ten or fifteen years has been that in the end the government official always ended up being guilty as charged. We just didn't run across people whose defense held up under close scrutiny." And a *New York Times* reporter on the Hamilton Jordan story explained that he believed Jordan guilty because "In every case that I can remember, the politician turned out to be lying."[78]

By the Reagan years, the investigative binge seemed over. In part, it could not last: no Watergates were turned up after years of digging. Journalists grew discouraged. In part, leaders in journalism came down hard on overzealous investigative work themselves. In part, Ronald Reagan was just terribly good at public relations, at least in his first term.

And, in part, the second myth of Watergate and the media took hold. Where the film *All the President's Men* glorified and popularized the journalism-in-Watergate myth, the second myth, Watergate-in-journalism, received filmic presentation in *Absence of Malice*. This 1981 film directed by Sydney Pollack, which brought in Oscars for best actor (Paul Newman) and best supporting actress (Melinda Dillon), announced itself in its opening sequence as the post-Watergate journalism film. Where *All the President's Men* closes with the soothingly old-fashioned staccato of teletype, *Absence of Malice* opens with shots of the high-tech laying out and printing of a newspaper page with photo-offset technology. *All the President's Men* implied that dubious reportorial tactics may be justified when the press takes out after a powerful public leader (who, indeed, turns out to be guilty of crimes); *Absence of Malice* condemned the tactics of a newspaper going after a private person (who, in fact, turns out to be not guilty). The audience that sees *All the President's Men* from the point of view of Woodward and Bernstein is tutored by the camera in *Absence of Malice* to watch the action from the point of view of journalism's victims. There is a scene in which victim Michael Gallagher (Paul Newman) comes to plead his case before the newspaper reporter, editor, and lawyer. In one powerful moment the audience looks up across the table, from Gallagher's view, to see reporter and editor, impassive, remote, unreachable, and unfeeling about Gallagher and the possibility they may be doing him an injustice. While the film makes no explicit reference to Watergate, the contrast to *All the President's Men* could not be more pointed.[79]

Despite all the suggestions of Watergate's influence on post-Watergate journalism, there is something remarkably elusive about it. The "null hypothesis," that Watergate did *not* change journalism at all, has some unlikely adherents. Carl Bernstein leaned toward the null hypothesis in remarks at the Kennedy School in 1989: "Watergate has not had the effect one would have hoped it would have . . . we haven't seen any truly significant breakthroughs in journalism" since Richard Nixon resigned.[80] Bob Woodward also inclined toward this view in suggesting some years ago that Watergate was a "blip" in the history of journalism, not the defining moment of a new era.[81]

After Watergate Woodward moved onward and upward to an editorial position at the *Post*, producing one book after another of reporting—after *The Final Days* (with Bernstein) there was *The Brethren* (with Scott Armstrong) and *Wired* (on John Belushi), *Veil* (on William Casey and the CIA) and *The Commanders* (on the Pentagon).[82] The triumph of each of these books—all best-sellers—was marred by continued criticism of Woodward's methods. Why the unattributed quotations? Why the un-named sources? What warrant is there for the reconstruction of exact dialogue at meetings that Woodward did not attend and that witnesses were asked to recall days, weeks, or even years later? This type of questioning was only encouraged by the fact that Woodward was Janet Cooke's editor for the "Jimmy's World" story that won a Pulitzer Prize in 1980 but then lost the prize when it turned out that the child heroin addict at the center of the story was the reporter's invention. Cooke was fired, and the *Washington Post*, Bob Woodward included, was red with embarrassment.

Woodward was controversial again as the editor on a story in 1979 concerning William Tavoulareas, chief executive officer of Mobil Oil. When I spoke with Woodward in 1991, he suggested that the Court of Appeals decision in the Tavoulareas libel suit against the *Washington Post* was a more important watershed in the history of journalism than was Watergate.

The *Tavoulareas* decision is indeed extremely interesting, but it, and Woodward's own role in it, may confirm rather than deny the importance of Watergate in journalism.

The story described Tavoulareas as "setting up" his son Peter in a firm that did business with Mobil. Tavoulareas sued the *Post* for libel for the story's implication that he had not borne his trust to Mobil stockholders in the decisions concerning his son. Tavoulareas won with the jury at the trial court in 1983. The judge overturned the verdict, however, ordering a "judgment notwithstanding the verdict," an option open to federal judges who find that no reasonable jury could have come to its verdict without misapplying the law. This decision was reversed by a three-judge panel of the appeals court in 1985, but this judgment itself was overturned when the full appeals court met to decide the case in 1987.

The myth of Watergate was curiously implicated in *Tavoulareas*. The *Washington Post* hired a private research firm to survey a sample of potential jurors to find if their sympathies would likely lie with the *Post* or with Mobil. They discovered a leaning in their favor; one *Washington Post* source said, "I guess we were associated with the downfall of Nixon, which in D.C. had to help us."[83]

So the *Post* requested a jury trial. In the trial, the *Post*'s attorney never mentioned Watergate. Woodward urged that he be questioned on the witness stand to bring out his role in Watergate, but the *Post* attorney said, "No, let them discover you're Robert Redford and that Ben is Jason Robards." He assumed that the *Post*'s role in Watergate would be so well known to District of Columbia jurors that the *Post* would win greater favor without pressing the point. None of the six jurors had seen *All the President's Men*, only one knew that Woodward or Bradlee had played a role in Watergate, and no one in the jury room mentioned Watergate.

The jurors focused on the question of whether the *Post* story on Tavoulareas was true or false and neglected the central matter of whether the journalists had pursued their story recklessly and with "actual malice." While the jurors ignored this question, the prosecution did not. It raised issues about malice that were rooted in Bob Woodward's Watergate-related career. Judge George MacKinnon, writing the majority opinion for the divided three-judge panel, leaned heavily on this evidence. MacKinnon argued that the jury could have reasonably considered the *Post*'s general orientation—including Woodward's own reputation for "high-impact investigative stories of wrongdoing"—as placing great pressure on reporters under his supervision to arrive at similar stories.[84]

When the full court reversed the three-judge panel in 1987, Judge Kenneth Starr, writing for the majority, observed that some of the evidence of "malice" that MacKinnon found was nothing more than an appropriately adversarial stance. "It would be sadly ironic for judges in our adversarial system to conclude," he wrote, "that the mere taking of an adversarial stance is antithetical to the truthful presentation of facts." For Judge MacKinnon, it was evidence of malice to say, in the words of the *Post*'s chief reporter on the story, that "it is not every day you knock off one of the seven sisters" (one of the seven largest oil companies). But for Judge Starr, this "is certainly not indicative of actual malice under the circumstances where, as here, the reporter conducted a detailed investigation and wrote a story that is substantially true."

As for the evidence of malice in Bob Woodward's use of the term "holy shit story" to describe the kind he looked for from his reporters, Judge Starr was equally unimpressed. Only if there is managerial pressure to produce "holy shit stories" without regard for their accuracy, he wrote, could it be evidence of malice. At no time did the evidence suggest Woodward was unconcerned about accuracy. And, indeed, the Tavoulareas story was, Starr repeated, thoroughly researched and "largely accurate." MacKinnon, in dissent, argued that the issue is not whether the *Post* "subjectively desired false stories" but whether "extra-heavy pressure to produce sensationalistic stories could motivate reporters to stretch the truth." But Starr held that, far from providing evidence of malice, pressure for high-impact investigative stories of wrongdoing was laudable: "We agree with the *Post* that the First Amendment forbids penalizing the press for encouraging its reporters to expose wrongdoing by public corporations and public figures. Rather, such managerial pressure is designed to produce stories that serve, as the panel majority rightly stated, 'one of the highest functions of the press in our society.' "[85]

Starr's decision not only backed up the *Washington Post* but provided a ringing defense of the right of the press to engage in aggressive, investigative reporting, seeking out wrongdoing in high places. But Woodward places too much weight on the majesty of the law, I think, to suggest that Starr's 1987 opinion will have greater influence in journalism in the long run than Woodward and Bernstein's 1972 and 1973 reporting on Watergate. He overestimates the power of a single judicial decision, especially one that proposes no new legal doctrine.

At the same time Woodward underestimates the power of a journalistic story become legend. The story about Watergate that has come down to us may matter much more than specific institutional changes that can be attributed to Watergate and Watergate alone. The story is in many respects distorted, overemphasizing the heroism of journalists, underestimating the heroism of bureaucrats, neglecting the role of other agents of investigation, and ignoring the accidents and luck that made the uncovering of Watergate possible. But that does not matter. Even when the revisionists have had their say, the enormity of what began with Woodward and Bernstein remains astonishing. That they did not uncover Watergate alone is true. The press as a whole during Watergate was, as before and since, primarily an establishment institution with few ambitions to rock establishment boats. But that doesn't matter either. What matters is that events, circumstances, and the energy, drive, ambition, competitiveness, and courage of some young reporters and their editors at a liberal Washington daily kept alive a story that eventually drove a president from office for the only time in our history. And that kernel of truth sustains the general myth and gives it, for all of its "inaccuracies," a kind of larger truth that is precisely what myths are for: not to tell us in empirical detail who we are but what we may have been once, what we might again become, what we would be like "if."

In that regard Leonard Downie was right to object to the skepticism implied in my use of the term "myth." Who cares if journalism in Watergate was generally lazy? Or if Judge Sirica or some FBI agents were as vital to Nixon's undoing as were Woodward and Bernstein? It does not matter, because the Watergate myth is sustaining. It survives to a large extent impervious to critique. It offers journalism a charter, an inspiration, a reason for being large enough to justify the constitutional protections that journalism enjoys.

A myth is not always invoked. It is what *Los Angeles Times* reporter Tom Rosenstiel calls an "institutional memory, sometimes slumbering, sometimes not, and it is kicked in sometimes by events." The journalists "trot out" this memory "on occasion when it's triggered, when it's appropriate, when we think it's safe, when we're not leading public opinion too much, when all the conditions and all the stars line up."[86] And if the myth of journalism-in-Watergate is not invoked, the companion myth of Watergate-in-journalism may be, the latter as antiheroic as the former is romantic.

Myths necessarily have multiple meanings; in fancier terms, they are "polysemic." They do not tell a culture's simple truths so much as they explore its central dilemmas. They can be read many ways, and the myth of Watergate journalism certainly has been. The myth has empowered the enemies of a bold journalism just as it has inspired practitioners of aggressive reporting. The Watergate myth of an independent and irresponsible "media" is as much the willful creation of Richard Nixon as the accidental invention of Woodward and Bernstein. For better and for worse, it is the crystallization of the hopes and fears and confusions of American society about its own increasingly prominent news media.

When I spoke with Steve Hess, he left me with a parting question: Are you prepared, he asked, to come to the conclusion that Watergate did not affect journalism? I waffled for a moment, then put on my best scientific front and said that of course, if that's where the evidence led me, I would be prepared to come to that conclusion, only I believed that the culture of journalism had changed even if the institutional apparatus had not. What

I did not see then, and believe I can argue now, is that myths may themselves become part of an institutional apparatus, like corporate goodwill, like any tradition, like language itself. While a tradition of muckraking precedes Watergate, Watergate gave it flesh and blood (Woodward and Bernstein), as well as an unforgettable knock-out-punch triumph (Nixon's resignation), however unfairly attributed to journalism. Watergate, by forcing a president to resign, was an exploding supernova in the sky of journalism, blotting out the record of investigative work during Vietnam. It was not only more salient, it was more consensual. Seymour Hersh's work in uncovering the My Lai massacre was too bloody and devastating and divisive a report to hold up as the epitome of American enterprise journalism. Watergate, at least retrospectively, could be widely accepted as a triumph not only of American journalism but of the American system of a free press.

I think the lingering doubt that Watergate left a lasting mark on journalism comes from a tendency to see "contingency" as the only way the past affects the present and to neglect the power of "continuity." Contingently, the most obvious impact of Watergate on the media was to establish the *Washington Post* as a significant rival to the *New York Times* in national political reporting. This has lastingly altered the map of political journalism. But it is not easy to agree on other permanent endowments of Watergate in the day-to-day activity of American journalists. Journalists do remember Watergate; whether they lived through it or not, "Watergate" holds a place in their understanding of what their job is and what it might be, what the significance of their work is and what it might be.

What is most important to journalism is not the spate of investigative reporting or the recoil from it after Watergate but the renewal, reinvigorization, and remythologization of muckraking. The muckraking theme has been powerful in American journalism for a century, even though its practice is the exception, not the rule. It is hard work. It is painstaking. It is expensive. It is often unrewarding. It runs against the ideological grain of professional neutrality. It has official celebrants within the world of journalism, especially in the form of the prestigious Pulitzer Prize for public service. Still, between Lincoln Steffens, Ida Tarbell, and Ray Stannard Baker in 1904, and Woodward and Bernstein in 1972 and 1973, it had no culturally resonant, heroic exemplars. But Woodward and Bernstein did not simply renew, they extended the power of the muckraking image. In the age of Steffens, the symbolically central White House seemed exempt from muckraking. Steffens tried his hand at it, only to be wined, dined, and charmed by Theodore Roosevelt.[87] Indeed, for the turn-of-the-century muckrakers, the federal government was a resource for pressuring state and local government, the primary seat of the corruption Steffens unearthed, not a locus for muckraking itself.

If President Nixon himself had not ultimately been implicated in the Watergate scandal, if the scandal had stopped with Jeb Magruder, no one would remember Watergate. If the scandal had stopped with Mitchell, Haldeman, Ehrlichman, and Dean, Watergate would be remembered as a great journalistic coup, bringing investigation into the White House itself. But it would not be the heart of American journalism mythology. Watergate found a president guilty of crimes, waist-deep in deception, and forced him from office. That makes Watergate, with all of its complexities for the press, the unavoidable central myth of American journalism.

CHAPTER 7

Memory Contained:
Conventionalizing Watergate

THE PAST CAN BE TRANSMITTED TO THE PRESENT IN WAYS THAT MAINTAIN (OR manufacture) emotional connections ("Remember the Alamo," "Remember the Maine," "Lest we forget") or in ways that modulate emotional intensity, seeking to secure a knowledge of the past while reducing the intensity of its grip on us. The two carriers of memory this chapter examines have modulated or tamed Watergate. Media coverage of notorious Watergate figures, focusing on persons rather than issues, creates celebrities whose meaning is assimilated to general cultural archetypes rather than to specific historical events. This kind of coverage, already in decline, will drop precipitously as people who lived through Watergate age and die. A more strongly institutionalized, more enduring carrier of memory, the history textbook, shares with media coverage of celebrities an inclination to minimize the drama of Watergate and particularly to neglect its political and partisan character. If Watergate should be remembered, if understanding it helps to understand our world today, then there is some question about how well "celebrity" as a cultural form of memory in the media or "lessons" as a cultural form in schoolbooks serve us.

CELEBRITY: WATERGATE'S LIVING MONUMENTS

It is an axiom in journalism that people make news. Whether it is *People* magazine's brand of celebrity news or the mainstream journalistic insistence on placing a "who" in every news story, people make news. People also make memories; we keep track of the recent past through individuals. Watergate stays alive for Americans in part because its key figures still live and the media remind us of them. Their lives serve as cultural markers and constituents of collective memory.

So do their deaths. At death, everyone involved in Watergate is publicly marked by its shadow. J. Fred Buzhardt, who died in 1978, was described in obituaries as "chief Watergate Counsel for former President Richard M. Nixon" in the papers of his home state of South Carolina as well as in the *New York Times* whose headline identified him as "Fred Buzhardt, Jr., Nixon's Counsel in Watergate."[1] Sen. Sam J. Ervin, in the U.S. Senate from 1954 to 1974, was remembered in the *Times* as "Ex-Senator Sam Ervin, Who Led Senate Watergate Inquiry."[2] The obituary for Robert McClory, who was an elected official for thirty-two years, including service in the House of Representatives from 1962 to 1982, remembers him simply as, "R. McClory; Backed Nixon's Impeachment." The lead paragraph notes that he was one of seven Republican congressmen on the House Judiciary Committee to vote for the "abuse of power" article of impeachment. No other political decision, preference, or act of leadership is mentioned.[3] The *Los Angeles Times* described John Mitchell upon his death as "Key Watergate Figure" and "the only attorney general in the nation's history ever to serve a prison sentence."[4] The same paper's obituary for Lawrence F. O'Brien was even more Watergate-centered: "Lawrence F. O'Brien, who while serving as Democratic National Committee chairman was the target of the Watergate break-in that spelled the downfall of then-President Richard M. Nixon, has died in New York City. He was 73." Five paragraphs follow about Watergate before any mention is made of O'Brien's role in managing John F. Kennedy's presidential campaign.[5]

When the news media chart events in the lives of people, they do not select randomly, even among certified famous people. They focus particularly on those whose stories represent or reflect on shared cultural presuppositions about what lives are supposed to be like, what we normally expect and what, in contrast, is ironic. This is not to say that individual celebrities are just placeholders for already established archetypes. Richard Nixon—like Marilyn Monroe, Michael Jackson, and Elvis Presley—does not snugly fit cultural archetypes even though Sen. Sam Ervin seemed to come straight out of Southern folklore or an Allen Drury novel. There is a complex interplay between traditional values, narratives, and literary conventions and the particularities of given individuals who become celebrities.

The one Watergate figure who is most meticulously charted, and with the most full-bodied sense of irony, is Richard Nixon, as if it were irony simply that he still lives, walks, talks. I will pay special attention to Nixon's portrait in the media in a later chapter. But other Watergate figures also have received ample press attention. G. Gordon Liddy is still followed in the press, not in a mood of irony or tragedy, as with Nixon, but with a sense of comedy. Liddy seemed always a kind of fictional character in Watergate, and the press could not help but note his move from dirty tricks to Hollywood acting. He has acted in several network television series (beginning with a guest appearance as the evil Capt. Real Estate on "Miami Vice" in 1985) and at least six (as of 1990) television or theatrical movies. He and Republican counsel to the Senate Watergate committee, Fred Thompson, another Watergate figure who turned to acting, appeared together as FBI agents in a movie, *Feds*.[6] Where others fled from Watergate, Liddy reveled in it, telling reporters how much he enjoyed it, even noting (in the course of promoting his 1990 novel, *The Monkey Handlers*) that prison had given him time to write.[7] When Liddy visited Washington in 1991, Paul Leeper, who arrested him in 1972 at the Watergate complex, and is now his friend, left him a gift bottle of wine at his hotel—where Leeper is fittingly the security director.[8] In 1991 Liddy met face-to-face on a cable news show with Jack Anderson, the journalist he had once proposed assassinating.[9] Liddy has turned himself into a kind of living Watergate icon, the license plate on his car reading, "H20GATE."[10]

Irony has been the leading trope in coverage of Jeb Stuart Magruder. Once described as a man "with a personal style as smooth as melted ice cream," he pleaded guilty in the summer of 1973 to conspiracy to obstruct justice, defrauding the United States, and wiretapping the Democratic National Committee headquarters.[11] At his sentencing a year later, Magruder said: "Somewhere between my ambition and my ideals I lost my ethical compass. I found myself on a path that had not been intended for me by my parents or my principles or by my own ethical instincts. It has led me to this courtroom."[12] This confessed loss of moral direction was the theme for Magruder's memoir, *An American Life*, which appeared in June 1974, to relatively sympathetic reviews.[13] Jeff Greenfield, for instance, reviewing it in the Sunday *New York Times*, thought well of the book ("written with restraint, regret and a fine ear and eye for anecdotal detail"), in part for its apparent honesty about "an amiably vapid young man who stumbled up and tumbled down the ladder of success without ever knowing where he was going, or why."[14]

In January 1975, having served seven months of his sentence, Magruder was released and passed largely, but not entirely, from public view. The *New York Times* found six months later (choosing the third anniversary of the break-in to track him down) that he had joined Young Life, a nondenominational Christian organization, as vice president for administration and communications.[15] The *Times* did not mention Magruder again, except in passing, until a reporter caught up with him in 1979 in Princeton, enrolled for a master of divinity degree and owner of a $270,000 Princeton house.[16] Graduated from Princeton, Magruder was serving as an assistant at the First Presbyterian Church of Burlingame, California, when he refused to comment on Watergate to the *Times* for their "where are they now" round-up on Watergate's tenth anniversary.[17]

Magruder successfully stayed out of the national public eye until, in a new position as minister of a church in Columbus, Ohio, he was appointed to head the city's Commission on Values and Ethics. Magruder acknowledged, "I'm aware that there might be some irony associated with that." The mayor of Columbus, Dana Rinehart, said, "Jeb Magruder is a fine man. He preaches every Sunday. He made a mistake and he paid for it."[18] *Parade* magazine did a two-page spread on Magruder in 1989.[19] "Today, at 54," the story reported, Magruder "is not just a respected member of his community but also a part of its collective conscience, a man to whom other people turn for guidance in times of moral crisis." Divorced and remarried, he felt his own troubles helped him as a counselor to his community. "I suppose I may still be held in disrepute by some people but with most people, the opposite is true. They say to themselves, 'This guy has been through divorce, prison, Watergate. I can tell him my problems. He'll understand. He won't be surprised that I'm getting a divorce or having trouble with my job.' " Readers could draw their own conclusions, of course, and see in Magruder evidence of American amnesia, but on the whole the article urges Magruder upon readers as a tribute to the nation of second chances and reborn lives. The reader learns nothing of Watergate; Magruder here is a living lesson about individual redemption, not about American political history.

To give a sense of the public attention paid through the years to Watergate figures, I want to examine media coverage of John Ehrlichman and John Dean. Each of them is of special interest not only because they were principals in Watergate but because they chose to write about their roles— and more. Ehrlichman has been the most prominent Watergate figure to turn his experience to fiction and to entertainment, Dean among the most prominent in turning to the lecture circuit. Both cases show that the news media share with the entertainment and education industries an institutional sponsorship of the memory of Watergate through individuals. What this kind of sponsorship does for historical memory, however, may be less than meets the eye.

JOHN EHRLICHMAN'S BEARD

In the years immediately after Watergate, John Ehrlichman was in the news because he was in the courts. (The legal system is itself an enormously influential institution of collective memory, but I will not be examining its special role in this study.) Because he was in the courts, he was not in the news for other reasons, prudently staying away from contact with the press while his case was pending.

By the time Richard Nixon resigned, Ehrlichman had been convicted of conspiring to violate the civil rights of Dr. Lewis J. Fielding, Daniel Ellsberg's former psychiatrist. Ehrlichman had directed the effort of the "plumbers" unit to break into Dr. Fielding's office in Beverly Hills, California, to seek material that could be used to damage the reputation of Daniel Ellsberg. Ehrlichman was also convicted on two counts of lying to a grand jury, and a week before the president resigned he was sentenced to twenty months to five years in prison.[20]

The following fall Ehrlichman was in the news often as the Watergate cover-up trial began before Judge John Sirica. In January 1975 a jury found Ehrlichman, along with Haldeman, Mitchell, and Robert Mardian, guilty on all counts—of conspiracy, obstruction, and two counts of perjury. In February he was sentenced to two and a half to eight years. Stories followed of Ehrlichman's expressed desire to use his expertise in land-use law on an Indian reservation rather than to serve a prison term; of the Indians' rejection of his offer;[21] of his disbarment recommended by the Washington State Bar Association; and of his disbarment approved by the State Supreme Court.[22]

Up to this point, while the newspaper or television was the carrier of Ehrlichman news, the judicial system was primarily responsible for generating it. After Ehrlichman's sentencing and disbarment, however, his place in the news was generated primarily by his own efforts to seek publicity and by the news media's efforts to exploit his notoriety. On 23 March 1975, Ehrlichman opened a new career as a writer with an op-ed column on alternatives to prison. Two weeks later, the *New York Times* reported in its "Notes on People" column that Ehrlichman, "wearing a beard that was apparently his own" (whose beard did the reporter imagine it might be?) had been seeking some kind of alternative service in New Mexico while free on bail, appealing his conviction. In October the *Times* reported that Ehrlichman had finished a novel, to be titled *The Company*, and again noted that he was "wearing the beard he has grown" while living in Santa Fe.[23]

As in much of journalism, the central point is unspoken. Ehrlichman and H. R. Haldeman were perceived as such stiff and unbending characters, staunch enemies of anything expressive, shaggy, or countercultural during their White House days, that the beard, even more than the literary accomplishments, signaled an ironic change in Ehrlichman's life. For the media, Ehrlichman fit the portrait of the right-wing loosening up, just as sixties' antiwar activists who turned to business or religion in the 1970s were for the media irresistible emblems of the Left turning conventional.

In 1976, while still appealing his convictions to the Supreme Court, Ehrlichman voluntarily entered prison.[24] But his literary career continued. He wrote two novels based on his Washington experiences. *The Company*, published by Simon & Schuster in 1976, followed the Watergate plot closely. *The Whole Truth*, published by Simon & Schuster in 1979, was a political thriller based more loosely on Ehrlichman's insider knowledge. In the meantime, the media briefly took notice of moments in his private life: buying a vacation home in Santa Fe with Rep. Paul McCloskey, the California Republican who introduced an impeachment resolution after President Nixon ordered the invasion of Cambodia in 1970; a prison furlough in 1978 to visit his ailing mother; the initiation of a suit against the government for return of personal property seized when he resigned.[25]

Ehrlichman wrote an unsympathetic review of former colleague H. R. Haldeman's *The Ends of Power* in 1978 for *Time*.[26] He did some free-lancing, writing for *Esquire* on undocumented Mexican workers, some of whom had been his prison mates at Safford Federal Prison Camp in Arizona.[27] He wrote on "Art in the Nixon White House" for *Art News*.[28] And he published his own Watergate memoir, *Witness to Power*, in 1982. At that point, seven years after Ehrlichman had grown his beard, the press still could not get over it, as in Peter Prescott's *Newsweek* review: "Ehrlichman may have changed his face—he wears a beard today that would have barred him from Nixon's rallies in 1968—but he hasn't changed his stripes."[29]

Soon after Iran-contra broke, Ehrlichman wrote a commentary on it for *Newsweek*.[30] On the fifteenth anniversary of the Watergate break-in in 1987, ABC reported that Ehrlichman had appeared in an ice-cream commercial but that adverse public reaction led the ice-cream manufacturer to pull the ad.[31] Ehrlichman makes public appearances as a commentator on public affairs, but he is generally far removed from the public eye, and the media no longer eavesdrop on his private affairs.

Both the publishing business and the television business, quite apart from the news media, kept Ehrlichman's name before the public for a decade. Ehrlichman was scarcely unique among Watergate figures in this respect. Watergate books were best-sellers throughout the Ford and Carter years. In 1974 *All the President's Men* dominated the best-seller charts for half the year, finally topped only by Marabel Morgan's *The Total Woman* among nonfiction books. In 1975 Theodore White's account of Watergate, *Breach of Faith*, was tenth on the list of nonfiction best-sellers, and Jimmy Breslin's *How the Good Guys Finally Won* was twentieth.[32] In 1976 Leon Jaworski's *The Right and the Power* was tenth on the list, selling 205,000 copies. Three Watergate books did even better. Charles Colson's *Born Again* was number five, selling 340,000 copies; John Dean's *Blind Ambition* was number eight, with 253,000 copies; and Carl Bernstein and Bob Woodward's *The Final Days* topped the charts with 630,000 copies.[33] *The Final Days* commanded what was at the time the biggest paperback reprint price ever, with Avon Books paying $1.5 million.

Less spectacularly, Watergate books stayed on the best-seller lists for a few years thereafter. In 1977 Victor Lasky's *It Didn't Start with Watergate* was number seventeen, with 119,000 copies sold. In 1978 Richard Nixon's memoirs was number six, with 262,000 in sales, and H. R. Haldeman's *The Ends of Power* was number eleven, with sales of 190,000.[34] In 1979 David Halberstam's book on journalism, with heavy attention to Watergate, was fifteenth on the list; in 1980 G. Gordon Liddy's autobiography, *Will*, was eighteenth.[35] After this, Watergate books did not rank among top best-sellers until *Silent Coup*, a book with novel answers to the questions of why there was a break-in at Democratic National Committee headquarters and who Deep Throat was, stayed on the *New York Times* best-seller list for three months in 1991.[36]

Both factual and fictional renderings of Watergate have received widespread public attention in part because Watergate coincided with, and no doubt played a part in stimulating, a "newsification" of popular entertainment. This is particularly notable in television. Although television news dates to the 1950s, only with the Vietnam War did it begin to take on a symbolic centrality for both Washington elites and the general public; the evening news show became the symbolic center of the national agenda and the national consciousness. At that point broadcasters realized news could be entertainment. In 1968, "60 Minutes" premiered and became in a few years the most popular program in the country. At the same time, local television news began to turn big profits. News took on a new commercial vitality.

While "60 Minutes" and other programs showed that news could be entertaining, other programs demonstrated that entertainment could center on news. "All in the Family" debuted in 1971. Within months it treated the subjects of homosexuality, cohabitation, race and racism, women's rights, and miscarriage. By the end of its first season, it was the top show in television. "Donahue," first syndicated out of Chicago in 1979, and later imitators provided televised sideshows featuring "real people" discussing their real problems or eccentricities. Made-for-TV movies dealt with "problems" from child abuse to chemical pollution of the environment to wife murdering of abusive husbands.

The result of this blending of news and fiction, information and entertainment, for individual psychology is anybody's guess. People still live their "real," bodily lives in their homes and workplaces and streets, as ever, but they also live alongside a hyper-reality on their television screens, radios, and newspapers. Contemporary consciousness threatens to become some kind of science fiction, two parallel worlds moving along in tandem, usually disconnected, only occasionally (and then sometimes jarringly) in touch. In any event, a huge and hungry entertainment machine eagerly capitalizes on popular, controversial events with dramatic potential.[37]

This publicity machine found its way to Watergate in both documentary and fictional forms. Documentaries include "Summer of Judgment: The Watergate Hearings," a two-hour PBS documentary airing on the tenth anniversary of the Senate hearings and "Nixon," a three-hour production, shown in 1990.[38] H. R. Haldeman turned his home movies into a television series, sold abroad but not in the United States.[39] Charles Colson's story became a full-length film screened primarily by church groups; it has also appeared as an inspirational comic book.[40] Watergate has been the subject of a number of made-for-television fictionalized accounts, notably a twelve-hour miniseries based on Ehrlichman's novel that opened the 1977–78 television season for ABC, one based on John Dean's *Blind Ambition*, one based on Gordon Liddy's *Will*, and the most recent one based on Woodward and Bernstein's *The Final Days*.[41] On each docudrama occasion, critics have worried over the confusing blend of fact and fiction. Daniel Schorr, for one, expostulated over the Ehrlichman "Washington: Behind Closed Doors," fearing that it might cause "staggering confusion" about what happened or what may have happened, and noting that "what is experienced on television becomes the operative reality, setting in motion its own train of events." He correctly recalled, however, that the docudramas did not initiate a trend to treating history as entertainment: viewers accomplished that on their own. In 1973, the Senate Watergate hearings became "substitute soaps," and viewers phoned the networks to suggest script changes or to ask that favorite witnesses like "that nice John Dean" return.[42] Terry Lenzner, a staff attorney for the Senate Watergate committee, recalls that people treated the Watergate hearings as a national call-in show, sending the committee their questions to ask witnesses the next day.[43]

JOHN DEAN'S MONEY

John Dean, like John Ehrlichman, was in the news in 1974 thanks to the judicial system. He appeared as a witness in the trial of Ehrlichman, Haldeman, Mitchell, and Mardian. Early in 1975, after serving four months of his sentence, he was released from prison and spoke to reporters about Watergate and about establishing a new life for himself. Dean discussed the financial hardships he had faced through the Watergate ordeal, saying he had "slowly liquidated almost everything I owned—my car, my house, my boat." He sold his Alexandria home for $135,000 to Sen. Lowell Weicker, who had served on the Senate Watergate committee. Dean said he planned to write a book on Watergate; his wife was already at work on one herself. He mentioned his intention to write a book of essays on the governmental process and a novel about the first black woman Supreme Court justice (neither ever materialized). He also said he would give a series of college campus lectures on Watergate. While he was "bothered by the idea of making money from the Watergate scandal," he added, "I don't know what else to do to make a living." He hoped that "some day maybe I will not be just John Dean, Watergate figure, but John Dean, something else."[44]

This is an ambition unlikely to find fulfillment. The leading issue in news about John Dean in the year after his release from prison was whether, or how much, criminals should profit from their crimes through public notoriety. The wages of sin seemed great, columnist Russell Baker suggested, citing a six-figure advance for Dean as "more money than Henry James earned from a lifetime of writing."[45] Dean, flying from California to Florida just after signing on with Simon & Schuster, was about to ask to borrow his neighbor's newspaper when the man jabbed his finger at a headline about Dean's contract, saying, "Isn't that disgusting, just disgusting!"[46]

If people did not like his publishing advances, they liked his lecture fees even less. The lecture controversy began over former Nixon press secretary Ron Ziegler when Boston University students backed away from a $3,000 speaker's fee they had offered him. At Michigan State the student government declared it would not pay its part of a $2,650 fee to Ziegler on the grounds that Ziegler had curtailed freedom of speech and press while serving the Nixon administration. Dean faced similar problems as he began his lecture tour. Faculty and students at Georgetown University signed petitions against the $3,000 fee that he was to receive for a speech there; University of Maryland students were debating whether to go ahead with a $3,000 fee. But six thousand people turned out for the first lecture of the tour that ultimately would gross $100,000. In all, Dean would give more than fifty lectures to a total audience he later estimated at more than three hundred thousand.[47]

The public lecture tour is an institution with deep American roots. A popular lecture system took shape in the United States in the 1840s and 1850s as an institution of education and entertainment. At that time it was a coherently organized, national system centered on a corps of paid professional lecturers who spoke at events sponsored by local organizations for a popular audience. Today the public lecture, sustained primarily by colleges and universities, keeps speakers before the public in two ways. First, of course, there is the sizable immediate audience that can see celebrated or notorious figures face to face. Television and radio have dimmed but by no means extinguished the popular appeal of the public lecture as entertainment. Attending a public lecture still provides a sense of occasion and an anticipation of the unexpected. Lecturers typically make at least passing reference to some local person, place, or event; they typically make themselves available for interviews in local media; their lectures, even if they have given the same one fifty times before elsewhere in the country, get covered in the local media. And this provides the second means by which the lecture circuit contributes to the collective memory: it recirculates the lecturer's name in the news media.

For Dean, however, there was at first more controversy about the fact that he was speaking, for sizable fees, than about anything he said. There was a spate of news stories and news commentary on whether crime should pay.[48] The issue plagued Dean, as it did Ziegler, and he decided to end his lecture tour, reportedly because the fees, and not Watergate, had become the chief topic of discussion.[49]

No sooner had the lecture fee issue begun to fade than the issue of "checkbook journalism" arose. On 24 March 1975 the *New York Times* reported that NBC paid John Dean (and Sirhan Sirhan) for interviews (although this was a sidelight to the story on CBS paying Bob Haldeman

$25,000 for an interview with Mike Wallace.[50] This story was corrected a week later: Dean was not paid for the NBC interview but gave the interview after NBC bought an option for the TV rights to his Watergate book.[51]

Dean's financial situation was again in the news a year later when he was hired by *Rolling Stone* magazine to cover the Republican National Convention. "Dean is a good writer with an extraordinary recall of detail," said editor Jann Wenner.[52] So Dean began a short-lived but eventful career as a journalist. At the end of September, at the height of the presidential campaign, Dean wrote of a racially offensive joke told to him by an unnamed cabinet official. *New Times* magazine picked up the incident and identified the cabinet officer as Secretary of Agriculture Earl Butz. Butz apologized for the incident, but it was a deeply embarrassing one, especially in the midst of a campaign, and Butz resigned.[53]

Dean's Watergate memoir, *Blind Ambition*, was published in 1976 and received respectful reviews from high-profile reviewers.[54] But apart from the odd story, Dean turned up thereafter in the *New York Times* only for general "where are they now" anniversary round-ups on Watergate figures. On the tenth anniversary of the Watergate break-in, Dean, having earned more than a million dollars for *Blind Ambition*, was still a client of the American Program Bureau, the lecture-tour agency, and was its single most-requested speaker on the college lecture circuit, outdoing other Watergate clients Bob Woodward, Sam Ervin, and E. Howard Hunt. In 1981 Dean made forty appearances at fees ranging from $2,000 to $5,000.[55]

In 1982 Dean published *Lost Honor*, a curious memoir concerned with his efforts to come to terms with Watergate. Wearing the mantle of the man who dares to tell all, he feels an investment in the nation's remembering Watergate and searches for signs that the lessons of Watergate live on. He is repeatedly disappointed. No, public opinion polls do not indicate a dramatic change of the public heart after Watergate. No, no "significant new laws" emerged from Watergate.[56] No, no lessons have been learned from Watergate. After the fifth anniversary of Nixon's resignation, Dean concludes that "post-Watergate morality" is dead. As for Watergate itself, "nobody really gives a damn!"[57] On the tenth anniversary of the Watergate break-in, Dean concluded that "it is clear that Watergate has had no lasting effect, has brought no real changes in government, and has had little impact on the people of the country."[58]

His book is meant to help remedy this. He wants to understand what happened to him. He wants to learn from Watergate. He quotes Thomas Hardy, "If way to the Better there be, it exacts a full look at the Worst."[59] *Lost Honor* is scarcely a full look at the Worst; in fact, the narrative thread that holds the book together is Dean's obsessive search for the identity of

Deep Throat, a search that is described in detail in the last, and longest, chapter of the book, complete with discussions with Bob Woodward, advice and colleagueship from *Time* reporter Hays Gorey, counsel from an unnamed *Washington Post* source (whom Dean calls "Deep Thought"), and finally the bill of particulars that leads Dean to name Alexander Haig as Deep Throat.

After this, Dean faded from public view. In 1986 *Forbes* caught up with him and his business activities. "I'm a gun for hire," he told *Forbes*. "Mainly I raise debt, but I also make sure the right lawyers are brought in and the right investment banking firm."[60] The *New York Times* business page surveyed the financial success of the Watergate figures and described Dean as employed as an investment banker. He only reluctantly agreed to be interviewed. "I just quietly want to do my own thing, without flash or splash. I'm trying to preserve my privacy."[61] He has successfully done just that.[62]

The prominence of some people in the news keeps Watergate alive in the culture. At the same time, there has been a censorship or self-censorship regarding others. Watergate is a stigma. Republican administrations have been loathe to revive the memory of Watergate by giving prominence to or recommending appointments that require congressional approval to Watergate figures. When they violate this unspoken prohibition, they have suffered the consequences. We have already seen this in reference to Judge Robert Bork, but there have been other cases, too. President Reagan tried to appoint Maurice Stans, finance committee chairman for CREEP, to a government position. Stans, insisting he did no wrong in Watergate, sought an appointment to help clear his name, and friends sought an ambassadorship for him. That was too prominent a position, Reagan aides thought, but the Reagan administration did try to locate for him what reporter Laurence I. Barrett called "a suitably obscure post." They settled on a seat on the Overseas Private Investment Corporation. Upon discovering that this required Senate confirmation, and learning from Sen. Howard Baker that this would mean a difficult floor debate, the Stans initiative died.[63]

Then there was a brief flurry over Republican presidential candidate George Bush's appointment of Frederick V. Malek to serve as his representative to the Republican National Committee in 1988. The *Washington Post* recalled that in 1971 Nixon had directed Malek, White House personnel chief, to investigate a "Jewish cabal" in the Bureau of Labor Statistics. Nixon was concerned that Jewish employees in that agency, whom Nixon believed to be unsympathetic to him, were inflating unemployment figures to embarrass him. Shortly thereafter, two Jewish senior agency officials were moved to less visible positions. With this incident revived, Malek resigned from the Republican post, Bush condemned anti-Semitism, and the issue died, but so did Malek's chance for a visible position in Republican circles.[64] In 1991 Bush tried Malek again, appointing him to a key position in his reelection campaign; the Nixon connection was raised in the press but led to no public outcry.[65]

All of this speaks to the continuous monitoring of public life by the mass media. I place some emphasis on the term "continuous." One of the features of contemporary experience is that social functions and cultural consciousness are continuously "on." For most Americans, gas and electricity and water are continuously on tap in ways that were not so a century ago when the pump had to be primed or the candles rekindled or the furnace stoked. The telephone keeps most of us continuously connected to distant family or to emergency services. The television differs from other forms of fiction and drama most of all in the continuousness of its presentation of material.[66] All-news radio and CNN make news headlines continuously available. Public opinion polling, once conducted occasionally, is now conducted for presidents and others on a more or less continuous basis. Intelligence gathering in the military and intelligence services has shifted from "batch" intelligence, gathered and then studied in batches, to "continuous" intelligence, a ceaseless monitoring of the world and unceasing analysis of the monitored data.[67]

If the world is not "on," an on/off switch is generally close at hand in contemporary society. Society, or a representation of the social, is continuously available. The media as an industry and education as an industry, with auxiliaries like the paid lecture circuits, keep in touch with a continuous, real-time presence of the world beyond people's face-to-face experience.

What does this do to memory? Certainly it keeps the past present in public discourse. Media monitoring of Watergate figures is more accessible and more intelligible to the general population than are congressional debates about reforming the special-prosecutor law or discussions of journalistic ethics inside journalism. But it may also be less consequential. In the immediate aftermath of Watergate, reports on Dean's prison sentence or Ehrlichman's court appearances were sober appendices to the Watergate book. But as attention to Dean, Ehrlichman, Magruder, and others shifted from "news" to "notes on people," media coverage communicated less and less about Watergate. If celebrities are known for their well-known-ness, as Daniel Boorstin memorably put it, notorious figures are after a time notorious primarily for their notoriety.[68] What established that notoriety recedes from view. Whatever serious issues there were, or might still be, over Watergate, do not get aired in popular media renderings of the Watergate figures. Instead, through this coverage Watergate is conventionalized and contained.

This flattening of Watergate is nowhere better illustrated than in that mournful footnote to Watergate, the story of security guard Frank Wills, whose conscientious attendance to his duties foiled the burglars in the Watergate break-in. The general media, print and broadcast, have paid some attention to Wills in part because he is taken to be the most prominent African American in the Watergate drama. (This is another instance in which the central role of a chronological account beginning with a burglary is taken for granted. Other African Americans played key roles in Watergate but have not become part of the conventional Watergate story and are not known by name to the general public: *Washington Post* editorial writer and writer of key Watergate editorials Roger Wilkins is well known only in journalistic circles, House Judiciary Committee members John Conyers and Barbara Jordan did not become popular television personalities or seek to capitalize on their Watergate roles, and members of the Watergate grand jury never became public figures.) On the third anniversary of the break-in, CBS noted that Wills was working as an actor in *All the President's Men,* the only Watergate figure to play himself in the movie.[69] The mainstream press covered Wills, but specialized black publications followed him more closely. In 1976 *Ebony* ran a "Speaking Out" column, by an African-American social work student, that held that "Frank Wills should not be forgotten so long as Richard M. Nixon is remembered." In 1984 *Jet* magazine ran a short article that noted that most key Watergate figures made a lot of money from books and lectures—but not Frank Wills. Indeed, Wills was twice arrested for shoplifting and in 1983 was sentenced to a year in jail for trying to steal a pair of tennis shoes.[70]

The theme is that crime pays in America, as long as you are white and privileged, and so these stories provide a racial counterpoint to the spate of stories critical of the way convicted Watergate felons made money out of their crimes.

But none of the stories about Frank Wills tell us very much about Frank Wills, let alone about Watergate, except to report the stark facts of his marginal economic existence. Wills, and Watergate, are appropriated for other narrative purposes. Whether this does anything in a more than momentary way to preserve a recollection of Watergate can be doubted. Just as Gordon Liddy became a joke, Jeb Magruder a lesson in redemption, John Ehrlichman a hirsute right-wing counterpart to sixties' radicals turned eighties' businessmen, and John Dean an emblem for outrage over why crime pays, the story of Frank Wills was appropriated for purposes that reveal nothing about Watergate or its place in American life.

LESSONS: WATERGATE FOR CHILDREN

Watergate is not much of a story for children, apart from the Woodward and Bernstein piece of it. A 1990 book for older children, *What Was Watergate?* by journalist Pamela Kilian, is the only book of its kind. It was written on the urging of an editor at St. Martin's who was stumped when looking for a book to help explain Watergate to his twelve-year-old son. While the book has sold tolerably well, Ms. Kilian's own thirteen-year-old provided a sober estimate of its market potential: "I'll read it when I have to do a school report, Mom."[71]

Watergate is not readily passed on to children. I was surprised, in speaking with a Washington attorney who had worked (along with his wife) as a staffer for the Senate Watergate committee, that they had never really discussed Watergate with their preteen children. He remembered trying once, but the kids were not interested. So here were both mother and father in a close brush with History, and the story had not entered into family legend.

If Watergate is not one of those historical episodes likely to thrill young people, still, it centers on children's most important political symbol: the president. Watergate must figure if only to explain, or explain away, our only officially discredited president. It is necessary also for the narrative succession that gets readers from Nixon to Ford. So Watergate will have at least a modest place in history textbooks; it may be less obvious why students need learn American history at all. Nineteenth-century American schoolchildren were not obliged to study American history or American literature. Not until the 1890s was American history regularly taught in public schools.[72] There is nothing writ in the stars about a national or state or local school board's insistence that its schools teach history. But in the United States, as in most, perhaps all, nation-states today, national history is a required school course. Schools are for the most part paid for and justified by the state. They are expected to train children in the adult competences that will benefit the nation. This includes education for citizenship, and citizenship training almost always suggests a study of the nation's history. In the United States, then, the memory of Watergate and of Nixon gets preserved through the institution of the schools and the presuppositions of nationalism, and through the medium of textbooks and other curricular aids as a teacher relays them to students.[73]

Distinctively pedagogical constraints emerge in telling the Watergate story in textbooks that do not appear elsewhere. Lessons taught to children must be, first of all, teachable. Frances Fitzgerald, in her incisive analysis of history textbooks, found that one of the most successful American history elementary school textbooks for the 1940s and 1950s, David Saville Muzzey's, succeeded for aesthetic, political, and pedagogical reasons. It was written in a lively style, it expressed the deep-seated view that the United States can right its own wrongs, and it assumed that children can learn elite politics more easily than social history. "Histories in which the main actors are institutions or social forces tend to lack surface attraction—an immediate appeal to the emotions," she argues, and "surface attraction" is necessary for children.[74] (It is also necessary for adults, though a bit less so.) She archly summarizes the lessons of history as they differ by grade: elementary school children learn they should love everyone; junior high children learn they should fight communism; and high school children learn they must face intractable problems.[75]

Textbook publishing is different from trade-book publishing in many ways. The textbook writers are dependent on a few, powerful institutional buyers whereas trade-book publishers sell to a mass market of individual purchasers. The Texas and California school systems, in particular, exercise enormous power in textbook publishing. Much as trade books seek controversy to attract reviews, headlines, and reader interest, textbooks avoid controversy to keep from offending anyone, particularly anyone who might raise public objections, begin a controversy, and force a school system to switch to a different publisher's wares.[76]

It would be surprising, then, to find in American history textbooks a clear expression of the Right's view that Watergate was a media-fostered scandal or the Left's view that Nixon was a product of, and scapegoat for, an imperial presidency and national security state inimical to democratic practices. There is not even a hint of the former view in any of the textbooks I have examined. There is discussion of the imperial presidency and of the dangers of secret government in several textbooks, but nowhere is there even an undertone that Nixon was a convenient scapegoat for an establishment that wanted to prevent more searching analysis of the troubles of the American system. Perhaps more surprising, only one textbook of the dozen I examined explicitly declares that the meaning of Watergate is controversial, even between the liberal view that the system almost didn't work and the conservative position that the system worked admira-

bly. A few others hint at controversy in the form, "Some people say
. . . while others believe that . . ." but the textbooks do not identify these
people by their political views. Indeed, they do not identify them at all and
do not suggest that the different opinions may reflect different politics. Nor
is there any suggestion of what might decide between different views.
Instead, the text moves into another topic or leaves controversy to a set of
"questions for discussion" in hope that the classroom teacher will take it
from there.

The nature of textbook writing is a good reminder that different versions of the past coexist not only because different people have different
interpretations of what happened but because people have different purposes for recalling the past and have different audiences they address. The
textbook version of history self-consciously seeks to teach lessons out of a
presumably consensual version of the past rather than to seek to establish
a preferred view among contested versions of the past. The version of
Watergate, or of any other event in the nation's past, that textbooks
provide is important because it is so powerfully institutionalized. It is the
only written place where most citizens will ever encounter very much of
the nation's past. But this does not make the textbook version of the past
"the" standard version of our history any more than pediatrics is the most
prestigious branch of medicine or Robert Schumann's "Album for the
Young" the best measure of his musical style and taste, even though it
remains his most often played composition.

The most cynical observer might imagine that there would be no mention of Watergate in the textbooks, it being by almost any measure such
a disreputable episode in our history. Richard Nixon himself once predicted that before long Watergate would be only a footnote in the textbooks.[77] But textbooks are not simple celebrations of the past: text writers
and publishers clearly feel an obligation to an established historical record.

Textbook writers not only mention Watergate but mention it with gravity. They typically suggest, however, that though Watergate was important, it was not a blemish on American character or institutions. Instead,
it demonstrated that the governmental machine of law, constitutional
order, and pluralistic dispersion of power survived despite a significant
challenge. In short, textbooks typically reinforce the conservative view of
Watergate. In Clarence L. Ver Steeg's *American Spirit: A History of the
United States*, Watergate is discussed in seven paragraphs on the Nixon
presidency. The emphasis is on the burglary and "lying, blackmail, spying,
and other such acts" connected with the reelection. The text states that
the tapes showed that "the President knew about the burglary and other
scandals. He had even tried to help cover them up." Nixon is ushered off

the stage with no mention that his culpability might reflect anything larger about American institutions.[78]

Winthrop D. Jordan, Miriam Greenblatt, and John S. Bowes put together an interestingly written, more evidently interpretive history, *The Americans: The History of a People and a Nation*. They acknowledge at the beginning of five pages on Watergate that "Historians will probably argue for years to come over the reasons for the events known collectively as Watergate." They say that some explanations have to do with the imperial presidency while others have to do with Richard Nixon's own personality. But even their unusually detailed treatment ends with the single most familiar textbook quotation on Watergate. It comes, of course, from Gerald Ford: "I believe that truth is the glue that holds governments together. . . . That bond, though strained, is unbroken. . . . My fellow Americans, our long national nightmare is over. Our Constitution works. Our great republic is a government of laws and not of men."[79]

Margaret Stimmann Branson's *America's Heritage* tutors younger students with a fairly heavy-handed moralism. She writes that "the record clearly shows that Richard Nixon did not plan the forced entry of Watergate." But she makes it clear she thinks he should have fired his aides as soon as he learned of their involvement with the break-in. Trying to cover up for them "was a very serious mistake. You know from your study of the Constitution that the President is responsible for carrying out the laws of the nation. The President takes a solemn oath to carry out the laws. But Nixon chose to forget about his responsibilities and his solemn promise." Still, it all came out okay. People everywhere, she said, wanted to know if the government "could stand up to such a great test. The Constitution and the government passed the test. Watergate proved once again how well designed they are."[80]

The great virtue of this position, for textbooks, is that it has a decisively uncontroversial air. It is endorsed by Gerald Ford, the president of the United States himself, after all. It also keeps the story centered on relations among branches of government, part of the lesson the textbook has been trying in any case to teach throughout. It removes the story from partisan politics in the unlikely event that students got the notion that politics was somehow involved. There is little or no attention to the fact that the executive branch of government at the time of Watergate was Republican and the legislative branch overwhelmingly Democratic. Indeed, most textbook versions of Watergate support Frances Fitzgerald's view that textbooks operate by the "natural-disaster theory of history." That is, there are problems in the world, but they are either natural disasters or technical difficulties or somehow vaguely mysterious. "In all history," if one believes the narrative strategy of most textbooks, "there is no known case of anyone's creating a problem for anyone else." Fitzgerald observes that in textbooks it was not Northerners or Southerners but "the era of Reconstruction" that created problems for the post-Reconstruction period. This natural-disaster theory of "authorless crimes," she suggests, is the pervasive, governing explanation of Watergate.[81] While this is generally true, Richard Nixon gets a measure of personal blame in some of the texts; the possibility of fundamental weaknesses in the political system or enduring dangers of unchecked executive power get no mention.

Omitting elements of partisanship that may have played a role in Watergate blocks out a likely source of controversy. Omitting the special prosecutor's office blocks out a likely source of confusion. In the textbooks designed for younger readers, the special prosecutor's office is either omitted or mentioned in passing. In Ernest R. May's *A Proud Nation*, for instance, the scant nine paragraphs devoted to Watergate make mention of the Ervin committee, the House Judiciary Committee, and the Supreme Court decision on the tapes, but neither Judge Sirica nor the special prosecutor's office.[82]

Also omitted from the May text is journalism. Journalistic investigators, like prosecutorial investigation, take a backseat in most textbooks to the roles of the familiar executive, legislative, and judicial (meaning the Supreme Court) branches of government. Some texts, like May's, and like Thomas Andrew Bailey and David M. Kennedy's *The American Pageant: A History of the Republic*, omit any mention of journalism at all. Since Bailey and Kennedy offer six pages on Watergate, compared to May's few paragraphs for the younger student, this is the more astonishing.[83] Even in a leading college textbook, journalism barely gets credited in the discussion of Watergate. In John Blum, William McFeely, Edmund Morgan, Arthur Schlesinger, Kenneth Stampp, and C. Vann Woodward, *The National Experience: A History of the United States*, seven pages on Watergate include only one mention of journalism. Woodward and Bernstein enter the story after the Senate votes in February 1973 to inquire into charges of election corruption, and they are described as "two young reporters on the *Washington Post*, [who] were meanwhile beginning to uncover sources in the executive branch, especially a mysterious and knowledgeable figure whom they identified only as Deep Throat."[84]

The omission of journalism is not, I think, motivated, as in the case of Stanley Kutler's history of Watergate, by an interpretation that Watergate was a constitutional crisis rather than a media-sponsored scandal. It derives instead from a desire to keep things simple, to show the virtues of the Constitution, to teach once more a lesson about the three co-equal branches of government. No text writer wants a "fourth branch of government" walking on stage at the eleventh hour. "The system that worked" is supposed to be the system of checks and balances of a government whose powers are divided among three branches that students have been reading about since early in the school year.

Textbooks are not the only historical sources for children. There are general history books for children for personal use. There is, as I have mentioned, Pamela Kilian's workmanlike, journalistic account, *What Was Watergate?* for juvenile readers.[85] Jim Hargrove's thirty-two-page picture book, *The Story of Watergate*, offers a lively chronological account of Watergate that ends with the familiar conclusion that "the scandal proved that the American system of government works." As for Nixon himself, "There are many, many examples of how he served his country well. Unfortunately, they are not a part of the story of Watergate."[86] *Mr. President*, a picture book of presidents, provides a one-line caption under Nixon's picture, "Richard Nixon, resigned under a cloud."[87] Frank Freidel's picture book, *The Presidents of the United States*, a publication of the White House Historical Association, offers one page of text on each president and a one-line summary of that page; Nixon's is, "The Watergate scandal forced Richard M. Nixon to resign the Presidency."[88] Vincent Wilson, Jr.'s *The Book of the Presidents*, a souvenir book now in its tenth edition, begins its one-page report on Nixon, "The first President to resign from office, Richard Nixon removed himself from the Presidency August 9, 1974, after investigations of the Watergate cover-up finally revealed that he had acted illegally and that it was clear that he could not survive the impeachment proceedings then in progress."[89] A reference book for young readers willing to draw a moral from the Nixon story, Wyatt Blassingame's *The Look-It-Up Book of Presidents* concludes four pages on Nixon this way: "Intelligent, well trained, with a natural instinct for politics, Nixon might have been one of the great Presidents. But he put politics above honesty. To get what he wanted he was willing to lie, and eventually he got caught."[90] Of the books I examined, only Dee Lillegard's *Richard Nixon*, a volume in the Childrens Press "Encyclopedia of Presidents" series, refuses to give even a hint of disapproval of Nixon's actions in Watergate: "In the calmer light of history, future generations will be able to weigh Richard Nixon's accomplishments against the mistakes revealed by Watergate."[91]

A card game on sale at the Smithsonian Museum in Washington, "Presidential Rummy," has a card for each president. Each card is half filled with a National Portrait Gallery oil painting of the president and the president's name and dates in office. There is some general information about the president's lifespan, home state, party, First Lady, and vice presidents. And there is a two- or three-sentence account of the highlights of the president's term in office. For Nixon, the card reads: "Nixon's term saw improved relations with the Soviet Union and Red China, the end of the war in Viet Nam, and astronauts on the moon. As a result of the Watergate scandal, he became the only President to resign." The only action clearly attributed to Nixon, in this thumbnail version of his presidential career, is resigning. Gerald Ford's card reads: "Ford is the only President who was never elected either President or Vice President. He was appointed Vice President when Spiro Agnew resigned and became President when Nixon resigned as a result of the Watergate scandal." In Ford's case, the only thing mentioned is how he came into office. Judging from these cards, he can be ranked with William Henry Harrison, whose card is dedicated to explaining how he died one month into his term. Neither is listed for any sin or glory apart from having been there.[92] Also available at the Smithsonian is a "Turn & Learn" board produced by OTT & Associates (1989) on "The Presidency." It offers only a line drawing of each president, below which are listed the president's dates in office, his party, his state, the length of his term in years and days, and his age at inauguration. An asterisk at the bottom of the Nixon entry says simply, "Resigned from office." When reduced and reduced again, that seems to be the residue of Richard Nixon for children.

Students who read textbooks will find descriptions of Watergate located between evasive neutrality and collective reaffirmation of the American system. Books for children preserve Watergate for future generations, but it is a thin preservation, a story deprived of both heroes and villains. As a tale told by a textbook, Watergate signifies only a reaffirmation of American government. It is a crisis contained, a drama tamed; the sense that "something happened" that might have happened otherwise is lost.

CHAPTER 8

Memory Engrained:
Post-Watergate Political Expectations

A LEGACY IN LANGUAGE

For people in public life, the language of Watergate still echoes through the corridors in the 1980s and 1990s.[1] In Peggy Noonan's memoir of her years writing speeches for Ronald Reagan, she recalls that, working in the White House, she wondered when she would "pass in the hall a meeting, or have a short conversation that turned out, in retrospect, to be touched by dark history—like the secretary in the office next to John Dean hearing, 'Mr. Liddy is here to see you, John,' or overhearing in the hall, 'Don Segretti, how are you, going to see Mr. Colson?' "[2] She remembers fantasizing Reagan's defending her speech drafts against other staffers who tried to edit it by calling her, "Hello, Peg? Your long national nightmare is over. If anyone tries to tamper with your work again you just tell them to dial G for Gippuh, got it?"[3] Ford's famous epitaph for Watergate was echoed and also mocked in the title of political journalist Sidney Blumenthal's book on the Reagan years, *Our Long National Daydream*.[4] The Watergate ghosts haunt the White House, Washington, newsrooms, wherever there is an attentive political public.

Well beyond Washington, Watergate is a cultural point of reference, available for almost any discussions of American politics or journalism. One sign of Watergate's cultural availability is that it has found its way into fiction as a reference point, too, quite apart from the direct fictionalizations of Watergate. Rex Stout's famous private investigator Nero Wolfe "probably knew more about every angle of Watergate than any dozen of his fellow citizens, for instance the first names of Haldeman's grandparents," the reader is told in the 1975 *Family Affair*. The murder victim in this novel is Harvey Bassett, a manufacturer of tape-recording equipment, who believed that President Nixon had "debased and polluted tape recorders" and was obsessed with Nixon and the Watergate tapes.[5] In the third of John Updike's *Rabbit* quartet, a novel whose action is set in 1979, the protagonist's mother-in-law discusses her deceased husband's views of Watergate. "You know I think it broke Fred's heart . . . Watergate. He followed it right to the end, when he could hardly lift his head from the pillows, and he used to say to me, 'Bessie, there's never been a President who hasn't done worse. They just have it in for him because he isn't a glamour boy. If that had been Roosevelt or one of the Kennedys,' he'd say, 'you would never have heard "boo" about Watergate.' He believed it, too.'"[6]

More recent fiction continues to employ Watergate as a common point of reference. In a 1983 novel by Michael Malone, the police detective-hero owns a poodle named Martha Mitchell; in a 1987 mystery novel Joan Hess makes references to Woodward and Bernstein; in a 1989 satire of the academic life, Gordon Liddy is mentioned.[7]

Television humor and fiction borrow from Watergate, too. The hit sitcom "Murphy Brown" has made reference to the Watergate break-in several times. "The Simpsons" has made allusions to Watergate, too.[8] References of this sort will not last beyond the generations that knew Watergate directly; they may be dying out already, as the fictionalizations themselves suggest. On the television series "thirtysomething," an episode aired during the 1990–91 season showed a Hollywood writers' conference with one writer suggesting the line, "They worked together on the high school newspaper, side by side, like Woodward and Bernstein." Another writer corrects: "You're dating yourself." In a 1991 mystery novel by Ralph McInerny, a student journalist asks a professor, "Do you remember Watergate?" "Don't you?" he responds. "I was a baby," she reminds him.[9]

Watergate references will "date," but some will gift into the general language and become part of common usage, shaping our thinking about politics even as their Watergate origins may become faint. William Safire lists more than a dozen "Watergate words" (a term he provides a separate entry itself) in *Safire's Political Dictionary*.[10] These include: plumbers, enemies lists, laundering, to deep-six, cover-up, smoking gun, firestorm, Saturday Night Massacre, to stonewall, dirty tricks, big enchilada, "up to speed," ratfucking, executive privilege, Oval Office, twisting slowly, slowly in the wind, at this point in time. Some of these terms are now rarely used, but others are in such common circulation that it is pointless to list instances—as with "smoking gun" or "cover-up" or "stonewalling." Two terms with at least loose connections to Watergate have come into general usage out of the Nixon era without any recognition of their political origin. "Oval Office" was not a term used to refer to the president's office until at least the Johnson administration (Eisenhower used the term "West Wing" to refer to the center of executive action). Safire recalls that the term "Oval Office," capitalized and unmodified, originated with Nixon aides to refer to a decision the president made without using his name. It was a way to make decisions less personal and less personally accountable, and it came into widespread use for the first time during Watergate. (The White House Historical Association's annual guide switched from the term "President's Office" to "Oval Office" in 1973.)[11] "Media," as I have already observed, is another term that owes much to Watergate.

The Woodward and Bernstein book title *All the President's Men*, itself borrowing from a nursery rhyme, has a cultural resonance and cultural echoes, as in Bill Moyers's repeated reference to "the President's men" in his PBS documentary on Iran-contra aired in 1990.[12] Reporter Tim Weiner uses the same phrase with the same overtones in a book on the Pentagon's "black budget" in 1990.[13] There is a similar borrowing in a *Common Cause* magazine article on potential conflicts of interest among the largest donors to President Bush's 1988 campaign, "All the President's Donors."[14] The accusatory connotations of the phrase are neutralized in a self-promotional Orange County magazine story on Orange County's Nixon-related citizens entitled, "All the President's Women and Men."[15]

Not only language-use but also language-avoidance stems from Watergate. The word "impeachment" was studiously avoided by Congress in the Iran-contra hearings and by Reagan's aides in their own discussions, just as the term "executive privilege" was avoided by President Reagan's attorneys in responding to Iran-contra–related inquiries after Reagan left office. During the 1976 election campaign, Gerald Ford avoided mentioning Watergate by name, and Jimmy Carter claimed, however disingenuously, that he would not use Watergate in his campaign. "It's one of those political charades," journalist Hugh Sidey complained, "that tries the American intelligence."[16] Congress changed the term "special prosecutor" to "independent counsel" when Title VI of the Ethics in Government Act was renewed in 1982, seeking to remove the stigma of the Watergate-era term.

The most obvious contribution of Watergate to the language is the suffix "-gate" to designate a scandalous event. This began almost instantly after

Watergate. William Safire credits "winegate," a scandal in France over the fraudulent mixing and labeling of millions of bottles of wine in November and December of 1974, as the first -gate.[17] He may underestimate his own role in writing on 12 September 1974 of the "Vietgate Solution," the notion of a package of pardons, for Watergate criminals on the one hand and Vietnam War draft resisters and military deserters on the other.[18] While this is different from the usage that became standard, it is the first mention I have found that detaches the "gate" from "Watergate" for some other purpose.

"Gates" and "Watergates" have since abounded. In the United States, some of the most prominent of these, where the "-gate" suffix became a standard appellation for the scandal, are "Koreagate," a scandal of the Korean CIA's efforts to buy influence with Congress, in 1977; "Lancegate," also in 1977; "Billygate," a scandal concerning President Carter's brother Billy and his relations with the Libyan government, in 1979; "Sewergate," a scandal involving the Environmental Protection Agency's top administrators, in 1983; "Debategate" or "Briefing-gate," an outcry in 1983 concerning the Reagan election campaign's apparent theft of a briefing book for the presidential debates from the Carter camp during the 1980 campaign.

In 1986 and 1987, "Irangate" or "Contragate" were terms in general use to describe the "Iran-contra affair," but neither seemed to take hold. (Why "Irangate" or "Contragate" never fully met with acceptance as appellations for the Iran-contra affair may reflect the fact that there was not a single "Iran-contra affair" but several reasonably separate "affairs," as Theodore Draper has argued.[19] Moreover, precisely because Iran-contra had the weight and dimension of Watergate, unlike any other political scandal in the interim, it required a naming of its own, not something derivative.)

Since Iran-contra, there has been "Section 8-Gate" (1989), a term congressional Democrats used to refer to a Reagan administration Housing and Urban Development Department scandal arising out of Section 8 of the National Housing law.[20] "The Senate's Watergate" (1990), according to the *Los Angeles Times*, was a common term for the Senate Ethics Committee investigation of the "Keating Five" for selling political favors to a savings and loan executive for campaign contributions (though I do not recall hearing it myself).[21] "Rubbergate" was a 1991 *Washington Times* coinage for a congressional check-kiting scandal.[22]

The usage of -gate is also international. South Africa had a "Muldergate" in 1978;[23] Germans likened a West German scandal in 1987 to Watergate;[24] in 1989 Solidarity's Citizens Committee announced "a Polish

Watergate" when it found an electronic bugging device in a regional election headquarters;[25] and in Canada, leaks of the government budget led to charges and countercharges of political skulduggery that borrowed liberally from Watergate talk. While this never became a "-gate" of its own, a columnist for the *Ottawa Citizen* wrote of Canadians' "Watergate Envy." He derided the House of Commons for reducing complex matters to the old Watergate question, "What did he know and when did he know it?" He criticized the media as much as the opposition parties for "needing a Canadian Watergate."[26] In 1991 the South African government's secret funding of the Inkatha Freedom Party, a rival to the African National Congress, became a major scandal known as "Inkatha-Gate."[27] In Argentina in 1991 a small left-wing party placed a television ad attacking President Carlos Saul Menem's position on the Malvinas war. When it became known that the Argentine intelligence service, whose initials are "S.I.D.E.," had secretly funded the ad, "SIDEgate" was born. A drug-money–laundering scandal involving President Menem's sister-in-law Amira Yoma became known as "Narcogate" or "Yomagate."[28] Also in 1991 a case of political murder in Puerto Rico became known as the "Watergate of Puerto Rico" and enlisted Sam Dash of Watergate fame to pursue its investigation.[29]

Why all this apparently endless use of "-gate" and the widespread borrowing of other Watergate words? What does all this language do?

Language has power. The Watergate scandal itself owes some of its prominence to the poetry of the word Watergate. The term was at first used only to refer to the building, as in "the Watergate" or "the Watergate hotel" or "Watergate complex." Or it was used adjectivally, as in "the Watergate caper," a term that appeared in the first *Washington Post* editorial on the subject on 21 June. Its usage as a freestanding noun did not become common in the media until the fall of 1972;[30] thereafter it seemed inescapable. I suspect that its capacity as a portmanteau term to refer equally to a set of abuses of power dating back several years, campaign law violations dating to 1972, obstruction of justice following the Watergate break-in, and general defensive behavior in the White House (like the keeping of an "enemies list") contributed to the belief that there was a pool of undifferentiated evil in the White House. A Washington correspondent wrote in 1924 that "Teapot Dome" was "an alluring and provocative name. It has a mysterious sound and comes trippingly from the tongue."[31] In Watergate as in Teapot Dome, a little poetry helped a scandal to cultural prominence.

Turning a scandal into a "-gate" has often been an effort to use the emotive power of language for political advantage. William Safire used "Lancegate" both to diminish the relative importance of Richard Nixon's guilt in Watergate and to underline the damaging implications of the Lance affair for Jimmy Carter. This usage was also a way to "presidential-ize" the scandal, to insist that it was Carter's scandal, not Lance's. "Briefing-gate" or "debategate," similarly, was an effort to turn what, so far as we know, was a relatively isolated infraction of fair-mindedness in a political campaign into a matter of considerable embarrassment to the Reagan administration. By the time of briefing-gate in 1983, "gating" every scandal was a practice that had plenty of critics. Stephen Chapman objected to "Sewergate" in his *Chicago Tribune* column, arguing that "the resemblance to Watergate lies in the press reaction, not the gravity of the alleged misdeeds." This use of "-gate," he held, had the effect both of inflating "ordinary bureaucratic wrangling" and of trivializing Richard Nixon's crimes.[32] "I find myself just bored to tears by someone sticking 'gate' after every little foible," political scientist Alan Westin told *Time* magazine in an interview related to "Briefing-gate." *Time*'s reporters concurred: "His point was well taken: the briefing book dispute did not remotely resemble a Watergate-class scandal."[33]

Languages differ, the linguist Charles Hockett once suggested, not in what they can express but in what they can express *easily*.[34] The vocabu-lary that is most readily available is the vocabulary most likely to give shape to political thought. No part of culture more directly expresses common understandings of the world than does language, and no part of culture is more widely shared. Language is what we think with. The vocabulary that becomes easily available for our thinking becomes a part of our thinking. Both cognitive step-stool and cognitive crutch for under-standing, it is through language that we construct our views and our responses to the world.

Quotation is the mechanism language uses to pay homage to the past. A word, phrase, or sentence whose general meaning was established by a particular speaker or for a particular occasion is plunked down in the present. This necessarily changes the meaning of the words (as Jorge Luis Borges so brilliantly demonstrates in "Pierre Menard, Author of the *Quix-ote*"). By drawing a past context into the present, quotation creates an ironic or parodic conversation between past and present. By repeating a phrase the audience knows to be tied to a particular past moment, quota-tion may take on the tone of incantation and evince reverence or irrever-ence, evoking in the audience attitudes toward the earlier event or even attitudes toward tradition itself. "The secret life of poetry," poet Mark

Strand has observed, is that "it is always paying homage to the past, extending a tradition into the present."[35] This is true not only of poetry but of language generally.

Linguistic representations may at first have very specific references: "Watergate" was originally a noun representing a building, later a general term referring to the set of abuses of power, dirty tricks, and paranoid practices of the Nixon White House. As time has passed, "Watergate" has come to mean "large and nefarious political scandal," and "-gate" has been sliced off to mean no more than "political scandal." The specific evocation of the Nixon administration recedes even as the term retains a diffuse rhetorical power. When in the Iran-contra affair people asked "what did the president know and when did he know it?" there was no doubt that the genie of Watergate was being intentionally conjured up. But quotations may shed their diacritical marks; today when people say "cover-up" or "stonewall" they do not necessarily recognize that a specific history brought these terms into general use. Yet even when the Watergate roots are forgotten, Watergate's legacy in language affects the presuppositions of political discourse. The words of Watergate have become engrained in our common language, the central storehouse of collective memory. They thereby shape our political thinking, our political dreaming, our expectations and anxieties about politics.

EXPECTATIONS

POST-WATERGATE MORALITY AND THE PRESIDENCY

In the years after Watergate, people began to speak of a "post-Watergate morality," the emergence of a newly stringent set of norms and expectations about the appropriate ethical conduct of men and women in public life. "Watergate," as Washington attorney and Nixon adviser Leonard Garment has ruefully observed, "marked the beginning of an unprecedented attempt to root out evil and wrongdoing from American politics and to promote virtue and rectitude in the country's public life."[36]

Where to locate this post-Watergate morality is not very clear. Is it to be found in the press? In the courts? In the minds of the public? It is hard to pinpoint the phenomenon, but it is just as hard to deny that something, somewhere we can label "post-Watergate morality" existed (at least for a time) and exercised real force on social relations. As long as people thought there was, or should be, a post-Watergate morality, it existed.

The past makes itself felt in the present, then, in part as a set of expectations about what the world will be like and should be like. It is an anchor for the imagination. When people make judgments about what the future is likely to hold, they do so from an empirical baseline—their sense, accurate or not, of what the past was like; at the same time, when they make judgments not about how people will act but about how they *should* act, they start from a moral baseline of codes, conventions, laws, sentiments, and sometimes, as in the case of Watergate, a powerful remembrance of past transgression.[37]

The power of Watergate to live on in cultural expectations has been most thoughtfully discussed in several essays by sociologist Jeffrey Alexander. Alexander finds in Watergate a practically perfect illustration of a sociological theory developed early in the twentieth century by French sociologist and social philosopher Emile Durkheim. Durkheim, one of the founding fathers of sociology, was intent on demonstrating that "social facts" have a real existence, something more than an aggregation of facts about individuals. He showed, for instance, that suicide rates vary systematically with social conditions and that one does not need to know anything about individuals in a given population to predict the rate of suicides in that population. Knowing large, measurable social factors like religious affiliation and economic conditions is enough to accurately predict how many people in a population will commit suicide.[38]

That suicide could be predicted without knowledge of individual psychology was a stunning demonstration. But Durkheim was not done. He was very interested in understanding the social nature of human systems of belief and, particularly, religious beliefs. Where do the basic ideas of religion come from? Empiricists who say that the categories of religious thought derive from experience cannot be right, Durkheim argues, because this would deny the essential feature of religious ideas: that people feel them as necessary, not contingent; they have a kind of weight and obligatoriness that rarely attends empirical knowledge. Then do people arrive at these ideas innately? Are they inborn in human cognition? This is more true to the weighty character of religious ideas, but it does not account for differences in religious ideas from time to time and society to society. Then what explanation can there be?

Durkheim's answer is that society is itself the source of religious beliefs. Looking at Australian aborigines in an effort to find a relatively pure and simple expression of religious ideas, Durkheim argued that when people worship a god, some invisible and transcendent power in the world, they are unknowingly responding to the transcendent force their own society exerts upon them. In the Australian case, the sense of power generated by society as a whole is created and sustained by the periodic gatherings of the aboriginal tribes, and the dancing, feasting, and celebrating they entail. These ritual gatherings could be enormously exciting and generate what Durkheim termed a "collective effervescence" whose weight and intensity would endure long after the ritual was over, especially when it was represented in sacred objects and ceremonies that sustained belief between tribal gatherings.[39]

The relevance of this, as many sociologists have argued, is that moderns are not so very different. Alexander finds a modern ritual, and a modern "collective effervescence," in America's collective experience of Watergate, particularly as people participated in its emotional turmoil through television.[40] The lingering influence of that collective experience, he argues, is what people refer to as "post-Watergate morality." "Americans talked incessantly in the period between 1974 and 1976 about the imperatives of 'post-Watergate morality.' They experienced it as an imperious social force which laid waste to institutions and reputations. 'Post-Watergate morality' was the name given to the effervescence from the ritual event. It named the revivified values of critical rationality, antiauthoritarianism, and civil solidarity, and it named the polluted values of conformity, personalistic deference, and factional strife."[41]

That naming, or rather, renaming, has provided or consolidated a changed and charged atmosphere of public discussion. Fifteen years after Watergate, a legal scholar could suggest that post-Watergate morality was still strong enough to make post-Watergate legislation redundant. "Ironically," Stephen Carter wrote in *Harvard Law Review*, "the same Watergate scandal that led to the Ethics in Government Act has brought about a post-Watergate morality that arguably makes the Act superfluous."[42] Is this post-Watergate morality or post-Watergate political culture awesome enough to obviate the need for government ethics legislation? What is it and where can it be located?

Where many observers have gone to find "post-Watergate morality" is to public opinion polls. While this is not a foolish move, it is also far from a conclusive one. What "post-Watergate morality" is supposed to mean, in public opinion findings, is a decline in confidence in government coupled with an inflation of expectations for the lawful behavior of public officials. But the decline in confidence that the polls certainly demonstrate cannot be traced specifically to Watergate. What the polls show is that confidence in government was declining from the Vietnam years on and that the decline of trust in government (as well as in just about every other major social institution) continued through the 1970s.[43]

Alexander may have taken the measure of post-Watergate morality better than Gallup, asking not what the public at large thinks but what policymakers and community leaders believe, rightly or wrongly, to be public pressures. If they act as if they are under the watchful surveillance of a post-Watergate morality, then, for all practical purposes, they are. Their believing makes it so.

And act that way they certainly have. This is not to say that corruption or other abuses of office necessarily declined or even that legal action against government officials became more severe, although the latter is true. But it does mean that elites lavished new attention on ethical issues in government and so altered the national political agenda. Law schools began to offer courses on legal ethics; Robert Stevens, historian of American legal education, writes that after Watergate "legal ethics became almost an industry in itself." Within a few years after Watergate, bar associations were demanding that the study of ethics be made compulsory in law schools.[44] Even the Boy Scouts rewrote their precepts to emphasize critical questioning as well as loyalty and obedience.[45]

Watergate and post-Watergate morality strengthened the hand of "public-interest" organizations and lobbies, most notably Common Cause. Founded by former Secretary of Health, Education, and Welfare John Gardner in 1970, Common Cause had an initial paid membership of 52,000. In 1971 the organization, still in its initial outreach, added 178,000 members. The following year 50,000 people joined the organization, but others failed to renew membership and total membership dropped from 232,000 to 197,000. Watergate turned this around. In 1973 and 1974, 264,000 people joined Common Cause, pushing its total membership from 197,000 to 315,000. Common Cause was indeed, as the *National Journal* later described it, the " 'open government' lobby that Watergate made a star."[46]

Membership has never again been so high (it was 273,000 in 1990) even though Common Cause has done what it can to keep the memory of Watergate alive in its solicitations of new members.[47] In direct-mail solicitation in 1977, Common Cause compared Koreagate to Watergate and enclosed a *San Francisco Chronicle* editorial that called for "someone like Sam Dash of Ervin Committee fame" to "get this Congressional Watergate behind us." In a 1980 solicitation, Common Cause chairman Archibald Cox writes that he was so impressed with the organization's efforts during Watergate that he joined up after he was dismissed as special prosecutor.[48]

Common Cause did indeed play its own role in Watergate, instituting a suit against the Committee to Re-Elect the President that helped forced disclosure of campaign contributions. It worked hard in lobbying for campaign finance reform and had an impact on the passage of the Federal Election Campaign Amendments of 1974. It pressed for election law reform in 1974 and 1975, its staff believing that "during the Watergate era, the chances of getting far-reaching reform might be better than at any subsequent time."[49] There is little doubt they were right. By December of 1974, forty-six states "energized by the Watergate scandals" had taken action to reduce the influence of money in elections and secrecy in legislative practices, two key Common Cause–sponsored reforms. In 1975 forty states strengthened open-government laws with Common Cause working as a lobbyist in every state legislature.[50] Between 1972 and 1982, forty-three states adopted new laws to control lobbyists, thirty-one adopted or strengthened laws requiring public officials to make financial disclosures, forty-five strengthened open-meeting laws, and almost all states passed new campaign-finance legislation.[51] In Washington, of course, as we have seen, there was a rash of post-Watergate legislation on ethics in government. In 1977 new codes of conduct were passed in both the House and the Senate with a set of rules for public financial disclosure, limits on outside earned income and gifts, a prohibition on using campaign funds for personal use, and other restrictions.[52] The collective effervescence of Watergate helped keep moral fervor alive in new rites (call them legislation) and new ceremonies of openness and democratic procedure. Post-Watergate morality existed well beyond Washington, affecting state capitals and local and municipal government as well. The sense of transgression in Watergate was not a specific response to a campaign-related burglary but a more generalized and diffuse sense of having been betrayed by a government operating in secret. Post-Watergate reforms tended to interpret Watergate as a set of threats to democratic governance through secrecy and deception.

Legislative activity is often ritual activity (which is not to say that it is "merely" ritual activity). There's no doubt Congress felt obliged not only to reform the political system but to *show* that it was busy reforming. Congressional action on post-Watergate reform was not only substantive, creating new laws with consequences for political behavior, but performative, demonstrating in the very act of deliberation that Congress was concerned about political ethics. Without doubting that legislators may have wanted to do good, it is clear they wanted also to look good.

The sense of a powerful post-Watergate morality in the Ford and Carter years was in decline by the time Reagan came to the presidency. Already in early 1979 the *New York Times* reported that "Some on Capitol Hill say the public has forgotten Watergate and that the pressure for reform has eased."[53] There seems wide agreement that by the early Reagan years "post-Watergate morality" was in decline. Political scientist James David Barber attributed this to an American inability to maintain high levels of righteous indignation for long periods.[54] Perhaps. But this scarcely seems an "American" characteristic. What may be more American is the ability to turn righteous indignation to political effect so readily. Many non-Americans were astonished at, and disdainful of, what they saw as an undue moralism or puritanism at work in Watergate.

FOREIGNERS' INCOMPREHENSION OF WATERGATE

One of the most peculiar features of Watergate is how it mystified foreigners. Most foreigners seem unable to understand why Nixon's misdeeds were scandalous, or why they should have brought down an administration whose foreign policy they admired. Writer C. P. Snow, for instance, interviewed on CBS in 1979, said, "Yes, Watergate, I can never understand how you became so astonishingly morally righteous about that. . . . It was a ridiculous incident. . . . What . . . they thought they were doing I don't know, but also the idea that this was the greatest crime since the Crucifixion, that also doesn't—strikes—strikes me as unreasonable."[55] British historian A. L. Rowse found Watergate (in the summer of 1973) a matter of "secondary or tertiary importance" that should be overlooked in relation to Nixon's important and valuable foreign policy. Other Britishers, including historian A. J. P. Taylor and legal scholar Arthur Goodhart, agreed.[56] Soviet leader Leonid Brezhnev in 1976 was reported to still admire Nixon and to be unable to understand what Nixon did that forced his resignation.[57]

I have found this incomprehension itself mystifying, a secret about Watergate deeper than Deep Throat and more compelling than the question of what the burglars were looking for. Why don't foreigners understand?

There seem to be several likely answers. One is that ours is a government where "checks and balances" and separation of powers are essential to the deepest core meaning of the Constitution. These features, the heart of our system, are for others bizarre and incomprehensible. Parliamentary governments are designed for unified government action as, of course, are nondemocratic governments. American constitutional government was born out of the Founding Fathers' deepest antipower instincts, to prevent hasty decision, to place checks on tyranny, and for better or for worse to hamstring executive authority.

That this is so, and that it is to conscientious Americans a sacred trust, is something foreigners do not generally fathom. Those catchphrases that are inescapable in elementary- and secondary-school American history courses—"checks and balances," "separation of powers," "separation of church and state," "freedom of the press," "executive, legislative, and judicial branches of government"—all speak to America's institutionalized anxiety about unitary and tyrannical political power.[58]

A second answer features less the constitutional peculiarities of the American system than the moral and puritan peculiarities of the American temper. We Americans simply expect our government and in particular our president to be virtuous as well as effective. We expect government policies to be moral as well as expeditious. This is not to say that other peoples expect their governments to be immoral, but there may be an unusual American spirit that the government is expressive of and representative of its people and that we cannot think well of ourselves if we cannot think well of our leaders. An Englishwoman told American political analyst Robert Goldwin that Watergate confirmed her view that Americans suffer from "moral greed." She and Europeans generally, Goldwin observes, thought that in Watergate "we were denigrating ourselves excessively."[59] If this is so, it may not be moralism deep in the American psyche, although I would not entirely discount (or entirely denigrate) this, but peculiarities of our political structure that require an attitude to the president different from European attitudes to their leaders. In the United States, the people are in a strong sense truly represented by the president. This can be said of neither king, who rules without representing, nor prime minister, who represents a party, not a people.[60]

Indeed, this suggests a third answer: Europeans treat the president as if he were a prime minister while Americans treat him as a democratic monarch.[61] David Riesman remarks that the American president is "our substitute for royalty." The president is encouraged "to transcend the ordinary and day-to-day," especially in a country where politicians have often (at least since the Progressive Era, this was not an invention of Jimmy Carter or Ronald Reagan) campaigned "against politics" itself. There is, Riesman added, "a mystique about the office of the President of the United States which is closely associated with the way in which Americans are tempted to turn questions of group or national interest into questions of morality."[62] The president represents, as no prime minister does, the nation and its peculiar sense of moral mission. British historian Hugh Trevor-Roper came to understand the seriousness with which Americans took Watergate when he compared Nixon to Charles I, not to a British prime minister: Watergate was about the limits of presidential power, not about a burglary, just as the English civil war was about the extent of the king's power, not about the ship-money tax that helped bring on the civil war: "No doubt, in the 1630s, foreigners thought the English very foolish to make such a fuss about ship-money when a firm and unhampered English government might have been effective in Europe. But the English thought first of their own liberties; and who shall say that they were wrong?"[63] It may have been Richard Nixon's central failing to think that the presidency belongs to he who occupies it and not to the culture. The "system that worked" to cut short Nixon's presidency was, and is, as much a system of cultural expectations about presidents as a constitutional system of legal constraints upon them.

Somewhere in the conjuncture of these answers is an explanation of Europeans' incomprehension of Watergate. The exceptional nature of the American political system with its separation of powers, its symbolically potent presidency, and its high regard for moral argument is difficult for foreigners who have not studied this society to grasp. This, at least, seems nearer the truth than the kinds of answers I have more often heard—ones that strangely get into explaining how Europeans are more sophisticated than Americans about scandal and that in France it is perfectly acceptable for leading politicians to have mistresses. I do not understand what the sexual morality of Europeans has to do with an incomprehension of Watergate. What this amounts to, in however addled a fashion, is an effort to link European incomprehension to something anthropologically deeper than formal political structures, something in the folkways and mores of a culture rather than something in its political institutions. There is a reluctance to see that politics in distant Washington, and Constitution-writing in the historically distant world of the Founding Fathers, influences not only the technical details of "how a bill becomes a law" but also the American heart, and what evokes anger or distress within it.[64] Politics is a part of culture, too.

Still, defining just what Americans expect of presidents or other elected officials is not easy to pin down and is not fully detailed in the Constitution. Watergate taught us that we could not trust Richard Nixon. But, as a government of "laws and not men," how could this come as a surprise? Do we not automatically distrust politicians? And if distrust of politicians is second nature, then what led to such fits of moral outrage in Watergate?

Americans do distrust politicians. That's what checks and balances are about. But American distrust is not simple. As Judith Shklar has observed, "One of the reasons why foreigners often fail to understand why Americans felt so betrayed by Richard Nixon is that they do not understand the importance of trust even in a political climate in which distrust is endemic."[65] In a democracy, particularly in American democracy, distrust is built in and maintained by law. But trust is also built into the culture and maintained by symbol, story, custom, and expectation. This cultural or symbolic dimension of trust and distrust centers on the president. As Shklar puts it, "representative democracy depends on a fine balance between trust and distrust, with the fear of betrayal lurking in just those places where trust is most hoped for."[66] In our system, people want to be able to trust most of all in the presidency. The president and the Supreme Court (but not the Congress) are expected to be, in American political culture, "like Caesar's wife and the British royal family, 'above suspicion.' "[67]

At the same time that we expect the president to be above suspicion, we assent to the proposition that "power corrupts" and "absolute power corrupts absolutely" (even though what Lord Acton wrote was that "power *tends to corrupt* and absolute power corrupts absolutely"). In fact, it is not so simple. Arnold Rogow and Harold Lasswell make a striking case that a number of American presidents who showed no moral compunctions in their rise to power were transformed into public servants of integrity by the expectations of the office. Chester Arthur, for instance, a product of New York Republican machine politics, though promoted to office by powerful and unscrupulous allies, sought in office to maintain the dignity of his position, refusing patronage demands of his New York Republican cronies, vetoing pork-barrel legislation, and abandoning his opposition to civil service reform to help pass the Pendleton Act.[68]

In the 1960s the presidency was widely idealized. To no one's surprise, studies disclosed that the president was the best-known figure in American politics, was greatly respected, and very favorably regarded by children. Adults, too, despite fluctuations, normally admired presidents, and they rallied around the president particularly in moments of international crisis.[69] Even so, the ambivalence Judith Shklar points to turned up well before Watergate, for instance, in the approval for strong presidents coupled with wide support for the constitutional amendment limiting a president's tenure to two terms in office.[70]

When it is said in Nixon's defense that others committed the same crimes, only Nixon got caught, there is truth in this. The "getting caught" is a central part of what happened. If trust is betrayed and we never know it, no sense of betrayal can arise. The wonderful, horrible accident of Watergate is that the general public and its representatives learned enough about how devastatingly trust had been abused to feel betrayed. The sense of betrayal went deep enough to raise in its wake the post-Watergate morality that, even in its now-attenuated form, shapes political life to this day.

Post-Watergate morality has had perhaps more critics than friends. It is said that post-Watergate journalists hold public officials to unreasonable standards of behavior and our culture unleashes them to pry into affairs that are neither their nor the public's business (see chapter 6). It is said that government is increasingly run by litigation, by prosecution, and by the judiciary, where what should be political decisions forged by consensus become legal decisions, made by technical judgments in response to litigation-happy prosecutors and pressure groups (see chapter 5). Political scientists Benjamin Ginsberg and Martin Shefter argue that "revelation, investigation, and prosecution" is a major new form of political combat made possible by a strengthened national news media and assertive federal bench.[71] Suzanne Garment fears that our politics have been overtaken by a "scandal machine."[72] People of merit are said to be discouraged from seeking public office because the scrutiny that post-Watergate journalism and post-Watergate disclosure laws would force upon them is more than they are willing to bear. "How are we going to get people into public office if we are going to make their life a nightmare when they get into public office?" Sen. John C. Danforth asked in the wake of the Bert Lance affair in 1977. "I'm very concerned about what's happening to government. I think we're eating ourselves alive."[73] The issue persists today. It is said that "ethics" has become a political weapon more than a genuine subject for public policy and that what was a "healthy concern with government ethics" may have turned into "an unhealthy obsession."[74]

This criticism is powerful. Through it, versions of Watergate are re-argued and renewed. If Watergate was a constitutional crisis, then post-Watergate morality is salutary, even if specific pieces of post-Watergate legislation can be criticized as excessive. But if Watergate was a scandal, then post-Watergate morality may be judged part of the extended run of its Congress and media show, a performance in which incumbents demonstrate their ethical uprightness to easily dazzled voters while journalists display their investigative zeal in a way that does more to polish their own reputation for brave independence than it does to improve the state of the nation. In my own view, there is truth on both sides of this argument. Because Watergate was both constitutional crisis and scandal, not one or the other exclusively, post-Watergate morality has been both laudable legal and moral corrective *and* dubious histrionics.

Changing expectations of political behavior, changing guidelines about the bounds of acceptable public discourse, and changing demands about our political institutions and the incumbents who make them run are a legacy of Watergate. These expectations surface occasionally in explicit reference to the Nixon years, but they are deeply engrained by now, operating underground, in the substratum of political culture. Our expectations about political life, and the language in which we are able to express them, both carry the past of Watergate into the present.

These resulting expectations and anxieties about politics are paradoxical. Not only is there an increased demand for higher morality in politicians, but there is lowered confidence that it will be forthcoming or, at least, less sense of shock when accusations of misconduct turn out to be true. This is especially true of the president. "Impeachment" of a president was not a part of the political vocabulary in 1972. To call for impeachment of a leading political figure was something generally associated with extremists or political cranks, like the John Birch Society's call for the impeachment of Chief Justice Earl Warren. Watergate changed this; there was now nothing, it seemed, a president might not conceivably stoop to. Impeachment was quickly on people's minds with Iran-contra, while in Watergate it became thinkable only after eighteen months of running battle and streaming revelations. But this is just one piece of the impact of Watergate on Iran-contra, a set of events that provides the single best case study of Watergate's enduring influence on American political culture.

CHAPTER 9

Memory Ignited:
The Metaphor of Watergate in Iran-Contra

ARLY IN NOVEMBER 1986, THE AMERICAN PRESS LEARNED FROM A LEBANESE magazine, *Al-Shiraa,* of American arms shipments to Iran. It quickly became apparent that the Reagan administration had been secretly selling arms to Iran to secure the release of Americans held hostage in the Middle East. More than two thousand TOW antitank missiles had been shipped to Iran with the understanding that Iran would arrange the release of American hostages in return. This was a violation of both administration policy and American law.

On its own terms, the arms-for-hostage policy had been a dismal failure. During the period of the arms-for-hostage deal, three hostages were released while three others were kidnapped. In larger terms, the policy was soon to be a major disaster for the Reagan administration. At first, President Reagan issued fumbling, false denials of an arms-for-hostage deal. His first instinct, Watergate notwithstanding, was to say little and hope the matter would blow over.[1] "How was it possible," *Washington Post* analyst Haynes Johnson wrote a few months later, "for anyone who occupied the White House in the 1980s to forget the lessons of Watergate?"[2]

But if Reagan had learned nothing from Watergate about respect for the law or the dangers of covert operations, his advisers learned a lot about how to respond to a major, potentially devastating, embarrassment. By mid-November there was growing suspicion in Washington of a "cover-up." Oliver North recalls that the administration's strategy in November was clearly that "this must not become another Watergate."[3] Attorney General Edwin Meese and his aides were "haunted" by the Watergate cover-up, as Theodore Draper puts it, and were "determined at all costs to avoid a repetition."[4] They feared that before they themselves made it public the *Washington Post* or another newspaper would discover that money earned from the arms sales to Iran were being secretly funneled to the Nicaraguan "contras" in their war against the Sandinista government. And so, on 25 November, realizing that this second cat could not long be kept in the bag, the president announced that Admiral John Poindexter was resigning, Lt. Col. Oliver North was fired, and the Department of Justice was investigating. Attorney General Edwin Meese then put the diversion of funds to the contras on the public record himself. Three weeks later, Lawrence Walsh was appointed independent counsel to investigate Iran-contra. The Nixon administration had waited ten months before extracting the resignations of H. R. Haldeman and John Ehrlichman, eleven months before appointing a special prosecutor.

Americans in Congress, in the media, in the White House, and in the general population saw the Iran-contra affair through the prism of Watergate. Already on 27 November the MacNeil-Lehrer News Hour spoke of "Iran-Gate."[5] Many columnists argued that the differences between the two events were far greater than the similarities, almost as if they had read Susan Sontag and were talking "against interpretation," warning of the oppression of a mistaken metaphor.[6] But they were inevitably drawn to the comparison, whether to endorse it (*The New Republic* declared "This is Watergate") or to criticize it (Tom Wicker wrote of "Two Different Gates.")[7] How people spoke of Iran-contra and how they refused to speak (the Congress wary of using the word "impeachment," the administration wary of invoking "executive privilege") was shaped directly by the recent memory of Watergate.

The power of the memory of Watergate was transmitted in a variety of ways. Through the careers of people who had been involved in Watergate or for whom it had left important lessons, through the Watergate-generated expectations people had come to have of the investigative skills of Congress and the press, through the almost visceral recall of the traumatic disruption of Washington life and national government Watergate occasioned, Watergate made its mark on Iran-contra. Though people may generalize lessons of the past to novel experiences they encounter, they most readily bring past experiences to bear on present situations that closely resemble the past.[8] People had to force the Korean bribes in Congress or Billy Carter's dealings with Libya into a "Koreagate" or a "Billygate," but scarcely anyone denied that Iran-contra had the proportions of a Watergate-size crisis. Indeed, one commentator after another pronounced Iran-contra a more serious and threatening set of events than

Watergate. In this way, not only was the unfolding of the Iran-contra scandal shaped by the ways Watergate remained in the public memory, but Watergate was revived in public memory, and to some extent reconfigured, because Iran-contra summoned it. This is a point that merits emphasis: It is not that people who forget the past are condemned to relive it but that people who live under conditions and remain allegiant to values obtained in the past are fated—for better and for worse—to keep the past in mind.

Once evoked—more than evoked, ignited—the Watergate memory became a powerful frame for examining Iran-contra. Principal players in the Iran-contra affair had been players, or close onlookers, in Watergate, too, and strong personal recollections shaped their action. Key institutions—the White House staff, the Congress, and the news media—had memories of their own. In culture or public discourse, Watergate served as a metaphor through which both insiders and onlookers came to understand Iran-contra. Watergate seems to have been what psychologist Jerome Bruner has called a "pre-emptive metaphor," a past, traumatic experience so compelling that it forces itself as the frame for understanding new experiences, even as it ensures a misunderstanding of the new experiences.[9] How did this persistence of vision of Watergate shape the unfolding and outcome of Iran-contra?

Watergate was more than a metaphorical framework, of course, for Iran-contra. It was also the legal framework. At the end of 1974, Congress passed the Hughes-Ryan amendment to require the president to personally "find" necessary any intelligence-community covert operation and to inform relevant committees in the Congress of the finding in short order. The provisions of this act were revised in the 1980 Intelligence Reorganization Act, still requiring the making of a "finding" and requiring timely congressional notification of it. A majority on the House Intelligence Committee wanted to pin down language to insist on prior notice but, deferring to a Democratic Senate and Democratic president, compromised on vaguer language. Rep. Louis Stokes later recalled that the argument for vagueness was that the memory of Watergate would keep presidents from withholding notification of covert action from Congress and that it was better "to proceed on the basis of an expectation of trust, rather than pursuant to a strict statute." In 1988 Stokes, speaking then as chair of the House Intelligence Committee, said, "And now I am here today, and, as Yogi Berra said, 'It's déjà vu all over again.' "[10]

A second legal legacy of Watergate to Iran-contra was the independent-counsel law. The prosecution of key Iran-contra figures, notably Oliver

North and John Poindexter, was undertaken by special prosecutor Lawrence Walsh, appointed under the provisions of the Ethics in Government Act of 1978.

There was a continuity of personnel as well as of legal mechanisms. There was continuity in the careers of people in the administration, the Congress, and the news media. Howard Baker, the ranking Republican on the Ervin Committee, became President Reagan's chief of staff after the Tower Commission report on Iran-contra helped make the position of then chief of staff Donald Regan untenable. Regan made the decision in November 1986 to cooperate fully with congressional inquiries, a policy that the free-lance conservative consultant Michael A. Ledeen, who served as an intermediary with the Israelis in setting up the arms-for-hostages plan, judged a "panicked" response. Ledeen has criticized Regan and his successors, Baker and David Abshire, for cooperating with the Congress rather than undertaking a direct investigation of their own. Abshire, an ambassador to NATO who was recalled to manage relations with the Tower Commission and the Iran-contra committees, had been assistant secretary of state for congressional affairs at the time of Watergate. Like Regan and Baker, he saw the Reagan presidency at stake. "Both Baker and Abshire had lived through Watergate," Ledeen observes, "and . . . assumed they were involved in a rerun of that trauma."[11] The policy of full cooperation with the Congress seems to me more realistic than panicky. In any event, it was certainly pursued with the breath of Watergate on the back of the administration's neck.

Patrick J. Buchanan, a speech writer close to Richard Nixon and one of the last loyalists in Nixon's final days in office, was communications director in the Reagan White House from early 1985 to early 1987. While he became a prominent voice in celebrating the heroism of Oliver North, he also recognized immediately that the Iran arms deal seriously jeopardized the administration. He advised Regan that it could impose "deep and permanent damage" on the administration. "The story will not die until some much fuller explanation—giving our arguments—is provided."[12] Larry Speakes, press secretary to Ronald Reagan, had been appointed a staff assistant to President Nixon in the last few months of the Nixon administration, serving primarily as press secretary for James St. Clair, the president's defense attorney. Speakes was among those who urged President Reagan to quickly acknowledge error in Iran-contra, and he had Watergate in mind as he gave this counsel: "The uproar over Iran reminded me of Watergate; I'm still convinced that if Nixon had taken responsibility and apologized early on, there never would have been an attempt to impeach him."[13] Speakes inherited the Reagan administration's good relations with the press, set up in part by David Gergen, White House director of communications, who left the White House in 1984. Gergen learned from the Watergate years, when he had been an assistant to Nixon speech writer Ray Price, the importance of establishing trust in the administration. He had seen firsthand how stonewalling backfired under Nixon, and he sought to set up good relations with the Washington press corps.[14]

Watergate may have had as much to do with the success of Reagan's first term as with the ignominious collapse of the second. Not only had Watergate weakened the center of the Republican Party, clearing the way for Reagan's conservative candidacy, but staffers who learned from Watergate helped shape Reagan's highly successful relations with Congress and the press. First-term chief of staff James Baker had come to Washington during the Ford administration. With a "personal memory of the forces that destroyed the Johnson and Nixon presidencies," he believed in pursuing policies only when he could enlist support in Congress, the press, and the public.[15] When he left the White House as chief of staff to run the Treasury Department, he was replaced by a much less experienced, much less savvy Donald Regan. He also took with him Richard Darman, who had headed the Legislative Strategy Group in the White House, the "command center" for congressional relations. Darman had been an assistant to Elliot Richardson during Watergate and supported Richardson in his refusal to fire Archibald Cox.[16] People who remembered Watergate helped keep Ronald Reagan out of trouble in his first term; their absence in the second term contributed to Iran-contra.

In the Congress, Sen. Daniel K. Inouye, a member of the Ervin committee, was chairman of the Iran-contra committee. His calm and fair-minded presentation of himself in the Ervin committee was a key factor in his selection to head the Iran-contra investigation. Two senators who served on the Iran-contra committee, William Cohen and Paul Sarbanes, had served on the House Judiciary Committee during Watergate and had voted to impeach Richard Nixon. So had Jack Brooks, who served on the House Iran-contra committee, and Peter Rodino.

Arthur Liman, chief counsel to the Senate Iran-contra committee, had his own connection to the events of Watergate: he served as a consultant to the California Bar Association in their effort to find a mechanism for Richard Nixon to resign from the California bar rather than be disbarred.[17] He served as a counsel in the proceedings that led to Nixon's disbarment in New York; this was, in fact, the only formal judicial proceeding (although a private one) in which Richard Nixon was tried and found guilty.[18]

When Inouye heard Meese's announcement about the diversion of arms-sale profits to the contras, he thought, "uh-oh, here we go again." Sen. Warren Rudman had the same reaction: "This is going to be a disaster," he told a fellow Republican, Sen. Paul Laxalt. "As a matter of fact, it's a lot like Watergate, Paul."[19] Inouye, selected to chair an investigating committee, told Rudman, selected as ranking minority member, that he didn't want the committee to repeat what he believed to be the mistakes of the Ervin Committee. There would be one professional staff, not separate majority and minority staffs, with a strong effort toward bipartisanship, not partisan bickering. He wanted junior as well as senior members of the committee to have equal opportunity to question key witnesses. In a gesture to promote bipartisanship, Inouye asked Rudman to serve as vice chair of the committee and to preside in his absence.[20] Inouye's efforts to streamline the inquiry also led the House and Senate panels to join their investigation rather than conduct parallel but separate investigations. He sought to avoid the confusion that competing House and Senate inquiries would surely create. This led to the unwieldy size of the committee for questioning public witnesses. Saved by memory from old errors, Inouye created new ones.

Inouye sought also to prevent what he believed to be serious damage to American national interests that the investigation could incur. Lance Morgan, press secretary for the Senate committee, recalls that Inouye emphasized this when they first met and repeated this point in every interview with reporters during the first weeks when he was setting up the committee.[21] Inouye wrote an op-ed piece for the *New York Times* warning that when the American presidency is in crisis domestically, American enemies take advantage abroad. After the Bay of Pigs, the Soviets felt bold enough to place missiles in Cuba; in the midst of Watergate, the Soviets threatened to intervene in the Middle East; eight weeks after Iran seized American hostages, the Soviets invaded Afghanistan. In the midst of Iran-contra investigations, what might the Soviets do next?[22] This view of the linkage of internal deliberative democracy and external exploitation of it called for extreme caution in coming to any conclusions that would weaken this president or his office, and great speed in bringing the investigation to a close.

Where Watergate personnel were not directly involved in Iran-contra in one way or another, they were enlisted as commentators or consultants on it. *Newsweek* called on John Ehrlichman and John Dean;[23] *U.S. News* collected quick quotes from John Doar and several congressmen and staffers associated with the House impeachment inquiry or the Senate Watergate committee.[24] Philip Lacovara, assistant prosecutor for Archibald Cox and Leon Jaworski, compared Iran-contra to Watergate for the *Los Angeles Times*.[25] Richard Nixon himself conferred with President Reagan twice by telephone in the early days of the scandal and spoke publicly about Iran-contra.[26]

There was also continuity in the general public; the public at large instantly saw the parallels to Watergate. In early December 1986, 55 percent of people in a national poll said they thought Iran-contra was at least as serious as the Watergate scandal.[27] In Watergate, Richard Nixon's first notable drop in public approval came ten months after the break-in. In Iran-contra, approval for Reagan dropped 21 percentage points within a week after the connection of the Iran arms sales to the Nicaraguan contras was revealed. Nearly half of Americans said they thought Reagan was lying in his denial of knowledge of the diversion of funds to the contras.[28] In a national poll conducted by the *Los Angeles Times* about the same time, 78 percent of Americans (including 85 percent of Democrats and 69 percent of Republicans) believed there was a White House cover-up and 60 percent felt the incident was at least as serious as Watergate.[29]

The polls provided good political reason for the administration to cooperate with the investigation. The *New York Times*/CBS News Poll conducted 7 and 8 December found that 26 percent of the public thought selling arms to Iran was the worst part of the crisis, 7 percent thought it was using the money to aid the contras, but 51 percent thought it was the way the administration "has handled the facts."[30] But what became the pivotal issue for Nixon—deception and cover-up—faded almost entirely from view for Reagan as the administration adopted a conciliatory stance toward investigators and removed key, high-ranking offenders North and Poindexter.

The polls themselves were a factor in Iran-contra, which they had not been in Watergate, and one much influenced by the Watergate precedent. Polls that showed large majorities of the population believed President Reagan was involved in Iran-contra and was lying when he claimed otherwise strengthened the resolve of the press and the Congress to pursue the matter. In Watergate, as Barry Sussman recalls, "the press had to be its own guide, but in Iran-contra it was hard for editors to say 'we don't want to look into this, nobody cares about it.' People cared about it and they thought the administration was doing really rotten things."[31] The pollsters, then, along with the press, the Congress, the administration, and the general public, had Watergate in mind as Iran-contra broke.

Watergate was the reference point for understanding Iran-contra from beginning to end, even if some analysts argued it was the wrong one. But what follows from this? The omnipresence of the Watergate metaphor does not mean that Iran-contra–era generals were simply refighting the last war. In this case, many of the generals realized they had the last war in mind but kept asking out loud if this was wise. From the beginning, people distinguished as well as compared the two scandals. The question remains: Was the Watergate metaphor consequential?

Some critics have argued that the media or the Congress remembered Watergate too well and were misled by the Watergate analogies they saw. This is based on the widely shared view that Iran-contra was ultimately a more serious and dangerous constitutional breach than Watergate. Critics, themselves guided by the Watergate metaphor, suggest that the failure to arrive at impeachment, the only appropriate constitutional remedy as they see it, is evidence of misperception at best, cowardice and conspiracy at worst.[32]

Scholars Michael Cornfield and David A. Yalof present a case against the press. They argue that "by continually comparing Iran-Contra with Watergate, journalists mitigated the very sense of crisis that their discomfiting news reports had fostered."[33] They see the Watergate metaphor serving the press by providing the framework for a "drama of a president under suspicion."[34] By doing so, it shifted the news from a story about foreign policy to a story about credibility. That made it more appealing because it was more familiar, more containable, more convenient to cover, and more amenable to presenting the media themselves as "watchdog" heroes. As we have seen, however, the credibility question was almost instantaneously the leading question in the public mind; if the media are guilty here, their crime lies in following public opinion.

The performance of the media in Iran-contra was also analyzed and criticized by Scott Armstrong in *Columbia Journalism Review*. Armstrong found the press corps to have been aggressive and effective in the first few months of the Iran-contra scandal but then, after the Tower Commission, it "mysteriously gravitated" toward the one question of whether Reagan knew of the diversion of funds from Iran arms sales to the contras. Meanwhile "reporters who had covered other aspects of the scandal were forced off the front page."[35] Again, the claim is that the Watergate question, "What did he know and when did he know it?" replaced the substantive policy question of how foreign policy should be conducted.

The argument against the Congress criticizes congressional leaders for, at least, failures of strategy and, in more assertive versions, failure of will or conspiratorial collaboration with the administration. This has been seen as another case of Watergate-on-the-brain. Michael Ledeen thought it clear that the Congress was overinfluenced by Watergate: "Just as generals prepared to fight the last war, the Congress prepared to replay Watergate." The consequence, for Ledeen's analysis, is that the Iran-contra committees chose as chief counsels men with courtroom, but not foreign policy, experience. This expressed the committees' Watergate-inspired view that there should be a legal or criminal rather than policy outcome: "The choice of attorneys proved that the committees' primary interest was in criminalizing the process, rather than investigating the many serious policy issues involved in the Iran-Contra affair."[36] Law professor Harold Hongju Koh argues similarly, in the most important evaluation of Iran-contra as a constitutional issue, that the congressional committees mistakenly fastened on the "what did he know and when did he know it" question. That question is of central interest only if impeachment, not policy review and reform, is the issue at hand. The committees' failure to locate a smoking gun "effectively mooted the impeachment question, leading several members to act as if their inquiry were exhausted."[37]

Critics of the handling of Iran-contra work within the Watergate framework as much or more than the Congress or the media they criticize. Thus some critics suppose that the absence of an impeachment means the Reagan administration got off scot-free. But not only were there legal proceedings against Admiral Poindexter (his conviction is on appeal), Colonel North (his conviction was overturned), and other lesser figures in Iran-contra; there was also public exposure through the press, the Tower Commission, and the Iran-contra committees. This severely weakened the Reagan administration in office and permanently marred the administration's place in the history books. Let me be specific.

Reagan's public approval never fully recovered after Iran-contra. In October 1986 his Gallup poll rating of "job performance" was 63 percent approving, 29 percent disapproving. His public approval rating reached a low, after the Tower Commission issued its report in February 1987, of 40 percent approval and 53 percent disapproval. It climbed back slowly thereafter, but never rose higher than 54 percent approval until the last measurement of the Reagan years in December 1988 brought it again to 63 percent.[38]

The power of public exposure—for its own sake—should not be underestimated. Senate counsel Arthur Liman took it to be the great triumph of the Iran-contra committees:

> I saw the capacity of this government, with a President who won 49 out of 50 states, one of the most popular presidents we ever had, I saw this government rise up and expose what happened. I looked at all the scandals that we have had and I say that in history there were many acts that remained buried, and that we live at a time when we are not afraid to put the spotlight

on, and we live in a country in which even on matters that involve or implicate national security in some undefined way like the Iran-Contra affair, we are willing to call all the witnesses before public television, we are willing to declassify tens of thousands of documents, we are willing to let all of the wrongdoing and errors, and lies, hang out there, we are willing to let our people make judgments on the credibility of these witnesses—and their judgments were very negative to the administration—and that to me is a sign of the strength and ethical sensitivity of the society, not of weakness and moral obtuseness.[39]

The Iran-contra committees were not as clear a force for public exposure and public education as they intended to be or as, in retrospect, Arthur Liman claims they were. The issues were confusing, and the committees had no homespun Sam Ervin to put them in comprehensible and epigrammatic terms. But I would not underestimate the power this public example set for high officials in Washington, and would-be high officials, as much as for the general public.

Public opinion forced President Reagan to replace chief of staff Donald Regan with Howard Baker, a chief of staff clearly favored by the administration's congressional critics. Reagan was also constrained in his choices for a successor at the CIA to William Casey and at the National Security Council for Admiral Poindexter. Oliver North's soldierly presence helped keep the Iran-contra hearing from being a complete rout for the administration, but "Olliemania" was much exaggerated; the administration by no means came out ahead in the public mind on the hearings.[40] Even before the hearings, the Tower commission report was a devastating blow to the administration's standing in Washington as well as in the country at large. As Benjamin Ginsberg and Martin Shefter observe, the only major initiatives the Reagan administration took after Iran-contra were ones that "coincided with the agenda of his liberal opponents," notably, arms control.[41] Before 1986 Reagan's vetoes were almost always sustained. After 1986, with the Senate back in Democratic hands and Reagan's public standing shaken, more veto overrides succeeded.[42]

Reagan's postpresidential career was sadly marred by Iran-contra. A man who might have ridden off into the sunset of history stumbled off, instead, his age showing more than his wisdom. Early in 1990, Reagan invoked executive privilege to prevent his White House diaries from being entered into evidence in the trial of Admiral Poindexter. This was not an easy maneuver in public relations terms, whatever its legal validity. The Los Angeles Times noted that Reagan's lawyers tried to avoid using the phrase "executive privilege" because "many still associate that phrase with former President Richard M. Nixon's attempts to disrupt investigations of the Watergate scandal of the early 1970s." Judge Harold Greene asked if the attorneys intended "a formal claim . . . of executive privilege, as that term is referred to in United States vs. Nixon." Attorney Theodore B. Olson, in some pique, replied, "Although the privilege for confidential presidential or executive branch communications has been described by various courts in various ways, no court has declared that the protections afforded the privilege . . . may be invoked only by reciting the phrase 'executive privilege.' "[43]

That was a minor embarrassment compared to what followed. Reagan appeared himself to answer questions. He testified under oath in an eight-hour videotaped deposition. The *Los Angeles Times* reported that he "often looked nervous, lost and even a little frightened" in his testimony, declaring 124 times in the course of eight hours, "I can't remember." The *Los Angeles Times* headline announced, "Reagan Retains Charm But Not His Memory."[44] A charming man, in the end, but very nearly a laughing stock.[45]

The fact that the Reagan administration suffered is scarcely evidence that it suffered enough; Reagan's embarrassment is not evidence that he should not have been impeached. Perhaps the most severe indictment of the Congress came in an article by investigative reporter Seymour Hersh in the *New York Times Magazine* in 1990, "The Iran-Contra Committees: Did They Protect Reagan?" Hersh answers his own question affirmatively. In a set of key decisions, he contends, the committee set up procedures that all but guaranteed Ronald Reagan's immunity. The Congress established an unrealistically short deadline for the committees to complete their work, demanding a full report within ten months. The committees did not make use of material evidence that might have pinpointed presidential involvement: presidential calendars, phone logs, or the tape-recorded phone calls of the president with foreign leaders. The committees made a clear decision to go after the president only for an "act of commission" rather than for acts of omission or negligence. Sen. Warren Rudman told Hersh that only a "conscious diversion" of Iranian arms funds to the contras would have been acceptable as an impeachable offense. And Hersh quotes chief Senate counsel Arthur Liman as saying that you cannot impeach in a nuclear age unless there is a smoking gun.[46]

When Liman made this statement in a debate with Hersh at Brown University in 1988, Hersh took him to task. Liman said he felt the sense of the committee was not to seek an impeachment without an airtight case. The short deadline, he said, while subject to change, was not subject to very much change. No evidence would have led to a successful impeachment unless Admiral Poindexter or Oliver North would incriminate the president, and there was no likelihood of that happening. The committees were determined that the hearings should come to a close before a scheduled summit with the Soviet Union in the fall of 1987. An impeachment inquiry that dragged on would have prevented a summit or a treaty coming out of it. Hersh responded, "What god damned business is it of yours as to the arms control treaty?"[47]

Hersh's report attracted vigorous dissent from Liman but a lot of attention and endorsements from *New York Times* and *Boston Globe* editorials.[48] It also received a reply in the form of an article by Theodore Draper in the *New York Review of Books*, who called it "sensationalism run amok" (as opposed to plain old ordinary sensationalism?).[49] What Hersh failed to acknowledge, I think—and Liman fully recognized—is that the Congress was engaged in an investigative-and-exposing, more than a prosecutorial, function. Liman, along with House counsel John Nields, conducted their inquiry within the framework of a committee unwieldy in size and deeply divided in loyalties. In the end not even one of the six Republican House members of the committee signed on to the majority report, although three of the five Senate Republicans (one of them William S. Cohen, who had served on the House Judiciary Committee in Watergate and voted for the articles of impeachment) went along with the strong indictment of the administration in the majority report. The Iran-contra committees did not choose for themselves an exclusively legal role nor solely a political role nor only a constitutional one, but muddled along with multiple voices and agendas in search of consensus.

So why was Reagan not impeached? According to Arthur Liman, Warren Rudman, and other principal figures in the investigation, he was not impeached because he committed no documented, impeachable offenses.[50] This seems to me disingenuous. A president can be impeached not only for directly engaging in criminal acts but for failing to fulfill his oath of office, failing to see in good faith that the laws of the land are executed. There is no "legal" bar to interpreting impeachment in this light; that is up to the Congress to determine.

In Watergate there was public discussion over what constituted an impeachable offense. Some people argued that impeachment was a political process rather than a legal or criminal proceeding, that the Constitution was intentionally vague in declaring impeachment a remedy for "high crimes and misdemeanors," and that it was therefore left to the Congress to determine for itself what constituted an impeachable offense. Others urged that "high crimes and misdemeanors" meant criminal activity and that no impeachment should proceed without evidence of serious criminal activity that a court of law would recognize. If the president had crossed the rather wavy line dividing executive from legislative power, that would not be grounds for impeachment; if the president in the exercise of his executive responsibilities had abused power, without specifically violating law, that would not be sufficient grounds either.

In Watergate crimes were committed, including most obviously the breaking and entering at the Democratic National Committee headquarters. But cautious voices defined the central question of impeachment, which was, in Howard Baker's memorable phrase, "What did the president know and when did he know it?" Only if the president knew his subordinates were engaged in criminal acts (rather than, more loosely, "dirty tricks") and only if the president knew of the criminal acts either before they took place or soon thereafter during the period when he repeatedly told the American people that White House personnel were not engaged in burglary or other nefarious activities, could impeachment be entertained. Only if hard evidence could be found of this—a smoking gun—should the president ultimately be removed from office through impeachment.

It is one of the interesting silences of Iran-contra that it gave rise to no literature or public discussion of impeachment. In Watergate, Raoul Berger's recently published treatise on impeachment was widely read and discussed.[51] Yale law professor Charles Black published a paperback impeachment primer. There he made it clear that "high crimes and misdemeanors" was not to be reduced to the simple displeasure of the Congress at the policies or practices of the president—impeachment was not a confidence vote in a parliamentary system. Nor did "high crimes and misdemeanors" refer simply to maladministration broadly. Nor did it refer to a president's responsibility for the misdeeds of subordinates; one could not attribute to the president guilt for all acts done by subordinates, Black wrote, because this was "totally incompatible with the flavor of criminality, of moral wrong" in the phrase "high crimes and misdemeanors."[52] The complicated area, Black argued, was that of negligence. Every leader is sometimes careless. The question is when carelessness becomes "so gross and habitual as to be evidence of *indifference* to wrongdoing."[53] Systematic indifference, he argued, as opposed to mere carelessness or oversight, might well be defined as impeachable. In Iran-contra, the Tower Commission labeled Reagan's carelessness a matter of managerial style rather than a criminal pattern of indifference to wrongdoing, but this is a matter of judgment the Congress might well have taken up.

The distinctive "styles" of Ronald Reagan and Richard Nixon did make translating the Watergate precedent to Iran-contra a tricky business. If ever a president would have known what his subordinates were up to, it was Richard Nixon, particularly subordinates involved in campaign activity where his interest was intense and his knowledge detailed. But if ever a president would not have known what his subordinates were up to, even if he had established guidelines of general policy they believed they were carrying out, it was Ronald Reagan. Reagan might well have been negligent in the extreme, grossly and habitually indifferent, but the chances of locating a "smoking gun" in his case seemed remote. In part, this was his manner. In part, it was a lesson of Watergate his administration learned: destroy the evidence. In part, it was that his subordinates, notably Admiral Poindexter, took a ramrod military attitude toward protecting their commander. Perhaps Reagan did not know the details of Iran-contra, but, if he did, there is little doubt that Poindexter would have lied and gone to prison to protect him. John Dean, in contrast, had not been prepared to fall on his own sword.

What did Ronald Reagan know and when did he know it? The prior question is, "Know about what?" Did he know that he was trading arms for hostages in violation of stated American policy? Yes, certainly, despite his later claims to the contrary. Here Watergate reforms made a smoking gun visible. Reagan signed a "finding" 5 December 1985 approving CIA involvement in shipping arms to Iran in exchange for the release of hostages. In a meeting on 7 December 1985, despite objections from Secretaries George Shultz and Caspar Weinberger, who advised him to cut his losses and extricate himself from the Iran initiative, and despite chief of staff Donald Regan's temporarily being won over to this position, Reagan chose to go ahead anyway. On this, Ronald Reagan made his own decision. He signed another finding 17 January 1986, supporting the Iran arms sales against the advice of both Shultz and Weinberger. The "prime mover" in the Iran initiative was Reagan himself. The Congress was not notified in a "timely" fashion of this action; it was not notified at all. So Reagan's action was not only hypocritical but a violation of law. On the diversion of funds from the Iran arms sales to the contras in violation of the Boland amendment, it is unclear what Reagan knew and when he knew it. It is clear only that he established an atmosphere in which aides had reason to believe that the president would approve extraordinary measures to aid the contras, perhaps even illegal measures.

What did he know and when did he know it? Was this in any event the right question to ask? Was it right to be searching for a smoking gun? Iran-contra committee investigator Pamela Naughton expressed some mystification about this: "I never understood why whether or not he knew about the diversion was such a critical issue. Somewhere along the line someone took Howard Baker's line—what did the president know and when did he know it—and framed it into the most narrow concept they could find. Which is really brilliant strategy on the part of White House attorneys." The congressional inquiry began to focus on whether Reagan knew about the diversion. "To me," Naughton recalls, "that was inconsequential. It was damning if he didn't. It was damning if he did."[54] But the Watergate precedent and the Howard Baker question seemed to powerfully color the Iran-contra inquiry. Howard Baker himself had a hand in this. Lance Morgan recalls, "The White House was very skillful, this is Howard Baker, in framing the whole issue as, hey, he didn't know about the diversion and the only thing that was impeachable was the diversion, and all they talked about was diversion, diversion, diversion." This drew attention away, Morgan believed, from the "very substantial constitutional crisis that was going on here."[55]

Richard Nixon's bad luck was that there was a smoking gun; Ronald Reagan's good luck may have been that the Watergate precedent made it seem natural to narrow the question in Iran-contra to the president's direct knowledge of specific criminal activity. The smoking gun, however, to mix metaphors, may have been a red herring. The emphasis on a smoking gun, the *New Yorker* wrote, encourages presidential aides "to break the law in ways they have reason to believe the President would like and at the same time, since they keep the details from him, enables them to provide him with 'future deniability.' " This is a recipe, the *New Yorker* concluded, for "government by plebiscite and junta. Every four years, we are to provide some leader with an immensely broad 'mandate,' and he will then leave it up to his colonels and admirals to carry out his programs in any way they see fit." And so, returning to the Watergate metaphor, the *New Yorker* ends with a plea for the Constitution: "The object in question is the body of the Constitution; when we find it with a hundred stab wounds, there's no point in looking for a smoking gun."[56]

So there is more than the Liman and Rudman way to read impeachment, but clearly they and many others foresaw political barriers to building support for articles of impeachment without a Watergate-style smoking gun. They recognized this long before all the information was in. Nobody wanted to hang Reagan, Senator Cohen told the *New York Times* 14 December 1986. "Nixon was dark, but Ronald Reagan is genial, uplifting, positive. Nobody's out to get him. He still has a reservoir of good will."[57] This is not as different from Watergate as it may seem. People tend to collapse the protracted history of Watergate, forgetting that Nixon was a popular president at the time of the break-in, even at the time of his second inauguration half a year later. Though he had enemies, to be sure, he had powerful allies, too, and so did "the presidency" in general. Nixon had strong support in the Congress until very late in the game; only the agonizingly extended course of events, with the repeated lies and denials from the White House that became more and more transparent, with more and more administration officials under indictment or found guilty of crimes, with more and more outrageous "surprises," finally eroded Nixon's position.

Moreover, where both the Ervin committee and later the House Judiciary Committee had renegade members willing to go out on a limb, to be outrageous, and to push the investigation, the Iran-contra committees were composed almost exclusively of congressional "heavies," responsible to a fault. There were no wild cards. Senator Inouye's insistence on a dignified procedure and the decision of House Democrats to choose committee chairs as members of the committee emphasized responsibility and caution from the beginning. The only incautious decision may have been to set a time limit for the investigation. This badly strained the investigating staffs and forced questioning of witnesses by legislators and staff not prepared for it.[58]

The size of the committee also led to the televisual impression, as Liman put it, that "Congress was both the interrogator and the judge," and many observers feel that this gave public viewers a sympathy for witnesses, particularly Colonel North, that further weakened any possible move for impeachment. Committee members felt undermined by the way they were perceived on television and particularly by the public approval for Colonel North during his testimony. Members were "so overwhelmed by his popularity, they declined to ask him some of the tougher questions drafted for them by the staff," according to a *New York Times* postmortem on the committee.[59]

So there are many reasons why Watergate ended in articles of impeachment and Iran-contra did not. Perhaps the strongest testimony to the power of the Watergate precedent is that the question itself is so often posed and the absence of impeachment so often taken as cause to indict the Congress and perhaps the media as well. But even now I have scarcely catalogued all the differences between Watergate and Iran-contra and, indeed, have neglected several of the most important ones. Watergate exploded six months before Nixon's reelection to a second term and heated up just a few months after he took the oath of office for a second time. In contrast, Iran-contra came out with just two years remaining in Reagan's second term. People remembered the ways in which Watergate had gummed up the work of government for two years and were reluctant to face that again.[60] Also, Reagan's policy of aiding the contras, even if carried out by unconstitutional means, served objectives that many Republicans and some Democrats in Congress were ready to defend. Nixon's misdeeds, in contrast, served no specific policy goals. Most important of all, whatever high crimes and misdemeanors occurred in Iran-contra, they were in the realm of foreign policy where the president ordinarily is granted considerable leeway, and they were undertaken by a president who sought to promote policies he believed in. They were not domestic crimes and misdemeanors in realms the Congress and the public monitor more closely, undertaken by a president intent on the self-serving objectives of his own reelection, the punishment of his "enemies," and the protection of his friends who committed crimes.

I think it's hard to imagine a cogent case that President Reagan did *not* commit an "impeachable" offense even if he did not directly and knowingly sanction illegality. He either set down policy to pursue getting the hostages back in ways that violated administration policy and laws governing covert operations and set down policy or established the atmosphere conducive to aiding the contras regardless of the will of Congress, or his "managerial style" was one of such grotesque negligence as to constitute a pattern of indifference. Either way, he laid the groundwork for foreign policy by secret junta.

In a sense, Reagan seems to have been both actively culpable and passively negligent. There is nothing to suggest his subordinates were violating his policy goals; they were in fact carrying them out. And there is everything to suggest Ronald Reagan did not know or want to know the details. If Nixon's presidency was a tragedy of overreaching ambition, of a fatal flaw and a mean spirit and of great opportunities lost, Ronald Reagan's presidency was an embarrassment. Marx's famous dictum is all too well illustrated, that history repeats itself, the first time as tragedy and the second time as farce.

This does not mean that either the congressional committees or the press failed in their duties. There were multiple reasons not to push Reagan from office, including the powerful fact that not enough votes could be mustered in the Congress to do so, no matter what the Iran-contra committees arrived at.

The character of Iran-contra may make us reconsider what was at issue in Watergate itself, making it clear, for instance, that Watergate was not in any conceivable way about national security. In light of a case where national security is plausibly involved, it is easier to recognize how disingenuous was the "national security" defense President Nixon has offered (and in the Richard M. Nixon Library and Birthplace still offers) for Watergate. At the same time, Iran-contra clarifies why the House Judiciary

Committee had been able to arrive at a bipartisan consensus on three articles of impeachment while failing to pass two others, especially the one that sought impeachment for the Nixon administration's carrying out a secret war in Cambodia. Neither in Watergate nor in Iran-contra was there a congressional consensus for strictly cutting back on presidential prerogatives in foreign affairs. We retain a system, oddly enough reinforced by both crises, of what Theodore Draper calls a "bifurcated presidency," where presidential action domestically is constitutionally limited while presidential action in foreign affairs may be arbitrarily exercised.[61]

In that sense, the Watergate and Iran-contra outcomes are more alike than may at first appear; both underwrite presidential prerogative in foreign policy. But part of the Watergate legacy is an expectation or demand for a fearless, aggressive press and a fearless, aggressive Congress. It is a demand for institutional heroism when presidential heroes turn out, at best, to have feet of clay or worse, to be chest-deep in the committing, condoning, or enabling of constitutional subversion. The Congress did not conspire to prevent Reagan's impeachment, but it did agree, by both intention and chance, not to insist on it.

What remains to be understood is not that President Reagan was not impeached but that President Nixon, for all intents and purposes, was. How could that have happened with a press that normally takes its cues from government officials? With a Congress that, even when roused for an investigative procedure, can rarely muster a stirring conclusion to it? With a judiciary that warily keeps a distance, whenever possible, from constitutional struggles between the executive and the legislature? And how, in Iran-contra, then, could critics have come to expect the press to be not only a watchdog but a bulldog that would not let go its prey? How could so many critics have come to expect the Congress, not even conducting an impeachment inquiry and scarcely the storm center of focused, univocal action, to bring a president to his knees without scorchingly good evidence, time to build public support, administration blunders to exploit, and a strategy to arrive at bipartisan consensus?[62]

My answer is that the memory of Watergate provided an irresistible metaphor to guide public discourse and public expectations about Iran-contra. Because Watergate was so traumatic, it proved no ordinary frame of reference but a "preemptive" metaphor that kept the administration from making the kind of errors that could have turned a scandal into a rout, instilled in the Congress a cautiousness about pursuing the president, and inspired in critics an expectation of decisive congressional action and media heroics.

It is possible to argue that actors in the Iran-contra drama manipulated the memory of Watergate to serve their predetermined policy objectives. Perhaps administration officials were not guided by Watergate as a preemptive metaphor but presumed that others would be. Officials who believed in cooperating with congressional inquiries then simply cried, "Watergate! Watergate!" to gain a rhetorical edge for decisions they had calculated independently. Perhaps Howard Baker cynically manipulated public discussion by reviving his "what did he know and when did he know it" question, centered on the diversion. Perhaps congressional leaders did not worry about creating national and international turmoil by pursuing impeachment of Ronald Reagan because they remembered Watergate but remembered it to gain a rhetorical advantage to pursue their predetermined aim of curbing their inquiries short of impeachment. This kind of argument, consistent with an "interest" theory of how people use the past, suggests that Watergate was a precedent people used in a calculated fashion to achieve personal or policy objectives shaped only by a shrewd assessment of the present situation. The past, in this view, is just another weapon in an arsenal of contemporary political conflict.

It is not an argument to dismiss out of hand. Certainly people use the memory of Watergate for rhetorical advantage and have sometimes done so in a calculating manner. But if there could ever be a demonstration that such a thing as a collective trauma exists in national affairs, apart from wars, depressions, and revolutions, Watergate would seem to be such a case. And if there could ever be a proof that the reignited emotional intensity of a past event shapes calculation, as much as calculation calls up some appropriate object from the past for rhetorical purposes, Iran-contra would seem to be such a case. The immediate recognition in the administration, the media, the Congress, and the public that Watergate, and nothing else, was conjured up by Iran-contra, was too instantaneous a reflex for calculation to have been at work. The self-conscious way in which administration officials sought to "apply lessons" from Watergate seems clearly the result of a quick, even panicked, search for guidance in events of living memory rather than a clever appeal to some common memory to legitimate a settled course of action.

If "interest theory" is not entirely persuasive in explaining the impact of Watergate on Iran-contra, might a cultural theory be better? It could be argued that the invocation of Watergate in Iran-contra was determined not by the power of Watergate's memory but by American culture's long-standing inclination to translate political complexities into moral simplicities. Then the emergence of post-Watergate morality and its application in Iran-contra would represent not a change in American politics but an intensification of one of its most deep-seated tendencies.

But what imagineable unfolding of Iran-contra would *not* be consistent with an established feature of American politics? Cultural inclinations are broad; historical outcomes, singular. Post-Watergate morality reawakened one American tradition—"good government" moralism—but not others, say, anti-intellectualism or the reputed American genius for compromise. Cultural traditions set outside limits within which the Iran-contra affair was confronted, but the well-remembered trauma of Watergate directed matters within those bounds. Watergate thereby helped both to restate and to reshape American political culture.

If the world of 1986 and 1987 had been a very different one from the world of 1973 and 1974, if post-Watergate reforms and morality and evaluations of the presidency and foreign affairs had changed radically enough so that the president could no longer presume a long leash in the conduct of foreign policy, and Congress would no longer grant him one, then there might not have been an Iran-contra affair and a reawakening of Watergate. If the world had changed enough, Watergate would have settled much more quickly into the dustbin of history. What keeps Watergate alive in collective memory is that the political conditions that gave rise to it are still with us. The world is in essential ways the same. George Washington remains prominently commemorated even after two hundred years not so much because of inertial power in the commemorative activities that have been established but because "the values he stood for in the late eighteenth century remain central to the political culture of the late twentieth century."[63] Nothing keeps the memory of the Holocaust more vital than the continuing presence of anti-Semitism, and nothing keeps the memory of American slavery more alive than continuing racism. Similarly, nothing keeps the memory of Watergate more alive than the continued vulnerability of the Constitution to the executives capacity and willingness to work outside the written law and consensual understandings of it.

CHAPTER 10

Memory Besieged:

Richard Nixon's Campaign for Reputation

How is he doing at the tidy-up, after the fuck-up and the cover-up? Not badly, I would say. The past disposes of itself in this country, except for the high points. So Nixon wore the wrong makeup once, and another time he got drunk and chewed out the press. Big deal. It's hard to convey the rich self-revelation of these moments to a generation that wasn't around at the time. All Nixon has to do now is flatten things out to the level where he has some company, where he's no worse than your average politician, and then murmur "Russia" and "China," and he's in. So far, time's bulldozer and his have done a pretty good job—except for one item: Watergate.[1]
                                                                          —Wilfrid Sheed

Will Richard Nixon be rehabilitated? Or, perhaps more accurately, will he be rehabilitated *again*? One of the notable features of Nixon's career has been his rise from defeat and his refashioning of a public image of himself: the "new Nixon" or the "new new Nixon." Could there be, after Watergate, yet another "new Nixon"?

Not, as it has turned out to date, without drawing enormous public attention to the very art of fashioning one. If a new post-Watergate Nixon exists in the public mind, it is the image of a man driven to remake his public reputation. The new Nixon is a post-modern one that has given up deeds for images altogether.[2] The question about the enduring reputation of Richard Nixon, the man and the president, is only in part whether détente with the Soviet Union and the opening to China will one day be judged achievements that outweigh the debacle of Watergate and the defeat of the United States in Vietnam. It is now also a question of how much Richard Nixon can be his own historian, how vulnerable history is to interest, and how powerful the manipulation of publicity in a world of continuous media voracity can be. It is a question about the meaning and making of reputations in contemporary life.

"Reputation" is another everyday concept that presumes the power of collective memory to make things happen. No one who has ever gone through high school would doubt that there is such a thing as "reputation" (or "popularity") that dramatically affects how people treat one another and what they expect of one another. A person's reputation is created by others out of his or her demeanor and deeds but also out of others' desire and envy, insecurity and fear, aspirations and hopes, and their partial or mistaken interpretations of the demeanor and deeds about which they weave reputations. Once constructed, a reputation, be it flattering or shattering, acts upon the individual, burdening, uplifting, or shaming, shaping that person's subsequent behavior in the world.

Reputation is a perfect illustration that we inhabit a socially constructed world. Reputation is a social construction based in part on the character of the subject but also on the character of the times and the social groups making use of the reputation, as well as the skill of the subject or that subject's friends or family in promoting and maintaining, or evading and escaping, a reputation over time.

This is demonstrated in several recent works focusing on how reputations are built and maintained.[3] In the most ambitious of these studies, Kurt and Gladys Lang have examined the posthumous reputation of nineteenth-century British etchers. Why did some of them, well regarded in their time, fade from memory? The Langs distinguish between two features of reputation: "recognition," the esteem in which an artist is held by insiders; and "renown," more general or public fame. Many artists who achieve both renown and recognition in their own day do not produce reputations that survive them.

For a reputation to be durable beyond the lifetime of the artist, the Langs cite four key factors. First, the artist can help promote an enduring reputation by producing works numerous enough and easily enough identified to interest dealers, collectors, and curators. Second, survivors of the artist who have an emotional or financial stake in the artist's reputation are critical in acting as the artist's agents posthumously. While a long life is useful to artists' reputations in enabling them to produce many works, a short life has an advantage, too. An artist cut down in the prime of life is more likely "to leave behind bereaved mothers and needy spouses with dependent children; they also leave people in their art world who, aware that life can be unfair, feel the need for some kind of memorial to mark the artist's departure, even if the oeuvre is not, by the usual measures, that extraordinary." Third, a reputation may be enhanced if the artist is linked to well-recognized artistic or literary circles or well-placed political or cultural elites. Being connected with an artistic movement is useful to reputation because "some of the glow from the luminaries then falls on the lesser figures within their orbit." Finally, reputation is also enhanced if there is some symbolic or ideological congruence between the artist and a larger movement or issue. Artists of the past whose work deals with the poor or dispossessed may be remembered or their reputation revived in eras of social reform; earlier women artists are today being rediscovered by feminist collectors, curators, and scholars. The Langs believe these four principles can guide general understanding of what makes for lasting eminence.[4]

Recognition, renown, reputation—these are the social vapors of personal identity that drive people both to achievements and to extraordinary efforts to interpret or reinterpret their achievements and to institutionalize, promote, or preserve the interpretation they favor. Richard Nixon was deeply concerned with his reputation or his public image when he was in office. But Nixon's career shows an unusual disjunction of a long record of active achievement in political office followed by another long record of active refashioning of his reputation during a kind of living, posthumous career. Metaphorically, Nixon died when he resigned the presidency and he has been his own survivor, entrusted to preserve and promote the reputation of the Nixon who died. How well has this survivor done his work?

Has Nixon been rehabilitated in public opinion? The final Gallup poll on whether Americans approved of the way Nixon was handling his office, conducted just days before he resigned, found 24 percent of the public, the lowest single rating since Truman, approving his conduct of office. In February and March 1976, 25 percent of respondents in a Gallup poll evaluated Nixon favorably or highly favorably; 29 percent did so in May. By this Gallup measure, Nixon has had a healthy, if unspectacular, recovery: 35 percent judged him favorably in 1978 and 39 percent in 1987 and 38 percent in 1990. (To get a sense of this comparatively, in the 1987 survey, Ronald Reagan was judged favorably by 62 percent of respondents, Ted Kennedy by 64 percent, Jimmy Carter 70 percent, and Jesse Jackson 51 percent. In 1990 Reagan again scored 62 percent, Kennedy 61 percent, Carter 67 percent, and Jackson 50 percent.)[5]

A Harris poll enables a more discriminating judgment by asking respondents to compare presidents across a number of distinct themes or issues. In 1976, 22 percent of Harris respondents judged Nixon tops among presidents since Franklin Roosevelt in foreign affairs, a higher score than any other president. This went as high as 30 percent in 1981, back to 26 percent in 1988 and 18 percent in 1990. In every year but two when the question has been asked, Nixon comes out first or in a tie for first (Kennedy edged out Nixon in the 1987 poll, Reagan in 1990). Nixon's foreign policy achievements were rated as outstanding from the beginning; the positive evaluation of them today is no evidence of "rehabilitation."[6]

Which president set the highest moral standards? Nixon is listed by 2 percent of respondents in 1981, 1987, and 1988, the best scores he ever received on this question. Who set the lowest moral standards? Sixty-three percent of respondents chose Nixon in 1976. While this dipped as low as 41 percent in 1987, there has never been even a close second, "not sure" usually coming in next with scores ranging from 10 to 19 percent. Still, people may forgive even if they do not forget. In 1975, in a Field poll in California, 51 percent thought Nixon had paid enough penalty, and 44 percent disagreed.[7] According to a 1976 *Newsweek* polling, 35 percent of people thought Ford rightly pardoned him; in 1982, 46 percent; and in 1986, 54 percent.[8]

Sometimes surveys have asked whether people would like to see Nixon play a role in public life. In 1977, 21 percent of people interviewed just after his first televised interview with David Frost (see below) said yes, but it is fair to say that the Frost interview, reviving Watergate's salience for respondents, depressed what would otherwise have been a higher figure. In 1982, 28 percent said Nixon should have a role in national affairs, even though 75 percent judged him guilty of crimes in Watergate. In 1986, 40 percent believed he should play a public role, a substantial increase, to be sure, but one that must be explained in part as validating the fact that Nixon by then had indeed reclaimed a public role.[9]

Public opinion measured by polls is obviously not the only measure of public reputation. Do politicians feel safer appearing publicly with Nixon today than they would have just after Watergate? Do people feel more secure to praise Nixon's presidency than they once did? By such indicators, Nixon's place in the world has certainly been markedly restored. But I think a close look at *how* Nixon's public appearances are publicly discussed will say more about his "rehabilitation" than the simple fact that he makes appearances.

Nixon has self-consciously sought to rebuild his reputation from the day he resigned. Within two weeks, *Newsweek* reported, "he was asking aides for memos war-gaming the restoration." One confidant said, "He has planned all this for years in a very cautious and painstaking fashion."[10] For several years after his resignation, Nixon stayed out of public view. His first break from postpresidency seclusion came in response to an invitation to visit the People's Republic of China in 1976. Ford administration officials expressed irritation and anger, worrying that Nixon's reemergence, just a few days before the New Hampshire primary, could hurt Ford in his primary fight with Ronald Reagan.[11] Sen. Barry Goldwater went so far as to suggest Nixon violated U.S. law (the Logan Act) by making statements in Peking about American foreign policy.[12] *Washington Post* columnist David S. Broder was bitter, seeing in the trip to Peking evidence that "there is nothing, absolutely nothing he will not do in order to salvage for himself whatever scrap of significance he can find in the shambles of his life."[13] The *Washington Post* editorialized on "Mr. Nixon's Kowtow," concluding that the only redeeming aspect of the trip to China "is the evidence it offers of how wise the American people were to drum this disgraced figure out of the White House 18 months ago."[14] The *Post* held that Nixon's visit encouraged the Chinese to believe they could manipulate the United States toward a more pro-Chinese, anti-Soviet policy than the Ford administration was following. The *New York Times*, similarly brusque, editorialized that the visit was in "shockingly bad taste," an inexcusable interjection in China's disagreements with the Ford administration and an unwarranted intrusion in the Republican primaries.[15] Two days after the New Hampshire primary, President Ford said that Nixon's trip "probably was harmful" to him in New Hampshire.[16]

Nixon's first major public appearance came the next year in a series of television interviews with David Frost. There had been reports as early as the spring of 1975 that friends of Nixon's were exploring efforts to organize a television interview for him to cover his growing legal expenses, then reported as reaching nearly $500,000. Nixon called off these initiatives.[17] But he agreed to the Frost proposal, earning a fee of $600,000 for his participation plus 20 percent of the profits.[18]

For Frost, the Nixon interviews were a big and perilous commercial venture. None of the networks would pay Frost's asking price for television rights, so Frost had essentially to create his own network of independent stations (and he denied the networks permission to use excerpts from the interviews in their regularly scheduled news broadcasts).[19] The result was a "media event" of enormous proportion. Weeks before the telecast, transcripts of Nixon White House tapes that had not previously been publicly released were leaked to the press and published in leading newspapers. All three evening newscasts led with the story, and *Time* and *Newsweek* both ran cover stories. The leaks were quickly challenged (by Charles Colson among others) as an effort to build an audience for the

Frost interviews. CBS Washington desk anchor Bruce Morton referred to it as "slick public relations" and "pretty high-class advertising."[20] But if CBS criticized the pre-interview publicity campaign, it also took a piece of that campaign for itself with "60 Minutes" interviewer Mike Wallace interviewing the interviewer, David Frost.[21]

The publicity work paid off. The audience for the first (of four) broadcast interviews was estimated at fifty million with about half of all people watching television tuned in.[22] In this first program, dealing primarily with Watergate, Nixon declared that he "did not commit a crime, an impeachable offense," but added, "those are legalisms." He said, "I let down our system of government."[23]

The Frost interview was the first occasion when Richard Nixon publicly discussed Watergate since the disclosure of the "smoking gun" tape. Nixon admitted to participation in the cover-up, but explained it as an effort to keep from hurting colleagues in his campaign and in the White House. CBS legal correspondent Fred Graham suggested that the news was not in what Nixon said but in the stunned and subdued way he sat when Frost pointed out that one is guilty of a crime regardless of one's motive. CBS called on Rep. Charles Wiggins, one of Nixon's strongest backers in the House Judiciary Committee, for comment: "He said that his motive was benign, namely, to protect the innocent and to contain a political problem. The President is wrong. That's not a defense."[24] Correspondent Graham declared, "legally there's virtually no question that that's not a legal defense. If you attempt to obstruct an investigation—and he admitted that he did, at least for a few days—that's a crime of obstruction—obstruction of justice. And if he had said that in a trial or an impeachment, it's pretty clear that he would have fallen flat on his face."[25]

Bruce Morton, in a commentary on the CBS Morning News, managed an odd sort of journalistic neutrality by criticizing both Frost and Nixon. Frost uncovered nothing new, according to Morton, left key questions unasked, and left important factual matters unresolved; similarly, Morton objected to Nixon's "motive" defense, contrasting his statement to Frost—"I didn't think of it as a cover-up"—with his 22 March 1973 taped comment to John Dean: "I want them all to stonewall it; let them plead the Fifth Amendment; cover-up or anything else, if it will save it—save the plan. That's the whole point." Did Nixon confess as the Frost fanfare suggested? No, he stopped short of admitting guilt. According to Morton, "Last night, he confessed to having heart; confessed to being compassionate; to caring for his friends, to wanting to avoid paying. He confessed to being a good guy, who loves his family and friends and country."[26]

The interview with David Frost stayed front-page news through its four weekly installments in May 1977. At the time, it was news with a special bite. On 19 May the *New York Times* published excerpts from the interview scheduled for airing that night in which Nixon declared that the president had the authority to order burglaries, eavesdropping, and other illegal acts against American dissidents, saying, "When the president does it, that means that it is not illegal." The reporter observed (and the reader could verify by glancing down the page to an adjacent story) that the telecast would take place a day after President Carter called for legislation to prohibit government wiretapping without prior court order.

Nixon did not control the Frost interviews themselves, and he had even less influence over their public reception or the news media's interpretations of them. In 1977 Watergate was recent memory and public property; people played back their own mental transcripts of the Watergate events against Nixon's efforts to present himself in the best possible light, and they found a mismatch.

In public discussion of the Frost interviews, a theme was sounded that came to dominate public accounts of the post-Watergate Nixon: that Nixon, sometimes with the connivance of the news media and the publicity industry, was polishing his own image for history. This meant that commentary, while focusing primarily on Nixon, up to his new tricks, looked also at the mechanics, commerce, and strategy of the nation's publicity machine.

The Frost interviews became a public topic themselves, occasioning news coverage, critical essays, and, ultimately, a book—Frost's own account of the shows.[27] They also evoked some of the first self-conscious, self-critical reflections by people publicizing Nixon who worried over their complicity in keeping his name before the public. David Frost was hurt by press reports that Nixon's own close friends Robert Abplanalp and Bebe Rebozo were his financial backers. But, Frost writes, he understood press skepticism about his enterprise: "A successful Nixon effort at revisionism could have had serious consequences. Had I been his willing accomplice, or (equally dangerous) his helpless victim, as he rewrote history, then abuses of power would have seemed ratified and courageous investigators would have appeared Cassius-like tormentors."[28] James Reston, Jr., a writer who helped Frost prepare the Nixon interviews, worried about this himself. He urged that the interviews probe the idiosyncratic mind and character of Nixon. "He feared," Frost wrote, "that our project could be the launching pad for this return to respectability, a disaster which could be averted only by a shrewd and informed exposition of his diabolical mind."[29]

In January 1978 Nixon's 1968 presidential rival Hubert Humphrey died, and services were held in the rotunda of the Capitol. Richard Nixon's attendance was amply noticed. When the Senate chaplain said, "It is in pardoning that we are pardoned," television cameras visually inscribed the memory of Watergate by focusing on Nixon, his head lowered in prayer. The *New York Times* noted in its front-page story on the memorial service that this was Nixon's first return to Washington "since he left it in disgrace 41 months ago"; there was a separate story inside on Nixon's return.[30]

Nixon waited four years after his resignation before making a live appearance before the general public. He went to a staunchly Republican community of five hundred people, Hyden, Kentucky, to dedicate a federally funded recreation center named for him. CBS News commentator Rod MacLeish said he was "the adored hero" of Hyden and that, whatever else one might say for or against him, Nixon remained "an American obsession." MacLeish called him, "the last vivid occupant of the White House."[31] Nixon gave a speech full of tough talk about foreign policy. He was wildly applauded when, referring to Daniel Ellsberg and the Pentagon Papers, he said, "I believe in freedom of information, but I think it's time we quit making heroes of people who take secret foreign policy documents and print them in the newspapers."[32]

The next major step in Nixon's return to public life was to renew his career as an author. Since his resignation, he has published eight books. The first and most important of these was his memoirs, published in 1978 to largely unflattering reviews. In the *New York Review of Books*, the best John Kenneth Galbraith could say was, "As committee work goes, this book is not badly written." James MacGregor Burns, in a lead review in the *New York Times Book Review*, took a centrist approach to the book, noting that it was part of a construction of a certain image of Nixon: "as we plow through the long narratives we sense always the brooding presence of a man constantly standing guard over his own image. That self-image now is of a President who was a superb foreign policy maker and peace maker, but whose achievements have been unfairly obscured by Watergate."[33]

Burns called the book Nixon's "final appeal to history," not foreseeing a spate of books to follow, plus a presidential library, plus public appearances. And he appears also to have misjudged the book's usefulness, predicting it would be a bible for Nixon revisionists who would cite chapter and verse to defend him. "For Richard M. Nixon and his band of followers it will be the ultimate Survivor's Kit."[34] It has not been used that way; Nixon's critics seem to cherish his memory more, or more publicly, than do his friends.

Autobiography is in the best of circumstances suspect as a window on the past. The autobiography written for a public figure by a ghost writer or, in this case, a ghost committee, is even more suspect. One written not as a final statement on a career but as a keystone in a second career dedicated to justifying the first is more suspect still. Nixon's is what Georges Gusdorf refers to as autobiography devoted exclusively to the public person; such a memoir, he writes, is always to a degree "a revenge on history," in contrast to an autobiography devoted to the private person wherein "the act of memory is carried out for itself, and recalling of the past satisfies a more or less anguished disquiet of the mind anxious to recover and redeem lost time in fixing it forever."[35] Certainly autobiography can be an effort by its author to understand the past, an effort at cleansing or purification. Its value to the biographer grows the more probingly confessional it is. Whatever embarrassment there may be in confession, the autobiographer can then feel he or she has made peace with the past or with his or her god, and may also believe, often rightly, that confession is a public service, enabling others in similar circumstances to understand or face their own unhappy pasts. This is not what Nixon produced. His autobiography is not a confession but a maneuver in his campaign for public sympathy and public acceptance. I think it confesses much more than reviewers at the time conceded, but it is illuminating largely as a further display of Nixon's characteristic public self, not as a peek at what may lie behind it.

In October 1981 Nixon joined Gerald Ford and Jimmy Carter to lead the official American delegation to the funeral of Anwar Sadat in Cairo. In March 1984 he spoke to sixteen hundred businessmen at the Economic Club of New York, where his speech was interrupted twenty times by applause and he received three standing ovations.[36] The American Society of Newspaper Editors gave him a friendly welcome in Washington the same spring, with nearly a minute of "enthusiastic applause."[37] But rehabilitation did not seem authoritatively accomplished until a 1986 *Newsweek* cover declared, "He's Back."[38] He seemed to be. The media paid regular attention to his private life, his aches and ailments, his buying and selling of homes, his daughter's pregnancy, his grandson's christening. He was reported to talk regularly to President Reagan.[39] He was consulted on his views on American presidential candidates.[40] In an article in *TV Guide*, he advised President-elect George Bush on how to handle the media, an act of chutzpah that *Los Angeles Times* TV critic Howard Rosenberg likened to "Dracula promoting a balanced diet."[41]

Nixon's views on China and the Soviet Union have been printed regularly in the media, both here and abroad.[42] His 1989 trip to China was widely covered;[43] in 1991 Nixon traveled to the Soviet Union, with "60 Minutes" tagging along as Nixon dispensed advice in Moscow that the Baltic states should have their independence.[44]

Nixon's "first high-profile visit" to Washington since leaving office was in 1990 when he revisited Capitol Hill. Republican congressional leaders were quick to praise his expert counsel on foreign affairs. Sen. Robert Dole held that Nixon was now fully rehabilitated. So did Secretary of State James Baker. Nixon bantered with reporters who dogged him about the past. Was he at peace with himself? He would not answer. Was his place in history assured? "I think my place in history has to be determined by other people," he replied.[45]

But was Nixon really back? From the moment *Newsweek* certified that he was, rehabilitation, not Richard Nixon, became even more prominently the main subject for public discussion of Nixon.[46] When Nixon published in 1990 a second autobiographical work, *In the Arena*, and gave *Time* an exclusive interview in connection with it, the publisher felt called on to justify such attention: "Why," he asked, "provide a platform for an ex-President who is plainly on a quest for historical redemption?"[47] Those in the news media who have participated in relegitimating Richard Nixon as a public figure clearly do so with second thoughts. And they do not always decide to go ahead. Former CBS correspondent Marvin Kalb, once wire-tapped at Richard Nixon's direction, now running a center for the study of the news media at Harvard, chose not to participate when asked to help with a 1990 PBS documentary on Nixon. "I will not contribute to the perpetuation of this man's prominence. He disgraced the office of the presidency and I don't feel that we should all be so constantly mesmerized." But he quickly added, "And yet, we are. And I am."[48]

In the *Time* interview, John Stacks and Strobe Talbott start right off with Watergate, but, following standard practice, they couch their interest in Watergate as a question about reputation: "How do you expect the Watergate affair to be judged in the future?" Nixon quoted Clare Booth Luce telling him after his trip to China that each person in history can be summed up in a single sentence and that his would be, "He went to China." Nixon said that historians are more likely to write, "He resigned the office." In this, to date, he seems to be correct. "The jury has already come in," he told the reporters candidly, "and there's nothing that's going to change it. There's no appeal."[49]

The culmination, to date, of Richard Nixon's return to public prominence came at the dedication of the Richard M. Nixon Library and Birthplace in Yorba Linda, California, in the summer of 1990. It was a ceremony notable for gathering four living presidents and ex-presidents: Bush,

Reagan, Ford, and Nixon (Jimmy Carter declining to attend). This was a grand media event. Local broadcast treated it that way. So did press photographs. The *Orange County Register*, for instance, displayed on its front page a big color picture of Richard and Pat Nixon receiving yellow roses from a Yorba Linda Brownie Scout. The *Los Angeles Times*'s front-page photo showed three Brownies in the same act of tribute. There was coverage of the ceremonial dinner the night before and of the luncheon of the four presidents at the library. The *Los Angeles Times* even ran a feature story on Salvador Avila, the self-made millionaire restaurateur and Mexican immigrant who, because Nixon has a special liking for Mexican food, catered the event.[50] But the pageantry and hoopla did not altogether displace another theme: "Is this rehabilitation?" The news media performed a rehabilitation and questioned it at the same time. ABC News correspondent Brit Hume opened his report by observing that the gathering of the four living Republican presidents and ex-presidents was occasioned not only by the opening of the library but by "the political rehabilitation of Nixon himself." So much for the self-fulfilling declaration that rehabilitation had already taken place. But then Hume closed his report this way: "At the end a spectacular balloon display worthy of a presidential campaign. Could it be? No, Nixon's 77 after all and there are limits to political rehabilitation even in America."[51] So what the journalist giveth, he quickly taketh away. He is rehabilitated, he is not rehabilitated. He is to be taken seriously, he is fair game for gentle mocking.

Newsweek headlined its coverage, "The Remaking of the President: Nixon Molds His New Library in His Own Image," reminding readers that the 5,500-square-foot building "just seven miles from Disneyland" as yet had no White House papers and would certainly not have the thousands of pages Nixon was suing to keep to himself.[52] It was a Potemkin Village of presidential libraries. The *Chicago Tribune* headline was, "Watergate's a Whisper as Nixon's Glorified at Library Dedication," observing that the presidents' tour of the library sidestepped the Watergate room.[53] The *San Francisco Chronicle*'s reporter joined two thousand first-day visitors to the museum and listened in as an aunt explained to an eleven-year-old nephew what the Watergate exhibit was about. "He almost got in trouble," she told him. "It was a close shave."[54] Nearly every news story noted that President Bush mentioned Watergate briefly in his public remarks and none of the three ex-presidents did.[55] The *San Francisco Chronicle* ran a box headlined, "W-Word Nearly Unspoken at Nixon Library Opening."[56]

ABC's "Nightline" ran a program on "The Resurrection of Richard Nixon." Historian Stephen Ambrose proclaimed the event the end of the rehabilitation story: "He has been, for sixteen years, running for the office of elder statesman, and he's now made it. This library represents his final resurrection, his total recovery from his disaster of 1974." That premature conclusion became the peg for ABC to narrate a history of the successful rehabilitation, even though historian Stanley Kutler later declared on the show that Watergate "is the spot that will not out."[57]

The news stories accompanying the opening of the Nixon Library bear out Kutler better than Ambrose. On 21 July 1990 the *Los Angeles Times* published a stunning story: that the one Watergate tape that the Nixon Library proudly had installed for visitors to listen to, the "smoking gun" tape of 23 June 1972, was heavily edited despite library officials' repeated assurances that the tapes presented at the museum would be left intact. The *Times* ran the full transcript of a portion of the tape, with the portions the library played in boldface and the ones edited out in standard type.[58]

The suggestion in this news story that the library was a continuation of the Watergate cover-up gained plausibility from other embarrassments at the library's opening. Library director Hugh Hewitt told the press that researchers would be screened and anyone seen as anti-Nixon would not be allowed to use the library. Hewitt cited Bob Woodward as an example of someone who would not be admitted. "I don't think we'd ever open the doors to Bob Woodward," he said. "He's not a responsible journalist."[59] Richard Nixon's spokesman, John Taylor, overruled Hewitt two days later.[60] But the damage was done. The *New York Times*'s front-page story on this gaffe opened, "There was one small wrinkle in the planning for the Richard Nixon Library and Birthplace here, one week before its dedication, and it involved a familiar question: What did Mr. Nixon know and when did he know it?"[61]

A more minor embarrassment, but still enough for page 3 in the *Los Angeles Times*, was criticism by Bush administration officials of Nixon's decision to allow only photographers, not reporters, to major portions of the library dedication. The rules were altered, but a White House aide said, "They just don't want anyone asking questions," and a library spokesman explained that it was "a space consideration" only. "We're not dealing with a cover-up."[62]

Still another embarrassment was to follow a few months later. The library's new director, John Taylor, who replaced Hugh Hewitt two months after the library opened, announced that the scheduled installation of the second and third Watergate tapes was being postponed. It was more important to use available funds, Taylor said, to mount a display of Pat Nixon's gowns and to acquire twenty-three Dwight D. Eisenhower oil paintings. Mr. Taylor said of the tapes, "I could have just spent $12,000 or $15,000 and gotten them in. But you've got to ask yourself what is more important."[63]

I have visited the Nixon Library myself four times. On my last visit, in August 1991, I read through pages of comments in the "guest book" displayed in the main entryway. There were occasional notes of objection—"History this isn't!" complained one couple—but most comments were very appreciative. "Our votes were well spent," wrote a couple from Norwood, Massachusetts. "Inspirational for my children," wrote a woman from nearby Riverside, California.

My own response has focused, of course, on how Watergate is presented in the museum. It is not neglected. A long, carpeted corridor, the last section of the exhibit space, is devoted to Watergate. This is a fairly dark, broad hallway. Ceiling lights shed eight spots of light along the way, of increasing size from a few inches in diameter to perhaps two feet across, leading the visitor's eyes up to a full-wall black and white photograph of Richard Nixon waving farewell from the plane as he leaves the presidency behind him. On the visitor's left is an illuminated wall of pictures, photographs, and documents entitled "Watergate: The Final Campaign" with a long panel of commentary just below. It explains that "Watergate is a word that has come to mean many things to many people. What it was before June 17, 1972 was a luxury apartment, office, and hotel complex in Washington, D.C. What it became over the course of the next twenty-six months was a catch-word for every misjudgment, miscalculation, or crime, imagined or real, that had ever been contemplated by anyone even remotely connected with the Nixon Administration." Moving down the corridor, the commentary holds that many people at the time portrayed Watergate "strictly as a morality play, as a struggle between right and wrong, truth and falsehood, good and evil. Given the benefit of time, it is now clear that Watergate was an epic and bloody political battle fought for the highest stakes, with no holds barred." Nixon in Watergate admitted to "inexcusable misjudgments." His opponents "ruthlessly exploited those misjudgments to further their own, purely political goals." As for the famous smoking gun tape available for listeners across the hallway, it was a conversation that lasted "more than an hour and a half," but included only "six minutes of discussion about Watergate." What is their significance? "These six minutes of conversation were and are the only evidence which suggest that President Nixon tried to curtail the investigation into Watergate to protect his people." The commentary holds that if the tape had been disclosed a year before it "probably" wouldn't have been treated as a smoking gun; the commentary acknowledges, however, that at the time it was devastating, and that all dissenters on the House Judiciary Committee changed their votes.

On the visitor's right are three stations with earphones for listening to excerpts from the "smoking gun" tape. The sign above each listening post is headed, "The June 23, 1972 Conversation." The text reads:

> On this recording, President Nixon can be heard approving a suggestion by his staff of a way to limit the FBI's investigation of the Watergate break-in. He also expresses relief at the apparent fact that no one from the White House was involved in the break-in. Then, in a diary note dictated by the President himself less than two weeks later, he describes learning of the FBI's concerns about White House pressure. He tells the FBI to go ahead with a complete and thorough investigation, and he tells his aides not to interfere with the FBI in any way.

The tape recording includes not only bits of the 23 June conversation and Nixon's diary note but extensive commentary on the conversation. It holds that "according to President Nixon's critics," the tape shows evidence of the crime of obstruction of justice. In fact, not just Nixon's critics but *all* of his most ardent defenders on the House Judiciary Committee agreed that the tape showed evidence of obstruction of justice. "Despite its fateful consequences," the commentary continues, "the so-called 'smoking gun' is not what it once appeared to be." Why? This is simply because, first, Nixon had already acknowledged (in May 1973) that he limited the FBI investigation, for legitimate national security reasons; the tape added only that he was "aware of the political consequences of Watergate as well." In fact, there was no national-security reason to limit the FBI investigation, and there is no indication that national security was anything other than a cover for asking the CIA to shoo away the FBI. Second, "no obstruction of justice, no Watergate cover-up occurred as a result of that June 23 conversation" because on 6 July Nixon told the FBI to go full steam ahead. This artfully ignores the fact that two critical weeks of obstruction of justice occurred before the phone call, that the crime of "obstruction of justice" need not persist for some given duration, and that there was bountiful evidence of the crime later, unrelated to the 23 June conversation: presidential approval of hush money to the Watergate burglars, suborning of perjury, and more. But for visitors to the Nixon Library, the recorded commentary frames the edited selections of tape and overpowers them, minimizing the damage the "smoking gun" does to Nixon's reputation.

Before leaving the library, the visitor may stop at a small auditorium just beyond the "smoking gun" tape to "Ask the President" one of perhaps a hundred questions by touching one of two computer screens. Nixon appears on video addressing the visitor's question. Again, Watergate is not ignored; quite a few questions address it:

On the smoking gun tape: "You just don't look at it in terms of words said at a time. You look at it in terms of what you did." And what he did, he says, is to tell the FBI to go ahead with the investigation two weeks later.

"Are you sorry for Watergate?" "There's no way that you could apologize that is more eloquent, more decisive, and more final or . . . which would exceed resigning the presidency of the United States. That said it all and I don't intend to say any more."

"How would you characterize Watergate?" "No one was killed at Watergate. No one profited from Watergate," Nixon replies, contrasting this to Teapot Dome and other presidential scandals. "No election was affected or stolen by it," though he adds that "some believe" the 1960 election was. So what was Watergate? "It was a political shenanigan—wrong, illegal, and very stupidly handled, true."

["If it were 1972 all over again, what would you have done differently about Watergate?" [In the weeks after the break-in,] "I wasn't thinking that much about Watergate. My main concern was about ending the war. . . . Frankly, I just didn't concentrate. That was my mistake." [If this is so, it is only because he believed his close attention to Watergate in the first week after the break-in had resolved the matter. By H. R. Haldeman's account and Nixon's own in *RN*, Nixon spoke about Watergate with Haldeman three times on 18 June and with Colson by phone at least once; on 19 June Nixon devoted three paragraphs in a diary to the topic of Watergate that he claims to have been the farthest thing from his mind; on 20 June he spoke with Haldeman twice and Colson once about Watergate and called Mitchell to discuss it in the evening; on 21 June he discussed Watergate with Haldeman and Ehrlichman; on 22 June with Haldeman; and on 23 June came the "smoking gun" conversation.][64]

Have all of Nixon's efforts "rehabilitated" him? Of course, the story of Richard Nixon is far from complete. There are insiders still to be heard from—Deep Throat, the Nixon daughters or sons-in-law, Alexander Haig. Maybe we will and maybe we won't hear from these people. This is beyond Nixon's control. Not fully beyond his control is whether the public will be able to hear the Nixon of 1972 to 1974 on tape, speaking to us again, unedited, as more tapes and papers are catalogued and made available at the National Archives. Special rules controlling access to the Nixon Presidential Materials went into effect in 1986, giving Nixon the right to contest release of materials as they are catalogued and made ready for public use. In 1987 Nixon contested the opening of fifteen thousand "Special File" documents, a matter still under administrative review. Should Nixon lose in his effort to block the release of these materials, he could take the matter to court.[65]

Nixon's representatives reviewed, but did not file objection to, the release of a number of White House tapes in June 1991. The response in the press was immediate and severe; this was the Nixon so many people had been grateful to see removed from office. On the tapes, Nixon comes across "paranoid, vengeful and mean-minded," according to *Newsweek*, the magazine that had announced Nixon's rehabilitation five years before.[66] *Time* headlined its story: "Notes from Underground: A Fresh Batch of White House Tapes Reminds a Forgiving and Forgetful America Why Richard Nixon Resigned in Disgrace." The tapes remind us, according to reporter Margaret Carlson, that "Nixon is not simply an author and global analyst but an unindicted co-conspirator who is lucky to have escaped prison." The tapes reveal "a deceitful, lowbrow, vindictive character, dangerously armed with the full power of the IRS, FBI and CIA, and all too willing to use it."[67] The *Wall Street Journal* reported that the tapes "recall the dark side of Richard Nixon—nasty, vindictive, profane, sometimes anti-Semitic, almost always on the lookout for ways to protect himself from what he perceived to be his many enemies."[68]

Commentary and news stories played the release of the tapes not as revealing anything new but as throwing a monkey wrench into Nixon's campaign for rehabilitation. The *Wall Street Journal* declared that "the rehabilitation of Richard Nixon hit a little snag yesterday." *Newsweek* asserted that "if Nixon's veneer of rehabilitative statesmanship has made folks forget why he needed Gerald Ford's presidential pardon, the pungent flavor of his unbuttoned chats should bring it back." The *New York Times* noted that sixty-four million Americans, a quarter of the population, had been born since Richard Nixon resigned. These younger people see him as a flickering image "drawn largely from Mr. Nixon's meticulously prepped role as eminence grise—in Beijing with Deng Xiaoping, in Moscow with Mikhail Gorbachev, in bookstores with weighty tomes on global politics or personal struggles. But"—and this is the "but" that constructs each of these stories—"like ordinary men, Mr. Nixon cannot entirely escape his past."[69]

That Richard Nixon can now write and speak and advise in public is a long way from demonstrating that his campaign for reputation has succeeded. His extravagant personal efforts at rehabilitation may demonstrate only the serious limitations a one-man-band faces in rewriting a well-known, well-documented, much cared about, recent and still controversial past. Nixon's reputation is not in any large part his to control. The more he hankers after rehabilitation without confronting what both foe and many sympathetic allies believe to be the shame of Watergate, the more the news media revive the liberal or conservative story of Watergate, drawing attention not so much to Nixon's version of the past but to the fact that he is self-servingly propounding one.[70]

William Safire and Stephen Ambrose both suggested in 1990 that Richard Nixon would appear at the 1992 Republican National Convention to make his rehabilitation complete.[71] By the time this book appears, whether Nixon did or did not speak at the convention will be decided. But either way, his rehabilitation will not be complete, his place in collective memory established in ways no personal effort of his, apart from the confession he has avoided for almost two decades, can dislodge.

Reputation is a valuable commodity. In business a firm's reputation is often treated as a material asset called "goodwill," the value of the brand names of products the firm sells or the value of loyal customers who have come to trust in the firm. The formation of reputation in the marketplace operates where consumers have imperfect information about the products before them, where they cannot fully judge the quality of a product before they put down their money and buy it. In these situations, reputation is a "signaling activity" where past quality is taken as an index of future quality.[72] Reputation is one of those powerful ways in which the past, or a version of the past, fairly or unfairly, exercises power in the present.

People have some power to affect their own reputations, retroactively, but it is limited. Nixon's reputation may shift here and there, but he is quite right that the one-liner that history books are so far bequeathing to him is, "The president who resigned." On reviewing the chronicle of Nixon's postpresidential reputation, the limits to Nixon's success are so striking that one cannot help but raise questions about the widely repeated fears of Nixon's rehabilitation. The reputation of Americans for historical amnesia seems so well established that journalists and social critics are obsessed with a fear of forgetting. Those who monitor Nixon's misstatements and misrepresentations of his past clearly feel they have the moral upper hand as they work to keep the record straight. I applaud their efforts; appalled myself at the treatment of Watergate at the Nixon Library, I have tried here to identify some of its errors.

But at the same time that I join in outrage at Nixon's manipulation of the past, I resist condemning American culture at large for forgetfulness. If we are too skilled at forgetting, we may also be unusually capable of forgiving, and for this there is reason to be grateful. Not Watergate, not even Vietnam became a Dreyfus affair. There is something admirable in Ford's act of pardon, even something to be grateful for in the acceptance of Nixon's provisional reentry in public life. As I toured the Nixon Library, still gnashing my teeth from the Watergate exhibit, I went out through the garden to the restored wood-frame house where Nixon was born in 1913. This is where he lived until he was nine, sharing with his brothers an attic room so small he could not stand up in it. He recalls in his memoirs, and I heard him repeat this in his remarks at the library's opening ceremonies, a vivid childhood memory: "Sometimes at night I was awakened by the whistle of a train, and then I dreamed of the far-off places I wanted to visit someday."[73] I pictured that boy and my mood changed as I approached the Nixon homestead. There is something simple and honest in the wood-frame house, and in Nixon's recollection of it, set off against the attractive, but massive and troubled "lie-brary," as one critic called it.[74] Here is something that gives pause, or should, in the midst of self-flattering feelings of moral indignation. There is something of this plain goodness in Nixon himself, I think, as redeeming as the house he was born in, although he may not know it or believe it, because it is not what he has honored in his own campaign for reputation.

PART III

REMEMBERING, FORGETTING, AND RECONSTRUCTING THE PAST

CHAPTER 11

The Resistance of the Past

BECAUSE IDEOLOGY IS POWERFUL, THE NEEDS AND DESIRES OF THE PRESENT urgent, and the pull of the self and its attachments strong, the past is forever subject to reconstruction and rewriting to accord with present views. That "history" should be so vulnerable often excites a special indignation. Few observations about Soviet intellectual life so powerfully affected American anti-Soviet views in the 1950s and 1960s as the oft-repeated fact that the Soviets rewrote their own (and the world's) history to glorify the Soviet state and the Communist party. There was a joke that it is harder for a Communist to predict the past than to predict the future, it changes so often.

This, of course, is supposed to be one of those things that distinguishes a free society from a totalitarian one. The Soviets rewrote history to accord with ideology; the West, in contrast, wrote history in unswerving allegiance to truth. We were saved, and the past protected, by the freedoms of a liberal society.

But today, more than forty years after George Orwell's Ministry of Truth, we are all Soviets in the eyes of many observers who examine how the contemporary world keeps track of its past. "The prime function of memory," writes David Lowenthal, "is not to preserve the past but to adapt it so as to enrich and manipulate the present."[1] The historical study of memory, writes historian David Thelen, explores how different human groups "selected and interpreted identifying memories to serve changing needs."[2] The presentism and self-servingness of memory affects professionals as well as the laity. Even historians, historians confess painfully, shape the past to their present wishes while claiming to shape their present views to accord with the "facts" of the past. "Presentism," as Arthur Schlesinger, Jr., has written, is the historians' original sin.[3]

At least the historians take up the Sisyphean struggle against their own prejudices; many others who have control over the way the past is reconstructed have no such scruples. When we recognize how much a nation's collective memory is shaped by maintainers of the past who are not professional historians at least putatively dedicated to scientific study and at least partially restrained by a community of criticism, but instead builders of monuments guided by commissions or writers of textbooks determined not to give offense or political leaders and political analysts transparently invoking the past to serve immediate political gain or to right old wrongs or settle old scores, there is no denying that much of the time the past is employed to legitimate present interests. "Interest theory" works. Orwell lives.

All this acknowledged, it is still unsatisfactory to see dominant versions of history as nothing more than texts freely constructed by today's powerful groups operating self-consciously and self-interestedly on the past. To hold this view is to take a position that can barely be stated without self-contradiction. If it is true that everyone understands the world in a way that legitimates pre-established interests and views (leave aside that people's views or beliefs about their own interests may be at odds with their "real" interests because they suffer from neurosis or because, simply, they do not have the relevant information to know their own interests), then *this* view, too, is but a legitimation of a pre-established interest.

Should we accord it special authority? I think there is a better way to understand how people construct the past. In some respects and under some conditions the past is highly resistant to efforts to make it over. Contrary to the anthropological view that history can be understood as "charter" for present-day social structures, or the sociological view that collective memory always is in the service of the present, or views in psychology that individual reconstructions of the past are invariably in the service of the ego, and contrary, too, to simplistic understandings of ideology or ideological hegemony, the past cannot be reconstructed at will.[4]

This is not to say that people don't try. Richard Nixon certainly has tried. People and organizations and nations strive to make the past their own and to remake it in a flattering light. Individuals, with enough motivation and little enough rationality, may rewrite the past entirely. Solipsism is possible. People can and do sometimes live in mental worlds they share with no one, or scarcely anyone, else. But in the normal run of events, this is rare. Even though the past is regularly reconstructed this is done within limits, stopped by the hard edges of resistance the past provides. The notion that we manufacture our own history and rewrite it according to the dictates of power, person, and privilege, that human societies are Oceanias where we remember and forget and reconstruct at will, denies the past any influence whatsoever. In effect, this view denies history. It is a misguided attempt to develop modes of explanation impervious to events. But a social science insensitive to historical contingency or to local variations will inevitably find itself surprised, its generalizations tripped up when a turn of events or a new location changes the context of action. What we should be seeking is a social study that acknowledges the contingency and continuity of human affairs.

As anthropologist Arjun Appadurai nicely put it, the past is a "scarce resource."[5] It is one that can occasion bitter conflict. Outside of a fully totalitarian society, and we have never seen one as airtight nor as lasting as Orwell's fictional one, no one who would remake the past can do so without encountering enormous obstacles. Some of the most important are:

1. *Living memory.* Memories become part of individual and group identities to which people are attached. Memories are commitments; memories are promises. People will not release important personal or group memories without a struggle. Revisionist history, whether it comes from a lone historian or a presidential commission, will have tough sledding if it contradicts the personal memories of individuals still living. President Ronald Reagan's abortive visit to the military cemetery at Bitburg in 1985 is a good example. Reagan's decision to visit this German military cemetery, in which members of Hitler's SS are buried, as part of the fortieth anniversary commemoration of World War II, was a thoughtless effort to paper over the past. It aroused an extraordinary storm of protest. French historian Henry Rousso, commenting on the response in France, concluded, "Bitburg is a good example of the political illusion of thinking it is possible to manipulate memory deliberately and with impunity." Reagan's effort to emphasize what unites us with Germans, by ignoring rather than confronting what profoundly separates us, almost accomplished the opposite of the reconciliation he sought. It brought to mind "everything that might divide the countries victimized by Nazism from a Germany searching legitimately to establish a clean slate."[6]

The power of living memory can be seen not only in political contexts. Thomas Kuhn's famous study of scientific revolution emphasizes that new scientific paradigms do not triumph over the old by converting people to their greater truth or beauty. Neither Copernicus nor Newton made many converts in their lifetimes. Kuhn quotes physicist Max Planck's observation that "a new scientific truth does not triumph by convincing its opponents and making them see the light, but rather because its opponents eventually die, and a new generation grows up that is familiar with it."[7] Memory, training, habit, and the long experience of seeing the world one way make it difficult to see, let alone accept, the world viewed differently. This cognitive conservatism is in many ways an unappealing rigidity in the human constitution. People rely all too much on their own experiences and memories. They learn more from past events the more their own "time, energy, and ego" are involved in the events themselves, as Robert Jervis observes. This is as much a source of misinformation as of knowledge, because people overgeneralize lessons from their own experience. As Jervis writes, "if people do not learn enough from what happens to others, they learn too much from what happens to themselves."[8]

Still, *my* cognitive failing in this respect is a protection against *your* efforts at a wholesale make-over of the past; your preoccupation with your own lived experience helps prevent me from effectively lying about you. The discussions of Watergate since 1974 bountifully illustrates this. Both political support for the independent counsel and antipathy to the law are overdetermined, motivated less by the practical benefits or risks of the statute than by the memory of its origins and approval or disdain for the version of Watergate it represents. The contest over the meaning of Watergate is as heated as it is because living memory keeps it so.

2. *Multiple versions of the past.* In liberal societies, multiple versions of the past can safely coexist. An all-powerful monolithic version of the past will not triumph in a pluralistic society where conflicting views have a good chance of emerging, finding an audience, and surviving. This is not to say that dominant views do not exist, simply that—again, in a liberal society—they are never invulnerable.

In the case of Watergate, what I have called the conservative and liberal views are the best-entrenched interpretations. They find repeated expression in the country's most powerful political, legal, and intellectual leadership, and they are taken for granted in the news media and in schoolbooks. This does not mean that other views are silenced, incapable of rallying people to their side, nor that they are too weak to influence the conservative and liberal viewpoints. In the wake of the 1975 investigations of the intelligence agencies, Article II abuse of power theories favored by the radical left and radical right gained some ground over Article I obstruction of justice theories, as I have suggested. In the wake of Iran-contra, anxieties about unaccountable executive conduct of foreign policy gave systemic theories added plausibility, although few people in the Congress or elsewhere were prepared to follow them through, any more than they were ready in 1974 to urge impeaching a president because he directed a secret war against a neutral nation.

Dominant groups (like other groups) do try, intentionally or intuitively, to make their own ideas common property and common sense, as a variety of studies of ideological "hegemony" have shown.[9] What is significant here is the incompleteness of this hegemonic process and the social mechanisms that keep it incomplete.

Liberal societies formally protect alternative pasts in two ways. First, there are social practices and mechanical technologies that maintain the integrity of documents through duplication. Thomas Jefferson observed that the best way to preserve documents from the past was to reproduce them in quantity. Worms, fire, the natural decay of paper, and changing political circumstance all threaten historical records. But Jefferson argued that the advent of printing changes this, and so he recommended as the best means to preserve the laws of Virginia "a multiplication of printed copies."[10] Social practice as well as mechanical capacities reinforce this. The United States government deposits documents in public libraries around the country. Parties to contracts sign two copies of the contract so that each party may retain a copy as safeguard against the other's misrepresentation or misremembering. Richard Nixon would not have been forced from office if people had not believed in the integrity of the mechanical reproduction of sound of the White House taping system. In this instance, it was not that there were multiple copies of the tapes but that the sheer multitude of tapes and the insuperable mechanical difficulties anyone would have faced in trying to rerecord and fake them guaranteed their authenticity. (Later, their integrity was guaranteed by their being deposited with Judge Sirica.)

Second, liberal societies may take measures to protect the existence of multiple versions of the past, which will invariably appear. Where societies are particularly heterogeneous and different groups within the societies have access to public media, different versions of the past emerge and compete with one another. But minority or subordinate groups may need support against dominant groups. In the United States, political traditions and institutions specifically honor and protect pluralistic understandings. The First Amendment's prohibition of established religion, for instance, protects pluralism and reduces the potentially all-encompassing reach of a Christian viewpoint in public forums. The First Amendment's prohibition of restraints on the press reduces the inclination of dominant political groups to censor views they disagree with.

Again, this is not to say that there is no dominant culture. Hegemonic ideology is at work. Jews, Muslims, and atheists know perfectly well that Christian culture is hegemonic in the United States. Blue-collar workers are well aware they do not sit astride the American cultural, political, or economic summits. African Americans or Hispanic Americans or other ethnic groups, even with a strong sense of the integrity of their own cultures, are also well aware that they define themselves and are defined in part by their relationship to dominant white middle-class society. Still, their separateness and the constitutional protections for it serve well to keep alive a variety of understandings of the American past. How an idea becomes hegemonic is an important issue, to be sure, and Marx's dictum that the ruling ideas of an age tend to be the ideas of the ruling class is unhappily the right place to start. But it is a starting point, not the finish line, of analysis.

In the case of Watergate, the executive, the courts and the Congress, and the news media that take them as their chief sources, largely control political memory. They establish the lines of consensus, theirs is a body of opinion hard to ignore. Seeking a solid core of meaning about Watergate as a point of departure, in this book I have turned to the articles of impeachment the House Judiciary Committee agreed to (and not the articles they defeated) as a baseline. I have also taken as valid the judgments of the courts on who obstructed justice, who lied to a grand jury, who was responsible for burglarizing Daniel Ellsberg's psychiatrist's office. These are not uncontestable matters. But they are not widely contested nor easily displaced from the center of gravity of our political conversation.

The power of living memory and the persistence of multiple versions of history are related. As people who lived through Watergate pass from the scene, conflict over its memory will decline, barring a particular event or change of circumstances that should happen to renew debate. The liberal version of Watergate, by now having largely completed its reforming tasks, is likely to fade more rapidly than "the system works" conservatism, complacently settling into the schoolbooks and implicitly reinforced every day that the political system endures without fundamental and manifest change. (Only conservatives—such as Suzanne Garment—ironically argue that post-Watergate reforms themselves have profoundly altered political institutions.) Imperial presidency or system theories grow faint, except when an explosion such as Iran-contra restores them to public view, because their premises have gone generally unaddressed and their criticisms unattended, the special prosecutor notwithstanding. "Nixon" theories tend to survive better; despite the pardon, Nixon's resignation provided them a fittingly dramatic climax.

3. A memory industry and memory professions. Some institutions and groups have a vested interest in memory itself. Of considerable importance, at least in the long run, is that the writing of history has been professionalized over the past century or a little more. Granted, professional historians, too, are people, subject to ideological blindnesses and shortsightedness, necessarily value-laden, inevitably located in the present. They are not free from the desire or the habit of distorting the past to serve their preconceptions, but they are vulnerable to professional criticism if they do this too often or too obviously.

We might distinguish three types of historians or roles historians play when they produce texts about the past. Each bears a different connection to legitimation. First, there are professional historians or scholar-historians, trained in universities to take on as their own a commitment to certain moral norms and purposes of historical research. They come to share a strong belief that they should work toward truthful accounts of the past and that they will accomplish this not only by devout attention to original sources but by making their work available for public comment and criticism in the community of scholars. The ultimate arbiters of their work are their professional colleagues.

Second, there are people who write school textbooks or others whose primary audience is one of novices, not peers. If the scholar-historian is guided above all by criteria of credibility as judged by colleagues, the educator-historian is guided most of all by criteria of teachability as measured by experienced hands in publishing companies, in the near term, and by marketplace sales in the long run. This adds constraints the scholar-historian does not have to face. Scholar-historians control their own writing within the limits imposed by norms of a community of professionals that the historian has more or less voluntarily accepted; in contrast, textbook writers are constrained by their publishers. Since textbooks can take years to write and are much more expensive to produce than a historiographic monograph, publishers are more conservative in their decisions about textbooks than about trade or scholarly books. As a result, textbooks are more intimately tied than professional historical writing to the "reproduction of culture" in a society.[11]

Even so, the textbook writer still has education in mind as a goal. However oversimplified the textbook—however overdramatized to hold students' interest, however overmoralized to fit conventional models of storytelling, however resistant to relaying to students the uncertainties and conflicts that characterize the work of scholar-historians, and however intent on burying controversy—the text writer still recounts a story of the past that is broadly in accord with available historical knowledge.

This is not necessarily so for the third type of historian, the politician-historian. The politician who creates historical texts does not seek to please professional colleagues nor to educate students but to celebrate and reaffirm local, state, regional, ethnic, party, or national solidarity. When the politician is the historian, or the historian a politician, then the argument that history is ideology or social "charter" is strong indeed. When Barry Schwartz studied the statues in the U.S. Capitol that have been placed there over two hundred years, he found, to no one's surprise, that the character of these art works accorded with the social and political conflicts of the periods in which they were commissioned.[12] States and politicians regularly use the past for political ends. If British historian J. H. Plumb is correct that the rise of a historical profession in the nineteenth century provided a new and positive force in world consciousness, a body of intellectuals devoted to telling the truth rather than to flattering the prince, he nonetheless neglected the expanding interest of nation-states in inventing pasts to suit their own needs.[13] The scholar-historian may have been on the ascendant for the past century, but so too is the educator-historian writing for the new centralized systems of public schooling and equally the politician-historian inventing civic holidays and state ceremonies, traditionalizing and legitimating new institutions of power.

If scholar-historians take on the role of the politician-historian, they are open to professional criticism; if they assume the role of the educator-historian, they may also lose professional regard. Professional honor and esteem accrue to historians only insofar as they focus on the pursuit of scholarship and abide by the professional norms of documenting their conclusions. This is not an iron-clad guarantee of their integrity, and the premium placed on originality or novelty may war with the pride in authenticity, but it is one of the best sorts of guarantees that fallible human societies have come up with.

With Watergate, scholar-historians have joined journalists as a kind of "truth squad" monitoring Richard Nixon's own effort to recapture history; to date, then, they have tended to speak more often in public and semiadversarial settings than the idealized scholar-historian role calls for. Less publicly visible, historians have also taken a professional interest in the preservation of Nixon administration documents in the National Archives; quite apart from any interest in a specific interpretation of Water-

gate or Nixon, historians as a group have a custodial interest in the maintenance of archives and documents that enable them to legitimately pursue
their craft. They are a special-interest group lobbying for the maintenance
of an authentic historical record.

4. The motive for history.
Examining the past is motivated not only
by a drive for legitimation. It is often a search for guidance. Powerful
groups as well as powerless groups sometimes seek to know the past to
learn lessons. When they do, they seek accurate knowledge. To see all
views of the past as aiming at legitimation is to betray an unduly narrow
grasp of human motivation and a restricted understanding of the uses of
history. People are not invariably seeking to legitimate their present interests. Sometimes people do not know what their present interests are and
know that they do not know. They seek information to arrive at a view.
They seek to know what is right, what is true. They seek some kind of
direction when they are aimless. They seek in the past some kind of anchor
when they are adrift. They seek a source of inspiration when they despair.

People are more often problem-solvers than they are legitimizers (legitimation may be one solution to a problem but it is not the best solution for
most problems). Richard Cyert and James March, in their study of formal
organizations, argue that organizations do not maximize their interests
but "satisfice" them, seeking the first available satisfactory solution to a
problem, not the best solution. They seek out new information with this
"problemistic" orientation. According to Cyert and March, problemistic
approaches to information-gathering are motivated by specific, immediate
problems, they are simple-minded in their strategies for seeking out relevant information, and they are biased.[14] But their bias is one of social
location and practical orientation, not ideological intention.

This model of information-seeking in organizations seems a plausible
model for the way in which individuals, groups, and organizations normally consult history (apart from those moments when the past is thrust
before them). The past is not generally mobilized only to legitimate; it is
often called up problemistically to resolve, calm, guide, instruct, clear the
decks, satisfy an opponent, mollify a superior or subordinate. Legitimation
is one aim of many for which the past may be mobilized.

Even while powerful groups may have a strong interest in history-as-
legitimation so far as widely distributed versions of the past are concerned,
they may have an equally strong interest in history-as-policy-lessons when
it comes to historiography they themselves will use. This is not to presume
that powerful groups see the past more clearly than anyone else. But
the strong motivation of people, powerful and powerless alike, to use ex-

perience to guide future decisions is an incentive for history writing markedly different from the drive for legitimation. In liberal societies this has enormous consequences. Histories prepared for one set of eyes have a way of becoming available to other sets of eyes. The "Pentagon Papers," a history of American policy-making in Vietnam prepared for internal use in the Department of Defense, was provided to the news media by Daniel Ellsberg and released with enormous repercussions for the conduct of the war and, indeed, for the whole presidency of Richard Nixon. Richard Nixon's tape recordings of his private conversations in the White House, intended for his own use in writing the history of his administration, became the decisive factor in bringing down his presidency. But the officials who commissioned the Pentagon Papers' study of the Vietnam War and even the president who commanded tape recordings in his own office had good reasons to seek accurate historical records.

5. *The treason of the history clerk.*   It is no accident that Orwell's Winston Smith, who came to be a doubter and a rebel in Oceania, was an insider. He was not just a consumer of cynically falsified versions of the past but a producer, a rewriter of news stories; Winston Smith and his coworkers, not Big Brother, put embarrassing stories down the memory hole, never to be seen again. There is an important lesson here: even in the computer age, human beings with human strengths and frailties are the cogs and wheels in any ideology machine or any machine of power and domination. Monkeys do not write textbooks, people do; moles do not write news stories, people do, including people of little power who have no ideological commitment to the work they are engaged in. These people who write the society's songs and stories, or print or distribute them, may face crises of conscience when they believe they are asked to falsify what they know. When this happens in a society that provides some rewards for truth tellers, even some legal protection for "whistle blowers," the clerks of the machines of domination may blurt out what they see as the truth.

In the United States today, there is a good market for insider accounts of history. The more scandalous the account, in fact, the larger the likely audience and the more certainly a publisher will be interested in it. Insiders, who may very well lose their jobs when they tell all, may be protected by the possibilities for sizable income in publishing. This is not to presume that making money is their chief motive. The motives of self-exoneration and self-justification may be stronger. For short-term corrections to the historical record, the forum for the clerk's treason is the news media, and the genre is the leak. Deep Throat, in my terms, was a history clerk. In the longer term, the forum is the publishing industry, and the genre is the memoir. In a liberal society with a publishing industry generally more interested in profits than in politics, there are great opportunities for ex-government officials or even, on occasion, ex-corporate officials to "tell all." In the most secret reaches of policy-making, notably in the Central Intelligence Agency, there are now contractual agreements to prevent employees from writing unauthorized accounts of their experiences, but this is the exception, not the rule, and a leaky exception at that.

In Watergate the threat of prosecution was the greatest spur to the defection of insiders. It appears that James McCord told the truth in part out of strong religious convictions, in part out of loyalty to the CIA that he feared would become the scapegoat for Watergate, and in part out of the hope Judge Sirica held out that he would receive a lighter sentence if he cooperated. John Dean told the truth as he saw it to win a lighter prison term. Why did so many people speak to Woodward and Bernstein for *The Final Days* so frankly and so intimately? It is easy to believe that self-justification was a strong motive, not to mention bitterness and a sense of betrayal. When they were ready to give voice to their feelings, Woodward and Bernstein and Simon and Schuster were ready to provide an outlet.

6. *Conventions of historiography and attitudes to history.*   There are cultural rules in a society about how to legitimately and coherently discuss the past. As Arjun Appadurai has argued, there is a cultural framework within which debates over the meaning of the past must take place. A culture must have some conventional agreements about the kinds of sources that will be accepted as credible, the kind of links that must be drawn between the present and the past for the relevance of the past to be credible, and the relative value to present concerns of different "depths" of time.[15]

One of the standard questions asked of Nixon administration figures who participated in an oral history session at the University of Virginia a few years ago was, "How do you think history will judge President Nixon?" No one found that an odd question. Arthur Burns, ambassador to the Federal Republic of Germany in the Reagan administration and chairman of the Board of Governors of the Federal Reserve System during most of the Nixon administration, asserted: "If we have peace over the next fifty years, I think Nixon will go down in the history books as one of our truly great Presidents. The Watergate episode will then receive a mere footnote in the history books."[16] "History," to the interlocutors at Virginia, seems to mean truth, balance, justice. When the question is, how will "history judge" Nixon, this seems to mean, "In truth, on balance, with justice, when the passions of the present are spent and the people with vested interests and allegiances gone, how will Nixon be measured?" To ask his associates the question of "how will history judge Nixon" is asking for more than their own considered judgment of Nixon's place in American life. It offers, in the question itself, a belief that in the long run people get what is their due, even if their own peers cannot see them clearly. The term "history" incorporates some godlike virtues of justice and truth and even mercy. Kenneth Thompson phrases the question, to Nixon's close associate Bryce Harlow, this way: "Do you think history will be kinder to Nixon than some writers are at the moment?"[17] Self and self-interest, in the American view of "history," must be excised. Historians with an evident self-interest or emotional allegiance will be not only professionally but popularly suspect.

Nixon himself has sometimes expressed a more savvy and skeptical view. Henry Kissinger assured him once that history would indeed judge him kindly, but Nixon replied, "It depends who writes the history."[18] On NBC's "Meet the Press" in 1988, Nixon gave a more ambivalent response: "History will treat me fairly. Historians probably won't because most historians are on the left, and I understand that."[19] Nixon doubles back here, away from his skepticism, to the popular view of a fair, impersonal "history."

More consistently skeptical about history, but on grounds different from Nixon's, are historians themselves. They are less afraid that historians are too politically engaged than that they are just too deeply human, too far from the truthful, balanced, judicious, merciful, godlike "history" of which the lay person speaks. Michael Howard, a British military historian, observes the difficulty of locating "lessons" in history. The lay person wants historians to be wise teachers, using the past to explain the present and guide us to the future, but what does he find instead? "Workmen, busily engaged in tearing up what he had always regarded as a perfectly decent highway; doing their best to discourage him from proceeding along it at all; and warning him, if he does, that the surface is temporary, that they cannot guarantee its reliability, that they have no idea when it will be completed, and that he proceeds at his own risk."[20] What Howard fails to observe is that these construction workers must operate with commonly accepted tools and abide by certain standard practices to be on the road crew at all.

7. *The ambiguity of stories.*   All stories can be read in more than one way. Although societies, by remembering some stories, may successfully repress others, every story contains its own alternative readings. Narratives are ambiguous or, to use a fancier term, polysemic. Take, for exam-

ple, the Hungarian celebration each 15 March of the proclamation in 1848 of Hungary as a constitutional monarchy and then, the next year, as an independent republic. Austria ultimately crushed that republic, with some help from Russia, but 15 March remains a nationalist holiday that the Communist government recognized and honored throughout its reign. But this was a dangerous memory for the authorities. In 1956 the Budapest uprising began at the statue of Jozef Bem, a Polish general who fought with the 1848 revolutionaries. On 15 March 1987, this statue was the site of a speech calling for the withdrawal of Soviet troops from Hungary. A political dissident recited a poem by a martyr of 1848, with its refrain, "We promise, we promise, we will not be slaves any longer." Demonstrators recited this and paraded through the streets of Budapest.[21] A celebration of the Hungarian state proved simultaneously, and inevitably, a rebel cry.

We need not leave Watergate to see similar complexity at work: Does Watergate teach that "the system worked" or that "the system almost failed"? Does it demonstrate that, as John Orman put it, "it can happen here or, alternatively, it cannot happen here"?[22] The same narrative plausibly gives rise to either conclusion. Does Watergate teach that an independent press is a bulwark of liberty? Or that a recklessly autonomous press is a threat to social order? If you tell the story of journalism-in-Watergate, you can take the former view; if you prefer the companion story of Watergate-in-journalism, you are more likely to take the latter. Both stories are plausible variants of the same narrative.

Those who see Watergate as a popular circus staged by liberals should not be shocked that others have taken this political theater at face value. Societies that did not have some faith in their own rituals or did not require rituals to affirm core values would be very odd societies indeed. It should neither surprise nor discourage those who believe in Watergate as a constitutional crisis that others can find in Watergate a scandal plot with potentially blasphemous lessons. The value of the Constitution will not be saved or lost by how people remember Watergate. The reverse may, in fact, be nearer the truth—that constitutionalist interpretations of Watergate will triumph or falter according to how highly we prize the Constitution.

8. Institutionalization of memory. The statue of Jozef Bem kept alive a history of Hungarian challenges to foreign domination. Of course, a more thoroughgoing regime than the Soviet-backed Hungarian Communist government might have removed the statue. Monuments can be razed. Monuments can even be changed: in Chivington, Colorado, a plaque commemorated a "battleground" where the state militia fought Cheyenne Indians in 1864. In 1985 the Colorado Native American Heritage Council won a new skirmish to replace the old marker with one that described the event as a "massacre" rather than a "battleground."[23]

Monuments, once installed, and markers, once engraved, are clearly not immutable. Still, they tend to persist. In a revolution, statues will be overturned, markers destroyed, street signs removed, calendars printed with new holidays, schoolbooks dumped and new texts commissioned. But most of the time people are surrounded with the evidence of other and older ways of being in the world. Architecture, to take the most solid example, embraces not only aesthetic values of a given age but social values and social relations. Language, to take the most ethereal, incorporates views and values that are extremely persistent; think how reluctantly, if at all, people of an older generation give up "Negro" for "black" or "the girls at the office" for "the women at the office." Think of how the language of Watergate survived to structure public thinking about Iran-contra and how it continues to shape our expectations of politics. Thoroughgoing ideological campaigns may seek to replace both old housing stock and old phrases with new, but there are few instances of this ever being attempted wholesale (the French Revolution was the first modern razing of the past) and no instances of its ever being altogether successful. Societies are pluralistic not only in the coexistence of different social groups but in the layering of the past in the present through cultural survival.

9. *The past as scar.* "The past is not dead," a William Faulkner character remarks in *Requiem for a Nun.* "It is not even past." Events of the past may be traumatic, twisting and torturing people and groups and leaving scars that cannot be covered over. This is a special case of the institutionalization of memory, but special enough to be listed separately. The past may traumatize anyone, even the rich or powerful. Court-packing accompanies Franklin Roosevelt in the history books, Chappaquiddick haunts Edward Kennedy, Watergate mocks Nixon. Even nontraumatic parts of the past persist over time through the cultural agency of careers, quotations and metaphors, celebrities, reforms and the other cultural mechanisms I have examined in this book. When the past is visibly, viscerally, or palpably alive in the present, it cannot be reorganized at will. The inescapability of the Watergate metaphor in Iran-contra is a good instance.

These points are ignored by the naive empiricist, who believes that there are hard facts that, accumulated, make up history; they are neglected also by the radical, relativist constructionist, who believes that there is only discourse and no independent world to which discourse is beholden. If these simple points were better recognized, then the view that powerful individuals or institutions easily have the resources to make us believe impossible things before or after breakfast would not have the large following it does. The construction of history—and of course it *is* a construction—is neither entirely free to follow the lead of power nor entirely bound by the discipline of hard facts.

Imagine the historian as a sculptor, facing a slab of marble. This sculptor-historian can make that marble into a variety of shapes, but not an infinite variety. The sculptor has freedom to interpret as he or she chooses, but the freedom is limited. The sculptor cannot with that marble slab and a finite set of tools, create a sculpture of greater mass than the slab available at the beginning. The sculptor cannot make a sculpture of wood or brass or Styrofoam. The sculptor cannot make a piece that will keep critics from comparing it and judging it by the standards of other marble sculpture nor can the sculptor do very much to make the piece one the critics will think to compare to sculptures of fabric or ice. The sculptor, and the historian, are at once free and constrained.

The past is with us, in various ways, whether we want it or not. In open societies, it is available in versions that no single person or group entirely controls. Sometimes, then, we remember the past despite ourselves. But should we seek to remember? Is remembering a moral imperative? We often talk about memory in moral terms. Bill Moyers, for instance, commenting on Richard Nixon's rewriting of Watergate history, urges: "Memory, you see, is indispensable to freedom. When there is nothing against which to measure what we're told today, we're at the mercy of those who destroy the past and publish new versions."[24] We are urged by historians and journalists and others to remember vigilantly. Legal scholar Anthony T. Kronman has argued that people should adopt toward the past a "custodial attitude." He writes, "That attitude is itself constitutive of our membership in the uniquely human world of culture; it is what makes us cultural beings. . . ." Kronman backs up his analysis by quoting Simone Weil, "The past once destroyed never returns. The destruction of the past is perhaps the greatest of all crimes. Today the preservation of what little of it remains ought to become almost an obsession."[25]

For our own time, there are two problems with this claim. First, surprisingly, the past can return from destruction. It is doing so in Eastern Europe and the former Soviet Union today. It is doing so in other states where tyrannies have restricted the telling of the past. It is doing so as subordinate groups in liberal societies reclaim pasts they never knew. This is not something that was obvious or anticipated until we began to see it happening before our eyes and one can scarcely fault Weil, writing under the shadow of Hitler, for missing it.

Second, in urging a moral obligation to remember, neither Weil nor Kronman clarifies what past we should remember. Every memory is necessarily also a forgetting since it is a choosing of what, among a multitude of possibilities, to keep in mind. Watergate so overwhelms our recollection of Richard Nixon that it removes from consideration not only the opening to China for which Nixon would like to be remembered but also the War in Vietnam.[26] Vietnam is generally remembered as Lyndon Johnson's war. Richard Nixon inherited it, surely, but he also extended it, presided over it, and finally brought it to an end without achieving the foreign policy objectives for which he justified prosecuting it for five years.

Watergate's "underlying issue," journalist Sidney Blumenthal has written, was Vietnam.[27] To the extent that this is so, almost all of the memories and narratives of Watergate are distortions, omitting Vietnam or crediting its importance and then leaving it to the side. Harold Hongju Koh has argued that the act of calling Watergate to mind so prominently during Iran-contra repressed the more significant precedent of Vietnam. The congressional and special-prosecutor investigations of Iran-contra pursued questions of individual ethics, he maintains, at the expense of reviewing policies and procedures of executive control over foreign policy established during Vietnam and never, Watergate notwithstanding, disestablished.[28]

Indeed, the investigation of Watergate itself in 1973 and 1974 can be judged a form of forgetting Vietnam. The impeachment resolution that took up questions of executive abuse of power in foreign policy—notably Nixon's secret, unauthorized bombing of Cambodia—could not gain a majority in the House Judiciary Committee. The impeachment inquiry drafted its own form of forgetting, one initiated by the investigators rather than the perpetrators of Watergate.

It is a curious irony that on 16 June 1972, as the Watergate burglars were preparing to break into the Democratic National Committee headquarters, John Paul Vann, one of the early heroes of the Vietnam military effort and one of its most prominent critics from within, was buried at Arlington Cemetery. Sitting in the second pew at the chapel at Arlington, just behind the immediate family, was Vann's close friend, Daniel Ellsberg, who watched General William Westmoreland, chief of staff of the army; General Bruce Palmer, vice chief of staff; and other pallbearers follow the coffin. After the funeral the Vann family went to the White House to accept for John Paul Vann the Presidential Medal of Freedom from Richard Nixon. Hours later the Watergate burglars were arrested.[29]

By remembering Watergate, do we forget Vietnam? If so, what is the virtue in this remembering? Even if there is merit in retelling the Watergate story without Vietnam, which retelling is to be enjoined? By remembering Watergate as an obstruction of justice, do we forget what it revealed about the contradictions between conducting an imperial foreign policy and maintaining a democratic society? By assigning blame to Richard Nixon, do we exonerate a political system that should be arraigned? By recalling the virtues of investigative reporting in this instance, do we excuse the irresponsibility and passivity of the press in other cases?

If a moral imperative to remember is to make any sense, it is necessary to accept a view of memory as a constructive act, not a neurological or documentary reflex. Yet it also requires acknowledging that there are limits to the pasts that can be constructed, that there is an integrity to the past that deserves respect. Only then is an imperative to study the past, to think and rethink it, to debate it, coherent. Only then is there a foundation for urging people to care about and care for fallible human truths, no matter how fragile or contestable. It is, indeed, the fragility of human truths that makes the duty of remembering so vital.

NOTES

Introduction

1. Charles Tilly, "Cities and Immigration in North America," *New School for Social Research Center for Studies of Social Change Working Paper* 88 (Sept. 1989): 3. For a powerful critique of the work of historical sociologists Theda Skocpol, Charles Tilly, and Immanuel Wallerstein as insufficiently mindful of path-dependence or the "eventfulness" of history, see William H. Sewell, Jr., "Three Temporalities: Toward an Eventful Sociology," in Terrence J. McDonald, ed., *The Historic Turn in the Human Sciences* (Ann Arbor: University of Michigan Press, forthcoming).

2. Stephen Jay Gould, *Wonderful Life: The Burgess Shale and the Nature of History* (New York: Norton, 1989).

3. For an extraordinary opportunity to look at the relations among national history, property, inheritance, and memory, someone should be studying the ways Eastern European nations are now returning to earlier owners property confiscated during the Nazi or Communist periods. See, for instance, Katie Hafner, "The House We Lived In," *New York Times Magazine*, 10 Nov. 1991.

4. If there are dangers in academicizing Watergate, imagine the dangers in academicizing the Holocaust! Yehuda Bauer has written thoughtfully on those dangers in *The Holocaust in Historical Perspective* (Seattle: University of Washington Press, 1978), pp. 30–49.

5. James Nuechterlein, "Watergate: Toward a Revisionist View," *Commentary* 68 (Aug. 1979): 38. Kurt and Gladys Lang told me in May 1991 that they had been advised not to write their book on Watergate and public opinion for just these reasons.

Chapter 1

1. House Committee on the Judiciary, *Impeachment of Richard M. Nixon, President of the United States*, 93d Congress, 2d session, 20 Aug. 1974, House Document 93-339, 1–4.

2. *New York Times*, 21 Feb. 1978, p. A-31; John W. Dean III, *Blind Ambition: The White House Years* (New York: Simon & Schuster, 1976); John W. Dean III, *Lost Honor* (Los Angeles: Stratford Books, 1982); Bob Woodward and Carl Bernstein, *All the President's Men* (New York: Simon & Schuster, 1974); Bob Woodward and Carl Bernstein, *The Final Days* (New York: Simon & Schuster, 1976); H. R. Haldeman with Joseph DiMona, *The Ends of Power* (New York: Times Books, 1978); John Ehrlichman, *Witness to Power: The Nixon Years* (New York: Pocket Books, 1982); G. Gordon Liddy, *Will: The Autobiography of G. Gordon Liddy* (New York: St. Martin's, 1980); John Sirica, *To Set the Record Straight: The Break-In, the Tapes, the Conspirators, the Pardon* (New York: Norton, 1979); Leon Jaworski, *The Right and the Power: The Prosecution of Watergate* (New York: Reader's Digest Press, 1976); Richard Ben-Veniste and George Frampton, Jr., *Stonewall: The Legal Case Against the Watergate Conspirators* (New York: Simon & Schuster, 1977); Samuel Dash, *Chief Counsel: Inside the Ervin Committee— the Untold Story of Watergate* (New York: Random House, 1976); Fred D. Thompson, *At That Point in Time* (New York: Quadrangle, 1975); Charles Colson, *Born Again* (Old Tappan, N.J.: Chosen Books, 1976); Jeb Stuart Magruder, *An American Life: One Man's Road to Watergate* (New York: Atheneum, 1974); Maurice H. Stans, *The Terrors of Justice: The Untold Side of Watergate* (New York: Everest House, 1978); James Doyle, *Not Above the Law: The Battles of Watergate Prosecutors Cox and Jaworski: A Behind-the-Scenes Account* (New York: Morrow, 1977); Tony Ulasewicz with Stuart A. McKeever, *The President's Private Eye: The Journey of Detective Tony U. from N.Y.P.D. to the Nixon White House* (Westport, Conn.: MACSAM Publishing, 1990).

3. Len Colodny and Robert Gettlin, *Silent Coup: The Removal of a President* (New York: St. Martin's, 1991).

4. Ethan Bronner, *Battle for Justice* (New York: Norton, 1989), p. 83.

5. Ibid., p. 274.

6. CBS Morning News, 8 Aug. 1975.

7. *Los Angeles Times*, 8 Aug. 1984, pp. I-1, 6.

8. Joan Hoff-Wilson, "Watergate Is Already a Dim and Distant Curiosity," *U.S. News & World Report*, 13 Aug. 1984, p. 59.

9. Diane Ravitch and Chester Finn, *What Do Our 17-Year-Olds Know?* (New York: Harper & Row, 1987), pp. 48, 84.

10. *Congressional Quarterly*, 27 Oct. 1973, p. 2838; Edward Mezvinsky, *A Term to Remember* (New York: Coward, McCann & Geoghegan, 1977), p. 70.

11. *New Orleans States-Item*, 22 Oct. 1973; *Chicago Tribune*, 22 Oct. 1973;

Charleston (W. Va.) *Gazette*, 23 Oct. 1973; *Honolulu Star-Bulletin*, 23 Oct. 1973. These editorials and others are reprinted in Evan Drossman and Edward W. Knappman, eds., *Watergate and the White House*, vol. 2 (New York: Facts on File, 1974), pp. 221–234.

12. See Seymour M. Hersh, "The Pardon," *Atlantic* (Aug. 1983), pp. 65, 68; J. Anthony Lukas, *Nightmare: The Underside of the Nixon Years* (New York: Viking, 1976; Penguin Books, 1988), p. 559; Theodore H. White, *Breach of Faith: The Fall of Richard Nixon* (New York: Atheneum, 1975; Dell, 1975), p. 35; *New York Times*, 25 Aug. 1974, pp. 1, 32.

13. Woodward and Bernstein, *The Final Days*, pp. 447–448.

14. NBC News Special, "Impeachment: The Committee Votes," 28 July 1974.

15. Vance Bourjaily, "The Triumph of Watergate: The Final Act," *American Heritage* 35 (1984): 32.

16. Stephen E. Ambrose, *Nixon: The Triumph of a Politician 1962–1972* (New York: Simon & Schuster, 1987), p. 558.

17. Of course, this varies by age. Watergate was judged most influential by people twenty-five to twenty-nine (21.2 percent), thirty to thirty-nine (21.5 percent) and fifty to fifty-nine (20.2 percent). Times-Mirror Center for People and the Press, *The People, the Press, and Politics 1990* (Washington, D.C.: Times-Mirror Center, 1990). The Times-Mirror poll was taken in May 1987. The question was, "Which one of the following major events most affected your political views?" See also Thomas J. Johnson, "The Resurrection of Richard Nixon: A Case Study of the Media's Effect on Collective Memory," Ph.D. diss., University of Washington (Ann Arbor: University Microfilms, 1989), pp. 123–126; and Howard Schuman and Jacqueline Scott, "Generations and Collective Memories," *American Sociological Review* 54 (1989): 359–381.

18. Dean, *Lost Honor*, p. 2.

19. *New York Times Book Review*, 9 Jan. 1983, p. 10. See also *New York Times*, 13 June 1982, p. IV-6.

20. Benjamin J. Stein, "Was Watergate Really Such a Big Deal?" *Washington Post*, 9 Aug. 1984, p. A-23. Leonard Garment asserted several years later that this is true even in Washington. Leonard Garment, "The Guns of Watergate," *Commentary* 83 (April 1987): 15.

21. Don Handelman, *Models and Mirrors: Towards an Anthropology of Public Events* (Cambridge: Cambridge University Press, 1990), p. 76.

22. Claude Lévi-Strauss, *Totemism* (Boston: Beacon Press, 1963), is the source of a tradition in anthropology of examining popular conceptual categories or cultural objects or cultural performances as "good to think with."

23. James MacGregor Burns, *The Crosswinds of Freedom* (New York: Knopf, 1989), p. 500.

24. Henry Steele Commager, "The Shame of the Republic," in Ronald Pym, ed., *Watergate and the American Political Process* (New York: Praeger, 1975), p. 20; reprinted from the *New York Review of Books*, 1973.

25. Henry F. Graff, "Unintended Fingerprints," *The New Leader*, 14–28 May 1990, p. 9.

26. John H. Schaar, *Legitimacy in the Modern State* (New Brunswick, N.J.: Transaction, 1981), p. 142. From "The Circles of Watergate Hell," written with Francis M. Carney; originally published in *American Review* 21 (Oct. 1974): 1–42.

27. Robert M. Herhold, "Letting Go of Richard Nixon," *The Christian Century*, 22–29 June 1977, p. 583.

28. Gore Vidal, "Nixon Without Knives," in *Fifty Who Made the Difference* (New York: Esquire Press Books, 1984).

29. Michael A. Genovese, *The Nixon Presidency* (Westport, Conn.: Greenwood Press, 1990), p. 2.

30. Roger Morris, "In a Shrine to History, Too Many Gaps," *Los Angeles Times*, 16 July 1990, p. B-5.

31. Tom Wicker, *One of Us: Richard Nixon and the American Dream* (New York: Random House, 1991).

32. Garry Wills, *Nixon Agonistes* (Boston: Houghton Mifflin, 1970; New American Library, 1979), p. vii.

33. Quoted in Fawn M. Brodie, *Richard M. Nixon: The Shaping of His Character* (New York: Norton, 1981), p. 18.

34. I do not think there is any reason to doubt that Nixon would have approved the plan, in the heat of an election year, if it had been presented to him. That is consistent with other activities he did approve or condone. But this is not at issue.

35. Lukas, *Nightmare*, p. 408.

36. White, *Breach of Faith*, p. 51.

37. Lukas, *Nightmare*, p. 1.

38. Ibid., p. xiv.

39. Godfrey Hodgson, *All Things to All Men: The False Promise of the Modern American Presidency* (New York: Simon & Schuster, 1980), p. 41.

40. Stanley Kutler, *The Wars of Watergate* (New York: Knopf, 1990), pp. xiii, 9, 10.

41. Ibid., p. xiii.

42. Ibid.

43. Marc Lackritz, personal interview, February 1991; Arthur Liman, remarks at Brown University, 1 Mar. 1988. Liman said, "Congressional investigations are extraordinary tools. They are awesome. All of us who remember the McCarthy days know that and we didn't want a repetition of that."

44. Robert Bellah, "Civil Religion in America," *Daedalus* 96 (1967): 1–21.

45. Jim Hougan, *Secret Agenda* (New York: Random House, 1984); and Colodny and Gettlin, *Silent Coup*.

46. David Wise, *The American Police State: The Government Against the People* (New York: Random House, 1976), pp. 141–186.

47. Lukas, *Nightmare*, pp. 197–203.

48. Wills, *Nixon Agonistes*, p. 548.

49. Bill Moyers, *The Secret Government: The Constitution in Crisis* (Cabin John, Md.: Seven Locks Press, 1988).

50. Walter Mondale, *The Accountability of Power: Toward a Responsible Presidency* (New York: David McKay, 1975), p. 190. See also TRB, "Facing the Music," *The New Republic*, 4 June 1977, p. 2. Not only liberals can take this view. Conservative social theorist Robert Nisbet insists on the role of accident in Watergate. See Robert Nisbet, *Twilight of Authority* (New York: Oxford University Press, 1975), pp. 45–47.

51. See Paul Johnson, "In Praise of Richard Nixon," *Commentary* 86 (Oct. 1988), pp. 50–53.

52. Paul Johnson, *Modern Times: The World from the Twenties to the Eighties* (New York: Harper & Row, 1983), p. 649. See also Paul Johnson, "Destiny Derailed, Then Triumphant," *Los Angeles Times*, 16 July 1990, p. B-5, in which Watergate is both a "witch hunt" and a "media putsch" again

53. Johnson, *Modern Times*, p. 653.

54. Johnson, "In Praise of Richard Nixon," p. 52.

55. San Francisco Bay Area *Kapitalistate* Group, "Watergate, or The Eighteenth Brumaire of Richard Nixon," *Kapitalistate* no. 3 (Spring 1975), p. 15.

56. Ibid., p. 18.

57. Barton J. Bernstein, "The Road to Watergate and Beyond: The Growth and Abuse of Executive Authority Since 1940," *Law and Contemporary Problems* 40 (1976): 84.

58. Noam Chomsky, "Watergate: A Skeptical View," *New York Review of Books*, 20 Sept. 1973, p. 8.

59. Leo P. Ribuffo, "Watergate & Mugwumps," *Dissent* (Winter 1974): 94–96, 123.

60. Hedley Donovan, *Right Places, Right Times* (New York: Henry Holt, 1989), p. 421.

61. Jonathan Rowe, telephone interview with author, December 1990.

62. Hugh Sidey, "The Man and Foreign Policy," in Kenneth W. Thompson, ed., *The Nixon Presidency* (Lanham, Md.: University Press of America, 1987), pp. 307–308.

63. Peter Schrag, "Watergate as Entertainment," *Social Policy* 5 (Sept./Oct. 1974): 23–26. If Watergate was entertainment, viewers could be not only engrossed but bored. Elizabeth Drew, who gave a speech in Richmond not long after Nixon's resignation, recalled talking with her hostess, a congressman's wife, before the speech. The hostess declared, "We had Senator Ervin here last year and thank God he didn't talk about Watergate. No one wants to hear about that." Elizabeth Drew, commencement address at Wellesley College, 27 May 1977. Introduced into the *Congressional Record* by Sen. Edward Kennedy, 95th Congress, 1st sess., 9 June 1977, v. 125, pt. 15, 18255.

64. Samuel Dash, *Chief Counsel*, p. 88.

65. Hodgson, *All Things to All Men,* p. 43.

66. Schrag, "Watergate as Entertainment," pp. 23–26.

67. I borrow this phrase from John J. MacAloon, "Steroids and the State: Dubin, Melodrama and the Accomplishment of Innocence," *Public Culture* 2 (1990): 41–64.

68. Leonard Garment, "The Guns of Watergate," p. 18.

69. Jeffrey C. Alexander, "Culture and Political Crisis: 'Watergate' and Durkheimian Sociology," in Jeffrey Alexander, ed., *Durkheimian Sociology* (New York: Cambridge University Press), p. 203.

70. See Jeffrey Alexander, "Constructing Scandal," *The New Republic,* 18 June 1987, pp. 18–19. I know of only one work that takes a broad, social scientific approach to the study of political scandals, and it usefully presents a set of case studies of political scandals from nine countries. See Andrei S. Markovits and Mark Silverstein, eds., *The Politics of Scandal: Power and Process in Liberal Democracies* (New York: Holmes & Meier, 1988).

Chapter 2

1. Leonard Garment, "The Guns of Watergate," *Commentary* 83 (April 1987): 15–23.

2. Samuel H. Day, Jr., "The Lessons of Watergate," *Bulletin of the Atomic Scientists* 31 (March 1975): 3–4.

3. C. Vann Woodward, ed., *Responses of the Presidents to Charges of Misconduct* (New York: Delacorte Press, 1974), p. xxv.

4. Victor Lasky, *It Didn't Start with Watergate* (New York: Dial Press, 1977).

5. Art Buchwald, "Instant Answers," part of *Watergate Classics,* a theater production of the Yale Repertory Theatre, 16 Nov. 1973 to 26 Jan. 1974. See *Yale/Theatre* 5 (Winter 1974): 124–126.

6. See Arthur Larson's and Martin Firestone's second thoughts on their campaign activities for Eisenhower in Fred W. Friendly, *The Good Guys, the Bad Guys and the First Amendment* (New York: Random House, 1976), p. 41.

7. An incipient feminist reading of Watergate, never very well developed, takes Martha Mitchell as a much-abused heroine whose integrity was one of the few obstacles to the successful cover-up; she is the Cassandra of Watergate. See Madeline Edmondson and Alden Duer Cohen, *The Women of Watergate* (New York: Stein and Day, 1975).

8. All of this is reported in J. Anthony Lukas, *Nightmare: The Underside of the Nixon Years* (New York: Viking, 1976; Penguin Books, 1988), pp. 211–228.

9. *New York Times,* 16 Oct. 1973, p. 8; *New York Times,* 2 Feb. 1975, p. 1. The CIA's deep implication in the Watergate cover-up is documented by David Wise, *The American Police State: The Government Against the People* (New York: Random House, 1976), pp. 246–257.

10. Richard M. Nixon, *RN: The Memoirs of Richard Nixon* (New York: Grosset and Dunlop, 1978), p. 638.

11. House Committee on the Judiciary, *Impeachment of Richard M. Nixon, President of the United States*, 93d Congress, 2d session, 20 Aug. 1974) House Document 339, p. 64.

12. Ibid., p. 69.

13. Nixon, *RN*, p. 834.

14. House Committee on the Judiciary, *Impeachment of Richard M. Nixon*, p. 89.

15. *New York Times*, 22 Nov. 1974, p. 21.

16. Nixon, *RN*, p. 850.

17. "Minority Views of Messrs. Hutchinson, Smith, Sandman, Wiggins, Dennis, Mayne, Lott, Moorhead, Maraziti and Latta," in House Committee on the Judiciary, *Impeachment of Richard M. Nixon*, p. 360.

18. Ibid., p. 361.

19. *New York Times*, 15 Sept. 1974, p. E-3.

20. Ibid. For the public response as measured by polls, see Gladys Engel Lang and Kurt Lang, *The Battle for Public Opinion: The President, the Press, and the Polls During Watergate* (New York: Columbia University Press, 1983), pp. 210–213.

21. "The Failure of Mr. Ford," *New York Times*, 9 Sept. 1974, p. 34; "Pardon for What?" *New York Times*, 10 Sept. 1974, p. 40; "Nightmare Compounded," *New York Times*, 11 Sept. 1974, p. 44.

22. Stephen E. Ambrose, *Nixon, vol. 3: Ruin and Recovery 1973–1990* (New York: Simon & Schuster, 1991), p. 462.

23. William F. Hildenbrand, U.S. Senate Oral History, National Archives, pp. 227–228. Republicans generally approved the pardon although Senators Edward Brooke, Jacob Javits, Lowell Weicker, and a number of senators facing tough reelection campaigns—Richard Schweiker of Pennsylvania, Marlow Cook of Kentucky, and Robert Packwood of Oregon—were critical. See *New York Times*, 9 Sept. 1974, p. 25; *New York Times*, 10 Sept. 1974, p. 28.

24. "Nixon's 'Mistakes,'" *New York Times*, 10 Sept. 1974, p. 41.

25. "A New Kind of Cover-up," *New York Times*, 10 Sept. 1974, p. 41.

26. "Pardon for What?" *New York Times*, 10 Sept. 1974, p. 40.

27. Arthur L. Liman and Steven B. Rosenfeld, "Rockefeller, Attica and Pardons," *New York Times*, 13 Sept. 1974, p. 37.

28. "Out of the Wreckage," *New York Times*, 12 Sept. 1974, p. 39.

29. Richard Ben-Veniste and George Frampton, Jr., *Stonewall: The Legal Case Against the Watergate Conspirators* (New York: Simon & Schuster, 1977).

30. Ibid., p. 308.

31. Ibid., p. 310.

32. Leon Jaworski, *The Right and the Power: The Prosecution of Watergate* (New York: Reader's Digest Press, 1976).

33. Benjamin J. Stein, "Was Watergate Really Such a Big Deal?" *Washington*

Post, 9 Aug. 1984, p. A-23. When the Watergate Special Prosecutor, Charles Ruff (the fourth and final prosecutor), packed up his tent on 19 June 1977, questions were left hanging. Rep. Elizabeth Holtzman criticized Ruff for not pursuing prosecutions of higher-ups for the Watergate break-in itself, the funds Howard Hughes provided Bebe Rebozo in 1970 on Nixon's behalf, the "sale" of ambassadorships to campaign contributors, the possible encouragement by Special Prosecutor Jaworski of Ford's pardon of Richard Nixon, and other matters. *Congressional Record*, 95th Congress, 1st session, 4 Aug. 1977, v. 123, pt. 21: 27144.

34. CBS Evening News, 8 Sept. 1974.

35. Daniel Schorr, *Clearing the Air* (Boston: Houghton Mifflin, 1977), p. 137.

36. William Colby, *Honorable Men: My Life in the CIA* (New York: Simon & Schuster, 1978), p. 340.

37. Schorr, *Clearing the Air*, p. 144.

38. Interestingly, the Church committee inherited some staff who had served on the Senate Watergate committee, not to mention some of the same offices. Gregory F. Treverton, *Covert Action: The Limits of Intervention in the Postwar World* (New York: Basic Books, 1987), p. 3.

39. Colby, *Honorable Men*, p. 411.

40. Ibid., p. 315.

41. Thomas Powers, *The Man Who Kept the Secrets: Richard Helms and the CIA* (New York: Knopf, 1979), p. 247.

42. Schorr, *Clearing the Air*, p. 161.

43. Ibid., p. 168. Robert Kennedy was "thoroughly briefed about the details of an attempt to murder Castro during his brother's presidency. The record is clear that the attempts to kill Castro continued. And the record is clear that despite his knowledge of the earlier attempt, Robert Kennedy did not protest to the CIA, to its director John McCone, to Helms, or to anyone else in the Agency for that attempt." Powers, *The Man Who Kept the Secrets*, p. 155. McNamara's testimony, according to the executive director of the Rockefeller Commission, attorney David Belin, could not be believed. He was covering up the fact that Kennedy administration officials knew of the assassination plots and encouraged them. Arthur Schlesinger, Jr., insists that Kennedy did not know of plots against Castro's life. See *The Cycles of American History* (Boston: Houghton Mifflin, 1986), p. 413. Belin believes that Robert Kennedy and Robert McNamara both actively encouraged Castro's assassination and that John Kennedy "knew and approved of their plans." See David Belin, *Final Disclosure: The Full Truth About the Assassination of President Kennedy* (New York: Charles Scribner's Sons, 1988), pp. 117–118. Belin had a special interest in this since he was counsel to the Warren Commission and the CIA withheld information from the commission concerning assassination plots aimed at Castro. See Belin, *Final Disclosure*, pp. 174–175.

44. Powers, *The Man Who Kept the Secrets*, pp. 119–120, ascribes these views to Richard Helms.

45. Ibid., p. 183.

46. Wise, *The American Police State*, p. 183.

47. Ibid., p. 184.

48. Marcus Raskin, *Notes on the Old System: To Transform American Politics* (New York: David McKay, 1974), quoted in Kevin P. Phillips, *Post-Conservative America* (New York: Random House, 1982), p. 68.

49. Theodore C. Sorensen, *Watchmen in the Night: Presidential Accountability After Watergate* (Cambridge: MIT Press, 1975), pp. 14–16.

50. House Committee on the Judiciary, *Impeachment of Richard M. Nixon, President of the United States*, 93d Congress, 2d session, House Document 93-339, pp. 217–219.

Chapter 3

1. We may sometimes speak of collective or social memory in organizations to refer to an organization's maintaining a "memory" through its standard operating procedures or through long-term employees who pass on unwritten institutional culture. See the literature on organizational learning and organizational memory, for instance, Bo Hedberg, "How Organizations Learn and Unlearn," in *Handbook of Organizational Design*, vol. 1 (New York: Oxford University Press, 1981), pp. 3–27; Lloyd S. Etheredge, "Government Learning: An Overview," in Samuel L. Long, ed., *The Handbook of Political Behavior*, vol. 2 (New York: Plenum Press, 1981), pp. 73–161; Barbara Levitt and James G. March, "Organizational Learning," *Annual Review of Sociology* 14 (1988): 319–340.

2. For discussion by psychologists on the social character of memory, see David Middleton and Derek Edwards, eds., *Collective Remembering* (Newbury Park, Calif.: Sage, 1990). Also relevant are Norman R. Brown, Steven K. Shevell, and Lance J. Rips, "Public Memories and Their Personal Context," in David Rubin, ed., *Autobiographical Memory* (Cambridge: Cambridge University Press, 1986), pp. 137–158; Elizabeth F. Loftus and Wesley Marburger, "Since the Eruption of Mt. St. Helens, Has Anyone Beaten You Up? Improving the Accuracy of Retrospective Reports with Landmark Events," *Memory and Cognition* 11 (1983): 114–120.

3. For an argument about the importance of positively valuing tradition and its remembrance, see Anthony T. Kronman, "Precedent and Tradition," *Yale Law Journal* 99 (March 1990): 1029–1068.

4. This is the judgment of Theodore S. Hamerow, *Reflections on History and Historians* (Madison: University of Wisconsin Press, 1987), p. 3.

5. Nathan Wachtel offers some reasons for this in his introduction in Marie-

Noelle Bourguet, Lucette Valensi, and Nathan Wachtel, eds., *Between Memory and History* (Chur, Switzerland: Harwood Academic Publishers, 1990), pp. 1–18. Historiography is traditionally the field that takes as its subject the writing of history itself. My impression is that historiography is increasingly historical itself, engaging less in analytical and methodological critiques of key historical works and more in social history, trying to understand and account for the rise of a historical profession in the past 150 years. See, for instance, Hamerow, *Reflections on History*. Other historians also have recognized the rise of a history profession as a key divide in the place of the past in cultural life. See J. H. Plumb, *The Death of the Past* (Boston: Houghton Mifflin, 1970), and Bernard Lewis, *History—Remembered, Recovered, Invented* (Princeton: Princeton University Press, 1975), pp. 53–55.

6. Peter Burke, "History as Social Memory," in Thomas Butler, ed., *Memory: History, Culture and the Mind* (Oxford: Basil Blackwell, 1989). The rise of oral history has spurred this along. So has the revolution in social history of the past generation that has made historians acutely aware of biases and conventions of their own profession, calling into question the privileged place of the historian as arbiter of the past. See the discussion in Marianne Debouzy, "In Search of Working-Class Memory: Some Questions and a Tentative Assessment," in Bourguet, Valensi, and Wachtel, *Between Memory and History*, pp. 55–76.

7. *Los Angeles Times*, 11 June 1988, p. 1. See also Nina Tumarkin, "Myth and Memory in Soviet Society," *Society* 24 (Sept./Oct. 1987): 69–72.

8. The most comprehensive recent indictment is Thomas C. Reeves, *A Question of Character: A Life of John F. Kennedy* (New York: The Free Press, 1991). On the biased presentation of Kennedy's memory at the Kennedy Library in Boston, see *Los Angeles Times*, 7 Nov. 1991, p. E-1.

9. Cited in Debouzy, "In Search of Working-Class Memory," in Bourguet, Valensi, and Wachtel, *Between Memory and History*, p. 60.

10. Barry Schwartz, Yael Zerubavel, and Bernice M. Barnett, "The Recovery of Masada: A Study in Collective Memory," *Sociological Quarterly* 27 (1986): 160. Schwartz's more recent work is not so staunchly Durkheimian but seeks a more powerful, and complex, understanding of a past "neither totally precarious nor immutable," a past that is not a foreign country but a familiar one, "its people different, but not strangers to the present." See Barry Schwartz, "Social Change and Collective Memory: The Democratization of George Washington," *American Sociological Review* 56 (1991): 234.

11. Carl Degler, "Why Historians Change Their Minds," *Pacific Historical Review* 45 (1976): 184.

12. Richard Handler and Jocelyn Linnekin, "Tradition, Genuine or Spurious," *Journal of American Folklore* 97 (1984): 276.

13. Anthony Giddens, *A Contemporary Critique of Historical Materialism* (Berkeley: University of California Press, 1981), p. 36. As soon as time is identified as a key dimension of humanness, one is obliged to recognize that

space is another. Perhaps time is more an Enlightenment dimension of human existence, since it leads, I think, to speaking of universals and universalities and continuities, where space forces us to contemplate differences and contextualities. In choosing to write about time rather than space, I no doubt emphasize one aspiration rather than another, one longing rather than another. An emphasis on time suggests a preoccupation with passing, aging, and death; an emphasis on space suggests a preoccupation with contingency, fixity, limits. A complete social theory, as Giddens especially has emphasized, will find a way to encompass both time and space. On the central importance of the lifetime as a framework for public discourse, see Michael Schudson, "When? Deadlines, Datelines, and History," in Robert Karl Manoff and Michael Schudson, eds., *Reading the News* (New York: Pantheon, 1986), pp. 87–88.

14. Bismarck is quoted in Robert Jervis, *Perception and Misperception in International Politics* (Princeton: Princeton University Press, 1976), p. 239, and Jervis makes the remark I have rephrased—that we do not in fact learn much from other people's experience. This is also suggested in an interesting volume by Robert A. Kann, in which he argues that a "restoration" of an overthrown political regime will not happen successfully unless it takes place within thirty-five to forty years. "The generation active in the public life of the original system must still be able to take an effective part in that of the restored system." Otherwise the will and the knowledge and the emotional attachment, presumably, would not exist. Robert A. Kann, *The Problem of Restoration: A Study in Comparative Political History* (Berkeley: University of California Press, 1968), pp. 78–79, 100.

15. Benjamin I. Schwartz, "On the New Turn in China," *Dissent* 36 (Fall 1989): 448–454, makes uses of this distinction between the "history of events" and "deep structure" in an effort to question it as he tries to understand the Chinese government's repression of student demonstrations in Tiananmen Square in June 1989. The power of events, of unpredictable origin with unpredictable but often stunning results, impressed a great many observers in the late 1980s, particularly in the wake of the revolutions of Eastern Europe and the end of the Cold War that no one—repeat, no one—had anticipated. It amounted, said political writer Peter Karman, to "yet another unforeseen outbreak of history. If life is what happens while people are busy making plans, history is what happens while they're making politics." "World Upsets Soviets and U.S. in Big Tussle," *In These Times*, 1–7 Nov. 1989, p. 3.

16. Fred D. Thompson, *At That Point in Time* (New York: Quadrangle, 1975), p. 12.

17. *U.S. News & World Report*, 18 Mar. 1974, p. 19.

18. Daniel Dayan and Elihu Katz, *Media Events: The Live Broadcasting of History* (Cambridge: Harvard University Press, 1992), pp. 118, 146.

19. Michael Cornfield, "The Watergate Audience: Parsing the Powers of the

Press," in James W. Carey, ed., *Media, Myths, and Narratives: Television and the Press* (Newbury Park, Calif.: Sage Publications, 1988), p. 195.

20. Mary McCarthy, *The Mask of State: Watergate Portraits* (New York: Harcourt Brace Jovanovich, 1974), p. 3.

21. In a 1985 national survey, people most often listed World War II (29.3 percent) or Vietnam (22.0 percent) as the first- or second-most important event of the past fifty years; then came space exploration (12.7 percent) and the Kennedy assassination (8.8 percent), with Watergate (2.8 percent) in fourteenth place. Howard Schuman and Jacqueline Scott, "Generations and Collective Memories," *American Sociological Review* 54 (1989): 359–381.

22. Two useful general discussions of commemoration are Paul Connerton, *How Societies Remember* (Cambridge: Cambridge University Press, 1989), pp. 41–71, and Edward S. Casey, *Remembering: A Phenomenological Study* (Bloomington: Indiana University Press, 1987), pp. 216–257.

23. Aphrodite Valleras, "Watergate Live," *The New Republic*, 19 July 1980, pp. 15–16. See also *New York Times*, 17 June 1980, p. II-9; *New York Times*, 7 Oct. 1980, p. II-2; and *New York Times*, 6 Sept. 1981, p. 41.

24. There has also been a kind of insider's, underground Watergate tourism in Washington. People who visited Peter Rodino's House office could view the five gavels, encased, that he used for the voting on each of the five articles of impeachment (two of the articles were defeated) in the House Judiciary Committee. Each gavel has the final vote engraved on it. Richard Nixon's old Oval Office desk, now in the office of the vice president in the Capitol, has become an object of interest for visitors who want to know where the microphones for the taping system were placed. Walter Mondale, when vice president, was known to get down on his hands and knees to point out the location of the taping system for visitors, and a member of Vice President Dan Quayle's staff has done the same more recently.

25. William Safire, "The Disappearance of Room 16," *New York Times*, 14 Sept. 1989, p. A-29.

26. *Washington Post*, 18 June 1982, p. C-1.

27. *Washington Post*, 24 Oct. 1983, p. C-1.

28. *Los Angeles Times*, 17 June 1982, p. 1.

29. Diane Ravitch, "Decline and Fall of Teaching History," *New York Times Magazine*, 17 Nov. 1985, p. 50.

30. Gloria Emerson, quoted in Lance Morrow, "The Forgotten Warriors," *Time*, 13 July 1981, p. 20. The catalog of such quotations is endless. A few more instances: "We live in the age of throwaway history. Nobody remembers what anyone said the day before yesterday. And if someone does have an inconvenient memory, they say it doesn't matter anymore." Alexander Cockburn, "Ashes and Diamonds," *In These Times*, 3–9 April 1991, p. 17. Robert G. Kaiser, a reporter for the *Washington Post*, in an article concerning Nixon's continuing fascination, holds, "First, we forget—we forget our own history just about as fast as it happens, often substituting historical myths that

suit our national self-image much better than historical realities." *Washington Post*, 5 Aug. 1984, p. C-1. See also Daniel Bell, *The End of Ideology* (New York: Free Press, 1962), p. 228, comparing American neglect of the past to British nurturing of memory. For a thoughtful analysis of American historical memory, see Michael H. Frisch, "The Memory of History," in Susan Porter Benson, Stephen Brier, and Roy Rosenzweig, eds., *Presenting the Past: Essays on History and the Public* (Philadelphia: Temple University Press, 1986), pp. 5–17.

31. Alexis de Tocqueville, *Democracy in America*, ed. J. P. Mayer, trans. George Lawrence (Garden City, N.Y.: Doubleday, 1969), p. 430.

32. Daniel Bell, "The End of American Exceptionalism," *The Public Interest* 41 (Fall 1975): 222.

33. On comity, see Richard Hofstadter, *The Progressive Historians: Turner, Beard, Parrington* (New York: Knopf, 1968; Vintage Books, 1970), p. 454; on the rise of a two-party system, see Richard Hofstadter, *The Idea of a Party System* (Berkeley: University of California Press, 1972). See also Daniel Bell's use of Hofstadter's notion of comity in Daniel Bell, "The End of American Exceptionalism."

34. Charles A. Miller, *The Supreme Court and the Uses of History* (Cambridge: Belknap Press of Harvard University Press, 1969), p. 176.

35. Michael Barrier, "Memories for Sale," *Nation's Business*, Dec. 1989, pp. 18–26.

36. For a valuable study of nostalgia, see Fred Davis, *Yearning for Yesterday* (New York: Free Press, 1979). Michael Kammen's series of important studies of American memory has been recently capped by *Mystic Chords of Memory: The Transformation of Tradition in American Culture* (New York: Knopf, 1991). This sprawling compendium of American attitudes to the past throughout history concludes that Americans have a greater tendency to experience amnesia than do people of many other nations but that this is a "matter of degree" rather than a radical difference. See page 701, especially.

37. See, for instance, Paul Gagnon, "Why Study History?" *Atlantic Monthly*, Nov. 1988, pp. 43–66, for a critique of the teaching of American history. See also Joseph Berger, "Arguing About America," *New York Times*, 21 June 1991, p. 1, on the treatment of minorities in New York public school social studies curricula.

38. Stephen Vaughn, ed., *The Vital Past: Writings on the Uses of History* (Athens: University of Georgia Press, 1985), p. 11.

39. Leonard W. Levy, *Original Intent and the Framers' Constitution* (New York: Macmillan, 1988). Levy argues, for instance: "Judges do not try to understand the past on its own terms, for its own sake, and as if they did not know how things turned out. Judges always *use* history. They turn to it only because they think it might help decide some issue posed in a case. They look for something to confirm a hunch or to illustrate a point that they have already decided on other grounds. . . . In short, judges exploit history by

making it serve the present and by making it yield results that are not historically founded" (p. 313). See also Mark Tushnet, *Red, White, and Blue: A Critical Analysis of Constitutional Law* (Cambridge: Harvard University Press, 1988), pp. 21–45, and William E. Nelson, "History and Neutrality in Constitutional Adjudication," *Virginia Law Review* 72 (1986): 1237–1296.

40. Robert Hewison, *The Heritage Industry: Britain in a Climate of Decline* (London: Methuen, 1987).

41. Martin Wiener, *English Culture and the Decline of the Industrial Spirit, 1850–1980* (Cambridge: Cambridge University Press, 1983). See also Patrick Wright, *On Living in an Old Country: The National Past in Contemporary Britain* (1985) and Patrick Wright, "Heritage and Danger: The English Past in the Era of the Welfare State," in Thomas Butler, ed., *Memory: History, Culture and the Mind* (Oxford: Basil Blackwell, 1989), pp. 151–182. David Lowenthal suggests that British perspectives on the past "differ more in style than in substance" from American views of the past. See David Lowenthal "The Timeless Past: Some Anglo-American Historical Preconceptions," *Journal of American History* 75 (1989): 1275.

42. Sheldon S. Wolin, *The Presence of the Past: Essays on the State and the Constitution* (Baltimore: Johns Hopkins University Press, 1989), p. 33.

43. There is a growing literature on American commemorations. See, for instance, David Glassberg, *American Historical Pageantry: The Uses of Tradition in the Early Twentieth Century* (Chapel Hill: University of North Carolina Press, 1990); Barry Schwartz, *George Washington: The Making of an American Symbol* (New York: Free Press, 1987); Wilbur Zelinsky, *Nation into State: The Shifting Symbolic Foundations of American Nationalism* (Chapel Hill: University of North Carolina Press, 1988); and, most recently, Michael Kammen, *Mystic Chords of Memory*.

Chapter 4

1. William Safire, *Before the Fall: An Inside View of the Pre-Watergate White House* (Garden City, N.Y.: Doubleday, 1975), pp. 3–6.

2. "On Being Wrong," *New York Times*, 13 Dec. 1973, in William Safire, *Safire's Washington*, (New York: Times Books, 1980), p. 24.

3. Quoted in Safire, *Safire's Washington*, p. 7.

4. "The Great Howcum," *New York Times*, 2 Aug. 1973, in Safire, *Safire's Washington*, p. 19.

5. "To 'Nixon People'," *New York Times*, 12 Aug. 1974, in Safire, *Safire's Washington*, p. 28.

6. "The New Torture," *New York Times*, 20 Dec. 1973, in Safire, *Safire's Washington*, p. 26; "Watergate's Third Crime," *New York Times*, 28 Oct. 1974, in Safire, *Safire's Washington*, p. 30.

7. "Who Else Is Guilty?" *New York Times*, 2 Jan. 1975, p. 33.

8. "The Thrill Is Gone," *New York Times*, 30 Jan. 1975, p. 35.

9. "Orchestrating Outrage," *New York Times*, 8 Dec. 1975, in Safire, *Safire's Washington*, p. 32.

10. Safire, *Safire's Washington*, p. 33.

11. "Three Attorneys General," *New York Times*, 10 May 1976, in Safire, *Safire's Washington*, p. 34.

12. Safire, *Safire's Washington*, p. 102.

13. "The Kennedy Transcripts," *New York Times*, 20 Feb. 1975, in Safire, *Safire's Washington*, p. 103.

14. "Nixon Never Did," *New York Times*, 5 June 1975, in Safire, *Safire's Washington*, p. 132.

15. "The President's Friend," *New York Times*, 15 Dec. 1975, in Safire, *Safire's Washington*, p. 105.

16. "Sauce for the Gander," *New York Times*, 26 Sept. 1974, in Safire, *Safire's Washington*, p. 163.

17. "Richard Redux," *New York Times*, 13 May 1976, in Safire, *Safire's Washington*, p. 240.

18. "Vic Lasky's Blockbuster," *New York Times*, 25 April 1977, p. 31.

19. Jules Witcover, *Marathon: The Pursuit of the Presidency 1972–1976* (New York: Viking Press, 1977), p. 111. See also Charles O. Jones, *The Trusteeship Presidency: Jimmy Carter and the United States Congress* (Baton Rouge: Louisiana State University Press, 1988), pp. xiii, 15, 217, for emphasis on Carter's presidency as a reaction to Watergate.

20. The Republicans did their best to show their own virtue in the face of Watergate, with Sen. Howard Baker, a Watergate hero, giving the keynote address at the 1976 Republican convention, arguing that the Republican party had faced Watergate, whereas Democrats had not confronted their own abuses, and attacked Democrats for "rattling the dusty old skeletons of Watergate all over again." CBS Morning News, 17 Aug. 1976.

21. James Wooten, *Dasher: The Roots and the Rising of Jimmy Carter* (New York: Summit Books, 1978), pp. 355–356.

22. Witcover, *Marathon*, p. 368.

23. CBS Evening News, 29 Oct. 1976.

24. Witcover, *Marathon*, p. 369.

25. Ibid., pp. 547–548

26. Ibid., p. 551.

27. Jimmy Carter, *Keeping Faith: Memoirs of a President* (New York: Bantam Books, 1982), p. 27.

28. *Washington Post*, 8 Jan. 1977, p. A-4; *New York Times*, 11 Jan. 1977, p. 22 and 16 Jan. 1977, p. 42.

29. *New York Times*, 23 July 1977, p. 1.

30. Clifford was counsel to Lance for his appearance before the Senate committee. See Clark Clifford, *Counsel to the President: A Memoir* (New York: Random House, 1991), pp. 631–632.

31. *New York Times*, 16 Sept. 1977, p. 22.
32. *New York Times*, 18 Sept. 1977, p. IV-1.
33. *Washington Post*, 26 July 1977, p. A-19.
34. *Washington Post*, 25 Aug. 1977, p. 1.
35. *New York Times*, 12 Sept. 1977, p. 33.
36. *New York Times*, 22 Sept. 1977, p. A-19.
37. *New York Times*, 26 Sept. 1977, in Safire, *Safire's Washington*, p. 270.
38. Frank J. Smist, Jr., *Congress Oversees the United States Intelligence Community, 1947–1989* (Knoxville: University of Tennessee Press, 1990), p. 54.
39. William Safire, "Lancegate: Why Carter Stuck It Out," *New York Times Magazine*, 16 Oct. 1977, p. 38.
40. Safire, "Lancegate: Why Carter Stuck It Out," p. 39.
41. Haynes Johnson and George Lardner, Jr., "The Political Price of Friendship," *Washington Post*, 25 Sept. 1977, p. C-1; personal interview with author, John G. Heimann, 12 Sept. 1991.
42. Safire, *Safire's Washington*, p. 259.
43. Ibid., p. 260.
44. Personal communication with author, 17 Sept. 1991.
45. All in op-ed columns in the *New York Times:* James Reston, "Carter, Panama and China," 24 Aug. 1977, p. A-19; Tom Wicker, "Georgia's Pattern," 26 Aug. 1977, p. A-21; James Reston, "Lance and the Georgians," 31 Aug. 1977, p. A-19; Anthony Lewis, "Judging Mr. Lance," 5 Sept. 1977, p. A-17. Reston in his 31 Aug. column called on Lance to resign, as did Lewis in his column.
46. Safire, *Safire's Washington*, p. 260.
47. Robert M. Kaus, "The Smokeless Gun: Billygate and the Press," *Washington Monthly*, 12 (Oct. 1980): 38–52.
48. "Waterquiddick," *New York Times*, 12 Nov. 1979, p. A-21.
49. "Lowering the Gate," *New York Times*, 15 Nov. 1979, p. A-31.
50. "Happy Watergate to You," *New York Times*, 14 June 1982, p. 19.
51. *New York Times*, 23 May 1991, p. A-15.
52. *New York Times*, 13 June 1991, p. A-19.
53. *New York Times*, 5 Sept. 1991, p. A-21.
54. "Cleaning Housegate," *New York Times*, 30 Sept. 1991, p. A-15.
55. Ned Pattison, "Ned Pattison's Unpublished Book," 1979, reports that the class was known as "Watergate babies" within a week of the election. This unpublished manuscript by Rep. Ned Pattison, one of the congressional class of 1974, was made available to me by his widow, Eleanor Pattison.
56. Eric M. Uslander and M. Margaret Conway argue for a direct impact of Watergate on voters' choices in "The Responsible Congressional Electorate: Watergate, the Economy, and Vote Choice in 1974," *American Political Science Review* 79 (1985): 788–803; while Gary C. Jacobson and Samuel Kernell argue for the importance of the mediating role of strategic elites, in

Strategy and Choice in Congressional Elections (New Haven, Conn.: Yale University Press, 1983), and in an exchange with Uslander and Conway, "Interpreting the 1974 Congressional Election," *American Political Science Review* 80 (1986): 591–595.

57. Burdett Loomis, *The New American Politician* (New York: Basic Books, 1988).

58. Sen. Tim Wirth, personal interview with author, February 1991, La Jolla, Calif.

59. Eric L. Davis, "Legislative Reform and the Decline of Presidential Influence on Capitol Hill," *British Journal of Political Science* 9 (1979): 465–479.

60. Ibid., p. 469.

61. Donald Brotzman, telephone interview with author, March 1991.

62. Sen. Tim Wirth, personal interview with author, February 1991, La Jolla, Calif.

63. Tom Downey, personal interview with author, February 1991, Washington, D.C.

64. Victor Veysey, personal letter to author, 26 Feb. 1991.

65. William Hudnut, personal letter to author, 25 Mar. 1991. In 1975 Hudnut ran successfully for mayor of Indianapolis and has served in that position since.

66. Ned Pattison, "Ned Pattison's Unpublished Book," pp. 38–39.

Chapter 5

1. Cited by William B. Spann, Jr., chairman of the American Bar Association Special Committee to Study Federal Law Enforcement Agencies, testimony Watergate Reorganization and Reform Act of 1975: Hearings Before the Subcommittee on Government Operations, 94th Congress, 1st session, S. 495 and S. 2036, pt. 2, 11 March 1976, S. 495, p. 159.

2. Quoted by Harold Seidman, political scientist, in a solicited letter to Abraham Ribicoff, Committee on Government Operations, for the 1975 considerations of S. 495; cited also by Rep. Robert Drinan in *Provision for Special Prosecutor: Hearings Before the Subcommittee on Criminal Justice*, House Committee on the Judiciary, 94th Congress, 2d session, 23 July 1976, p. 17.

3. *Hearings Before the Subcommittee on Criminal Justice*, 26 Aug. 1976, pp. 142, 176.

4. Senate Committee on Governmental Affairs, *Hearings Before the Subcommittee on Oversight of Government Management*, 97th Congress, 2d session, on S. 2059, 28 April 1982, p. 47.

5. *Watergate Reorganization and Reform Act of 1975: Hearings Before the Senate Committee on Government Operations*, 94th Congress, 1st session, S. 495 and S. 2036 3, 4, 8 Dec. 1975 and 11 Mar. 1976, pt. 2, p. 1.

6. *Hearings Before the Senate Committee on Government Operations*, 29–31 July 1975, S. 495 and S. 2036, pt. 1, p. 5. For similar comments, see also

Walter Mondale, *The Accountability of Power: Toward a Responsible Presidency* (New York: David McKay, 1975), pp. 161–162.

7. *Hearings Before the Senate Committee on Government Operations*, Pt. 1, p. 95.

8. *Hearings Before the Senate Committee on Government Operations*, S. 495 and S. 2036, 3, 4, 8 Dec. 1975 and 11 March 1976, pt. 2, p. 7.

9. *Hearings Before the Senate Committee on Government Operations*, 29–31, July 1975, S. 495 and S. 2036, pt. 1, p. 3.

10. *Hearings Before the Senate Committee on Government Operations*, pt. 2, p. 37.

11. Ibid., p. 40.

12. Sen. Howard Baker, *Hearings Before the Senate Committee on Government Operations*, 29–31 July 1975, S. 495 and S. 2036, pt. 1, p. 28.

13. Ibid., p. 38.

14. Ibid., John Glenn comments, pt. 1, p. 38.

15. Ibid., Leon Jaworski testimony, pt. 1, p. 105.

16. Ibid., Henry Ruth testimony, pt. 1, p. 121.

17. Cited in Terry Eastland, *Ethics, Politics and the Independent Counsel: Executive Power, Executive Vice 1789–1989* (Washington, D.C.: National Legal Center for the Public Interest, 1989), p. 44.

18. Griffin B. Bell with Ronald J. Ostrow, *Taking Care of the Law* (New York: Morrow, 1982), p. 37.

19. Senate Committee on Governmental Affairs, *Special Prosecutor Provisions of Ethics in Government Act of 1978: Hearings Before the Subcommittee on Oversight of Government Management*, 97th Congress, 1st session, 20 and 22 May 1981, p. 95.

20. "The Law's Heavy Hammer," *Washington Star*, 1 Dec. 1979, reprinted in ibid., pp. 456–457.

21. "The Special Prosecutor Rides Again," *Washington Post*, 16 Sept. 1980, ibid., pp. 457–458.

22. Senate Committee on Governmental Affairs, *Ethics in Government Act Amendments of 1982: Hearings Before the Subcommittee on Oversight of Government Management*, 97th Congress, 2d session on S. 2059, 28 April 1982, p. 63.

23. Senate Committee on Governmental Affairs, *Oversight of the Independent Counsel Statute: Hearings Before the Subcommittee on Oversight of Government Management*, 100th Congress. 1st session, 19, 20 Mar. 1987, p. 26.

24. Oral argument, 28 April 1988, in Philip B. Kurland and Gerhard Casper, eds., *Landmark Briefs and Arguments of the Supreme Court of the United States: Constitutional Law 1987 Term Supplement*, vol. 177, *Morrison v. Olson* (1988) (University Publications of America, 1989), p. 37.

25. *Morrison v. Olson* 487 U.S. 653. The only dissent was a characteristically fiery one from Justice Antonin Scalia, who argued that the statute obviously infringed on the separation of powers. "If to describe this case is not to decide

it, the concept of a government of separate and coordinate powers no longer has meaning."

26. William French Smith, "Independent Counsel Provisions of the Ethics in Government Act," in L. Gordon Crovitz and Jeremy A. Rabkin, eds., *The Fettered Presidency: Legal Constraints on the Executive Branch* (Washington, D.C.: American Enterprise Institute, 1989), pp. 253–261.

27. See Stephen L. Carter, "The Independent Counsel Mess," *Harvard Law Review* 102 (Nov. 1988): 105–141; special issues of *American University Law Review* 38 (Winter 1989) and *American Criminal Law Review* 25 (Fall 1987); and Thomas S. Martin and David E. Zerhusen, "Independent Counsel—Checks and Balances," *George Washington Law Review* 58 (Feb. 1990): 534–548.

28. Eastland, *Ethics, Politics*.

29. Suzanne Garment, *Scandal: The Culture of Mistrust in American Politics* (New York: Random House, 1991).

30. Eastland, *Ethics, Politics*, p. x.

31. Garment, *Scandal*, pp. 9–10.

32. Ibid., p. 108.

33. Katy Harriger, *Symbol of Justice: The Special Prosecutor in American Politics* (Lawrence: University Press of Kansas, forthcoming).

34. Edward H. Levi testimony, *Provision for Special Prosecutor: Hearings Before the Subcommittee on Criminal Justice*, 23 July 1976.

35. Benjamin Ginsberg and Martin Shefter, *Politics by Other Means: The Declining Importance of Elections in America* (New York: Basic Books, 1990).

36. Harriger, *Symbol of Justice*.

37. The best summary of this post-Watergate legislation is Stanley Kutler, *The Wars of Watergate* (New York: Knopf, 1990), pp. 574–611.

38. Would it have passed without the congressional outrage about the Saturday Night Massacre? A *Congressional Quarterly* analysis found few congressmen who claimed Watergate matters affected their votes. On the other hand, the House had sustained all five previous presidential vetoes in 1973, and congressional leaders, both Clement Zablocki, the chief proponent of the bill, and William Mailliard, its chief opponent, believed Watergate helped create the climate for the successful override. See *Congressional Quarterly Weekly Report 31* (10 Nov. 1973): 2943–2944, 2985–2986.

39. There is a vast literature now on the intelligence agencies and their legal standing. See William Colby, *Honorable Men: My Life in the CIA* (New York: Simon & Schuster, 1978); Loch K. Johnson, *A Season of Inquiry: The Senate Intelligence Investigation* (Lexington, Ky.: University Press of Kentucky, 1985) and *America's Secret Power: The CIA in a Democratic Society* (New York: Oxford University Press, 1989); Rhodri Jeffrey-Jones, *The CIA and American Democracy* (New Haven, Conn.: Yale University Press, 1989); Thomas Powers, *The Man Who kept the Secrets: Richard Helms and the CIA* (New York: Alfred A. Knopf, 1979); Frank J. Smist, Jr., *Congress Oversees*

NOTES TO PAGES 98–101

the United States Intelligence Community, 1947–1989 (Knoxville: University of Tennessee Press, 1990); Gregory F. Treverton, *Covert Action: The Limits of Intervention in the Postwar World* (New York: Basic Books, 1987); Stansfield Turner, *Secrecy and Democracy: The CIA in Transition* (Boston: Houghton Mifflin, 1985); David Wise, *The American Police State: The Government Against the People* (New York: Random House, 1976); and Bob Woodward, *Veil: The Secret Wars of the CIA 1981–1987* (New York: Simon & Schuster, 1987).

40. David H. Flaherty, *Protecting Privacy in Surveillance Societies* (Chapel Hill: University of North Carolina Press, 1989), p. 314.

41. James Rule, Douglas McAdam, Linda Stearns, and David Uglow, *The Politics of Privacy* (New York: Elsevier, 1980), p. 64.

42. Andrew S. McFarland, *Common Cause: Lobbying in the Public Interest* (Chatham, N.J.: Chatham House, 1984), p. 129. Gary Jacobson also indicates that the vividness of the Watergate scandal helped the tough 1974 amendments to pass. See Gary Jacobson, *Money in Congressional Elections* (New Haven, Conn.: Yale University Press, 1980), pp. 180, 182, 191.

43. Sen. Claiborne Pell supported the reforms, holding that they might not "eradicate future Watergates" but would discourage "a climate in which power is abused by the clever at the expense of the unwary." Sen. Lowell Weicker, Jr., opposed the public financing provision, holding that it "is not magical Clorox guaranteed to end forever the dirty laundry of Watergate." In the House, too, where floor debate took place in the days just before Nixon resigned, Watergate rhetoric was thrown back and forth between Republicans and Democrats. See *Congressional Quarterly Almanac*, 30 (1974): 618, 629, 631, 632.

44. Joel L. Fleishman, "The 1974 Federal Election Campaign Amendments: The Shortcomings of Good Intentions," *Duke Law Journal* (1975): 851–899.

45. *New York Times*, 21 Nov. 1974, p. 1; *New York Times*, 22 Nov. 1974, p. 21.

46. *Hearings Before the Senate Committee on Government Operations*, 29–31 July 1975, S. 495 and S. 2036, pt. 1, p. 2.

47. CBS Evening News, 29 Oct. 1976.

48. *Special Prosecutor Provisions of Ethics in Government Act of 1978: Hearings Before the Senate Subcommittee on Oversight of Government Management*, 20 and 22 May 1981, p. 89.

49. *Hearings Before the Senate Committee on Government Operations*, on S. 495 and S. 2036, 3 Dec. 1975, pt. 2, p. 8.

50. *New York Times*, 23 Jan. 1977, p. VI-33. This conservative view is restated in the report of the President's Commission on Federal Ethics Law Reform in 1989. The report concluded that laws do not create virtue but define a standard for honest citizens. "Laws can be persuasive and effective, but only in an atmosphere created by emphatic leadership at the top, leadership which asserts ethical norms as the universal standard of conduct across the Government, leadership that is replicated at every echelon of Government." President's Commission on Federal Ethics Law Reform, *To Serve With*

Honor (Washington, D.C.: Government Printing Office, 1989), p. 114. See also L. H. LaRue, *Political Discourse: A Case Study of the Watergate Affair* (Athens: University of Georgia Press, 1988), which takes a close look at the metaphor of a "government of laws and not of men" (p. 67).

51. The phrase "government of laws and not of men" has a long tradition, which Justice Antonin Scalia recalled in his dissenting opinion in *Morrison v. Olson* (1988). It comes from the Massachusetts Constitution of 1780 establishing separation of powers among the executive, legislative, and judicial branches of government. The Constitution held that the legislative department should never exercise executive or judicial powers, the executive should never exercise legislative or judicial powers, and the judicial department should never exercise legislative or executive powers "to the end it may be a government of laws and not of men." The power of this quotation, for Scalia, was that this essential affirmation of lawful rule was originally invoked not against executive abuse of power or against a leader's going beyond legally constituted authority in general but against one governmental branch's encroachment upon the duly constituted authority of another's. *Morrison v. Olson* 487 U.S. 654 at 697.

52. Richard Ben-Veniste and George Frampton, Jr., *Stonewall: The Legal Case Against the Watergate Conspirators* (New York: Simon & Schuster, 1977), pp. 394–395.

Chapter 6

1. Quoted in Justin Kaplan, *Lincoln Steffens* (New York: Simon & Schuster, 1974), p. 151.
2. Wilfrid Sheed, *Essays in Disguise* (New York: Knopf, 1990), p. 148.
3. Larry Sabato, *Feeding Frenzy* (New York: Free Press, 1991), p. 61.
4. Karen Rothmyer, *Winning Pulitzers* (New York: Columbia University Press, 1991), p. 9.
5. Thanks to Michael Cornfield who, by the example of his own work, has led me to think more seriously about narratives about journalism as well as narratives in journalism.
6. Katherine Graham interviews, 21 Dec. 1984 and 4 Sept. 1985, Poynter Institute for Media Studies "NewsLeaders" series, St. Petersburg, Fla.
7. Ben Bagdikian, "The Fruits of Agnewism," *Columbia Journalism Review* 11 (Jan./Feb. 1973): 9–21.
8. Katherine Graham interviews, 21 Dec. 1984 and 4 Sept. 1985.
9. Howard Bray, *The Pillars of the Post* (New York: Norton, 1980), pp. 125–126.
10. Katherine Graham interviews, 21 Dec. 1984 and 4 Sept. 1985.
11. Epstein's essay originally appeared in *Commentary* 58 (July 1974): 21–24;

reprinted in Edward Jay Epstein, *Between Fact and Fiction: The Problem of Journalism* (New York: Vintage Books, 1975), pp. 19–33.

12. Katherine Graham, "The Activism of the Press," *Nieman Reports* (Spring 1974): 21–25.

13. Thomas Edsall, personal interview with author, 13 Feb. 1991, La Jolla, Calif.

14. Larry Sabato, *Feeding Frenzy*, pp. 86–93.

15. See, for instance, S. Robert Lichter, Stanley Rothman, and Linda S. Lichter, *The Media Elite: America's New Powerbrokers* (Bethesda, Md.: Adler & Adler, 1986).

16. Barry Sussman, *The Great Cover-Up: Nixon and the Scandal of Watergate* (New York: Crowell, 1974), pp. 130–131.

17. Ben Bagdikian, personal interview with author, 5 Aug. 1990, Berkeley, CA.

18. Sanford Ungar, *The Papers & The Papers: An Account of the Legal and Political Battles over the Pentagon Papers* (New York: Columbia University Press, 1972, 1989), pp. 130–147.

19. Chalmers Roberts, *In the Shadow of Power: The Story of the Washington Post* (Cabin John, Md.: Seven Locks Press, 1989), p. 441.

20. Stephen E. Ambrose, *Nixon: The Education of a Politician 1913–1962* (New York: Simon & Schuster, 1987), p. 664.

21. Timothy Crouse, *The Boys on the Bus* (New York: Random House, 1973), but see Edith Efron, *The News Twisters* (Los Angeles: Nash Publications, 1971).

22. Michael A. Genovese, *The Nixon Presidency* (Westport, Conn.: Greenwood Press, 1990), p. 48.

23. Bagdikian, "The Fruits of Agnewism," 9–21. As for network television coverage of Watergate, it appears generally to have been scrupulously neutral. See Marlene Schuler Daniels, "Carbon Copy News: A Content Analysis of Network Evening News Coverage of Watergate." M.A. diss., University of Wisconsin–Madison, 1976.

24. Godfrey Hodgson, *All Things to All Men: The False Promise of the Modern American Presidency* (New York: Simon & Schuster, 1980), pp. 193–194.

25. Leonard Downie, personal interview with author, 28 Feb. 1991, Washington, D.C.

26. Quoted in Chalmers Roberts, *In the Shadow of Power*, p. 495.

27. Maxwell E. McCombs, "Testing the Myths: A Statistical Review 1967–86," *Gannett Center Journal* (Spring 1988): 101–108.

28. When Ben Bagdikian commented on a draft of this chapter that included this paragraph, it reminded him that a senior editor at the *Atlantic* at the last minute removed a paragraph explaining that the influx of students into journalism did not start with Woodward and Bernstein; the editor, Bagdikian recalls, was "obsessed with" the impression that it all began with Watergate (personal communication with author, 16 Oct. 1991).

29. Dina Rasor, an enterprising Washington journalist, recalls that as a teenager during Watergate, she came to view the press as the "defenders of truth,

justice, and the American Way." Dina Rasor, *The Pentagon Underground* (New York: Times Books, 1985), p. 49.

30. Thomas Edsall, personal interview with author.

31. *San Diego Union*, 6 Jan. 1990, p. A-17. Nessen spoke at a symposium on "The Presidency, The Press and the People," organized by the University of California, San Diego, and later broadcast on PBS.

32. David S. Broder, *Behind the Front Page: A Candid Look at How the News Is Made* (New York: Simon & Schuster, 1987), p. 167.

33. Michael K. Deaver with Mickey Herskowitz, *Behind the Scenes* (New York: Morrow, 1987), p. 148.

34. Peter Kaye, "When the White House Speaks, the World Listens," *KPBS on Air*, Jan. 1990, p. 16.

35. Leonard Downie, personal interview with author.

36. Gerald Warren, personal communication with author, 13 Nov. 1991.

37. Ben Bradlee, personal interview with author, 27 Feb. 1991, Washington, D.C.

38. Steven Brill, "Back on the Beat with Woodward and Bernstein," *Esquire* Dec. 1983, p. 503.

39. William Goldman, *Adventures in the Screen Trade* (New York: Warner Books, 1983), pp. 115–116.

40. CBS Morning News, 5 April 1976.

41. Nat Hentoff, "Woodstein in the Movies," *Columbia Journalism Review* (May–June 1976): 46.

42. Vincent Canby, "Two Exhilarating Thrillers, Plotted by Hitchcock and Nixon," *New York Times*, 11 April 1976, p. II-1.

43. Barbara Stubbs Cohen, personal interview with author, 25 Feb. 1991, Washington, D.C.

44. Bob Woodward and Carl Bernstein, *The Final Days* (New York: Simon & Schuster, 1976).

45. CBS Morning News, 5 April 1976.

46. William B. Arthur, *The Courier-Journal* (Louisville), 21 Mar. 1974.

47. *New York Times*, 2 Dec. 1974. p. A-29.

48. *New York Times*, 4 May 1976, p. 14.

49. John Osborne, "The Woodstein Flap," *The New Republic*, 24 April 1976, p. 8. Thomas Powers predicted in *Commonweal* that *The Final Days* would outlast its critics, as did Peter Prescott in *Newsweek*. They may be right, although my impression is that *All the President's Men*, because it found a cherished niche in the journalism school curriculum, and because the film still enhances its value, is the far more familiar work today. See Thomas Powers, "The Nixon Finale," *Commonweal*, 7 May 1976, pp. 307–309 and Peter Prescott, "Instant History," *Newsweek*, 3 May 1976, pp. 89–90.

50. James Fallows, "The New Celebrities of Washington," *New York Review of Books*, 12 June 1986, p. 42.

51. In a recent brochure from a Washington speakers bureau advertising a stable

of "history makers, trailblazers, entrepreneurs, explorers, news breakers, pioneers, discoverers, educators, experts," nearly half of the speakers listed are journalists (eighteen of forty-two speakers are known primarily as journalists). Cosby Bureau International, 1991.

52. The best evidence on the status of Washington journalists comes from studies by Stephen Hess in *The Washington Reporters* (Washington, D.C.: The Brookings Institution, 1981), pp. 158–165; and *Live from Capitol Hill! Studies of Congress and the Media* (Washington, D.C.: The Brookings Institution, 1991), pp. 110–130. Hess's surveys do not indicate any marked rise in educational attainment in the past generation among Washington journalists. He did not gather data on income. Anecdotal evidence suggests skyrocketing incomes, at least among an elite of Washington reporters. See Jacob Weisberg, "The Buckrakers," *The New Republic*, 27 Jan. 1986, pp. 16–18; and Carol Matlack, "Crossing the Line?" *National Journal*, 25 Mar. 1989, pp. 724–729.

53. Benjamin Bradlee, personal interview with author.

54. This is a topic that has been written about extensively. See in particular Jonathan Schell, *The Time of Illusion* (New York: Knopf, 1976); William Safire, *Before the Fall: An Inside View of the Pre-Watergate White House* (Garden City, N.Y.: Doubleday, 1975); Genovese, *The Nixon Presidency;* William Porter, *Assault on the Media: The Nixon Years* (Ann Arbor: University of Michigan Press, 1976); Thomas Whiteside, "Shaking the Tree," *The New Yorker* 51 (17 March 1975): 41–91.

55. Safire, *Before the Fall*, p. 341.

56. See Schell, *Time of Illusion*, pp. 24, 55.

57. Sig Mickelson, *The Electric Mirror: Politics in an Age of Television* (New York: Dodd, Mead, 1972), p. 4, finds this a turning point in government-television relations.

58. Charles Peters, "Why the White House Press Didn't Get the Watergate Story," *Washington Monthly*, July/Aug. 1973; reprinted in David Saffell, ed., *Watergate: Its Effects on the American Political System* (Cambridge, Mass.: Winthrop Publishers, 1974), p. 31.

59. Safire, *Before the Fall*, p. 351.

60. The Kraft case has a particularly detailed history. See David Wise, *The American Police State: The Government Against the People* (New York: Random House, 1976), pp. 3–30 and also Joseph Kraft, "Reflections on a Personal Wiretap," *Washington Post*, 12 June 1973, p. 21.

61. Genovese, *The Nixon Presidency*, p. 54.

62. Daniel Schorr, *Clearing the Air* (Boston: Houghton Mifflin, 1977), pp. 30–34, 53–57.

63. Herbert G. Klein, *Making It Perfectly Clear* (New York: Doubleday, 1980), p. 109; the Haldeman memo was written on 4 Feb. 1970.

64. Klein, *Making It Perfectly Clear*, p. 125; Larry Higby's letter is dated 16 Sept. 1970.

65. George W. Johnson, *The Nixon Presidential Press Conferences* (New York: Earl M. Coleman Enterprises, 1978), pp. 369, 373. Nixon repeats this line in a video display at the Richard Nixon Library and Birthplace; his hostility to the press remains implacable.

66. Harry S. Ashmore, "Nixon's Regime Gave News Media Identity Separate from Public's," *Phoenix Gazette*, 10 Dec. 1973. Ashmore attributes this view to Lisagor and endorses it.

67. Safire, *Before the Fall*, pp. 343, 351.

68. See Sabato, *Feeding Frenzy*, p. 45.

69. Theodore White, *The Making of the President, 1960* (New York: Atheneum, 1961).

70. American Society of Newspaper Editors, *Problems of Journalism* (Washington, D.C., 1983), p. 114.

71. See Michael Schudson, *Discovering the News* (New York: Basic Books, 1978), pp. 189–190.

72. Barry Sussman, personal interview with author, Jan. 1991, Washington, D.C.

73. Steve Hess, personal interview with author, Jan. 1991, Washington, D.C.

74. *Washington Post*, 5 Aug. 1977, p. A-21.

75. Benjamin Bradlee, personal interview with author.

76. "Carter and the Press: One Good Month," interview with Jack Nelson, *Washington Journalism Review* 13 (Jan./Feb. 1991): 17.

77. James Deakin, *Straight Stuff: The Reporters, the White House, and the Truth* (New York: Morrow, 1984), p. 295.

78. Jody Powell, *The Other Side of the Story* (New York: Morrow, 1984), p. 173.

79. For reviews of *Absence of Malice* that comment on *All the President's Men*, see David Ansen, "Wayward Press," *Newsweek*, 23 Nov. 1981, p. 125; Richard Schickel, "Lethal Leaks," *Time*, 23 Nov. 1981, p. 98; and Stanley Kauffmann, "The Facts of Some Matters," *The New Republic*, 23 Dec. 1981, pp. 24–25. Discussions of how journalists respond to *Absence of Malice* also include comments on *All the President's Men* in the *New York Times*, 15 Nov. 1981, p. II-1 and in the *Washington Post*, 18 Nov. 1981, p. B-1.

80. "Bernstein Chides News For Its Over-Confidence," *Harvard Crimson*, 21 Mar. 1989.

81. *Washington Post*, 8 Aug. 1984, p. A-12.

82. Bob Woodward and Scott Armstrong, *The Brethren* (New York: Simon & Schuster, 1979); Bob Woodward, *Wired: The Short Life and Fast Times of John Belushi* (New York: Simon & Schuster, 1984); *Veil: The Secret Wars of the CIA, 1981–1987* (New York: Simon & Schuster, 1987); *The Commanders* (New York: Simon & Schuster, 1991).

83. Steven Brill, "Inside the Jury Room at the *Washington Post* Libel Trial," *American Lawyer* 4 (Nov. 1982): 1, 89–93.

84. This account of the courtroom and jury room follows Brill, "Inside the Jury Room."

85. *William P. Tavoulareas v. Washington Post*, 817 F. 2d 762 (D.C. Cir. 1987); Kenneth Starr, at 795–97; George MacKinnon, at 834.
86. Tom Rosenstiel, personal communication with author, 16 Jan. 1991, Washington, D.C.
87. Kaplan, *Lincoln Steffens*, pp. 145–146.

Chapter 7

1. J. Fred Buzhardt obituaries from a variety of South Carolina papers were placed in the *Congressional Record* by Sen. Strom Thurmond; 29 Jan. 1979, *Congressional Record*, v. 125, pt. 1 14/15: 1270–1275.
2. *New York Times*, 24 Apr. 1985, p. B-12.
3. *Los Angeles Times*, 26 July 1988, p. I-20.
4. *Los Angeles Times*, 10 Nov. 1988, p. I-8.
5. *Los Angeles Times*, 29 Sept. 1990, p. A-30. See also the obituary for Joseph J. Maraziti, one of Nixon's defenders on the House Judiciary Committee in *Chicago Tribune*, 23 May 1991, p. II-9.
6. *Los Angeles Times*, 22 Sept. 1990, p. F-2 (San Diego County edition); *Milwaukee Sentinel*, 14 Aug. 1990, p. III-2.
7. On enjoying Watergate, see *Milwaukee Sentinel*, 14 Aug. 1990, p. III-2. On prison and writing, see *Los Angeles Times*, 7 Nov. 1990, p. B-1. See G. Gordon Liddy, *The Monkey Handlers* (New York: St. Martin's Press, 1990).
8. *Los Angeles Times*, 7 Feb. 1991, p. E-1.
9. *Los Angeles Times*, 13 June 1991, p. A-25.
10. Liddy reported this on the cable television talk show he hosts, CNBC's "Talk Live," during a program in the fall of 1991.
11. *New York Times*, 17 Aug. 1973, p. 9.
12. *New York Times*, 22 May 1974, p. 1.
13. Jeb Stuart Magruder, *An American Life: One Man's Road to Watergate* (New York: Atheneum, 1974).
14. Jeff Greenfield, review of *An American Life*, by Magruder, *New York Times Book Review*, 30 June 1974, p. 4. See also Christopher Lehmann-Haupt in the daily *New York Times*, 25 June 1974, p. 35.
15. *New York Times*, 18 June 1975, p. 38.
16. *New York Times*, 9 May 1979, p. III-16.
17. *New York Times*, 17 June 1982, p. 27.
18. *New York Times*, 9 Oct. 1988, p. I-28.
19. Michael Ryan, " 'We Can Come Back'," *Parade*, 14 May 1989, pp. 12–13.
20. *New York Times*, 1 Aug. 1974, p. 1.
21. *New York Times*, 22 Feb. 1975, p. 1; 23 Feb. 1975, p. 31; 25 Feb. 1975, p. 10; 28 Feb. 1975, p. 66.
22. *New York Times*, 15 Mar. 1975, p. 13, and 26 Mar. 1975, p. 31.
23. *New York Times*, 17 Oct. 1975, p. 28.

24. *New York Times*, 29 Oct. 1976, p. 1.
25. *New York Times*, 12 Nov. 1977, p. 19; 31 Jan. 1978, p. 14; 26 July 1978, p. 16.
26. John Ehrlichman, review of *The Ends of Power*, by H. R. Haldeman, *Time*, 6 Mar. 1978, pp. 26–27.
27. John Ehrlichman, "Mexican Aliens Aren't a Problem . . . They're a Solution," *Esquire*, Aug. 1979, pp. 54–64.
28. John Ehrlichman, "Art in the Nixon White House," *Art News*, May 1982, pp. 74–81.
29. Peter S. Prescott, "Ehrlichman's Poison Pen," *Newsweek*, 15 Feb. 1982, p. 80.
30. *Newsweek*, 8 Dec. 1986, pp. 51–52.
31. ABC World News Tonight, 17 June 1987.
32. Theodore H. White, *Breach of Faith: The Fall of Richard Nixon* (New York: Atheneum, 1975); Jimmy Breslin, *How the Good Guys Finally Won: Notes on an Impeachment Summer* (New York: Viking, 1975).
33. Leon Jaworski, *The Right and the Power: The Prosecution of Watergate* (New York: Reader's Digest Press, 1976); Charles Colson, *Born Again* (Old Tappan, N.J.: Chosen Books, 1976); John W. Dean III, *Blind Ambition: The White House Years* (New York: Simon & Schuster, 1976); Bob Woodward and Carl Bernstein, *The Final Days* (New York: Simon & Schuster, 1976).
34. Victor Lasky, *It Didn't Start with Watergate* (New York: Dial Press, 1977); Richard Nixon, *RN: The Memoirs of Richard Nixon* (New York: Grosset and Dunlop, 1978); H. R. Haldeman, with Joseph DiMona, *The Ends of Power* (New York: Times Books, 1978).
35. David Halberstam, *The Powers That Be* (New York: Alfred A. Knopf, 1979); G. Gordon Liddy, *Will: The Autobiography of G. Gordon Liddy* (New York: St. Martin's Press, 1980). This information is from *The Bowker Annual of Library and Book Trade Information* (New York: R. R. Bowker, various years). The *Annual* takes its statistics about best-sellers from *Publishers Weekly*.
36. Len Colodny and Robert Gettlin, *Silent Coup: The Removal of a President* (New York: St. Martin's Press, 1991).
37. For a more extensive discussion of newsification, see Michael Schudson, "National News Culture and the Rise of the Informational Citizen," in Alan Wolfe, *America at Century's End* (Berkeley: University of California Press, 1991), pp. 265–282.
38. "Summer of Judgment: The Watergate Hearings" is a production of WETA, Washington, D.C., and "The American Experience: Nixon," WGBH/Thames Television production. The latter is reviewed by Walter Goodman, *New York Times*, 15 Oct. 1990, p. B-6.
39. CBS Evening News, 11 Feb. 1982.
40. CBS Evening News, 11 Feb. 1982. The Colson comic book is in the Richard Nixon collection at Whittier College.

41. "Washington: Behind Closed Doors," a Paramount-ABC miniseries starring Cliff Robertson and Jason Robards, created by David Rintels, aired 6 Sept. to 11 Sept. 1977. See Les Brown, "Ehrlichman Novel to Open ABC Season," *New York Times*, 29 June 1977, p. III-24. "Blind Ambition," starring Martin Sheen, aired in four parts on CBS 20 May to 23 May 1979. Reviews by John J. O'Connor, *New York Times*, 18 May 1979, p. III-26; Bruce Henstell, *New York Times*, 20 May 1979, p. II-1. "Will" was televised 10 Jan. 1982. See John J. O'Connor, "Is This Autobiography Really Necessary?" *New York Times*, 10 Jan. 1982, p. II-23. "The Final Days" appeared 29 Oct. 1989, a three-hour ABC production starring Lane Smith. It was previewed in the *Los Angeles Times* Calendar, 4 June 1989, p. 7, and reviewed by the *Los Angeles Times* television critic Howard Rosenberg 27 Oct. 1989, p. F-32 and the *New York Times* television critic John J. O'Connor 29 Oct. 1989, p. II-33. It was a cover story in *TV Guide:* Michael Leahy, "The Nixon Drama Revisited— Has TV Got It Right?" 28 Oct. 1989, pp. 2–4; it received harsh criticism from Leonard Garment, 30 Oct. 1989, *New York Times*, p. I-19. "Will" appeared some time before February 1982. A videotaped drama originally performed on stage in Los Angeles, "Secret Honor," was produced and directed by Robert Altman in 1984.

42. Daniel Schorr, "The Danger of Blurring Fact and Fantasy," *New York Times*, 7 Aug. 1977, p. II-1.

43. Interviewed on "Summer of Judgment: The Watergate Hearings," aired on PBS in 1983.

44. *New York Times*, 16 Jan. 1975, p. 33.

45. Russell Baker, "Go Ye and Sin Unto the Upper Brackets," *New York Times*, 21 Jan. 1975, p. 33.

46. John W. Dean III, *Lost Honor* (Los Angeles: Stratford Press, 1982), p. 18.

47. Ibid., pp. 43, 46.

48. See *New York Times*, 3 Feb. 1975, p. 13; *New York Times*, 4 Feb. 1975, p. 29; Tom Wicker, "Fat Fees and Free Speech," *New York Times*, 2 Feb. 1975, p. E-15; "News of the Week," *New York Times* 9 Feb. 1975, p. IV-4; *New York Times* 23 Feb. 1975, p. 39 (photo); *New York Times*, 23 Feb. 1975, p. 57; 27 Feb. 1975, p. 12 (report of a bomb threat at Westchester Community College); 28 Feb. 1975, p. 17.

49. "Fee Issue Leads Dean to End Lecture Tour" *New York Times*, 17 Mar. 1975, p. 23 (AP).

50. John J. O'Connor, "TV Review," *New York Times*, 24 Mar. 1975, p. 62.

51. Les Brown, "Networks Reviewing Policies on Paying for Exclusive Interviews," *New York Times*, 2 April 1975, p. 78.

52. *New York Times*, 2 June 1976, p. 31.

53. Dean had one more surprise for the Ford White House. In mid-October, early copies of his *Blind Ambition* appeared in bookstores. The book alleged that the Nixon White House had used Gerald Ford to block an early Watergate investigation by Rep. Wright Patman in September 1972. Congressional

Democrats asked Watergate Special Prosecutor Charles Ruff to investigate, but Ruff concluded that the matter was not under his jurisdiction, and it was not pursued.

54. Major reviews of *Blind Ambition*, by John Dean: James Q. Wilson, "The Greasy Pole," *Commentary* 63 (Feb. 1977): 66–68; Garry Wills, "Gadarene White House," *Saturday Review*, 11 Dec. 1976, pp. 64–67; Nicholas von Hoffman, "Leakage," *New York Review of Books*, 25 Nov. 1976, pp. 8–9; J. Anthony Lukas, "Blind Ambition," *New York Times Book Review*, 31 Oct. 1976, pp. 3, 12–13.

55. *New York Times*, 17 June 1982, p. D-18. The other leading Watergate lecturer has been Gordon Liddy, said to have grossed $150,000 in fifty-four lectures in the fall of 1980. See Michael Posner, "Tough Guy on the Campus Star-maker Circuit," *MacLean's*, 26 Jan. 1981, p. 10. See also CBS Evening News, 14 Nov. 1980, and CBS News, 17 Sept. 1981, reporting on Liddy's sharing a platform with Daniel Ellsberg at Syracuse University.

56. Dean, *Lost Honor*, p. 252.

57. Ibid., p. 264.

58. Ibid., p. 2.

59. Ibid., p. 358.

60. M. Beauchamp, "Wages of Fame," *Forbes* 137 (21 Apr. 1986): 140–141.

61. *New York Times*, 13 July 1986, p. III-1.

62. The 1991 publication of *Silent Coup: The Removal of a President*, by Len Colodny and Robert Gettlin (New York: St. Martin's Press, 1991), brought Dean briefly back into the public eye. The book pictures him as the mastermind of Watergate, entrapping the president in his snares. Dean issued a statement calling the book "absolute garbage." See *Washington Post*, 21 May 1991, p. C-1.

63. Laurence I. Barrett, *Gambling with History: Ronald Reagan in the White House* (Garden City, N.Y.: Doubleday, 1983), p. 460. Maurice H. Stans sought also to clear his name in a book, *The Terrors of Justice: The Untold Side of Watergate* (New York: Everest House, 1978).

64. *Los Angeles Times*, 12 Sept. 1988, p. I-1.

65. *Los Angeles Times*, 2 Dec. 1991, p. 1.

66. See Martin Esslin, *The Age of Television* (San Francisco: W. H. Freeman, 1982).

67. See Paul J. Bracken, *The Command and Control of Nuclear Forces* (New Haven, Conn.: Yale University Press, 1983).

68. Daniel Boorstin, *The Image, or What Happened to the American Dream* (New York: Atheneum, 1962), p. 57.

69. CBS Morning News, 17 June 1975. See also *Time*, 28 Feb. 1983, p. 25.

70. Russell Mootry, Jr., "Frank Wills Must Not Be Forgotten!" *Ebony*, June 1976, p. 100. See also "Watergate Figures Made Millions, Wills $2,000," *Jet* 2 July 1984, p. 34; S. Booker, "Frank Wills, Ten Years After Watergate, Faces Dismal Future in Georgia," *Jet*, 10 Sept. 1984, pp. 22–24; Jill Nelson-Ricks,

"The Dog Days of Frank Wills," *Essence*, Nov. 1984, pp. 93–94, 142; "Caught in the Act" (editorial), *New York Times*, 18 Feb. 1983, p. 30.

71. Pamela Kilian, personal communication with author, 20 Aug. 1991; Kilian, *What Was Watergate? A Young Reader's Guide to Understanding an Era* (New York: St. Martin's Press, 1990).

72. Frances Fitzgerald, *America Revised: History Schoolbooks in the Twentieth Century* (Boston: Atlantic Monthly Press, 1979), p. 48.

73. The teacher may work against, as well as with, the textbook lesson, or may simplify lessons of complex textbooks or complexify lessons of simple ones. To read textbooks is not necessarily to know what lessons children learn from them. John Wills demonstrates this in "Public Education and Political Discourse: Classroom Histories of the Cold War" (Ph.D. diss., University of California, San Diego, 1990).

74. Fitzgerald, *America Revised*, p. 69.

75. Ibid., p. 143.

76. Ibid., p. 46.

77. Robert Sam Anson, *Exile: The Unquiet Oblivion of Richard M. Nixon* (New York: Simon & Schuster, 1984), p. 274.

78. Clarence L. Ver Steeg, *American Spirit: A History of the United States* (Boston: Allyn & Bacon, 1985), p. 682.

79. Winthrop D. Jordan, Miriam Greenblatt, and John S. Bowes, *The Americans: The History of a People and Nation* (Evanston, Ill.: McDougal, Littell, 1985), p. 787; The Ford quotation can also be found in James West Davidson and John E. Batchelor, *The American Nation* (Englewood Cliffs, N.J.: Prentice-Hall, 1986), pp. 677–678. Ernest R. May, *A Proud Nation* (Evanston, Ill.: McDougal, Littell, 1985), p. 729; and other textbooks.

80. Margaret Stimmann Branson, *America's Heritage* (Lexington, Mass.: Ginn and Co., 1986), pp. 556–562.

81. Fitzgerald, *America Revised*, p. 158.

82. May, *A Proud Nation*, pp. 727–728.

83. Thomas Andrew Bailey and David M. Kennedy, *The American Pageant: A History of the Republic* (Lexington, Mass.: D. C. Heath, 1987), pp. 889–895.

84. John M. Blum, William S. McFeely, Edmund S. Morgan, Arthur M. Schlesinger, Jr., Kenneth M. Stampp, and C. Vann Woodward, *The National Experience: A History of the United States* (San Diego: Harcourt Brace Jovanovich, 1989), p. 790.

85. Kilian, *What Was Watergate?*

86. Jim Hargrove, *The Story of Watergate* (Chicago: Childrens Press, 1988).

87. George Sullivan, *Mr. President: A Book of U.S. Presidents* (New York: Scholastic, 1989), p. 142.

88. Frank Freidel, *The Presidents of the United States* (Washington, D.C.: White House Historical Association, 1981).

89. Vincent Wilson, Jr., *The Book of the Presidents* (Brookeville, Md.: American History Research Associates, 1989), p. 78.

90. Wyatt Blassingame, *The Look-It-Up Book of Presidents* (New York: Random House, 1984), p. 135.

91. Dee Lillegard, *Encyclopedia of the Presidents: Richard Nixon* (Chicago: Childrens Press, 1988), p. 89.

92. "Presidential Rummy: An Educational Card Game," Safari Limited, Miami, Fla., an authorized product of the Smithsonian Institution.

Chapter 8

1. A good round-up of famous Watergate phrases is in Stanley I. Kutler, "Wordwars," *Christian Science Monitor*, 10 Sept. 1987, p. 14, a column prompted by the reprise of Watergate phrases and Watergate themes in Iran-contra.

2. Peggy Noonan, *What I Saw at the Revolution* (New York: Ballantine Books, 1990), p. 245.

3. Noonan, *What I Saw at the Revolution*, p. 94.

4. Sidney Blumenthal, *Our Long National Daydream* (New York: Harper & Row, 1988).

5. Rex Stout, *A Family Affair* (New York: Bantam Books, 1975), pp. 25, 86. Other references to Watergate on pp. 16, 70.

6. John Updike, *Rabbit Is Rich* (New York: Ballantine Books, 1981), p. 94.

7. Michael Malone, *Uncivil Seasons* (New York: Pocket Books, 1983) p. 9; Joan Hess, *Dear Miss Demeanor* (New York: Ballantine Books, 1987), p. 90; Anne Bernays, *Professor Romeo* (New York: Weidenfeld & Nicolson, 1989), p. 144.

8. "Murphy Brown," 24 June 1991 (rerun from the 1990–91 season); "The Simpsons," 26 Sept. 1991.

9. "thirtysomething," episode aired 21 May 1991. The quotations here may not be exact; Ralph McInerny, *The Search Committee* (New York: Atheneum, 1991), p. 57.

10. William Safire, *Safire's Political Dictionary* (New York: Random House, 1978), pp. 779–780.

11. Ibid., pp. 499–500.

12. "High Crimes and Misdemeanors," PBS, broadcast 27 Nov. 1990.

13. Tim Weiner, *Blank Check: The Pentagon's Black Budget* (New York: Warner Books, 1990), p. 2. "I heard the President's men telling transparent lies about what the White House was doing in Central America." Allan Goodman, former senior staff member in the CIA and associate dean of the School of Foreign Service, Georgetown University, summarizing the Tower Commission report, held that the CIA was "under the control of the president's men," in "Reforming U.S. Intelligence," *Foreign Policy* 67 (Summer 1987): 121. These are notable uses of a telling phrase, particularly in an era when the normal usage would be more sensitive to gender: "the President's

men and women" or, more likely, "the President's aides." The gender-insensitivity of "the President's men" would not pass were it not for its cultural resonance.

14. Jean Cobb, Jeffrey Denny, Vicki Kemper, and Viveca Novak, "All the President's Donors," *Common Cause* (Mar./April 1990).

15. *Orange Coast* 16 (July 1990): 98–112.

16. CBS Morning News, 21 July 1976.

17. Safire, *Safire's Political Dictionary*. On the winegate scandal, see *New York Times*, 1 Nov. 1974, p. 1; *Washington Post*, 30 Oct. 1974, p. E-1; *Los Angeles Times*, 19 Dec. 1974, p. 1; *Washington Post*, 19 Dec. 1974, p. C-3.

18. William Safire, "The Vietgate Solution," *New York Times*, 12 Sept. 1974, p. 39.

19. Theodore Draper, *A Very Thin Line: The Iran-contra Affairs* (New York: Hill & Wang, 1991).

20. *Newsweek*, 12 June 1989, p. 18.

21. *Los Angeles Times*, 11 Feb. 1990, p. 1 (San Diego County edition).

22. See William Safire, *New York Times Magazine*, 20 Oct. 1991, p. 18. There have been dozens of other appropriations of "-gate" for other events where the usage did not become common currency. In 1978 President Carter's adviser on drugs and narcotics, Dr. Peter Bourne, was found to have written a prescription for amphetamines to a fictitious person; he immediately left his White House position but not before some people referred to the episode as "Pillgate." In 1983 the *Wall Street Journal* (15 July, p. 26) labeled as "ethics-gate" what it found an excessive and dangerous concern for virtue in public life. In 1989 journalist Hendrik Hertzberg dubbed "Atwatergate" a controversy about Republican National Committee chairman Lee Atwater (*The New Republic*, 3 July 1989, p. 4). In 1991 the *Los Angeles Times* applied "Darylgate" to an outcry over police brutality in Los Angeles that led to criticism of Police Chief Daryl Gates. (See the Conrad cartoon 15 Mar. 1991, p. B-7, San Diego County edition.) Also in 1991, the *New York Times* (26 Mar. 1991, p. A-14) headlined an editorial, "A Scientific Watergate?" commenting on a case of alleged scientific fraud.

23. Mervyn Rees and Chris Day, *Muldergate* (Johannesburg: Macmillan South Africa, 1980).

24. See *Der Spiegel*, 29 Sept. 1986 and 6 Oct. 1986.

25. *San Diego Union*, 11 May 1989, p. A-11 (Reuters).

26. Charles Gordon, "Watergate Envy: It's a Scandal," *MacLean's*, 26 June 1989, p. 9.

27. *Los Angeles Times*, 23 July 1991, p. A-1.

28. Information gathered by Silvio Waisbord. See also *New York Times*, 7 Aug. 1991, p. A-4 for an account of Yoma-gate. See *Los Angeles Times*, 17 Aug. 1991, p. A-21 for a reference to the term "Yoma-gate" being used in the Argentine press.

29. National Public Radio, "All Things Considered," 8 Dec. 1991.

30. This is from an unpublished manuscript by Ronald D. Brunner and Raymond Hopkins that examined the changing use of the term "Watergate" systematically in a number of leading news sources.

31. Cited in J. Leonard Bates, "Watergate and Teapot Dome," *South Atlantic Quarterly* 73 (Spring 1974): 145.

32. Stephen Chapman, "Searching for a New Watergate," *Chicago Tribune*, 24 Feb. 1983.

33. *Time*, 11 July 1983, p. 12.

34. Charles Hockett, "Chinese vs. English: An Exploration of the Whorfian Hypothesis," in H. Hoijer, ed., *Language in Culture* (Chicago: University of Chicago Press, 1954), p. 122.

35. Mark Strand, "Slow Down for Poetry," *New York Times Book Review*, 15 Sept. 1991, p. 36.

36. Leonard Garment, "The Guns of Watergate," *Commentary* 83 (April 1987): 15.

37. Amos Tversky and Daniel Kahneman, "Availability: A Heuristic for Judging Frequency and Probability," *Cognitive Psychology* 5 (1973): 207–232. See also Daniel Kahneman, Paul Slovic, and Amos Tversky, *Judgment Under Uncertainty* (Cambridge: Cambridge University Press, 1982).

38. Emile Durkheim, *Suicide* (New York: Free Press, 1951).

39. Emile Durkheim, *Elementary Forms of the Religious Life* (Winchester, Mass.: George Allen & Unwin, 1915; New York: Free Press, 1965).

40. Alexander is not alone among sociologists in this observation, but he has produced the most subtle and substantial analysis. See also Albert Bergesen and Mark Warr, "A Crisis in the Moral Order: The Effects of Watergate upon Confidence in Social Institutions," in Robert Wuthnow, ed., *The Religious Dimension: New Directions in Quantitative Research* (New York: Academic Press, 1979), pp. 277–295, and Robert Wuthnow, *The Restructuring of American Religion* (Princeton: Princeton University Press, 1987), p. 200.

41. Jeffrey C. Alexander, "Culture and Political Crisis: 'Watergate' and Durkheimian Sociology," pp. 187–224 in Jeffrey C. Alexander, ed., *Durkheimian Sociology* (New York: Cambridge University Press), p. 212. See also Jeffrey C. Alexander, "Three Models of Culture and Society Relations: Toward an Analysis of Watergate," in Jeffrey C. Alexander, *Action and Its Environments* (New York: Columbia University Press, 1988), pp. 153–174.

42. Stephen L. Carter, "The Independent Counsel Mess," *Harvard Law Review* 102 (1988): 136.

43. Seymour Martin Lipset and Everett Carl Ladd, *The Confidence Gap: Business, Labor, and Government in the Public Mind*, rev. ed. (Baltimore: Johns Hopkins University Press, 1987).

44. Robert Stevens, *Law School: Legal Education in America from the 1850s to the 1980s* (Chapel Hill: University of North Carolina Press, 1983), pp. 237–238.

45. Alexander, "Culture and Political Crisis," p. 214.

46. Neal R. Peirce and Jerry Hagstrom, "The 'Open Government' Lobby Is Closing in on New Frontiers," *National Journal* 9 (31 Dec. 1977): 2012.

47. "Common Cause Annual Membership Counts," 4 Feb. 1991, Common Cause, Washington, D.C.

48. Common Cause papers, Box 120, Mudd Manuscript Library, Princeton University. Common Cause still trades on Watergate. In a membership solicitation I received in 1989, a letter from Common Cause chairman Archibald Cox begins, "Dear Friend: The years since the Watergate scandal have seen a skyrocketing growth in contributions from political action committees—the PACs."

49. Andrew S. McFarland, *Common Cause: Lobbying in the Public Interest* (Chatham, N.J.: Chatham House, 1984), p. 134.

50. Common Cause Governing Board minutes, 24–25 Oct. 1975, Appendix H, draft report by Bruce Adams on "OUTS"—"Open Up The System" activity.

51. "Post-Watergate Reforms," memo from Common Cause, Washington, D.C., 14 June 1982, 7 pp.

52. Ann McBridge, "Ethics in Congress: Agenda and Action," *George Washington Law Review* 58 (Feb. 1990): 456.

53. "How to End Watergate" (editorial), *New York Times*, 10 Jan. 1979, p. 22.

54. *New York Times*, 29 Mar. 1983, p. A-18.

55. CBS Morning News, 22 Jan. 1979.

56. All cited in Hugh Trevor Roper, "Nixon—America's Charles I?" *The Spectator*, 11 Aug. 1973, pp. 176–177.

57. *New York Times*, 30 Sept. 1976, p. 47.

58. Hannah Arendt has argued that foreigners do not comprehend a nation governed by a written constitution. Some transgressions that others might not intuitively "feel" to be crimes are crimes in the United States by virtue of written constitutional prohibitions. I am not persuaded. The written nature of the Constitution may have something to do with its symbolic power in American culture, but it is more likely its identification with our origins than its written-ness that gives it such authority. The Constitution stands astride our origins, it defines our union, and the Supreme Court operates in a way to create an ongoing illusion of our unbroken continuity with the principles and purposes of its drafters. Hannah Arendt, "Home to Roost: A Bicentennial Address," *New York Review of Books*, 26 June 1975, p. 4.

59. Robert A. Goldwin, *Why Blacks, Women, and Jews Are Not Mentioned in the Constitution, and Other Unorthodox Views* (Washington D.C.: American Enterprise Institute, 1990), p. 22.

60. For an instructive comparison of presidents and prime ministers, see Richard Rose, "Presidents and Prime Ministers," *Society* 25 (Mar./April 1988): 61–67, and Richard Rose, "Government Against Sub-governments: A European Perspective on Washington," in Richard Rose and Ezra N. Suleiman, eds., *Presidents and Prime Ministers* (Washington, D.C.: American Enterprise Institute, 1980), pp. 284–347.

61. See the comments on the presidency by J. G. A. Pocock, "States, Republics, and Empires: The American Founding in Early Modern Perspective," in Terence Ball and J. G. A. Pocock, eds., *Conceptual Change and the Constitution* (Lawrence: University Press of Kansas, 1988), pp. 73–75.

62. David Riesman, "Attitudes Toward President Nixon: A Case of American Exceptionalism in Relation to Watergate," *Tocqueville Review* 4 (1982): 284.

63. Trevor Roper, "Nixon—America's Charles I?" p. 177.

64. As a sociology student, my reading of Tocqueville was almost exclusively of the second volume, *Democracy in America*, rather than the first. The first volume analyzes political institutions, the second social and moral features of American society. As Tocqueville knew, though the separation of political science from sociology and anthropology may tend to obscure it, political institutions not only grow out of but contribute powerfully to the social, moral, and emotional landscape of a society.

65. Judith Shklar, *Ordinary Vices* (Cambridge: Harvard University Press, 1984), p. 184.

66. Ibid., p. 190.

67. Arnold A. Rogow and Harold D. Lasswell, *Power, Corruption, and Rectitude* (Englewood Cliffs, N.J.: Prentice-Hall, 1963), p. 63.

68. Ibid., pp. 36–37.

69. See Fred I. Greenstein, "More on Children's Images of the President," pp. 281–286; and "Popular Images of the President," pp. 287–296, both in Aaron Wildavsky, ed., *The Presidency* (Boston: Little, Brown, 1969).

70. A study of the political views of Detroit citizens conducted by Roberta Sigel found that the public wanted to endow the president with "very full powers" but also found people "genuinely concerned over a possible abuse of power," and so they approved time limits on the exercise of power. Roberta S. Sigel, "Image of the American Presidency: Part II of An Exploration into Popular Views of Presidential Power," p. 308 in Wildavsky, *The Presidency*.

71. Benjamin Ginsberg and Martin Shefter, *Politics By Other Means: The Declining Importance of Elections in America* (New York: Basic Books, 1990), pp. 26–31.

72. Suzanne Garment, *Scandal: The Culture of Mistrust in American Politics* (New York: Random House, 1991). See also Arthur Maass, "U. S. Prosecution of State and Local Officials for Political Corruption: Is the Bureaucracy Out of Control in a High-Stakes Operation Involving the Constitutional System?" *Publius* 17 (Summer 1987): 195–230. See also *New York Times* editorial, 18 Jan. 1977, p. 18; Irving Kristol, "Post-Watergate Morality: Too Good for Our Good?" *New York Times Magazine*, 14 Nov. 1976, p. 35; "Public Virtue, Private Rights" (editorial), *Washington Post*, 9 Apr. 1979, p. A-18.

73. *New York Times*, 25 Sept. 1977, p. IV-1.

74. Bruce Jennings, "Ethical Politics vs. Political Ethics: Too Much of a Good Thing?" *Journal of State Government* 62 (1989): 173–175. A new state ethics

law in New York in 1991 required extensive financial disclosure from municipal officials across the state, precipitating scores of resignations of people who did not find their service on public boards and authorities should demand such invasion of privacy. See *New York Times*, 18 May 1991, p. 14.

Chapter 9

1. Lou Cannon, *President Reagan: The Role of a Lifetime* (New York: Simon & Schuster, 1991), p. 680. Cannon's narrative of Iran-contra seems to me particularly lucid, and I have generally followed it here.
2. *Washington Post*, 4 Mar. 1987, p. A-2.
3. *Time*, 28 Oct. 1991, p. 36.
4. Theodore Draper, *A Very Thin Line: The Iran-Contra Affairs* (New York: Hill & Wang, 1991), p. 522.
5. Michael Cornfield and David Yalof, "Innocent by Reason of Analogy: How the Watergate Analogy Served Both Reagan and the Press During the Iran-Contra Affair," *Corruption and Reform* 3 (1988): 191.
6. Susan Sontag, *Illness as Metaphor* (New York: Farrar, Straus & Giroux, 1978), and *Against Interpretation, and Other Essays* (New York: Farrar, Straus & Giroux, 1966).
7. "This Is Watergate" (editorial), *The New Republic*, 16 Mar. 1987, p. 7; Tom Wicker, "Two Different Gates," *New York Times*, 12 Dec. 1986, p. A-35. See also Philip Geyelin, "Compared to Watergate," *Washington Post*, 22 Feb. 1987, p. C-7; Jody Powell, "Watergate *Does* Offer Lessons," *Los Angeles Times*, 5 Dec. 1986, p. II-5; Edwin Yoder, Jr., "It Won't Fit in the Watergate Mold," *Washington Post*, 18 Dec. 1986, p. A-27; Richard Cohen, "No Comparisons Needed," *Washington Post*, 2 Dec. 1986, p. A-19; David Ignatius and Michael Getler, "This Isn't Watergate—But the Moral Is the Same," *Washington Post*, 1 Mar. 1987, p. D-1. James David Barber, "How Irangate Differs from Watergate," *New York Times*, 9 Aug. 1987, p. E-25; Meg Greenfield, "When Men Act Like Boys," *Washington Post*, 26 May 1987, p. A-21; George McGovern, "On Nixon and Watergate, Reagan and Iran," *New York Times*, 6 Jan. 1987, p. A-21; Lawrence Meyer, "Here We Go Again," *Washington Post*, 7 Dec. 1986, p. D-5.
8. This appears to be true for the practice of literacy, for instance, and the cognitive skills acquired in literacy. See Sylvia Scribner and Michael Cole, *The Psychology of Literacy* (Cambridge, Mass.: Harvard University Press, 1988).
9. Jerome Bruner, *Toward a Theory of Instruction* (Cambridge: Belknap Press of Harvard University Press, 1966), p. 136.
10. House Permanent Select Committee on Intelligence, *Hearings Before the Subcommittee on Legislation*, 100th Congress, 2d session, 24 Feb. and 10 Mar. 1988, p. 4.

11. Michael A. Ledeen, *Perilous Statecraft: An Insider's Account of the Iran-Contra Affair* (New York: Charles Scribner's Sons, 1988), p. 251.

12. Jane Mayer and Doyle McManus, *Landslide: The Unmaking of the President 1984–1988* (Boston: Houghton Mifflin, 1988), p. 300.

13. Larry Speakes, *Speaking Out* (New York: Avon Books, 1988), pp. 353–354. See also his remarks at a symposium of former press secretaries convened at the University of California, San Diego, in January 1990. "We attempted to convince the President to say, 'I take full responsibility.' But we knew that in this day and age . . . we would have never been able to say, 'It's not in the national interest to talk any more about it.' We couldn't have gotten away with what Kennedy was able to do 30 years before." *Los Angeles Times*, 8 Jan. 1990, pp. B-1, 12.

14. Mark Hertsgaard, *On Bended Knee: The Press and the Reagan Presidency* (New York: Schocken Books, 1989), pp. 15–16, 39.

15. David S. Broder, "Another President Loses IIs Way," *Washington Post*, 19 Nov. 1986, p. A-19.

16. Cannon, *President Reagan*, pp. 113, 551.

17. *New York Times*, 9 July 1976, p. A-12; *New York Times*, 18 Sept. 1974, p. A-24.

18. *New York Times*, 20 Sept. 1975, p. 1. Liman also coauthored a *New York Times* op-ed piece upon Ford's pardoning of Nixon, urging the pursuit of further legal action against Nixon. Arthur L. Liman and Steven B. Rosenfeld, "Rockefeller, Attica and Pardons," *New York Times*, 13 Sept. 1974, p. A-37.

19. Daniel Inouye and Warren Rudman quoted in Haynes Johnson, *Sleepwalking Through History* (New York: Norton, 1991), pp. 324, 327.

20. Johnson, *Sleepwalking*, p. 328.

21. Lance Morgan, personal interview with author, Feb. 1991, Washington, D.C.

22. Daniel K. Inouye, "More Serious Than Watergate," *New York Times*, 3 May 1987, p. E-27.

23. John Ehrlichman, "The Taste of Ashes," *Newsweek*, 8 Dec. 1986, pp. 51–52; John Dean, "John Dean on Ollie: The Ugly Road Ahead," *Newsweek*, 20 July 1987, pp. 28–29.

24. *U.S. News & World Report*, 22 Dec. 1986, p. 22.

25. Philip Lacovara, "Iran Affair Is Higher Drama than Watergate, But Watergate Had Nixon," *Los Angeles Times*, 30 July 1987, p. II-5.

26. *New York Times*, 2 Dec. 1986, p. A-15; *Washington Post*, 10 Dec. 1986, p. 1; *New York Times*, 10 Dec. 1986, p. 9.

27. Gerald M. Boyd, "Many in Poll Say Reagan Is Lying on Diversion of Funds from Iran," *New York Times*/CBS News Poll, p. 9.

28. *New York Times*, 10 Dec. 1986, p. 1.

29. *Los Angeles Times*, 15 Dec. 1986, p. 1.

30. *New York Times*, 10 Dec. 1986, p. 9.

31. Barry Sussman, personal interview with author, Feb. 1991, Washington, D.C.

32. I did not come upon anyone, in my interviews or in print, who claimed that Watergate raised more serious constitutional issues than did Iran-contra. This strikes me now as very odd indeed, because there is an obvious case to be made. Iran-contra was an operation entirely in the realm of foreign policy and was an extension of the presidential prerogative in foreign policy in ways that everything in postwar American politics pointed to. The minority report of the Iran-contra committees denies that the White House even violated the reporting requirements on covert operations, holding that the National Security Administration was excluded from them. So Iran-contra, by this view, was an ill-advised escapade, but not even technically illegal, let alone wantonly outlaw. Watergate, in contrast, was a perversion of the electoral process and an obstruction of the judicial process through a well-considered conspiracy involving the president and his closest associates. Whether this is the "right" way to compare the events is less important than the fact that it is a plausible reading and that it did not come up in public commentary on Iran-contra. This makes it more clear to me that Watergate was invoked for rhetorical purposes; calling Iran-contra "worse than Watergate" was a way to demand attention. See Anthony Lewis, "Ronald Milhous Reagan," *New York Times*, 22 May 1987, p. A-31; Inouye, "More Serious than Watergate," p. E-27.

33. Cornfield and Yalof, "Innocent by Reason of Analogy," p. 186.

34. Ibid., p. 192.

35. Scott Armstrong, "Was the Press Any Match for All the President's Men?" *Columbia Journalism Review* 29 (May/June 1990): 30.

36. Ledeen, *Perilous Statecraft*, p. 247.

37. Harold Hongju Koh, *The National Security Constitution: Sharing Power After the Iran-Contra Affair* (New Haven, Conn.: Yale University Press, 1990), p. 19.

38. George Gallup, Jr., *The Gallup Poll: Public Opinion 1989* (Wilmington, Del.: Scholarly Resources, 1990), pp. 4–6; and the *Gallup Report* 277 (October 1988): 26.

39. From transcript of debate between Arthur Liman and Seymour Hersh at Brown University, Providence, R.I., 1 Mar. 1988.

40. David Thelen, personal communication with author, Jan. 1992. Thelen, a historian, has been analyzing constituents' letters to several Iran-contra committee congressmen.

41. Benjamin Ginsberg and Martin Shefter, *Politics By Other Means: The Declining Importance of Elections in America* (New York: Basic Books, 1990), p. 148.

42. Koh, *National Security Constitution*, pp. 189, 314. Not all agree that Reagan was hurt. "The most remarkable thing about President Reagan's role in the Iran and Contra affairs," Theodore Draper wrote, "is that he came out of them without anything more than a temporary dip in his political standing." It seemed that way to many people at the time, but I do not think a full

examination supports this. See Theodore Draper, *A Present of Things Past: Selected Essays* (New York: Hill and Wang, 1990), p. 240.

43. *Los Angeles Times*, 8 Feb. 1990, p. 25.
44. *Los Angeles Times*, 23 Feb. 1990, p. 1.
45. A *Los Angeles Times* Poll found that 28 percent of people in a national survey judged Ronald Reagan "above average" as a president, 39 percent "average," and 33 percent "below average." More people judged him among the worst presidents (15 percent) than among the best (8 percent). *Los Angeles Times*, 4 Nov. 1991, p. 1.
46. Seymour Hersh, "The Iran-Contra Committees: Did They Protect Reagan?" *New York Times Magazine*, 29 April 1990, p. 47.
47. Liman and Hersh debate, Brown University.
48. "Iran-Contra's Unfollowed Leads," *New York Times*, 2 May 1990, p. 26; "An Iran-Contra Postscript," *Boston Globe*, 3 May 1990.
49. Theodore Draper, "Was There a Missing Witness?" *New York Review of Books*, 31 May 1990, pp. 44–45. Draper criticized especially Seymour Hersh's contention that a certain James Radzimski, administrative assistant on the National Security Council staff, should have been publicly questioned, because in one interview with committee investigators he purportedly linked President Reagan to approval of diverting arms sale funds to the contras. But, says Draper, his testimony did no such thing; Draper concludes, as did some members of the Iran-contra committees, that Radzimski before the television lights "would have been a laughingstock." Pamela Naughton, who was among the sources for Hersh's story, was an investigator for the House Iran-contra committee and believes Radzimski was a credible witness, a career military person with a fine record, the highest possible security clearances, and no indication that he held strong political views (personal interview with author, 19 Mar. 1991, San Diego, CA.)
50. Arthur L. Liman, "Road to Impeachment Requires Evidence," letter to *New York Times Magazine*, 3 May 1990; Sen. Warren Rudman, letter to *Boston Globe*, dated 4 May 1990. Both Liman and Rudman emphasize that Special Prosecutor Lawrence Walsh's investigation, though taking several years longer, has found no evidence of any impeachable offense or criminality on the part of the president.
51. Raoul Berger, *Impeachment* (Cambridge: Harvard University Press, 1973).
52. Charles L. Black, *Impeachment: A Handbook* (New Haven, Conn.: Yale University Press, 1974), p. 46.
53. Ibid., p. 47.
54. Pamela Naughton, personal interview with author.
55. Lance Morgan, personal interview with author.
56. "Talk of the Town," *New Yorker*, 27 July 1987, p. 21.
57. *New York Times*, 15 Dec. 1986, p. II-14.
58. Pamela Naughton, personal interview with author, on the composition of the committees and its consequences.

59. Stephen Engelberg with David Rosenbaum, "What the Iran-Contra Committees Wish They Had Done Differently," *New York Times*, 20 Nov. 1987, p. 1.

60. William D. Ruckelshaus, "Watergate's Costs," *New York Times*, 18 June 1982, p. 31.

61. Draper, *A Very Thin Line*, p. 598.

62. Peter Rodino reports that though the question of impeachment did not come up directly in the Iran-contra committees' deliberations, he does not think the committees would have supported a move toward impeachment if pressed, he recalls, "Even during the beginning of the Nixon investigation, before the Saturday night massacre, it was talked about, but there was no real headstrong, no momentum to consider impeachment." Personal telephone interview with author, 6 May 1991.

63. Barry Schwartz, *George Washington: The Making of an American Symbol* (New York: Free Press, 1987), p. 200. John Rodden makes a similar point about the continued vitality of the reputation of George Orwell: "Orwell is 'alive today' as a public literary figure partly because the political and technological developments of mid-century which initially conditioned his reputation—the Cold War, the Bomb, the specter of totalitarianism, the agonies of the Left, the advent of the 'media age,' the rise of the 'organization man' are themselves still 'alive today.' " John Rodden, *The Politics of Literary Reputation: The Making and Claiming of "St. George" Orwell* (New York: Oxford University Press, 1989), p. 404.

Chapter 10

1. Wilfrid Sheed, *Essays in Disguise* (New York: Knopf, 1990), p. 155.

2. This was also the Nixon of the Nixon presidency, according to Jonathan Schell, *The Time of Illusion* (New York: Knopf, 1976), pp. 126–133. See also Stephen E. Ambrose, *Nixon: Ruin and Recovery 1973–1990* (New York: Simon & Schuster, 1991), p. 136.

3. See especially Richard A. Posner, *Cardozo: A Study in Reputation* (Chicago: University of Chicago Press, 1990); John Rodden, *The Politics of Literary Reputation: The Making and Claiming of "St. George" Orwell* (New York: Oxford University Press, 1989); and Jane Tompkins, *Sensational Designs: The Cultural Work of American Fiction 1790–1860* (New York: Oxford University Press, 1985), for its chapter on Nathaniel Hawthorne's reputation.

4. Gladys Engel Lang and Kurt Lang, *Etched in Memory: The Building and Survival of Artistic Reputation* (Chapel Hill: University of North Carolina Press, 1990), pp. 318–319, 330, 331.

5. *The Gallup Poll 1979* (Wilmington, Del: Scholarly Resources, 1980), p. 37; Norman Ornstein, Andrew Kohut, and Larry McCarthy, *The People, the Press, and Politics* (Reading, Mass.: Addison-Wesley, 1987) p. 128; Times-

Mirror Center for the People and the Press, *The People, the Press, and Politics 1990* (Washington, D.C.: Times-Mirror Center, 1990).

6. The Harris Poll, no. 6, 1981; no. 30, 1985; no. 13, 1987; no. 97, 1988; no. 2, 1991.
7. *New York Times*, 15 Mar. 1975, p. 10.
8. *Newsweek*, 19 May 1986, p. 29.
9. *Los Angeles Times* 17 July 1990, p. E-1; ABC/*Washington Post* Poll, Survey 0054, June 1982. In the 1986 *Newsweek* poll, 39 percent reported they would like to see Nixon in some public capacity as an ambassador or presidential adviser.
10. *Newsweek*, 19 May 1986, p. 27.
11. "Nixon Comes Back into the Limelight—and Controversy," *U.S. News & World Report*, 1 Mar. 1976, p. 24.
12. *New York Times*, 26 Feb. 1976, p. 3.
13. David S. Broder, "Nixon's China Trip: 'Nothing Shames Him'," *Washington Post*, 25 Feb. 1976, p. A-15.
14. "Mr. Nixon's Kowtow," *Washington Post*, 21 Feb. 1976, p. A-16.
15. "Illegitimate Spokesman," *New York Times*, 24 Feb. 1976, p. A-34.
16. *New York Times*, 27 Feb. 1976, p. 1.
17. *New York Times*, 27 Mar. 1975, p. I-13.
18. David Frost, *"I Gave Them a Sword": Behind the Scenes of the Nixon Interviews* (New York: Morrow, 1978), p. 21.
19. Price was the primary, but not sole, consideration. CBS was concerned about maintaining control over production of CBS news programs. CBS executive Richard Salant was also sensitive to charges of "checkbook journalism," having been criticized for paying H. R. Haldeman $100,000 for two one-hour interviews in 1975. See "60 Minutes," 1 May 1977.
20. CBS Morning News, 2 May 1977.
21. "60 Minutes," 1 May 1977.
22. CBS Evening News, 5 May 1977.
23. On the CBS Morning News, 5 May 1977, Sam Ervin declared in response, "He's still covering up." In *Newsweek* (16 May 1977, pp. 33, 34), Leon Jaworski expressed disappointment at Nixon's failure to face up to his crimes, while former Nixon speech writers Patrick Buchanan and Ray Price expressed resentment of the Nixon haters, predicting such people would not let Nixon's remorse be the act of healing they believed it might be.
24. Rep. Charles Wiggins, CBS Evening News, 5 May 1977.
25. CBS Morning News, 5 May 1977.
26. Ibid.
27. See for instance, Colin L. Westerbeck, Jr., "The Last Syllable of Recorded Time," *Commonweal*, 27 May 1977, pp. 339–340; Frank Getlein, "Nixon Without Dietrich," Ibid., pp. 324–326; "Watching Nixon," *Newsweek*, 16 May 1977, pp. 28–40; and Frost, *"I Gave Them a Sword."*
28. Frost, *"I Gave Them a Sword,"* p. 35.

29. Ibid., p. 44.
30. *New York Times*, 16 Jan. 1978, p. A-1; p. A-24.
31. CBS Evening News, 1 July 1978. There had been a more low-key public appearance earlier at a charity golf tournament. Stephen E. Ambrose, *Nixon: Ruin and Recovery 1973–1990* (New York: Simon & Schuster, 1991), p. 487.
32. *New York Times*, 3 July 1978, p. 1.
33. Cited reviews of *RN*, by Richard M. Nixon, are John Kenneth Galbraith, "The Good Old Days," *New York Review of Books*, 29 June 1978, p. 3; and James MacGregor Burns, "A Final Appeal to History," *New York Times Book Review*, 11 June 1978, p. 1.
34. Burns, "A Final Appeal," p. 54.
35. Georges Gusdorf, "Conditions and Limits of Autobiography," in James Olney, ed., *Autobiography: Essays Theoretical and Critical* (Princeton, N.J.: Princeton University Press, 1980), pp. 36–37.
36. Robert Kaiser, "What Power Does He Hold over Us?" *Washington Post*, 4 Aug. 1984, p. C-1.
37. *New York Times*, 10 May 1984, p. B-17.
38. *Newsweek*, 19 May 1986, pp. 26–34.
39. ABC Weekend Report, 11 May 1986, from *Newsweek* interview with Nixon.
40. On the 1980 election, *Washington Post*, 8 Sept. 1980, p. A-4; on Democrats in 1984, *Washington Post*, 28 Jan. 1984, p. A-3, and 13 May 1984, p. C-5; on Mario Cuomo, ABC News, 6 Sept. 1987; on the Democratic ticket, ABC News, 15 July 1988; on the 1988 election, *Washington Post*, 11 Apr. 1988, p. A-4.
41. *Los Angeles Times*, 18 Jan. 1989, p. VI-1.
42. For instance, see Nixon's articles on China in the *Los Angeles Times*, 25 June 1989, p. V-1, or *Die Zeit* (Germany), 7 July 1989, p. 7; and his articles on the Soviet Union in *Time*, 18 Dec. 1989, p. 94 ("Should the U.S. Help Gorbachev?") and the *Los Angeles Times*, 15 April 1990, p. M-1 ("We're Not Cold War Victors Yet").
43. See Roger Morris, "Just Like Old Times, Except . . ." *Los Angeles Times*, 11 Nov. 1989, p. B-8.
44. *New York Times*, 23 Mar. 1991, p. A-13. See also *New York Times*, 7 April 1991, p. E-3. (But observe that this short article in the "Week in Review" section was accompanied by a drawn silhouette of the familiar ski-nose profile topped by a Russian fur hat, a less than dignified presentation.)
45. *Los Angeles Times*, 9 Mar. 1990, p. A-1.
46. See, for instance, Bob Woodward's view that the cover story was "the most prominent event in Nixon's elaborate campaign to rehabilitate himself in the eyes of the American public and, more importantly, of history" and his warning that we should "beware of unindicted, pardoned co-conspirators bearing their own versions of history." Bob Woodward, "The Revisionist Nixon: Sinner in Shining Armor," *Washington Post*, 2 Oct. 1988, p. C-1.
47. Louis A. Weil III, "From the Publisher," *Time*, 2 April 1990, p. 6.

48. Marvin Kalb, personal interview with author, Nov. 1990, Cambridge, MA.
49. "Interview: Paying the Price," *Time*, 2 April 1990, p. 46.
50. *Orange County Register*, 17 July 1990, p. 1; *Los Angeles Times*, 17 July 1990, p. 1; *Los Angeles Times*, 9 July 1990, p. E-1.
51. ABC World News Tonight, 19 July 1990.
52. *Newsweek*, 30 July 1990, p. 24.
53. *Chicago Tribune*, 20 July 1990, p. I-5.
54. *San Francisco Chronicle*, 21 July 1990.
55. See, for instance, *Washington Post*, 20 July 1990, p. A-5; *Miami Herald*, 20 July 1990, p. A-1.
56. "W-Word Nearly Unspoken at Nixon Library Opening," *San Francisco Chronicle*, 20 July 1990, p. 1.
57. "Nightline," ABC News, 19 July 1990. Stephen Ambrose was widely quoted to the same effect. He told the *Los Angeles Times*, "It's a symbolic redemption, a final recovery. . . . It's absolutely the capstone to his life, and it makes it all worthwhile." *Los Angeles Times*, 17 July 1990, p. A-1.
58. This story was picked up in Sidney Blumenthal, "The Last New Nixon," *The New Republic*, 20–27 Aug. 1990, p. 43.
59. *Los Angeles Times*, 8 July 1990, p. A-1.
60. Catherine Gewertz, "Nixon Drops Restrictions to His Library," *Los Angeles Times*, 10 July 1990, p. A-3.
61. Seth Mydans, "Nixon Library Set to Open, with Disputes Old and New," *New York Times*, 16 July 1990, p. A-1.
62. David Lauter, "Planned Press Curbs at Nixon Dedication Eased," *Los Angeles Times*, 19 July 1990, p. A-3.
63. Seth Mydans, "Nixon Center Delays Access to Tapes," *New York Times*, 9 Nov. 1990, p. A-14.
64. Richard Nixon, *RN: The Memoirs of Richard Nixon* (New York: Simon & Schuster, 1978, 1990), pp. 626, 632, 635, 637, 638; and H. R. Haldeman with Joseph DiMona, *The Ends of Power* (New York: Times Books, 1978), pp. 7–27.
65. Clarence Lyons, acting director, Nixon Presidential Materials staff, National Archives, telephone interview with author, 20 Sept. 1991.
66. *Newsweek*, 17 June 1991, p. 32.
67. Margaret Carlson, "Notes from Underground," *Time*, 17 June 1991, p. 27.
68. *Wall Street Journal*, 5 June 1991, p. 1.
69. *New York Times*, 9 June 1991, p. E-5. See also *New York Times*, 11 June 1991, p. A-18; *New York Times*, 5 June 1991, p. A-1; *Washington Post*, 5 June 1991, p. A-1, and *Washington Post*, 7 June 1991, p. A-2.
70. Ellen Goodman argues that there should be no forgiveness of Nixon if he does not repent, that confession is the price of rehabilitation. "Ford Forgave Him, Many Forgot Him; Now Nixon's Back, Still Owing Repentance," *Los Angeles Times*, 22 April 1988, p. II-7.
71. "Nightline," ABC News, 19 July 1990.

72. Carl Shapiro, "Premiums for High Quality Products as Returns to Reputations," *Quarterly Journal of Economics* 98 (1983): 659–679.
73. Nixon, *RN:* p. 3.
74. Jon Wiener, "Inside the Nixon Liebrary," *The Nation*, 10 Sept. 1990, pp. 242–245.

Chapter 11

1. David Lowenthal, *The Past Is a Foreign Country* (Cambridge: Cambridge University Press, 1985), p. 210.
2. David Thelen, "Memory and American History," *Journal of American History* 75 (1989): 1123.
3. Arthur Schlesinger, Jr., *The Cycles of American History* (Boston: Houghton Mifflin, 1986), p. 373. See T. G. Ashplant and Adrian Wilson, "Present-Centred History and the Problem of Historical Knowledge," *The Historical Journal* 31 (1988): 253–274.
4. On history as charter, see Bronislaw Malinowski, *Magic, Science and Religion* (Garden City, N.Y.: Doubleday, 1954), pp. 96–126. For the views of Maurice Halbwachs, see Maurice Halbwachs, *The Collective Memory*, trans. Francis J. Ditter and Vida Yazdi Ditter (New York: Harper & Row, 1980).
5. Arjun Appadurai, "The Past as a Scarce Resource," *Man* (N.S.) 16 (1981): 201–219.
6. Henry Rousso, "The Reactions in France: The Sounds of Silence," in Geoffrey Hartman, ed., *Bitburg in Moral and Political Perspective* (Bloomington: Indiana University Press, 1986), p. 62.
7. Thomas S. Kuhn, *The Structure of Scientific Revolutions* (Chicago: University of Chicago Press, 1962), p. 150.
8. Robert Jervis, *Perception and Misperception in International Politics* (Princeton: Princeton University Press, 1976), p. 240.
9. See Todd Gitlin, *The Whole World Is Watching* (Berkeley: University of California Press, 1978), for a leading analysis of how the news media during the 1960s did, in fact, "trivialize" and "marginalize" the views of antiwar protesters.
10. Quoted in Elizabeth Eisenstein, *The Printing Press as an Agent of Change* (Cambridge: Cambridge University Press, 1979), p. 116.
11. Michael Apple, "The Culture and Commerce of the Textbook," *Journal of Curriculum Studies* 17 (1985): 147–162.
12. Barry Schwartz, "The Social Context of Commemoration: A Study in Collective Memory," *Social Forces* 61 (1982): 374–402.
13. J. H. Plumb, *The Death of the Past* (Boston: Houghton Mifflin, 1970).
14. Richard Cyert and James March, *A Behavioral Theory of the Firm* (Englewood Cliffs, N.J.: Prentice-Hall, 1963), pp. 121–122.
15. Appadurai, "The Past as a Scarce Resource," p. 203.

16. Kenneth Thompson, ed., *The Nixon Presidency* (Lanham, Md.: University Press of America, 1987), p. 161.
17. Thompson, *The Nixon Presidency*, p. 25.
18. Henry Kissinger, *The White House Years* (Boston: Little, Brown, 1979), p. 1209.
19. "Meet the Press," 10 April 1988. (Washington, D.C.: Kelly Press, 1988), p. 20.
20. Michael Howard, *The Lessons of History* (Oxford: Clarendon Press, 1981), p. 10.
21. *New York Times*, 16 Mar. 1987, p. 3.
22. John Orman, *Presidential Secrecy and Deception: Beyond the Power to Persuade* (Westport, Conn.: Greenwood Press, 1980), p. 123.
23. *New York Times*, 22 Sept. 1985, p. 40.
24. CBS Evening News, 9 April 1984.
25. Anthony I. Kronman, "Precedent and Tradition," *Yale Law Journal* 99 (1990): 1068. The quotation from Weil is from *The Need for Roots* (New York: G. P. Putnam's, 1952), Arthur Wills translation, pp. 51–52.
26. It also removes from memory the vital initiatives Nixon took toward stabilizing relations with the Soviet Union and getting disarmament off square one. Watergate, one former National Security Council staff member told me, was a tragedy most of all because it set back enormously important arms negotiations.
27. Sidney Blumenthal, *Pledging Allegiance: The Last Campaign of the Cold War* (New York: HarperCollins, 1990), p. 12.
28. Harold Hongju Koh, *The National Security Constitution: Sharing Power After the Iran-Contra Affair* (New Haven, Conn.: Yale University Press, 1990), pp. 3–4.
29. Neil Sheehan, *A Bright Shining Lie: John Paul Vann and America in Vietnam* (New York: Vintage Books, 1988), pp. 3–31.

INDEX